Folk Devils and Moral Panics

'[Cohen's] analysis is richly documented and convincingly presented . . .
Altogether this is a book full of insight, which should lead us to a painful
reappraisal of our traditional methods and indeed our whole philosophy
for coping with deviants and handling rebellious youth.'

New Society, of the first edition

Stanley Cohen's study of deviant groups – society's 'folk devils' – and the
public and media reaction to them, is both a classic and a very current work
of sociology. The book's conclusion is no less applicable today than when it was
first published, thirty years ago: 'More moral panics will be generated and
other, as yet nameless, folk devils will be created . . . our society as presently
structured will continue to generate problems for some of its members . . .
and then condemn whatever solution these groups find.'

In his new introduction to the third edition, Stanley Cohen reviews recent
sociological theory and criticism about the concept of 'moral panics' and
discusses the moral panics generated around the 'folk devils' of this day and age:
ecstasy and designer drugs; the death of James Bulger; the 'Name and Shame'
campaign against suspected paedophiles, and the vilification of 'bogus' asylum
seekers.

Stanley Cohen is Professor of Sociology at the London School of Economics.
His best-known books include *Folk Devils and Moral Panics* (first edition, 1972),
Psychological Survival: Long Term Imprisonment (1973); *Visions of Social Control*
(1985); *Against Criminology* (1988) and *States of Denial: Knowing About Atrocities
and Suffering* (2000).

Folk Devils and Moral Panics

The Creation of the Mods and Rockers

3r

Stanley Cohen

Routledge
Taylor & Francis Group

LONDON AND NEW YORK

First published 1972 by MacGibbon and Kee Ltd;
reprinted in paperback 1973 by Paladin;
and with a new Introduction 1980
by Martin Robertson & Company Ltd

Second edition published 1987 by Basil Blackwell Ltd

Third edition first published 2002 by Routledge
2 Park Square, Milton Park, Abingdon, Oxon, OX14 4RN

Simultaneously published in the USA and Canada
by Routledge
270 Madison Ave, New York, NY 10016

Reprinted 2004 (twice), 2005, 2006, 2007, 2008 (twice), 2009, 2010

Routledge is an imprint of the Taylor & Francis Group, an informa business

© 1972, 1980, 1987, 2002 Stanley Cohen

Typeset in Perpetua by
Keystroke, Jacaranda Lodge, Wolverhampton
Printed and bound in Great Britain by
TJ International Ltd, Padstow, Cornwall

British Library Cataloguing in Publication Data
A catalogue record for this book is available from the British Library

Library of Congress Cataloging in Publication Data
Cohen, Stanley.
  Folk devils and moral panics / Stanley Cohen. – 3rd ed.
    p. cm.
  Originally published: New ed. Oxford : M. Robertson, 1980. With new introduction.
  Includes bibliographical references and index.
  1. Young adults – Great Britain – Case studies. 2. Deviant behavior. 3. Subculture –
Great Britain. I. Title.

HQ799.8.G7 C63 2002
305.5′6–dc21   2002032633

ISBN10: 0–415–26711–0 (hbk)
ISBN10: 0–415–26712–9 (pbk)

ISBN13: 978–0–415–26711–3 (hbk)
ISBN13: 978–0–415–26712–0 (pbk)

Contents

Moral Panics as Cultural Politics

Introduction to the Third Edition

Folk Devils and Moral Panics was published in 1972. It was based on my PhD thesis, written in 1967–69 and the term 'moral panics' very much belongs to the distinctive voice of the late Sixties.[1] Its tone was especially resonant in the subjects then shared by the new sociology of deviance and the embryonic cultural studies: delinquency, youth cultures, subcultures and style, vandalism, drugs and football hooliganism.

When the **Second Edition** appeared in 1980, I wrote an Introduction ['Symbols of Trouble', reprinted here unchanged] that dealt almost entirely with the 'Folk Devils' part of the book's title (the Mods and Rockers), especially the developments in subcultural theories of delinquency associated with the Birmingham Centre for Contemporary Cultural Studies. In this Introduction to the **Third Edition**, I deal only with the 'Moral Panics' part of the title: reviewing uses and criticisms of the concept over the last thirty years. This is followed by a *Selected Reading List*.

There are three overlapping sources for this review:

First, is the stuff itself, thirty years of moral panics. Whether or not the label was applied and/or contested at the time or afterwards, there are clusters of reactions that look very much like 'classic' moral panics.

Second, the same public and media discourse that provides the raw evidence of moral panic, uses the concept as first-order description, reflexive comment or criticism.[2] These are short-term reactions to the immediate ('the current moral panic about paedophiles') and long-term general reflections on the 'state-of-our-times'.

Third, is the meta-view from academic subjects, notably media and cultural studies, discourse analysis and the sociology of deviance, crime and control. Here the concept has been adapted and adopted, expanded and criticized, and included as a 'Key Idea' in sociology and a standard entry in textbooks and dictionaries.[3]

Calling something a 'moral panic' does not imply that this something does not exist or happened at all and that reaction is based on fantasy, hysteria, delusion and illusion or being duped by the powerful. Two related assumptions, though, require attention – that the attribution of the moral panic label means that the 'thing's' extent and significance has been exaggerated (a) in itself (compared with other more reliable, valid and objective sources) and/or (b) compared with other, more serious problems. This labelling derives from a wilful refusal by liberals, radicals and leftists to take public anxieties seriously. Instead, they are furthering a politically correct agenda: to downgrade traditional values and moral concerns.

Carry on Panicking

The objects of normal moral panics are rather predictable; so too are the discursive formulae used to represent them. For example:

They are *new* (lying dormant perhaps, but hard to recognize; deceptively ordinary and routine, but invisibly creeping up the moral horizon) – but also *old* (camouflaged versions of traditional and well-known evils). They are damaging *in themselves* – but also merely *warning signs* of the real, much deeper and more prevalent condition. They are *transparent* (anyone can see what's happening) – but also *opaque*: accredited experts must explain the perils hidden behind the superficially harmless (decode a rock song's lyrics to see how they led to a school massacre).

The objects of moral panic belong to seven familiar clusters of social identity:

1. Young, Working-class, Violent Males

Working-class yobs are the most enduring of suitable enemies. But the roles they played over these decades – football hooligans, muggers, vandals, loiterers, joy riders and mobile phone snatchers – were not represented by distinctive subcultural styles. There is too much fragmentation to identify dominant subcultures. Loyalties – whether to fashion, musical style, or football – are too diffuse to match each other. Under the exclusionary regimes set up in the Thatcher years and adapted by New Labour, the losers drop quietly off the board, too quietly for any public displays like the Mods and Rockers. Each of the 1992 riots on out-of-town council estates (in Bristol, Salford and Burnley) was short-lived and self-contained. Only the identities and barriers of race have been further strengthened. With the constant exception of football hooliganism, most crowd scenes of these years (mobs, riots, public distur-bance) have been organized on ethnic lines (Brixton, Leicester and Bradford).

Away from the crowds two very different cases stand out, both known by the names of the victims. One, the Jamie Bulger story, was utterly unique, yet triggered off an immediate and ferocious moral panic; the other, the Stephen Lawrence case, despite being indeed a harbinger of things to come, produced a late, slow running and ambiguous reaction, never reaching full panic status.

On 12 February 1993, two 10-year-old boys, Robert Thompson and Jon Venables, led away 2-year-old James Bulger from a shopping centre in Bootle (Liverpool). They walked with him for some two and a half miles to a railway line and then battered him to death. The number of 'Children Who Kill Children' is minute and not increasing. It was precisely the rarity of the event and its context that made it so horrible. Long before the trial began in November the Bulger story had become a potent symbol for everything that had gone wrong in Britain: a 'breed' of violent children, whether feral or immoral; absent fathers, feckless mothers and dysfunctional underclass families; the exploitation of children by TV violence and video nasties; anomic bystanders – on the grainy screen of the defective CCTV they watch as the toddler (arm stretched up, between the two older boys, one in step, the other moving grimly ahead) is led to his death.

The Sun instantly called for 'a crusade to rescue a sick society'. A few days later, the shadow Home Secretary, Tony Blair, referred to the week's news as 'hammer blows struck against the sleeping conscience of the country, urging us to wake up and look unflinchingly at what we see'. *The Independent* (21 February 1993) used Blair's phrase to headline its leading article '*The Hammer Blow To Our Conscience*'. 'Britain is a worried country,' it stated, 'and it has a good deal to be worried about.' By the end of the week, Britain was 'examining the dark corners of its soul' (*The Economist*, 27 February 1993). The only bit of late modernist reflexivity came from someone who makes a living from moralizing: Archbishop George Carey warned about the dangers of 'lapsing into moral panic'.

One such danger is a ready susceptibility to simple explanations. A throwaway remark by the trial judge – 'I suspect that exposure to violent video films may in part be an explanation' – quickly became a factoid that the last video rented by one of the boys' father was *Child's Play 3* (a nasty video indeed in which a child 'kills' a manic doll). This had 'chilling parallels' to the murder of Jamie Bulger; the two boys 'may' have watched it (*Daily Mail*, 26 November 1993). The panic turned on media violence. *The Sun* staged a public burning of horror videos; reports claimed that *Child's Play* had been removed from video shops; Scotland's largest video chain burnt its copies. Four months later, a senior Merseyside police inspector revealed that checks on the family homes and rental lists showed that neither *Child's Play* nor anything like it had been viewed.

The search for meaning and causes is of course not always spurious, simple-minded or mythical. Public opinion, social scientific theories and poetic imagination[4] had to strain themselves to make sense of such an event. But during moral panics and media frenzies the atypical case is compressed into general categories of crime control (such as 'juvenile violence'). The explanatory theory is based on too few cases; injustice results by targeting too many cases.

Stephen Lawrence was an 18-year-old black youth from South London. On the evening of 22 April 1993, while standing at a bus stop with a friend he was taunted with racial abuse by a group of five or six white youths. They then stabbed him in the chest and he died some hours later.

This was to become another boundary marking case. It was not as unusual as the Bulger story, but just as rich and received more intense public and media exposure over a much longer period. The visible failure to bring the known group of suspects to trial led to continuous revelations of police incompetence and racism. After six years of persistent campaigning and claims-making (by various civil liberties organizations, anti-racist groups and the local black community including Stephen Lawrence's parents), an inquest, a botched private prosecution, a flawed internal police review, and a Police Complaints Authority investigation, eventually a £3 million Judicial Inquiry was set up (chaired by a retired judge, Sir William Macpherson). It published its 335-page Report in February 1999.[5] The Report generated enormous public attention and an iconic policy agenda still refers to policing 'after Macpherson' or 'after the Stephen Lawrence Report'.[6]

At first glance, all the ingredients for a moral panic were in place. The Report itself took a moral stand against the persistent racism it had identi-fied. For example: 'Stephen Lawrence's murder was simply and solely and unequivocally motivated by racism. It was the deepest tragedy for his family. It was an affront to society, and especially to the local black community in Greenwich' (Para. 1.11); 'Nobody has been convicted of this awful crime. This is also an affront both to the Lawrence family and the community at large' (Para. 1.12). Professional incompetence and poor leadership were important reasons for the police failure, but the overarching problem was 'pernicious and persistent institutional racism', police failure to respond to the concerns of ethnic minorities and 'discrimination through unwitting prejudice, ignorance, thoughtlessness and racist stereotyping' (Para. 6.34).

Why did all this not quite add up to a moral panic? Despite the continued use of Stephen's name, public attention shifted from the victim to the police. With the quick departure from the scene of the suspected offenders (their culture of violence and racism soon forgotten) the police became the *only* object of attention. The Macpherson Report found a divided organization sending out contradictory and confusing messages marked by an 'alarming inability to see how and why race mattered'.[7] Precisely because of this 'inability' the police could hardly be expected to carry the full burden of the Lawrence fiasco, and even less, the damaging indictment of 'institutionalized racism'. There was no one else to blame – but the police were just unsuitable as folk devils. Moreover they had the power to deny, downplay or bypass any awkward claims about their culpability.[8]

The right wing press, especially the *Daily Mail* and the *Daily Telegraph*, claiming to speak on behalf of all British society, directly aided the police. These papers applied, with astonishing accuracy, methods that could appear in a manual on '*How To Prevent a Moral Panic*'. The notion of 'institutionalized racism' was denounced as meaningless, exaggerated and too sweeping; the term could stir up resentments among ordinary people (stigma and deviancy amplification theory); it besmirches the whole police force because of a few blameworthy individuals; the British are a tolerant people who have marginalized the far right and allowed racial minorities to be integrated and accepted. The Report, proclaimed the *Telegraph*, could have come from a 'loony left borough'. Some of its conclusions 'bordered on the insane'. Macpherson (a witch finder looking for thought-crimes) was a useful idiot duped by the 'race relations lobby' (*Sunday Telegraph* 21 and 28 February 1999 and *Daily Telegraph*, 26 February 1999).

In the end, the Lawrence case lacked three of the elements needed for the construction of a successful moral panic. First, a *suitable enemy*: a soft target, easily denounced, with little power and preferably without even access to the battlefields of cultural politics. Clearly not the British police. Second, a *suitable victim*: someone with whom you can identify, someone who could have been and one day could be anybody. Clearly not inner-city young black males. Third, a consensus that the beliefs or action being denounced were not insulated entities ('it's not only this') but integral parts of the society or else could (and would) be unless 'something was done'. Clearly if there was no institutionalized racism in the police, there could not be in the wider society.

2. School Violence: Bullying and Shootouts

The 'Blackboard Jungle' (the name of the 1956 movie) has long served, in Britain and the USA, as a vivid image about the menacing violence of inner-city schools. Violence is seen as a constant daily backdrop: pupils against each other (bullying, playing dangerous macho games, displaying weapons); teachers against pupils (whether formal corporal punishment or immediate rage and self-protection).

There have been sporadic outcries about this backdrop of school violence and related problems such as truancy, large-scale social exclusion into special classes or units and more recently the neighbourhood pusher selling drugs at the school gate. Fully-fledged moral panics need an extreme or especially dramatic case to get going. The age-old rituals of bullying in classroom and playground (girls, for once, getting a fair share of attention) are usually normalized until serious injury or the victim's suicide.

A recent example is the run of high school massacres and shooting sprees. The first images – from the USA in the mid-nineties – were quite unfamiliar: school grounds taped off by police; paramedics rushing to wheel off adolescent bodies; parents gasping in horror; kids with arms around each other; then the flowers and messages at the school gates. In the late nineties, when these events were still rare, each new case was already described as 'an all-too-familiar story'. The slide towards moral panic rhetoric depends less on the sheer volume of cases, than a cognitive shift from 'how could it happen in a place like this?' to 'it could happen anyplace'. In the USA at least, the Columbine Massacre signalled this shift.

On 20 April 1999 two male students dressed in black (one 17 years old, the other just 18) walked into the 1,800 student Columbine High School in the quiet town of Littleton, Colorado. They were armed with shotguns, a handgun and a rifle. They started shooting, initially targeting known athletes, killing a teacher and twelve fellow students and then shot themselves. How could this have happened? As *Time* magazine posed the question: 'The Monsters Next Door: What Made them Do It?' (3 May 1999). British newspaper headings (the archetypal carriers of moral panics) had already covered a range of explanations. On the print day after the event (22 April) the *Daily Mail* went for ideological motivation ('Disciples of Hitler'). *The Independent* preferred psychopathology ('The Misfits Who Killed For Kicks') as did the *Sunday Times* (25 April): 'Murderous Revenge of the Trench-coat Misfits'. *The Guardian* side-stepped the problem of motivation and went for the liberal middle path issue: 'The Massacre that Challenges America's Love Affair with the Gun' (22 April).

This scurrying around for a causal theory – or, at least, a language for making sense – is found in all moral panic texts. If indeed, in President Clinton's words, Columbine had 'pierced the soul of America' we must find out why *this* event happened and how to stop it happening *elsewhere*. Moreover, if this happened in a place like Columbine (and most school massacres do happen in such ordinary places) then it could well happen elsewhere.

As these stories unfold, experts such as sociologists, psychologists and criminologists are wheeled in to comment, react and supply a causal narrative. Their ritual opening move – 'putting things in perspective' – is not usually very helpful: 'Schools Still Safest Place For Children; Many More Dead at Home Than in Classroom.'

3. *Wrong Drugs: Used by Wrong People at Wrong Places*

Moral panics about psychoactive drugs have been remarkably consistent for something like a hundred years: the evil pusher and the vulnerable user; the slippery slope from 'soft' to 'hard' drugs; the transition from safe to dangerous; the logic of prohibition. New substances are just added to the list: heroin, cocaine, marijuana and then the Sixties drugs of amphetamines (very much the Mod pill) and LSD. Then a string of substances: designer drugs, PCP, synthetic drugs, ecstasy, solvents, crack cocaine and new associations: acid-house, raves, club culture, 'heroin chic' supermodels.

In Britain, Leah Betts joined James Bulger as a melodramatic example of a moral panic generated by the tragic death of one person. On 13 November 1995, 18-year-old Leah Betts collapsed soon after taking an ecstasy tablet in a London nightclub, was taken to hospital and went into a coma. By the next day – for reasons not altogether clear – the story made instant panic headlines: the anguish of Leah's parents; the evil pushers of poison; the insistent message 'it could be your child'. Leah died two days later. Her parents began to appear regularly in the media to warn of the dangers of ecstasy. They became instant experts and moral guardians – disagreeing with them would be insensitive to their grief. The warning was symbolically sharpened by Leah's respectable home background: father an ex-police officer, mother had worked as a drug counsellor. This meant, explained the *Daily Express*, that drugs were a 'rotten core in the heart of middle England'. Leah was the girl next door.

This episode has been much analysed: the story itself, the media reaction, the left liberal counter-reaction (attacking the media-spread panic) and even a left liberal reaction against the counter-reaction for being just a mirror-image, merely inverting one simple message into another equally simple.[9]

Instead of: a monolithic popular youth culture promotes drug use and normal-izes other anti-social actions and attitudes, we have: panic coverage by a monolithic media promotes a false consensus that alienates occasional drug users into further marginalization.

This was to be a long-running story. Nearly six months later, anxieties were still being raised: 'Even the best parents, raising the most level-headed children, fear that one of them somehow might be next weekend's Leah Betts, who died after taking Ecstasy' (*Daily Telegraph*, 12 April 1996). Fourteen months after Leah's death, the pop star Noel Gallagher had to apologize to her parents for saying that ecstasy use was commonplace and harmless among some young people. In March 2000, about five years after the event, Leah's mother was widely quoted as 'hitting out' at a Police Federation inquiry that suggested relaxing some drug laws. Leah's father was still a recognizable authority: 'Ecstasy Victim's Dad in Drug Danger Alert' (*Birmingham Evening Mail*, 12 October 2000); 'Leah Drug Death Dad Not here to Preach' (*Bolton, UK Newsquest Regional Press*, 18 May 2001).

4. Child Abuse, Satanic Rituals and Paedophile Registers

The term 'child abuse' contains many different forms of cruelty against children – neglect, physical violence, sexual abuse – whether by their own parents, staff in residential institutions, 'paedophile priests' or total strangers. Over the last decade, public perceptions of the problem have become increasingly focused on sexual abuse and sensationally atypical cases outside the family.

Reactions to the sexual abuse of children rest on shifting moral grounds: the image of the offender changes; some victims appear more suitable than others.[10] A series of stories over the last twenty years about serious abuse in children's homes and other residential institutions revealed not panic or even anxiety, but a chilling denial. The victims had endured years of rejection and ill-treatment by their own parents and the staff supposed to care for them. Their complaints to senior staff and local authority officials and politicians were met with disbelief, collusion and a tight organizational cover-up. There have been repeated waves of denial, exposure then denunciation. The same pattern applies to those traditional folk devils, paedophile priests.[11]

In the mid-1980s, however, a succession of highly publicized child deaths under more 'ordinary' circumstances, led to a very different type of panic. Into the familiar criminal triangle – child (innocent victim); adult (evil perpetrator) and bystanders (shocked but passive) – appears the social worker, trying to be rescuer but somehow ending up being blamed for the whole mess. Social workers and social service professionals were middle-class folk devils: either gullible wimps or else storm troopers of the nanny state; either uncaring cold hearted bureaucrats for not intervening in time to protect the victim or else over-zealous, do-gooding meddlers for intervening groundlessly and invading privacy.

The Cleveland child sexual abuse scandal of 1987 marked the peak of this period and condensed its themes: the tensions between social work, medicine and the law; social workers as anxious, demoralized and particularly vulnerable as a predominantly female profession. [12] For three months from April that year, a cluster of some 120 children (average age between 6 and 9) had been diagnosed as having been sexually abused in their families. In June, a local newspaper published a story about confused and angry parents who claimed that their children had been taken from them by local authority social workers on the basis of a disputed diagnosis of sexual abuse made by two paediatricians in the local hospital. The *Daily Mail* ran the story on 23 June ('Hand Over Your Children, Council Orders Parents of 200 Youngsters').

The resulting moral panic became a pitched battle of claims and counter-claims. So busy were the key players in fingering each other – social workers, police, paediatricians, doctors, lawyers, parents, local and national politicians, then a judicial inquiry – that there was not even minimal consensus about what the whole episode was about.

Another episode was more fictitious and one of the purest cases of moral panic. Superimposed on the very real phenomenon of childhood sexual abuse and incest, came the 'recovered memory' of childhood incest: bitter debates about the existence of repressed (and recovered) memories of childhood sexual abuse. In these therapeutic interstices, came the story of 'ritual child abuse', 'cult child abuse' or 'Satanic abuse'. In around 1983, disturbing reports began circulating about children (as well as adults in therapy who were 'recovering' childhood memories) alleging that they had been sexually abused as part of the ritual of secret, Satanic cults, which included torture, cannibalism and human sacrifice. Hundreds of women were 'breeders'; children had their genitals mutilated, were forced to eat faeces, were sacrificed to Satan, their bodies dismembered and fed to participants – who turned out to be family members, friends and neighbours, day-care providers and prominent members of the community. Claims-making for various parts of this story joined conservative Christian fundamentalists with feminist psychotherapists.

One form of sexualized violence against children does not generate counter-claims about its existence nor any moral disagreement: the abduction and sexual killing of children, especially girls. This strikes a depth of horror in us all. There is a panicky sense of vulnerability – both in the sense of statistical risk (these events seem to be happening more often) and emotional empathy (How would I feel if this happened to my child?). The script becomes more familiar: child disappears on way home from school; the police set up investigation team; school friends, neighbours, teachers interviewed; frantic, distraught parents make appeals on TV; members of public join police in searching fields and rivers . . .

These offenders are pure candidates for monster status. The July 2000 abduction and murder of 8-year-old Sarah Payne led to the *News of the World* 'crusade' (its own word), a series of classic texts of monster-making. The 23 July front page reads: 'NAMED AND SHAMED. There are 110,000 child sex offenders in Britain . . . one for every square mile. The murder of Sarah Payne has proved police monitoring of these perverts is not enough. So we are revealing WHO they are and WHERE they are . . . starting today.' The lists of names and the rows of photos reflect what the paper assumes and constructs as the primeval public anxiety: 'DOES A MONSTER LIVE NEAR YOU?' Check the list, then read on: 'WHAT TO DO IF THERE IS A PERVERT ON YOUR DOORSTEP.' The paper called for information about convicted sex offenders to be made publicly available and itself published over the next two weeks photos, names and addresses of 79 convicted sex offenders.

Many obvious and worrying issues were raised: how the list was constructed (partly from Scout Association records: *Scouting Out the Beasts*, the paper explained); how downloading child porn or the seduction of a 14-year-old schoolboy by his mid-thirties female teacher belong to the same category as the sexual murder of a child; the counter-productive effect of driving already monitored offenders underground; the media's own freedom to publish. The special dangers of vigilantism and lynch mobs soon appeared with crowd protests calling for named and shamed offenders to be moved out of neighbourhoods or council housing estates. Attention focused on the Paulsgrove estate near Portsmouth – where each night for a week crowds of up to 300 marched upon houses of alleged paedophiles.

Public figures had to express sympathy with the parents and share their moral revulsion but also distance themselves from the mob. This was easily done by repeating the inherently negative connotations of lynch mob and mob rule, the primitive, atavistic forces whipped up by the *News of the World*.[13] The rational polity is contrasted to the crowd: volatile, uncontrollable and ready to explode.

5. Sex, Violence and Blaming the Media

There is a long history of moral panics about the alleged harmful effects of exposure to popular media and cultural forms – comics and cartoons, popular theatre, cinema, rock music, video nasties, computer games, internet porn.[14] For conservatives, the media glamorize crime, trivialize public insecurities and undermine moral authority; for liberals the media exaggerate the risks of crime and whip up moral panics to vindicate an unjust and authoritarian crime control policy. In these 'media panics', the spirals of reaction to any new medium are utterly repetitive and predictable. With historical incorporation: 'the intense pre-occupation with the latest media fad immediately relegates older media to the shadows of acceptance.'[15]

The crude model of 'media effects' has hardly been modified: exposure to violence on this or that medium causes, stimulates or triggers off violent behaviour.[16] The continued fuzziness of the evidence for such links is overcompensated by confident appeals to common sense and intuition. When such appeals come from voices of authority (such as judges) or authoritative voices (experts, professionals, government inquiries) the moral panic is easier to sustain, if only by sheer repetition. The prohibitionist model of the 'slippery slope' is common: if 'horror videos' are allowed, then why not 'video nasties?' Child pornography will be next and finally the legendary 'snuff movies.' Crusades in favour of censorship are more likely to be driven by organized groups with ongoing agendas.

Some recent media panics are more self-reflective – anticipating having to defend themselves against the accusation of spreading a moral panic. The media play a disingenuous game. They know that their audiences are exposed to multiple meanings and respond differently to the 'same' message. They use this knowledge to support their indignation that they could have any malignant effect; they forget this when they start another round of simple-minded blaming of others. The powerful, increasingly homogenized and corporate news media blame *other* media forms. But their own effect is the most tangible and powerful, shaping the populist discourse and political agenda-setting. This has happened most obviously in my next two examples: welfare cheats and bogus asylum seekers.

6. Welfare Cheats and Single Mothers

The cutbacks in welfare state provisions during the Thatcher years were accompanied by the deliberate construction of an atmosphere of distrust.

Widespread folk beliefs – the assumption that significant numbers of welfare claims were bogus or fraudulent, made by people taking advantage of ('ripping off') the welfare state – were given official credibility. Governments confirmed the need for institutional practices (laws, administrative procedures) that would firmly and reliably weed out the fake from the real. Legal changes assume, along with the public culture, 'not just that each claimant is *potentially* a fraudster but that he/she is probably so'.[17]

'Welfare cheats', 'social security frauds' and 'dole scroungers' are fairly traditional folk devils. So too are unmarried mothers. Over the 1980s, though, there was a 'kind of subdued moral panic' about young, unemployed girls becoming pregnant, staying single and taking themselves out of the labour market by opting for full-time motherhood, becoming dependent on welfare benefits rather than a male breadwinner.[18] The campaign ran most stridently from 1991 to 1993. Conservative politicians explicitly linked the goal of reducing government expenditure with moral exhortation for people to take responsibility for their own lives. 'Girls' were depicted as getting pregnant in order to be eligible for state benefits, even 'extra handouts' or to jump the queue for public housing. The 1993 'Back to Basics' campaign in Britain cynically constructed the single mother as a potent moral threat.[19] The abuse directed at lone parents led an *Independent* editorial (11 October 1993) to note that 'Conservative politicians are subjecting them to a vilification that would be illegal if addressed to racial minorities.'

The image of single mothers as irresponsible adults and ineffective parents helps to legitimize and entrench shrinking public provisions.[20] There are further causal leaps: 'feckless mothers' get pregnant to obtain state welfare; they raise children who will be the criminals of the future; absent fathers are present somewhere, unemployed and also living off the state. All this points to the same underclass culture that created the problem in the first place. But the real problem is none other than: the future of the nuclear family.

7. Refugees and Asylum Seekers: Flooding our Country, Swamping our Services

In media, public and political discourse in Britain the distinctions between immigrants, refugees and asylum seekers have become hopelessly blurred. Refugee and asylum issues are subsumed under the immigration debate which in turn is framed by the general categories of race, race relations and ethnicity. The framing itself does not necessarily imply racism. There are domains of British society where racism is subdued or at least contested. Conservatives may well flirt with the idea that 'political correctness' is a leftist moral panic, but political instinct tells them to condemn their members for telling racist jokes.

No such sensitivity is extended to refugees and asylum seekers. Over the 1990s and throughout Europe a 'hostile new agenda' emerged.[21] At one level, there is the repeated and ritualistic distinction between genuine refugees (still entitled to compassion) and bogus asylum seekers (no rights, no call on compassion). But this distinction hides the more profound sense in which the once 'morally untouchable category of the political refugee'[22] has become deconstructed.

Governments and media start with a broad public consensus that *first*, we must keep out as many refugee-type of foreigners as possible; *second*, these people always lie to get themselves accepted; *third*, that strict criteria of eligibility and therefore tests of credibility must be used. For two decades, the media and the political elites of all parties have focused attention on the notion of 'genuineness'. This *culture of disbelief* penetrates the whole system. So 'bogus' refugees and asylum seekers have not really been driven from their home countries because of persecution, but are merely 'economic' migrants, attracted to the 'Honey Pot' of 'Soft Touch Britain'.

In tabloid rhetoric, especially the *Daily Mail* (whose campaign of vilification is too deliberate and ugly to be seen as a mere moral panic), the few nuances in these assumptions disappear: the untypical is made typical; the insulting labels are applied to all. (The bogus/genuine dichotomy appeared also in 58 per cent of all relevant articles over 1990–1995 in *The Guardian, The Independent* and *The Times*; one-third of *Guardian* and *Independent* references either criticized this idea or were citing others.[23])

This area is crucially different from my other six examples. First, although there have been intermittent panics about specific newsworthy episodes, the overall narrative is a single, virtually uninterrupted message of hostility and rejection. There is a constant background screen, interspersed with vivid little tableaux: Tamils at the airport, stripping in protest; Kurds clinging to the bottom of Eurostar trains; Chinese suffocating to death in a container lorry. Second, these reactions are more overtly political than any others – not just because the problem is caused by global political changes, but because the reactions have a long history in British political culture. Moreover, successive British governments have not only led and legitimated public hostility, but spoken with a voice indistinguishable from the tabloid press.

The media's lexicon of verbal abuse has kept up a constant level of bigotry. A recent analysis shows Scottish newspapers highlighting the same negative words and racial stereotypes; presenting asylum myths as fact; openly hostile about the presence of asylum seekers in Britain and openly suggesting they go back to their country of origin.[24] (Note though that only 44 per cent of references were judged as wholly negative, 21 per cent as balanced and 35 per cent as positive.)

A socio-linguistic study in a quite different cultural context – Austrian newspaper reports on the Kurdish asylum seekers in Italy in 1998 – nicely identifies the 'metaphors we discriminate by'.[25] Three dominant metaphors portray asylum seekers as *water* ('tidal waves'), as *criminals* or as an *invading army*. The repetition of these themes in relatively fixed lexical and syntactic forms shows them as the 'natural' way of describing the situation. The 'naturalization' of particular metaphors can blur the boundaries between the literal and the non-literal.

Similar metaphors – plus a few others – appear in British newspapers:

- Water is represented as *Flood, Wave, Deluge, Influx, Pour(into), Tide* and *Swamp*. As in 'Human Tide Labour Would Let In' (*The Sun*, 4 April 1992).
- Refugees are more criminal and more violent: 'Thousands have already [come to Britain] bringing terror and violence to the streets of many English towns' (*Sunday People*, 4 March 2001). 'An asylum free-for-all is a time bomb ticking away . . . that could one day explode with terrifying public violence' (*Scottish Daily Mail*, 13 April 2000). Their primal dishonesty is that they are *Cheats, Fakes, Bogus* and *Liars*. 'Fury as 20,000 Asylum cheats beat the System to Stay in Britain; Get them Out' (*Daily Express*, 30 July 2001).
- Refugees are *Scroungers* and *Beggars*, always looking for *Handouts* and trying to *Milk* the system.
- This is easy because Britain is a *Haven* with generous provisions (*Milk and Honey*) and is such a *Soft Touch*: 'Don't Let Britain Be A Soft Touch' (*Sunday Mirror*, 4 August 2001); 'Labour has made UK a haven for Refugees' (*Daily Mail*, 7 August 1999); Britain as 'the number one destination for asylum-seekers' (*Daily Telegraph*, 19 February 2001); 'the Costa del Dole for bogus refugees' (*Scottish Sun*, 11 April 2000).
- These metaphors and images are usually combined: 'Soft Touch That Lets in the Refugee Tricksters' (Press Association, 4 November 1999); 'Bogus Asylum Seekers That Keep on Flooding Into Britain: Britain a Soft Touch on Asylum' (*Daily Express*, 26 April 2001); 'We resent the scroungers, beggars and crooks who are prepared to cross every country in Europe to reach our generous benefits system' (*The Sun*, 7 March 2001).

- The headlines of 'Straight Talking', David Mellor's regular column in the *People* make up a collage of these themes: 'Why we must turn back the Tide of Dodgy Euro Refugees' (29 August 1999); 'Send Spongers Packing Before We Are Over-run' (13 February 2000); 'Kick Out All This Trash' (5 March 2000). Then, after all this, 'When Telling the Truth is Called Racism' (16 April 2000).

The immediate effects of such sustained venom are easy to imagine, but harder to prove. In three days in August 2001 a Kurdish asylum seeker was stabbed to death on a Glasgow housing estate and two other Kurds attacked. The UNHCR issued a statement saying that this was predictable given the 'climate of vilification of asylum seekers that has taken hold in the UK in recent years'. This branding has become so successful that the words 'asylum seeker' and 'refugee' have become terms of abuse in school playgrounds.

Because this area is so obviously political, a strong opposition has been generated. Many NGOs – from human rights, civil liberties and anti-racist directions – give explicit attention to combating the pernicious effects of panic discourse. More specialist groups such as the Press Trust and RAM (Refugees, Asylum-seekers and the Mass Media) work only on countering media images and myths.

In May 2002, the Labour government announced a new round of plans under the slogan of 'zero acceptance': shut the Sangatte refugee camp on the French side of the Channel Tunnel; intercept boats carrying illegals; speed up deportation procedures. Under the heading 'Asylum: 9 out of 10 are Conmen' the *Daily Star* (22 May 2002) launched a typical side panic against 'turncoat immigration officers'. Immigration officers, trained at the taxpayers' expense, are quitting their jobs and using their expertise to set up lucrative consultancies to advise waves of bogus asylum seekers on how to beat the system.

Extensions

The concept of moral panic evokes some unease, especially about its own morality. Why is the reaction to Phenomenon A dismissed or downgraded by being described as 'another moral panic,' while the putatively more significant Phenomenon B is ignored, and not even made a candidate for moral signification?

These are not just legitimate questions but *the* questions. Like the folk objections against labelling, social constructionist or discourse theory in general, they strengthen the very position they are trying to attack. Such questions can only be posed if the lack of congruence between *action* (event, condition, behaviour) and *reaction* is correctly understood to be normal and obvious. To point to the complexities of the relationship between social objects and their interpretation is not a 'criticism' but the whole point of studying deviance and social control. Some trivial and harmless forms of rule-breaking can indeed be 'blown out of all proportion'. And yes, some very serious, significant and horrible events – even genocide, political massacres, atrocities and massive suffering – can be denied, ignored or played down.[26] Most putative problems lie between these two extremes –exactly where and why calls for a comparative sociology of moral panic that makes comparisons within one society and also between societies. Why, thus, does rate X of condition Y generate a moral panic in one country but not in another with the same condition?

All this certainly demands a rather clearer definition of the concept. Commentators have distinguished the separate elements in the original definition:[27] (i) *Concern* (rather than fear) about the potential or imagined threat; (ii) *Hostility* – moral outrage towards the actors (folk devils) who embody the problem and agencies (naïve social workers, spin-doctored politicians) who are 'ultimately' responsible (and may become folk devils themselves); (iii) *Consensus* – a widespread agreement (not necessarily total) that the threat exists, is serious and that 'something should be done'. The majority of elite and influential groups, especially the mass media, should share this consensus. (iv) *Disproportionality*: an exaggeration of the number or strength of the cases, in terms of the damage caused, moral offensiveness, potential risk if ignored. Public concern is not directly proportionate to objective harm. (v) *Volatility* – the panic erupts and dissipates suddenly and without warning.

I will return to these elements, especially the last two. Before that, a list of more sophisticated theories not available thirty years ago.

1. Social Constructionism

Folk Devils and Moral Panics was informed by the sixties fusion of labelling theory, cultural politics and critical sociology. Today's students of moral panics do not have to engage with this theoretical mix-up. They can go straight into the literature on social constructionism and claims-making.[28] This is a well-developed model for studying the contested claims that are made – by victims, interest groups, social movements, professionals and politicians – in the construction of new social problem categories.

Typical cases include: drunken driving, hate crime, stalking, environmental problems, psychiatric categories such as PTSD (Post Traumatic Stress Disorder) and various dependencies, eating disorders and learning disorders. Moral enterprise comes from many different directions: traditional 'disinterested' forces (such as the helping professions), interest groups (such as pharmaceutical companies) and the rainbow coalition of multi-cultural and identity groups, each claiming its own special needs and rights. The rhetoric of victim-hood, victim and victimization is the common thread in these newer forms of claim-making: secondary victims, such as Mothers Against Drunk Driving (MADD) look for tougher punishment; animal rights campaigners look for the criminalization of cruelty towards victims who cannot speak; putative victims, such as sick Gulf War veterans, want official recognition of their syndrome and consequent compensation.

Social problem construction always needs some form of enterprise. It does not, however, need a moral panic. When this rather special mode of reaction takes place, it may strengthen (and then be absorbed by) the construction process. Or it never reaches this point – remaining a shriek of indignation that leads nowhere.

'But is there anything out there?' Constructionists have a range of well-rehearsed responses to this question. In the 'strong' or 'strict' version there are constructs and nothing but constructs all the way down; the sociologist is merely another claims-maker; in 'weak' or 'contextual' constructionism, the sociologist can (and should) make reality-checks (to detect exaggeration) while simultaneously showing how problems are socially constructed. I would also distinguish between *noisy* constructions – where moral panics appear (usually at an early stage) and may be associated with a single sensational case – and *quiet* constructions, where claims-makers are professionals, experts or bureaucrats, working in organizations and with no public or mass media exposure.

2. Media and Cultural Studies

At their point of origin in the sixties, concepts like 'moral panic' and 'deviancy amplification' were symbiotically linked to certain assumptions about the mass media. Vital causal links were taken for granted – notably that the mass media are the primary source of the public's knowledge about deviance and social problems. The media appear in any or all of three roles in moral panic dramas: (i) *Setting the agenda* – selecting those deviant or socially problematic events deemed as newsworthy, then using finer filters to select which of these events are candidates for moral panic; (ii) *Transmitting the images* – transmitting the claims of claims-makers, by sharpening up or dumbing down the rhetoric of moral panics; or (iii) *Breaking the silence, making the claim*. More frequently now than three decades ago, the media are in the claims-making business themselves. Media exposures – whether *The Guardian's* tale of government sleaze or *The Sun's* headline 'Would You like a Paedophile as Your Neighbour?' – aim for the same moral denouement: 'We Name the Guilty Men.'

These years have seen major developments in discourse theory and analysis. I would now be expected to *interrogate* the speeches by Brighton magistrates or editorials from the *Hastings Observer* as *texts* or *narratives* in order to *problematize* their *mediated representation* of the *distant other's* stance to a *posited external world*. All this is far away from what I now see as the book's weakest link: between moral panics and folk devils. The many robust critiques of simple 'stimulus/response' and 'effects' models have hardly touched the thin idea of media-induced deviancy amplification. This is not causation in the constructionist sense – moral panics 'cause' folk devils by labelling more actions and people – but causation in the positivist sense and without the inverted commas. This psychology still uses concepts such as triggering off, contagion and suggestibility. Later cognitive models are far more plausible. For those who define and those who are defined, sensitization becomes a matter of cognitive framing and moral thresholds. Rather than a stimulus (media message) and response (audience behaviour) we look for the points at which moral awareness is raised ('defining deviance up') or lowered ('defining deviance down').

These years have also seen some substantive changes in the media coverage of crime, deviance and social problems. One study of crime reporting in Britain over the last five decades finds that crime is increasingly portrayed as a pervasive threat not just to its vulnerable victims, but to ordinary people in everyday life.[29] Attention shifts away from offence, offender and the criminal justice process and towards a victim-centred cosmology. If the offenders' background, motivation and context become less salient so they are easier to demonize. This contrast between dangerous predators and vulnerable innocents allows the media to construct what Reiner terms 'virtual vigilantism'. This can be seen throughout the new realities of 'tabloid justice'[30] and in the victim culture encouraged by talk shows such Jerry Springer's.

These Durkheimian boundary setting ceremonies continue to be staged by the mass media. But they have become desperate, incoherent and self-referential. This is because they run against shifts in media representation of crime and justice since the late sixties: the moral integrity of the police and other authorities is tarnished; criminality is less an assault on sacred and consensual values than a pragmatic matter of harm to individual victims. Above all, crime may be presented as part of the wider discourse of risk. This means that moral panic narratives have to defend a 'more complex and brittle' social order, a less deferential culture.

3. Risk

Some of the social space once occupied by moral panics has been filled by more inchoate social anxieties, insecurities and fears. These are fed by specific risks: the growth of new 'techno-anxieties' (nuclear, chemical, biological, toxic and ecological risk), disease hazards, food panics, safety scares about travelling on trains or planes, and fears about international terrorism. The 'risk society' – in Beck's well-known formulation – combines the generation of risk with elaborated levels of risk management plus disputes about how this management is managed. The construction of risk refers not just to the raw information about dangerous or unpleasant things but also to the ways of assessing, classifying and reacting to them. Newly refined methods of predicting risk (like actuarial tables, psychological profiling, security assessments) become themselves objects of cultural scrutiny. If these methods reach quite different conclusions – Prozac is a safe drug; Prozac is a dangerous drug – the discourse shifts to the evaluative criteria or to the authority, reliability and accuracy of the claims-maker. Even further from the original 'thing' the shift takes a moral turn: an examination of the character and moral integrity of the claims-makers: Do they have a right to say this? Is their expertise merely another form of moral enterprise?

Reflections on risk are now absorbed into a wider culture of insecurity, victimization and fear. Both the technical question of risk analysis and the wider culture of risk-talk, have influenced the domain of deviance, crime and social control. This is self-evident in crime control policies such as *Situational Crime Prevention* that are grounded in the model of risk and rationality. Contemporary crime control ideology has not been wholly taken over by the 'new penology', based on prevention, rational choice, opportunity, actuarial modelling, etc. In one view, these new methods of governance and management are still being 'interrupted' by episodic spasms of old morality. Another view sees the theorists and managers of the criminal justice system employing the rhetoric of risk – while the public and mass media continue with their traditional moral tales.[31] Neither view does justice to the now stylized (almost self-parodying) screams of tabloid panics nor the real anger, resentment, outrage and fear of the crowd banging the sides of the security van outside the trial of a sex offender.

The global scope of the risk society, its self-reflective quality and its pervasiveness create a new backdrop for standard moral panics. Perceptions of heightened risk evoke images of panic. And in populist and electoral rhetoric about such issues as fear of crime, urban insecurity and victimization, the concepts of risk and panic are naturally connected. The realm of political morality, however, is just about distinctive enough for the BSE ('mad cow disease') or foot and mouth disease panics not to be *moral* panics. Only if risk analysis becomes perceived as *primarily* moral rather than technical (the moral irresponsibility for taking this risk) will this distinction wither away. Some argue that this has already happened. The story of HIV-AIDS shows how the clearly organic nature of the condition can be morally constructed and result in changed value positions about sexuality, gender and social control. The demography of risk was informed from the outset by the ascription of moral failures to homosexuals and other groups.

This is not quite the same as claiming that the language of the risk society has taken over or should take over the moral framework.[32] Public talk about child neglect, sexual abuse or predatory street crime strongly resists the language of probabilities. Clever statistics about your low risk of becoming a victim are no more consoling than a message from medical epidemiology that you are in a low risk category for the disease that you are actually suffering.

More interesting than 'applying' risk theory to the study of moral panics is to remember that most claims about relative risk, safety or danger depend on political morality. As Douglas originally argued, substantial disagreements over 'what is risky, how risky it is and what to do about it' are irreconcilable in purely objective terms. Moreover the perception and acceptance of risk is intimately tied to the question of who is perceived to be responsible for causing the hazard or damage to whom.[33] This allocation of blame is intrinsic to moral panics.

Criticisms

Armed or not with these newer theoretical extensions, we can approach some recurring criticisms of moral panic theory.

1. Why 'Panics?'

In disputes about definition, the term 'panic' has caused unnecessary trouble. I believe that it still makes some sense as an extended metaphor and furthermore, that there are indeed similarities between *most* moral panics and *some* other panics.

The term is unfortunate, though, because of its connotation with irrationality and being out of control. It also evokes the image of a frenzied crowd or mob: atavistic, driven by contagion and delirium, susceptible to control by demagogues and, in turn, controlling others by 'mob rule'. Newspaper reports over the last decade have referred to: *in the grips (or climate) of a moral panic . . . hit the moral panic button . . . a moral panic has broken out (or struck, been unleashed) . . . moral panic merchants (or mongers) . . . seized by a moral panic.* I invited further criticism by using two rather special examples of mass panics: first, collective delusions and urban myths – implying that these perceptions and beliefs were based on hallucinations, entirely imagined realities and second, natural disasters – evoking images of a hysterical crowd, utterly out of control, running for their lives from an imminent danger.

After being at first apologetic and accepting the downgrade of 'panic' to a mere metaphor, I remain convinced that the analogy works. Recent sociological literature on disasters and environmental problems has broadened the definition of the social. This is a denaturalization of nature. The contingencies of ordinary social life – the divisions of power, class and gender – influence the risks and consequences of exposure to such events. Models of 'environmental justice' show how dangers such as proximity to nuclear waste are socially determined. And just as Erikson used seventeenth century witch-hunts and religious persecution to understand how deviance and social control test and reinforce moral boundaries (see Chapter 1) he later showed how catastrophes may be treated as social events.[34] These 'technical' disasters are 'the new species of trouble', in contrast to traditional 'natural' disasters. They have become 'normal accidents', catastrophes embedded within the familiar: the collapse of a football stand, a rail crash, a bridge falling, the sinking of a channel ferry, a botched cancer screening programme. The resultant reactions are not as homogenous, automatic or simple as they are supposed to be in contrast with the complexities of moral discourse. Indeed the reactions are similar to the highly contested terrain of all moral panics.[35]

The criteria by which certain media driven narratives are easily recognized as moral panics need more careful explanation: drama, emergency and crisis; exaggeration; cherished values threatened; an object of concern, anxiety and hostility; evil forces or people to be identified and stopped; the eventual sense of the episodic and transitory, etc. Many such criteria are self-evident. Thompson correctly notes, though, that two of them are genuinely problematic: first, *disproportionality* and second, *volatility*.[36] While conservatives complain that moral panic theorists use disproportionality in a highly selective way that barely hides their left liberal political agenda, the critique of volatility comes from radicals to whom the assumption of volatility is not solid or political enough.

2. Disproportionality

The very usage of the term moral panic, so this argument starts, implies that societal reaction is disproportionate to the actual seriousness (risk, damage, threat) of the event. The reaction is always *more* severe (hence exaggerated, irrational, unjustified) than the condition (event, threat, behaviour, risk) warrants. Why is this just assumed? And on what grounds is the sociologist's view always correct, rational and justified?

Even in these limited terms, the assumption of disproportionality is problematic. How can the exact gravity of the reaction and the condition be assessed and compared with each other? Are we talking about intensity, duration, extensiveness? Moreover, the argument goes, we have neither the quantitative, objective criteria to claim that R (the reaction) is 'disproportionate' to A (the action) nor the universal moral criteria to judge that R is an 'inappropriate' response to the moral gravity of A.

This objection makes sense if there is nothing beyond a compendium of individual moral judgements. Only with a prior commitment to 'external' goals such as social justice, human rights or equality can we evaluate any one moral panic or judge it as more specious than another. Empirically, though, there are surely many panics where the judgement of proportionality can and should be made – even when the object of evaluation is vocabulary and rhetorical style alone. Assume we know that, over the last three years, (i) X% of asylum seekers made false claims about their risk of being persecuted; (ii) only a small proportion (say 20 per cent) of this subgroup had their claims recognized; and (iii) the resultant number of fake asylum seekers is about 200 each year. Surely then the claim about 'the country being flooded with bogus asylum seekers' is out of proportion.

This, needless to say, is not the end of the matter: the counter-claim may lead only to another round of claims-swapping. But this does not make questions of proportion, congruence and appropriateness unimportant, irrelevant or out of date (because all there is, after all, is representation). The core empirical claims within each narrative can usually be reached by the most rudimentary social science methodology. It would be perverse to dismiss such findings merely as one 'truth claim' with no 'privileged status'. Claims about past statistical trends, current estimates and extrapolations to the future are also open to scrutiny.

The problem is that the nature of the condition – 'what actually happened' – is not a matter of just how many Mods wrecked how many deck-chairs with what cost, nor how many 14-year-old girls became ill after taking which number of ecstasy tablets in what night club. Questions of symbolism, emotion and representation cannot be translated into comparable sets of statistics. Qualitative terms like 'appropriateness' convey the nuances of moral judgement more accurately than the (implied) quantitative measure of 'disproportionate' – but the more they do so, the more obviously they are socially constructed.

The critics are right that there is a tension between insisting on a universal measuring rod for determining the action/reaction gap – yet also conceding that the measurement is socially constructed and all the time passing off as non-politically biased the decision of what panics to 'expose'.

3. Volatility

Every critique from the 'left' starts by citing *Policing the Crisis*, the 1978 study by Hall and his colleagues about media and political reactions to street violence, especially mugging, carried out by black youth. This critique contrasts labelling theory's supposed separate and free-floating moral panics, each dependent on the whims of moral enterprise (Satanic cults this week, single mothers the week after) with a theory of state, political ideology and elite interests, acting together to ensure hegemonic control of the public news agenda. Far from being isolated, sporadic or sudden, these are predictable moves from one 'site' of tension to another; each move is patrolled by identical and integrated interests.

In some theories, this is less a contrast than a sequence. Discrete and volatile moral panics might indeed once have existed but they have now been replaced by a generalized moral stance, a permanent moral panic resting on a seamless web of social anxieties. The political crisis of the state is displaced into softer targets, creating a climate of hostility to marginal groups and cultural deviance. Even the most fleeting moral panic refracts the interests of political and media elites: legitimizing and vindicating enduring patterns of law and order politics, racism and policies such as mass imprisonment.[37] The importance of the media lies not in their role as transmitters of moral panics nor as campaigners but in the way they reproduce and sustain the dominant ideology.

This sequential narrative – from discrete to generalized, volatile to permanent – sounds appealing. But when did it happen? And what exactly was the shift? Thompson's claim, for example, that moral panics are succeeding each other more rapidly does not deny their volatility. His claim that they are becoming more all pervasive (panics about child abuse extend to the very existence of the family) is not, however, a shift because the appeal to pervasiveness ('it's not only this') was a defining feature of the concept.

The notion of a 'permanent moral panic' is less an exaggeration than a oxymoron. A panic, by definition, is self-limiting, temporary and spasmodic, a splutter of rage which burns itself out. Every now and then speeches, TV documentaries, trials, parliamentary debates, headlines and editorials cluster into the peculiar mode of managing information and expressing indignation that we call a moral panic. Each one may draw on the same stratum of political morality and cultural unease and — much like Foucault's micro-systems of power — have a similar logic and internal rhythm. Successful moral panics owe their appeal to their ability to find points of resonance with wider anxieties. But each appeal is a sleight of hand, magic without a magician. It points to continuities: in space (*this sort of thing . . . it's not only this*) backward in time (*part of a trend . . . building up over the years*) a conditional common future (*a growing problem . . . will get worse if nothing done*). And for a self-reflexive society, an essential meta-message: *This is not just a moral panic.*

The element of volatility should be studied in two ways. First, why do full-blown panics ever end? My original answers were only guess-work: (i) a 'natural history' which ends with burn out, boredom, running out of steam, a fading away (ii) the slightly more sophisticated notion of cycles in fashion — like clothing styles, musical taste; (iii) the putative danger fizzles out, the media or entrepreneurs have cried wolf once too often, their information is discredited; (iv) the information was accepted but easily reabsorbed whether into private life or public spectacle — the end result described by the Situationists as *recuperation*. A second question concerns failed moral panics. Why despite having some ingredients, did they never quite take off: alcopops; computer hackers; cults, new age travellers; lesbian mums; commercial surrogate births; the Dunblane school shooting; baby-snatching from hospitals; cloning . . .

The volatility issue needs careful steering. If the idea of panic is domesticated under the dull sociological rubric of 'collective behaviour', the political edge of the concept is blunted. In this tradition, a moral panic merely reflects fears and concerns that are 'part of the human condition', or the 'maverick side of human nature' and 'operates outside the stable, patterned structures of society'.[38] The opposite is true: without the 'stable, patterned structures' of politics, mass media, crime control, professions and organized religion, no moral panics could be generated or sustained.

McRobbie and Thornton are correct that today's more sophisticated, self-aware and fragmented media make the original notion of the spasmodic ('every now and then') panic out of date.[39] 'Panic' is rather a mode of representation in which daily events are regularly brought to the public's attention:

> They are a standard response, a familiar, sometimes weary, even ridiculous rhetoric rather than an exceptional emergency intervention. Used by politicians to orchestrate consent, by business to promote sales . . . and by the media to make home and social affairs newsworthy, moral panics are constructed on a daily basis.[40]

But surely not quite a 'daily basis'. Moral panic theory indeed must be updated to fit the refractions of multi-mediated social worlds. But the unexpected, the bizarre and the anomalous happen: the James Bulger murder is neither a daily event nor a familiar story. The repertoire of media and political discourses has to design special conventions to translate anomalies into everyday, long-term anxieties. But they still have to remain within the format of the transitory and spasmodic – the essence of news.

The fragmentary and the integrated belong together: moral panics have their own internal trajectory – a microphysics of outrage – which, however, is initiated and sustained by wider social and political forces.

4. Good and Bad Moral Panics?

The criticism that 'moral panic' is a value-laden concept, a mere political epithet, deserves more complicated attention than it receives. It is obviously true that the uses of the concept to expose disproportionality and exaggeration have come from within a left liberal consensus. This empirical project is concentrated on (if not reserved for) cases where the moral outrage appears driven by conservative or reactionary forces. For cultural liberals (today's 'cosmopolitans'), this was an opportunity to condemn moral entrepreneurs, to sneer at their small-mindedness, puritanism or intolerance; for political radicals, these were easy targets, the soft side of hegemony or elite interests. In both cases, the point was to expose social reaction not just as over-reaction in some quantitative sense, but first, as *tendentious* (that is, slanted in a particular ideological direction) and second, as *misplaced* or *displaced* (that is, aimed – whether deliberately or thoughtlessly – at a target which was not the 'real' problem).

As the term itself became diffused and explicitly used in the media, the liberal/anti-authority origin of its birth made it more openly contested. A popular strand in Thatcherite Conservatism was indeed to uphold *exactly* the

meta-politics and causal theories that fuelled moral panics and to attack
the derogatory use of the concept as a symptom of being 'out of touch' with
public opinion and the fears of 'ordinary people'. This populist rhetoric
remains in New Labour – with the attractive twist that many with roots in
Guardian liberalism (and who had used the concept earlier) now turn on the
'jargon-laden left' for using the term so selectively.

In the British public arena the debate is frozen at this level of journalistic
polemics. An imaginary sequence:

- *The Sun* reports that a 14-year-old school-girl in Oldham attacked a male
  teacher with a pair of scissors after he reprimanded her for using dirty
  language. The teacher's wound needed hospital treatment. The girl is
  'of Asian origin'; the teacher is white. The police are investigating the
  incident; the local MP claims that such violent attacks by girls have
  doubled in this year. The story, with standard elaborations (the girl's father
  was an asylum seeker; teachers in other schools were too scared to speak
  out), runs in the tabloids for two more days.

- On the fourth day, *The Guardian* publishes an op-ed article by one of its
  think-piece journalists. She urges caution before a fully-fledged moral
  panic breaks out. The police, the school, the education authority and the
  police deny that such incidents are increasing; no one knows where
  the MP got his statistics. The teacher's wound was superficial. Such
  irresponsible reporting plays into the hands of extremist parties running
  for the local election. The *real* problems in places like Oldham are institutionalized racism in the schools and the special pressures that immigrant
  parents place on their daughters.

- On the day after, a *Daily Telegraph* editorial denounces the *Guardian* piece
  for deliberately trying to evade and distort the issue in the name of political
  correctness. Once again, the label of 'moral panic' is being used to play
  down the fears and anxieties of ordinary people – teachers, pupils, parents
  – who have to live every day in an atmosphere of violence. It now appears
  that the local schoolteachers' union had warned two months ago that
  school violence was driving teachers into leaving the profession.

This sequence allows for somewhat different readings of the relationships
between moral panics and political ideology. (i) The weakest version sees the
concept as a neutral descriptive or analytical tool, no different from other
terms in this area (such as 'campaign' or 'public opinion'). It just so happens
that the term has been used by left liberals (and their sociological cronies) to

undermine conservative ideologies and popular anxieties by labelling their concerns as irrational. But the term remains neutral and its usage could easily be reversed. (ii) In a slightly stronger version, the liberal appropriation of the term has gone too far for any reversal. We cannot expect to find conservatives trying to expose liberal or radical concerns as being 'moral panics'. (iii) A third version goes further. The genealogy of the term, its current usage and its folk meaning allow for one reading only: the term is not just 'value laden' but intended to be a critical tool to expose dominant interests and ideologies. The school violence sequence depicts one round in the battle between cultural representations.

These positions rest on shifting sands. In some cases, the logic of labelling social reaction as a moral panic may indeed lead to varieties on non-intervention (leave things alone): either because reaction is based on literal delusion or because the problem does not deserve such extravagant attention. The difficult cases are more interesting – the existence of the problem is recognized, but its cognitive interpretation and moral implications are denied, evaded or disputed.

Such reactions form exactly the discourse of denial: *literal denial* (nothing happened); *interpretative denial* (something happened, but it's not what you think) and *implicatory denial* (what happened was not really bad and can be justified). Instead of exposing moral panics, my own cultural politics entails, in a sense, *encouraging* something like moral panics about mass atrocities and political suffering – and trying to expose the strategies of denial deployed to prevent the acknowledgement of these realities. All of us cultural workers – busily constructing social problems, making claims and setting public agendas – think that we are stirring up 'good' moral panics. Perhaps we could purposely *recreate* the conditions that made the Mods and Rockers panic so successful (exaggeration, sensitization, symbolization, prediction, etc.) and thereby overcome the barriers of denial, passivity and indifference that prevent a full acknowledgement of human cruelty and suffering.

The pathetic ease and gullibility with which the mass media are lured into conventional moral panics may be contrasted to the deep denial behind their refusal to sustain a moral panic about torture, political massacres or social suffering in distant places. Public and media indifference are even attributed to deep states such as 'compassion fatigue'.[41] Moeller describes a cognitive and moral stupor in which attention thresholds have risen so rapidly that the media try even more desperately to 'ratchet up' the criteria for stories to be covered. In the hierarchy of which events and issues will be covered, a footballer's ankle injury will get more media attention than a political massacre.

Sometimes (as Moeller shows in her analysis of the coverage of the Bosnian and Rwandan stories) the media try to create moral concern, but struggle against a palpable audience denial. This was less compassion fatigue than compassion avoidance: 'confronted with the images of putrefying corpses or swollen bodies bobbling along river banks they looked away – even when they believed that the story was important.'[42] The shifting thresholds of attention she describes – the bewildering ways in which compassion rises and falls, the blurred boundaries of what is accepted as normal – look just like the volatility of moral panics.

I concluded my book with a vague prediction that more 'nameless' folk devils would be generated. The current causes of delinquency are clearer now: the climate of distrust and Darwinian individualism generated by Thatcherism and sustained in New Labour; under-regulated market economies; privatiza-tion of public services, welfare state cutbacks, growing inequality and social exclusion. Delinquents are nameless not in the banal sense that I meant (not being able to predict the names of the subcultural styles that would replace 'Mod' and 'Rocker') but because they remain as anonymous as the schools, housing estates, urban sprawls from which they came. Pictorial and verbal imaginations are applied more readily to the naming of social controls: Crime Watch, Situational Crime Prevention, Closed Circuit Television, Zero Tolerance, Three Strikes and You're Out, Anti Social Behaviour Orders. Social policies once regarded as abnormal – incarcerating hundreds of asylum seekers in detention centres, run as punitive transit camps by private companies for profit – are seen as being normal, rational and conventional.

The idea that social problems are socially constructed does not question their existence nor dismiss issues of causation, prevention and control. It draws attention to a meta debate about what sort of acknowledgement the problem receives and merits. The issue indeed is *proportionality*. It is surely not possible to calibrate exactly the human costs of crimes, deviance or human rights violations. The shades of intentionally inflicted suffering, harm, cruelty, damage, loss and insecurity are too complex to be listed in an exact, rational or universally accepted rank order of seriousness. But some disparities are so gross, some claims so exaggerated, some political agendas so tendentious that they can only be called something like, well, 'social injustice'.

Sociologists have no privileged status in pointing this out and suggesting remedial policies. But even if their role is relegated to being merely another claims-maker, this must include not only exposing *under-reaction* (apathy, denial and indifference) but making the comparisons that could expose *over-reaction* (exaggeration, hysteria, prejudice and panic). These 'reactions' may be compared to the perceptual realm occupied by the sociology of risk: assessing not the risk itself nor its management, but the ways it is perceived. Even if there is no question of physical danger (death, infliction of pain, financial loss), the drawing and reinforcement of moral boundaries is as similar as Mary Douglas's comparison between physical and moral pollution. People's perceptions of the relative seriousness of so many different social problems cannot be easily shifted. The reason is that cognition itself is socially controlled. And the cognitions that matter here are carried by the mass media.

This is why moral panics are condensed political struggles to control the means of cultural reproduction. Studying them is easy and a lot of fun. It also allows us to identify and conceptualize the lines of power in any society, the ways we are manipulated into taking some things too seriously and other things not seriously enough.

Notes and References

1 The term 'moral panic' was first used by Jock Young in 'The Role of the Police as Amplifiers of Deviancy, Negotiators of Reality and Translators of Fantasy', in S. Cohen (Ed.), *Images of Deviance* (Harmondsworth: Penguin, 1971), p. 37. We both probably picked it up from Marshall McLuhan's *Understanding Media*, published in 1964.

2 Between 1984 and 1991 (inclusive) there were about 8 citations of 'moral panic' in UK newspapers; then 25 in 1992, then a sudden leap to 145 in 1993. From 1994 to 2001, the average was at 109 per year.

3 Kenneth Thompson's *Moral Panics* (London: Routledge, 1998), appeared in the Routledge 'Key Ideas' series. For definitions, see Allan G. Johnson, *Blackwell Dictionary of Sociology* (Oxford: Blackwell, 2000) and Karim Murji, 'Moral Panic' in *Dictionary of Criminology*, London, Sage, 2001.

4 Blake Morrison, *As If* (Cambridge: Granta, 1997).

5 Sir William Macpherson, *The Stephen Lawrence Inquiry* (London: HMSO, 1999).

6 Two useful examples: Eugene McLaughlin and Karim Murji, 'After the Stephen Lawrence Report', *Critical Social Policy* 19 (August 1999), pp.371–85; Alan Marlow and Barry Loveday (Eds), *After Macpherson: Policing After the Stephen Lawrence Inquiry* (Lyme Regis: Russell House Publishing, 2000).

7 McLaughlin and Murji, op. cit. p.372.

8 As *The Sun*'s front page proclaimed: 'Britain Backs Our Bobbies: Sun Poll Boosts Under-Fire Cops' (1 March 1999).

9 Karim Murji, 'The Agony and the Ecstasy: Drugs, Media and Morality', in Ross Coomber (Ed.), *The Control of Drugs and Drug Users: Reason or Reaction?* (London: Harwood Publishers, 1998).

10 Phillip Jenkins, *Moral Panic: Changing Concepts of the Child Molester in Modern America* (New Haven, Yale University Press, 1998).

11 See Phillip Jenkins, *Pedophiles and Priests: Anatomy of a Contemporary Crisis* (Oxford: Oxford University Press, 1996).

12 For two different, but complimentary, views see Beatrix Campbell, *Unofficial Secrets: Child Sexual Abuse – The Cleveland Case* (London: Virago, 1989) and Nigel Parton, *Governing the Family: Child Care, Child Protection and the State* (London: Macmillan, 1991), especially Chapter 4 'Sexual Abuse, the Cleveland Affair and the Private Family'.

13 For an analysis of newspaper coverage of the series of 'anti-paedophile crowd actions' in Britain over summer 2000, see John Drury, '"When the mobs are looking for witches to burn, nobody's safe" talking about the reactionary crowd', *Discourse and Society* 13, 1 pp. 41–73.

14 On the history of media panics about the appearance of new forms of media, see Kirsten Drotner, 'Modernity and Media Panics', in M. Skovmand and K.C. Schroder (Eds), *Media Cultures: Reappraising Traditional Media* (London: Routledge, 1992) and 'Dangerous Media? Panic Discourses and Dilemmas of Modernity', *Pedagogica Historica* 35, 3 (1999), pp. 593–619.

15 Drotner, op. cit. p.52.

16 For a recent review (concentrating on highly publicized violent crimes) see Martin Barker and Julian Petley (Eds), *Ill Effects: The Media-Violence Debate* (London: Routledge, 2001).

17 Grainne McKeever, 'Detecting, Prosecuting and Punishing Benefit Fraud: The Social Security Administration (Fraud) Act 1997', *Modern Law Review* 62 (March 1999), p.269.

18 Angela McRobbie, 'Motherhood, A Teenage Job', *Guardian* (5 September 1989).

19 A. Ward, *Talking Dirty: Moral Panic and Political Rhetoric* (London: Institute for Public Policy Research, 1996).

20 P.M. Evans and K.J. Swift, 'Single Mothers and the Press: Rising Tides, Moral Panic and Restructuring Discourses', in S.M. Neysmith (Ed.), *Restructuring Caring Labour: Discourse, State Practice and Everyday Life* (Oxford, OUP, 2000).

21 J. Doly *et al.*, *Refugees in Europe: The Hostile New Agenda* (London: Minorities Rights Group, 1997).

22 Robin Cohen, *Frontiers of Identity: The British and the Others* (London: Longman, 1994).

23 Ron Kaye, 'Redefining the Refugee: The UK Media Portrayal of Asylum Seekers', in Khalid Koser and Helma Lutz (Eds), *The New Migration in Europe: Social Constructions and Social Realities* (London: Macmillan Press, 1998), pp. 163–82.

24 See the report by Oxfam's UK poverty programme in Scotland, *Asylum: the Truth Behind the Headlines* (Oxfam, February 2001). This project monitored six

Scottish papers over a two-month period (March–April 2000): a total of 263 articles on asylum and refugee issues.

25 E. El Refaie, 'Metaphors we Discriminate by: Naturalized Themes in Austrian Newspaper Articles about Asylum Seekers', *Journal of Sociolinguistics* 5, 3 (August 2001), pp.352–71.

26 Stanley Cohen, *States of Denial: Knowing About Atrocities and Suffering* (Cambridge: Polity, 2001).

27 For example, Erich Goode and Nachman Ben-Yehuda, *Moral Panics: The Social Construction of Deviance* (Oxford: Blackwell, 1994).

28 See **Selected Reading List** below for references on constructionism.

29 Robert Reiner, 'The Rise of Virtual Vigilantism: Crime Reporting Since World War II', *Criminal Justice Matters* 43 (Spring 2001).

30 Richard.L. Fox and Robert Van Sichel, *Tabloid Justice: Criminal Justice in an Age of Media Frenzy* (Boulder: L. Rienner Publishers, 2001).

31 David Garland, *The Culture of Control* (Oxford: Oxford University Press, 2001).

32 Sheldon Unger, 'Moral Panic versus the Risk Society: Implications of the Changing Sites of Social Anxiety', *British Journal of Sociology* 52, pp. 271–292.

33 Mary Douglas's main publications on the subject (*Risk and Culture* and *Risk and Blame*) are presented in Richard Farndon, *Mary Douglas: An Intellectual Biography* (London: Routledge, 1999), pp 144–67.

34 Kai T. Erikson, *Everything in Its Path: Destruction of Community in the Buffalo Creek Flood* (New York: Simon and Schuster, 1976).

35 See Phil Scraton, *Hillsborough: The Truth* (Edinburgh: Mainstream, 2001).

36 Thompson, op. cit. pp. 8–11.

37 See William J. Chambliss, 'Crime Control and Ethnic Minorities: Legitimizing Racial Oppression by Creating Moral Panics', in Darnell Hawkins (Ed.), *Ethnicity, Race and Crime* (Albany: State University of New York Press, 1995).

38 Goode and Ben-Yehuda, op. cit. p.104.

39 Angela McRobbie and Sarah L. Thornton, 'Rethinking "moral panic" for multi-mediated social worlds', *British Journal of Sociology* 46 (December 1995), pp. 559–74.

40 ibid. p. 560.

41 Susan D. Moeller, *Compassion Fatigue: How the Media Sell Disease, Famine, War and Death* (New York: Routledge, 1999).

42 ibid. p. 306.

Thanks to Kate Steward and Andy Wilson for their help with this 'Third Edition'.

Selected Reading List
(1982–2002)

I. General, Theoretical, Historical

Nachman Ben-Yehuda, *The Politics and Morality of Deviance: moral panics, drug abuse, deviant science, and reversed stigmatization*, SUNY Press, Albany, 1990.

Joel Best, 'But Seriously Folks: the limitations of the strict constructionist interpretation of social problems', in Miller and Holstein (q.v.).

Joel Best, 'Debates about Constructionism', in E. Rubington and M. Weinberg, eds, *The Study of Social Problems*, Oxford University Press, New York, 1995.

Joel Best, *Random Violence: how we talk about new crimes and new victims*, University of California Press, Berkeley, 1999.

Joel Best, ed., *Images of Issues: typifying contemporary social problems*, Aldine de Gruyter, New York, 1999.

Joel Best, *Damned Lies and Statistics: untangling numbers from the media, politicians and activists*, University of California Press, Berkeley, 2001.

Erich Goode and Nachman Ben-Yehuda, *Moral Panics: the social construction of deviance*, Blackwell, Cambridge, Massachusetts, 1994.

P. R. Ibarra and John Kitsuse, 'Vernacular Constituents of Moral Discourse: an interactionist proposal for the study of social problems', in Miller and Holstein (q.v.).

Philip Jenkins, *Intimate Enemies: moral panics in contemporary Great Britain, Social Problems and Social Issues*, Aldine de Gruyter, New York, 1992.

Angela McRobbie and Sarah L. Thornton, 'Rethinking "Moral Panic" for Multi-Mediated Social Worlds', *British Journal of Sociology* 46/4 (1995).

Kate Marshall, *Moral Panics and Victorian Values*, 2nd ed., Junius Publications, London, 1986.

Gale Miller and John A. Holstein, eds, *Constructionist Controversies: issues in social problems theory*, Aldine de Gruyter, New York, 1993.

Geoffrey Pearson, 'Scare in the Community: Britain in a moral panic', *Community Care* (1995).

Gary Potter and Victor Kappeler, eds, *Constructing Crime: perspectives on making news and social problems*, Waveland Press, Prospect Heights III, 1996.

Theodore Sasson, *Crime Talk: how citizens construct a social problem*, Aldine de Gruyter, New York, 1995.

Elaine Showalter, *Hystories: hysterical epidemics and modern culture*, Columbia University Press, New York, 1997.

Malcolm Spector and John Kitsuse, *Constructing Social Problems*, Aldine de Gruyter, New York, 1987.

Kenneth Thompson, *Moral Panics*, Routledge, London/New York, 1998.

Sheldon Ungar, 'Moral Panic versus the Risk Society: the implications of the changing sites of social anxiety', *British Journal of Sociology* 52/2 (2001).

Andrew Ward, *Talking Dirty: moral panic and political rhetoric*, Institute for Public Policy Research, London, 1996.

II. Mass Media and Moral Panic

Gregg Barak, ed., *Media, Process and the Social Construction of Crime: studies in newsmaking criminology*, Garland Publishing, New York/London, 1994.

Kirsten Drotner, 'Dangerous Media? Panic Discourses and Dilemmas of Modernity', *Pedagogica Historica* 35/3 (1999).

John Eldrige, *The Mass Media and Power in Modern Britain*, Oxford University Press, Oxford, 1997.

B. Franklin and J. Petley, 'Killing the Age of Innocence: newspaper reporting of the death of James Bulger', in Jane Pilcher and Stephen Wagg, eds, *Thatcher's Children? Politics, Childhood and Society in the 1980s and 1990s*, Falmer Press, London, 1996.

Arnold Hunt, '"Moral Panic" and Moral Language in the Media', *British Journal of Sociology* 48/4 (1997).

Sarah Kember, 'Surveillance, Technology and Crime: the James Bulger case', in Martin Lister, ed., *The Photographic Image in Digital Culture*, Routledge, London, 1995.

David Kidd-Hewitt and Richard Osborne, eds, *Crime and the Media: the post-modern spectacle*, Pluto Press, London, 1995.

Angela McRobbie, 'The Moral Panic in the Age of the Postmodern Massmedia', in A. McRobbie, ed., *Postmodernism and Popular Culture*, Routledge, London, 1994.

Philip Schlesinger and Howard Tumber, *Reporting Crime: the media politics of juvenile justice*, Oxford University Press, Oxford, 1994.

Michael Welch, Melissa Fenwick and Meredith Roberts, 'Primary Definitions of Crime and Moral Panic: a content analysis of experts' quotes in feature newspaper articles on crime', *Journal of Research in Crime and Delinquency* 34/4 (1997).

III. Applications and Case Studies

1. Juvenile Delinquency and Youth Subcultures

Ulf Boethius, 'Youth, the Media and Moral Panics', in J. Fornas and G. Bolin, eds, *Youth Culture in Late Modernity*, Sage, London, 1995.

Sheila Brown, 'Representing Problem Youth: the repackaging of reality', in S. Brown, ed., *Understanding Youth and Crime: listening to youth?*, Open University Press, Buckingham, 1998.

Colin Hay, 'Mobilization through Interpellation: James Bulger, juvenile crime and the construction of a moral panic', *Social and Legal Studies* 4 (June 1995).

Bernard Schissel, *Blaming Children: youth crime, moral panic and the politics of hate*, Fernwood, Halifax, NS, 1997.

John Springhall, *Youth, Popular Culture and Moral Panics: penny gaffs to gangsta-rap, 1830–1996*, St Martin's Press, New York, 1998.

Sarah Thornton, 'Moral Panic, the Media and British Rave Culture' in A. Ross and T. Rose, eds, *Microphone Friends: youth music and youth culture*, Routledge, London, 1994.

P. A. J. Waddington, 'Mugging as a Moral Panic: a question of proportion', *British Journal of Sociology* 37/2 (1986).

Marjorie Zatz, 'Chicano Youth Gangs and Crime: the creation of a moral panic', *Contemporary Crises* 11 (1987).

2. School Violence

R. Burns and C. Crawford, 'School Shootings: the media and public fear: ingredients for a moral panic,' *Crime, Law and Social Change* 32/2 (1999).

Elizabeth Donohue, *et al.*, *School House Hype: school shooting and the real risks kids face in America*, Justice Policy Institution, Washington DC, 1998.

Mike Kennedy, 'The Changing Face of School Violence', in *Under Siege: Schools as the New Battleground*, publisher unknown, 1999.

Donna Killingbeck, 'The Role of Television News in the Construction of School Violence as a "Moral Panic"', *Journal of Criminal Justice and Popular Culture* 8/3 (2001).

John Springhall, 'Violent Media, Guns and Moral Panics: the Columbine High School massacre', *Pedagogica Historica* 35/3 (1999).

3. Panics about the Media

Martin Barker, *The Haunt of Fears: the strange history of the British horror comics campaign*, Pluto Press, London, 1984.

Martin Barker, *The Video Nasties: freedom and censorship in the arts*, Pluto Press, London, 1984.

Martin Barker, 'Frederic Wertham: the sad case of the unhappy humanist', in
J. A. Lent, ed., *Pulp Demons: international dimensions of the postwar anti-comics
campaign*, Associated University Presses, Cranbury, 1999.

Martin Barker and Julian Petley, eds, *Ill Effects: the media/violence debate*, 2nd ed.,
Routledge, London, 2001.

Shearon A. Lowery, 'Seduction of the Innocent: the great comic book scare', in
S. A. Lowery and M. L. DeFleur, eds, *Milestones in Mass Communication Research:
media effects*, Longman, New York, 1983.

Shearon A. Lowery and Melvin L. DeFleur, 'The Invasion from Mars: radio panics
America', in S. A. Lowery and M. L. DeFleur, eds, *Milestones in Mass
Communication Research: media effects*, Longman, New York, 1983.

John Martin, *The Seduction of the Gullible: the curious history of the British 'video nasties'
phenomenon*, Procrustes Press, Nottingham, 1997.

4. Bad Drugs

Chris Baerveldt, *et al.*, 'Assessing a Moral Panic Relating to Crime and Drugs Policy
in the Netherlands: towards a testable theory, *Crime, Law and Social Change* 29/1
(1998).

Theodore Chiricos, 'Moral Panic as Ideology: drugs, violence, race and punishment
in America', in M. J. Lynch and E. B. Patterson, eds, *Justice with Prejudice: race
and criminal justice in America*, Harrow and Heston, Guilderland NY, 1997.

M. Collin, *Altered State: the story of ecstasy culture and acid house*, Serpent's Tail,
London, 1997.

Cottino and M. Quirico, 'Easy Target and Moral Panic: the law on drug addiction
No. 162 of 1990, *The Scandinavian Journal of Social Welfare* 4/2 (1995).

Eric Goode, 'The American Drug Panic of the 1980s: social construction or
objective threat?', *International Journal of Addiction* 45/5 (September 1990).

Andrew Hill, 'Acid House and Thatcherism: noise, the mob and the English
countryside', *British Journal of Sociology* 53/1 (2002).

5. Pornography

Varda Burstyn, 'Political Precedents and Moral Crusades: women, sex and the
state', in V. Burstyn, ed., *Women against Censorship*, Douglas and MacIntyre,
Vancouver, 1985.

Gary Kinsman, 'Danger Signals: moral conservatism, the media and the sex police',
in G. Kinsman, ed., *The Regulation of Desire: sexuality in Canada*, Black Rose
Books, Montreal, 1987.

Theresa Murray and Michael McClure, *Moral Panic: exposing the religious right's agenda
on sexuality, Listen up!*, Cassell, London, 1995.

Simon Watney, *Policing Desire: pornography, AIDS and the media*, University of
Minnesota Press, Minneapolis, 1987.

6. Threatened Children: Child Abuse – Sexual and Satanic

Joel Best, *Threatened Children: rhetoric and concern about child-victims*, University of Chicago Press, Chicago, 1990.

Joel Best, *Troubling Children: studies of children and social problems*, Aldine de Gruyter, New York, 1994.

Mary deYoung, 'Speak of the Devil: rhetoric in claims-making about the satanic ritual abuse problem', *Journal of Sociology and Social Welfare* 23 (1996).

Mary deYoung, 'Another Look at Moral Panics: the case of satanic day care centers', *Deviant Behavior* 19/3 (1998).

Philip Jenkins, *Moral Panic: changing concepts of the child molester in modern America*, Yale University Press, New Haven, CT, 1998.

Philip Jenkins and Daniel Maier-Katkin, 'Satanism – Myth and Reality in a Contemporary Moral Panic', *Crime, Law and Social Change* 17/1 (1992).

Jean S. LaFontaine, *Speak of the Devil: tales of satanic abuse in contemporary England*, Cambridge University Press, Cambridge, 1998.

James T. Richardson, *et al.*, eds, *The Satanism Scare*, Aldine de Gruyter, Hawthorn, 1991.

Jeffrey S. Victor, *Satanic Panic: the creation of a contemporary legend*, Open Court, Chicago, 1993.

Jeffrey S. Victor, 'Fundamentalist Religions and the Moral Crusade against Satanism: the social construction of deviant behavior', *Deviant Behavior* 15 (1994).

Jeffrey S. Victor, 'Moral Panics and the Social Construction of Deviant Behavior: a theory and application to the case of ritual child abuse', *Sociological Perspectives* 41/3 (Fall 1998).

7. Welfare Issues and Single Mothers

Lisa D. Brush, 'Worthy Widows, Welfare Cheats: proper womanhood in expert needs talk about single mothers in the US 1900–1988', *Gender and Society* 11/6 (1997).

Kate Cregan, '(S)he was Convicted and Condemned', *Social Semiotics* 11/2 (2001).

Dean Hartley and Peter Taylor-Gooby, *Dependency Culture: the explosion of a myth*, Harvester Wheatsheaf, London, 1992.

O. Linne and M. Jones, 'The Coverage of Lone-Parents in British Newspapers: a construction based on moral panic?', *Communication Abstracts* 24/1 (2001).

Bronwyn Naylor, 'The "Bad Mother" in Media and Legal Texts', *Social Semiotics* 11/2 (2001).

Anne Phoenix, 'Social Constructions of Lone Motherhood', in E. Bortoloaia Silva, ed., *Good Enough Mothering?: Feminist Perspectives on Lone Mothering*, Routledge, London, 1996.

8. Refugees and Asylum Seekers

Colin Campbell and Elaine Clark, '"Gypsy Invasion": a critical analysis of newspaper reaction to Czech and Slovak Romani asylum-seekers in Britain', *Romani Studies* 10/1 (1997).

Lorna Chessum, 'Race and Immigration in the Leicester Local Press 1945–62', *Immigrants and Minorities* 17/2 (1998).

Ron Kaye, 'Redefining the Refugee: the UK media portrayal of asylum seekers', in K. Koser and H Lutz, eds, *The New Migration in Europe: social constructions and social realities*, Macmillan, Basingstoke, 1998.

9. Miscellaneous

Thomas Acton, 'Modernisation, Moral Panics and the Gypsies', *Sociology Review* 4/1 (1994).

G. Fordham, 'Moral Panic and the Construction of a National Order: HIV/AIDS risk groups and the moral boundaries in the creation of a modern Thailand', *Critique of Anthropology* 21/3 (2001).

Sheldon Ungar, 'Hot Crises and Media Reassurance: a comparison of emerging diseases and Ebola Zaire', *British Journal of Sociology* 49/1 (1998).

B. Williams, 'Bail Bandits: the construction of a moral panic', *Critical Social Policy* 13/1 (1993).

Preface to First Edition

The exigencies of life in general and academic life in particular have transformed a study which started its life as an instant sociological response to the immediate, into a piece of historical sociology. Who on earth is still worried about the Mods and Rockers? Who – some might even ask – *were* the Mods and Rockers? I too would have preferred this book to have appeared when the phenomenon it describes was still a contemporary one, but sustained by friends and colleagues I carried on writing in the belief that this study has implications beyond its immediate subject matter. For the most part I have resisted the temptation to make such implications explicit or up to date; I will have failed if they are not transparent enough for the reader to make himself. The processes by which moral panics and folk devils are generated do not date.

Some of the research on which this book is based originated as part of a Ph.D. thesis, and I am grateful to Terence Morris who supervised my work during those years. My greatest debt since then is to David Downes for his constant help and encouragement, and subsequently to all my other friends in and around the National Deviancy Conference among whom – most invidiously – I single out Stuart Hall, Paul Rock, Ian Taylor, Laurie Taylor and Jock Young.

Sarah Stubbs typed various drafts with a speed and efficiency which I could never match and my wife Ruth helped me in many ways.

S.C.
1971

Symbols of Trouble

Introduction to the Second Edition

Taken as an instant pop sociological response to the immediate and newsworthy problems of the day, this book was 'out of date' even when it originally appeared in 1972. Such an enterprise is anyway best left to good journalists who know far better than sociologists about reacting to the contemporary and – moreover – about meeting deadlines.

But then, as now, I would want to justify this piece of historical reconstruction as having implications somewhat beyond the immediate and topical. It matters neither here nor there that there is now (1980) a major Mod revival, spinning its way through music, fashion, colour supplement journalism and even two full-length movies from *The Who*, trying to recreate the spirit of the Brighton beaches.

We need to look beyond these ephemera. Admittedly, the assertion in my original preface that the processes by which moral panics and folk devils are generated do not date was a little brash in implying that I had cleverly succeeded in uncovering these processes. But I doubt that later developments have changed this picture. My pessimistic concluding words have, alas, also been justified: 'More moral panics will be generated and other, as yet nameless folk devils will be created. This is not because such developments have an inexorable inner logic, but because our society as present structured will continue to generate problems for some of its members – like working-class adolescents – and then condemn whatever solution these groups find.'

One cannot let things rest at this point, though. Indeed, a defect of the book was the impression it sometimes might have conveyed of a certain timelessness, an unveiling of a set of consequences insulated from history and politics. This is what Barthes calls the 'miraculous evaporation of history from events'. While having to leave the actual text intact for this edition (with the exception of a few minor corrections) I want to use this introduction to comment on recent theoretical developments in the study of delinquency and subcultures, which are very much concerned with re-inserting the historical and the political. Given my limited space, I can do little more than give a critical guide to this literature and also (more than the original text) address issues within the sociological debate rather than looking to a more general audience.

I refer to theoretical developments rather than actual historical occurrences because I do not believe that anything which has actually happened or has been 'discovered' (about youth, popular culture, delinquency, mass media reporting) in the decade since the research was completed needs extended reconstruction here. True, the substance of this period has been continually interesting: the skinhead years, the brief glamrock interlude, the punk explosion, the revival of both the Teds and the Mods, the continued noise of football hooliganism. But to re-examine the subject of post-war British youth subcultures is not quite the same as constructing, say, a revised historiography of World War II: there are no new archives to be opened, no secret documents to be discovered, no pacts of silence to be broken. There are just the same (rather poor) sources of information from the same (often inarticulate) informants. The question is what new sense can be made of this 'same' data.

And this decade has been one of quite phenomenal growth in the relevant 'making sense' fields such as deviancy theory and cultural studies. These years saw the novelty of the labelling perspective in the sociology of deviance being challenged by Marxism, which at the same time (in combination with various branches of structuralism and semiotics) established virtual hegemony over the cultural studies field. And in theorizing about delinquent subcultures, there was a leap straight from the functionalism of the original American theory to various types of neo-Marxism. The interactionist/labelling intervention hardly registered here. *Folk Devils and Moral Panics* certainly relied heavily on labelling theory, but never suggested that the origins of the behaviour itself could be explained by anything other than a slightly tougher version (via Downes) of original subcultural theory. Despite my pains to avoid this, the book was still misinterpreted (together with most labelling studies) as implying that there is no need for a structural explanation of the subculture in its own right.

It is quite true, of course, that the book was more a study of moral panics than of folk devils. Influenced by labelling theory, I wanted to study reaction; the actors themselves just flitted across the screen. Now – to redress this balance but also because this is where the most creative and challenging work has been done during this decade – I want to concentrate more on action. Accordingly – still following this rather abstract distinction between actor and audience, action and reaction, behaviour and labelling – I will reverse the book's sequence and consider action first.

Action

Traditional subcultural theory of delinquency is too well known to have to expound here.[1] The intellectual offspring of two oddly matched but conventional strands of American sociology – functionalist anomie theory and the Chicago school – and the political offspring of the end of ideology era, it has shaped sociological visions of delinquency for twenty-five years. Like all intellectual departures – particularly those influenced by political considerations and particularly those in the deviancy field[2] – when new subcultural theory appeared in Britain at the beginning of the seventies[3] it was concerned to show how radically it differed from tradition. And it could hardly have *looked* more different.

It was not just the switch from functionalist to Marxist language but the sense conveyed of why this switch 'had' to take place. The context was light years away from America in the mid-fifties: a sour, post welfare state Britain which had patently not delivered the goods; the cracking of all those interdependent myths of classlessness, embourgeoisement, consumerism and pluralism; the early warnings of economic recession and high (particularly juvenile) unemployment; the relative weakness of recognizably political resistance.

No tortuous sociology of knowledge is needed to see how this context 'influenced' the theories; the context was explicitly woven into the theories' very substance. History and political economy became open rather than hidden; the 'problem' of the working-class adolescent was seen not in terms of adjustment, or providing more opportunities to buy a larger share of the cake, but of bitter conflict, resistance and strife. The delinquent changed from 'frustrated social climber'[4] to cultural innovator and critic. What was really happening on the beaches of Brighton and Clacton – as well as earlier at the Teddy Boy dance halls and later on the football terraces and punk concerts – was a drama of profound symbolic resonance. Subculture was, no less, a political battleground between the classes.

I will come back in more detail to this framework. It is worth noting, though, that for all its obvious novelty and achievement – it is now simply not possible to talk about delinquent subcultures in the same way – the new theory shares a great deal more with the old than it cared to admit. Both work with the same 'problematic' (to use the fashionable term): growing up in a class society; both identify the same vulnerable group: the urban male working-class late adolescent; both see delinquency as a collective solution to a structurally imposed problem. For example, while its tone and political agenda is distinctive enough, Willis's statement of what has to be explained is not too far away from the original theories:

> . . . the experience and cultural processes of being male, white, working class, unqualified, disaffected and moving into manual work in contemporary capitalism.[5]

These common assumptions must be emphasized precisely because they do *not* appear in the rhetoric of moral panics or in conventional criminology or in the official control culture.

Beyond this, of course, there are the novelties and differences to which this Introduction will now turn. These lie primarily in the levels of sophistication and complexity which the new theories have added, in the location of delinquency in the whole repertoire of class-based negotiations and in the rescuing of traditional subcultural theory from its historical flatness by placing both the structural 'problem' and its subcultural 'solution' in a recognizable time and place. Of course – as I will point out again – most delinquency is numbingly the same and has never had much to do with those historical 'moments' and 'conjunctures' which today's students of working-class youth cultures are so ingeniously trying to find. But whatever the object of attention – 'expressive fringe delinquency' (as I originally called it) or ordinary mainstream delinquency – the new theories distinguish three general levels of analysis: *structure, culture* and *biography*. I will adopt (and adapt) these headings to organize my review.

(i) *Structure* refers to those aspects of society which appear beyond individual control, especially those deriving from the distribution of power, wealth and differential location in the labour market. These are the structural 'constraints', 'conditions', 'contingencies' or 'imperatives' which the new theory identifies in general terms – and then applies to the group most vulnerable to them, that is, working-class youth. In old subcultural theory, these conditions constitute the 'problem' to which (ii) the *culture* is the solution. More broadly, culture refers to the traditions, maps of meanings and ideologies which are patterned responses to structural conditions; more narrowly *sub*culture is the specific, especially symbolic form through which the subordinate group negotiates its position. Then (iii) there is *biography*: broadly, the pattern and sequence of personal circumstances through which the culture and structure are experienced. More narrowly: what the subculture means and how it is actually lived out by its carriers.

Much of the new work of British post-war youth cultures is a teasing out of the relationships between these three levels. And all of this work is more or less informed by the Marxist categorization of structure, culture and biography as the determinate conditions ('being born into a world not of your own choosing') to which the subculture is one of the possible working-class responses ('making your own history').[6]

1. Structure / History / Problem

In the more one-dimensional world of the original theories, working-class kids somehow hit the system – as represented variously by school, work or leisure. To use the common metaphor: the theories explained how and why kids would kick a machine that did not pay; no one asked how the machine was rigged in the first place. The new theories are very much concerned with how the machine got there. From a general analysis of post-war British capitalism, specific features – particularly the pervasiveness of class – are extracted and historicized. Their impact on the working class – and more particularly, its community and its most vulnerable members, adolescents – is then identified as a series of pressures or contradictions stemming from domination and subordination.

✳ To determine what the old theories would classify as the 'problem' to which delinquency is the 'solution', one must 'situate youth in the dialectic between a "hegemonic" dominant culture and the subordinate working-class "parent" culture of which youth is a fraction'.[7] The conventional assumptions of the old ✳ theories are thus politically (and alas, linguistically) retranslated. In so doing, the individualistic bias of those theories (the assumption that status frustration, alienation or whatever, somehow had to be psychologically recognized) is removed. By stating the problem in historical or structural terms, there is no necessary assumption that it has to be present in a realized conscious form. Ethnographic support (in the form of statements about the 'system', the 'authorities', the 'fucking bosses') is occasionally cited but clearly the theories would not be embarrassed without this support. (I will return later to the question of consciousness.)

Let me list three representative such attempts to find the structural problem; each is a Marxist revision of the liberal or social-democratic assumptions behind the equivalent traditional theories.

Phil Cohen's influential work[8] is thus a radicalized and historically specific rendering of traditional accounts of working-class culture and community. He uses a particular delinquent youth culture, the skinheads, and a particular place, the East End of London, to analyse the destruction of the working-class community and the erosion of its traditional culture. Kinship network, neighbourhood ecology, local occupational structure, depopulation, the destruction of communal space, immigration, post-war redevelopment and housing, the stress on the privatized space of the family unit . . . all these vectors of life so commonly ignored in standard delinquency theory, are assembled into a model of the internal conflicts in the parent (i.e. adult) culture which come to be worked out in terms of generational conflict. These conflicts (or contradictions) register most acutely on the young and might appear at all sorts of levels: at the ideological, between the traditional working-class puritanism and the new hedonism of consumption; at the economic, between the future as part of the socially mobile élite (the future 'explored' by the Mods) and the future as part of the new lumpen (represented by the skinhead inversion of the glossy element in Mod style). The latent function of the subculture is 'to express and resolve, albeit magically the contradictions which remain hidden or unresolved in the parent culture'.[9] Delinquent cultures retrieve social cohesive elements destroyed in the parent culture.

My next example is Corrigan – and this time, the target is the social democratic view of educational disadvantage. The persistent theme in his ethnography of 14–15-year-old boys in two Sunderland working-class schools, is power and subordination. Far from being a public sports track in which the earnest working-class youth's striving for status and mobility is thwarted by his deprived background, the school is a hidden political battleground, a setting in which the historical role of compulsory state education in attacking working-class culture is re-enacted each day. Bourgeois morality, values, discipline and surveillance, on the one hand; the continuous 'guerrilla warfare' of truancy, mucking about, 'dolling off' and getting into trouble, on the other. The kids simply do not *see* the world in the same way as the school; their 'problem' is how to resist and protect themselves from an alien imposition, not how to attain its values.

Then there is Willis – whose target is also liberal ideologies about education, opportunity and work (and who provides the most sophisticated theory of the interplay between structure, culture and biography). His ethnographic picture – based on two years' work with boys in a Midlands comprehensive school, 'Hammertown', and then another year as they moved into work – is similar to Corrigan's, but even bleaker and darker. Again, there is the metaphor of a 'permanent guerrilla war' – and the bland sociological notion of a 'counter culture' is replaced by 'caged resentment which always stops just short of outright confrontation'.[10] The boys' class culture is devoted to subverting the institution's main aim: making them work. But also – and here lies the subtlety and originality of Willis's thesis – this culture, with its values of chauvinism, solidarity, masculinity and toughness, contains also the seeds of the boys' defeat. The same transcendance of the school system – the refusal to collude in the elaborate pretence of qualifications, useless certificates, vocational guidance and careers advice – signals insertion into a system of exploitation through the acceptance of manual labour. (Willis's view of culture – 'not simply layers of padding between human beings and unpleasantness'[11] – as a creative appropriation in its own right, in fact undermines the whole solution/problem framework. The solution, ironically, is the problem: the boys eventually collude in their own domination.)

Each of these formulations – and other allied work – needs, and no doubt will receive, separate criticism. I want to mention here just one general problem: the over-facile drift to historicism. There are too many points at which the sociological enterprise of understanding the present is assumed to have been solved by an appeal to the past. No doubt it is important to see today's school in terms of the development of state education in the nineteenth century; to specify the exact historical transformations in the working-class neighbourhood; to define football hooliganism in terms of the erosion of the sport's traditions by bourgeois entertainment values,[12] or to explain an episode of 'Paki-bashing' by skinheads not in terms of a timeless concept of racial prejudice but by the place of migrant workers in the long historical drama of the collapse and transformation of local industry.[13] In each case the connections sound plausible. But in each case, a single and one-directional historical trend is picked out – commercialization, repression, bourgeoisification, destruction of community, erosion of leisure values – and then projected on to a present which (often by the same sociologist's own admission) is much more complicated, contradictory or ambiguous.

The recent enthusiasm with which criminologists have taken up the new 'history from below' derives from a common spirit.[14] The enterprise of bestowing meaning to certain contemporary forms of deviance was identical to the rescuing of groups like Luddites from (in E. P. Thompson's famous ringing phrase) 'the enormous condescension of posterity'. The appeal to history, though, is a hazardous business – especially in the form I will later discuss of trying to find actual continuities in resistance. I am less than convinced that any essentialist version of history – such as the dominant one f a free working class interfered with since the eighteenth century by the bourgeois state apparatus – is either necessary or sufficient to make sense of delinquency or youth culture today. It also leads to such nonsense as the assertion that *because* of this historical transformation, each working-class adolescent generation has to learn anew that its innocent actions constitute delinquency in the eyes of the state.

2. Culture / Style / Solution

Above all else, the new theories about British post-war youth cultures are massive exercises of decoding, reading, deciphering and interrogating. These phenomena *must* be saying something to us – if only we could know exactly *what*. So the whole assembly of cultural artefacts, down to the punks' last safety pin, have been scrutinized, taken apart, contextualized and re-contextualized. The conceptual tools of Marxism, structuralism and semiotics, a Left-Bank pantheon of Genet, Levi-Strauss, Barthes and Althusser have all been wheeled in to aid this hunt for the hidden code.[15] The result has been an ingenious and, more often than not, plausible reading of subcultural style as a process of generating, appropriating and re-ordering to communicate new and subversive meaning.

Whether the objects for decoding are Teddy Boys, Mods and Rockers, skinheads or punks, two dominant themes are suggested: first that style – whatever else it is – is essentially a type of *resistance* to subordination; secondly, that the form taken by this resistance is somehow *symbolic* or *magical*, in the sense of not being an actual, successful solution to whatever is the problem. The phrase 'resistance through ritual' clearly announces these two themes.

The notion of resistance conveys – and is usually intended to convey – something more active, radical and political than the equivalent phrases in old subcultural theory. It is not a question any more of passive adaptation or desperate lashing out in the face of frustrated aspirations, but of a collective (and, we are sometimes asked to believe) historically informed response, mediated by the class-culture of the oppressed. The following is a list of the terms actually used in the literature to convey this reaction:

in relationship to dominant values:

either: *resistance*: attack, subversion, overturning, undermining, struggle, opposition, defiance, violation, challenge, refusal, contempt

or: *transformation*: transcendence, reworking, adaption, negotiation, resolution, realization *in relationship to traditional working-class values*:

either: *defend*: safeguard, protect, preserve, conserve

or: *recapture*: reappropriate, retrieve, reassert, reaffirm, reclaim, recover

Clearly, the nuances of these words convey somewhat different meanings but there are common threads particularly in the recurrent theme of *winning space*. Territoriality, solidarity, aggressive masculinity, stylistic innovation – these are all attempts by working-class youth to reclaim community and reassert traditional values.

Sociologically more opaque than this notion of resistance is the reciprocal[16] idea that this process (whether conceived as defence, re-working, re-assertion or whatever) is somehow a symbolic one.[17] Again it is instructive to list the actual words used to convey this meaning: ritualistic; imaginary; mythical; fantastic; metaphorical; magical; allegorical; ideological; suppressed; displaced; dislocated. There appear to be three contexts in which such concepts are invoked:

(i) When the target for attack is inappropriate, irrational or simply wrong in the sense that it is not logically or actually connected with the source of the problem. Thus Teddy Boys attacking Cypriot café owners, Mods and Rockers attacking each other, skinheads beating up Pakistanis and gays, or football hooligans smashing up trains, are all really (though they might not know it) reacting to other things, for example, threats to community homogeneity or traditional stereotypes of masculinity. To quote Cohen and Robins on the Arsenal youth end: 'It's as if for these youngsters, the space they share on the North Bank is a way of magically retrieving the sense of group solidarity and identification that once went along with living in a traditional working-class neighbourhood.'[18]

(ii) The second (and allied) meaning is that the solution is 'always and only' magical in that it does not confront the real material bases of subordination and hence lacks the organization and consequences of a genuinely political response. Such attempts to deal with contradictions and subordination 'crucially do not mount their solutions on the real terrain where the contradictions themselves arise and . . . thus fail to pose an alternative, potentially counter hegemonic solution'.[19] The gestures are as effective as sticking pins into kewpie dolls or as neurotic defence mechanisms like displacement or suppression. The bosses, educational disadvantage, unemployment, the police, remain where they were. Relations with the state are 'd at an imaginary level '. . . not in the sense that they are illusory, but ...they enfold the human beings who find themselves in confrontation in a common misrecognition of the real mechanisms which have distributed them to their respective positions'.[20] It is a staged shadow boxing, a very bad case indeed of false consciousness.

(iii) The final (and more conventional) meaning of symbolic, is simply that the subcultural style stands for, signifies, points to or denotes something beyond its surface appearance. The Mods' scooters, the skinheads' working boots, the punks' facial make-up are all making oblique, coded statements about relationships – real or imaginary – to a particular past or present. Objects are borrowed from the world of consumer commodities and their meanings transferred by being reworked into a new ensemble which expresses its opposition obliquely or ironically.

Hebdige captures all these three meanings:

> These 'humble objects' can be magically appropriated; 'stolen' by subordinate groups and made to carry 'secret meanings which express, in code, a form of resistance to the order which guarantees their continued subordination.'[21]

Both these themes of *resistance* and *symbols* are rich and suggestive. I have only the space to mention, somewhat cryptically, a few of the problems they raise.

The first arises from the constant impulse to decode the style in terms *only* of opposition and resistance. This means that instances are sometimes missed when the style is conservative or supportive: in other words, not reworked or reassembled but taken over intact from dominant commercial culture. Such instances are conceded, but then brushed aside because – as we all know – the style is a *bricolage* of inconsistencies and anyway things are not what they seem and so the apparently conservative meaning really hides just the opposite.

There is also a tendency in some of this work to see the historical development of a style as being wholly internal to the group – with commercialization and co-option as something which just happens afterwards. In the understandable zeal to depict the kids as creative agents rather than manipulated dummies, this often plays down the extent to which changes in youth culture are manufactured changes, dictated by consumer society.[22] I am not aware of much evidence, for example, that the major components in punk originated too far away from that distinctive London cultural monopoly carved up between commercial entrepreneurs and the lumpen intellectuals from art schools and rock journals. An allied problem is the often exaggerated status given to the internal circuit of English working-class history. The spell cast on the young by American cultural imperialism[23] is sometimes downgraded. Instead of being given a sense of the interplay between borrowed and native traditions[24] we are directed exclusively to the experiences of nineteenth century Lancashire cotton weavers.

This is inevitable if the subculture is taken to denote some form of cumulative historical resistance. Where we are really being directed is towards the 'profound line of historical continuity' between today's delinquents and their 'equivalents' in the past. And to find this line, we have to ask questions like 'How would "our" hooligans appear if they were afforded the same possibilities of rationality and intelligibility say as those of Edward Thompson?'[25]

To afford them these possibilities, what these theorists have to do is subscribe to what Ditton nicely calls the dinosaur theory of history.[26] A recent zoological argument apparently proposes that dinosaurs did not after all die out: one group still lives on, known as – birds! Similarly, historical evidence is cited to prove that mass proletarian resistance to the imposition of bourgeois control did not after all die out. It lives on in certain forms of delinquency which – though more symbolic and individualistic than their progenitors – must still be read as rudimentary forms of political action, as versions of the same working-class struggle which has occurred since the defeat of Chartism. What is going on in the streets and terraces is not only not what it appears to be, but moreover is really the same as what went on before. And to justify this claim, a double leap of imagination is required. In Pearson's example, the 'proof' that something like Paki-bashing is a 'primitive form of political and economic struggle' lies not in the kids' understanding of what it is they are resisting (they would probably only say something like, 'When you get some long stick in your 'and and you are bashing some Paki's face in, you don't think about it') but in the fact that the machine smashers of 1826 would *also* not have been aware of the real political significance of their action.[27]

This seems to me a very peculiar sort of proof indeed. If ever Tolstoy's remark applied, it might be here: 'History is like a deaf man replying to questions which nobody puts to him.'[28]

This leads on to the vexing issue of consciousness and intent, a problem present even when the appeal is to symbols rather than history. Now it would be as absurd to demand here that every bearer of symbols walk around with structuralist theory in his head, as it would be to expect the oppressed to have a detailed knowledge of dialectical materialism. It seems to me, though, that *somewhere* along the line, symbolic language implies a knowing subject, a subject at least dimly aware of what the symbols are supposed to mean. To be really tough-minded about this, our criterion for whether or not to go along with a particular symbolic interpretation should be Beckett's famous warning to his critics: 'no symbols where none intended'.

And at times, the new theories would seem to accept such a tough criterion. Clark, for example, insists at one point 'that the group self-consciousness is sufficiently developed for its members to be concerned to recognize themselves in the range of symbolic objects available'.[29] More often than not, though, this tough criterion of a fit, consonance or homology between self-consciousness and symbolism is totally ignored and the theory is content to find theoretical meanings (magic, recovery of community, resistance or whatever) quite independent of intent or awareness. Indeed Hebdige – who is more sensitive than most to this problem – ends up by conceding 'It is highly unlikely . . . that the members of any subcultures described in this book would recognize themselves reflected here.'[30]

Some inconsistencies arise – I think – from a too-literal application of certain strands in structuralism and semiotics. Hebdige, for example, uses Barthes' contrast between the obviously intentional signification of advertisements and the apparently innocent signification of news photos to suggest that subcultural style bears the same relationship to conventional culture as the advertising image bears to the less consciously constructed news photo. In other words, subcultural symbols are, obviously and conspicuously, fabricated and displayed. This is precisely how and why they are subversive and against the grain of mainstream culture which is unreflexive and 'natural'. But in the same breath, Hebdige repeats the semiotic article of faith that signification need not be intentional, that Eco's 'semiotic guerrilla warfare' can be conducted at a level beneath the consciousness of the individual members of a spectacular subculture – though, to confuse things further 'the subculture is still at another level an intentional communication'.[31]

This leaves me puzzled about the question of intent. I doubt whether these theories take seriously enough their own question about how the subculture makes sense to its members. If indeed not all punks 'were equally aware of the disjunction between experience and signification upon which the whole style was ultimately based' or if the style made sense for the first wave of self-conscious innovators from the art schools 'at a level which remained inaccessible to those who became punks after the subculture had surfaced and been publicized'[32] – and surely all this must be the case – then why proceed as if such questions were only incidental? It is hard to say which is the more sociologically incredible: a theory which postulates cultural dummies who give homologous meanings to all artefacts surrounding them or a theory which suggests that individual meanings do not matter at all.

Even if this problem of differential meaning and intent were set aside, we are left with the perennial sociological question of how to know whether one set of symbolic interpretations is better than another – or indeed if it is appropriate to invoke the notion of symbols *at all*. Here, my feeling is that the symbolic baggage the kids are being asked to carry is just too heavy, that the interrogations are just a little forced. This is especially so when appearances are, to say the least, ambiguous or (alternatively) when they are simple, but taken to point to just their opposite. The exercise of decoding can then only become as arcane, esoteric and mysterious as such terms as Hebdige's imply: 'insidious significance', 'the invisible seam', 'secret language', 'double meaning', 'second order system', 'opaque sign', 'secret identity', 'double life', 'mimes of imagined conditions', 'oblique expression', 'magical elisions', 'sleight of hand', 'present absence', 'frozen dialectic', 'fractured circuitry', 'elliptic coherence', 'coded exchanges', 'submerged possibilities', etc.

This is, to be sure, an imaginative way of reading the style; but how can we be sure that it is also not imaginary? When the code is embedded in a meaning system already rich in conscious symbolism, then there are fewer problems. For example, when Hebdige is writing about black rasta culture,[33] the connections flow smoothly, the homology between symbols and life could hardly be closer. The conditions in the original Jamaican society, Rastafarian beliefs, the translation of reggae music to Britain . . . all these elements cohere. A transposed religion, language and style create a simultaneously marginal and magical system which provides a subtle and indirect language of rebellion. Symbols are *necessary*: if a more direct language had been chosen it would have been more easily dealt with by the group against which it was directed. Not only does the system display a high degree of internal consistency – particularly in its references to the historical experience of slavery – but it refers directly to patterns of thought which are *actually* hermetic, arcane, syncretic and associative.

If such patterns have to be forced out of the subject-matter, though, the end result is often equally forced. When any apparent inconsistencies loom up, the notion of 'bricolage' comes to the rescue: the magic ensemble is only *implicitly* coherent, the connections can be infinitely extended and improvised. And even this sort of rescue is too 'traditional', and 'simple' we are now told: instead of a reading being a revelation of a fixed number of concealed meanings, it's really a matter of 'polysemy': each text is seen to generate a potentially infinite range of meanings. Style fits together precisely because it does not fit; it coheres 'elliptically through a chain of conspicuous absences'.[34]

This is an aesthetics which may work for art, but not equally well for life. The danger is of getting lost in 'the forest of symbols'[35] and we should take heed of the warnings given by those, like anthropologists, who have searched more carefully in same forests than most students of youth culture. Thus in trying to interpret what he calls these 'enigmatic formations', Turner is aware of certain frontiers to the anthropologist's explanatory competence.[36] Some method or rules of guidance are needed. It would do no harm, for example, to follow his distinction between the three levels of data involved in trying to infer the structure and property of symbols and rituals: first, the actual observable external form, the 'thing'; secondly, the indigenous exegetics offered either by ritual specialists like priests (esoteric interpretations) or by laymen (exoteric interpretations); and finally the attempt by the social scientist to contextualize all this, particularly by reference to the field: the structure and composition of the group that handles the symbol or performs mimetic acts with reference to it.

Having made a simple enough distinction like this, it is then possible to proceed to the interesting complications: the problem of intent; of polysemy (a single symbol standing for many things); how people's interpretations of what they are doing might contradict how they actually behave; under what conditions the observer must go beyond indigenous interpretations because of what he knows of the context. All this requires great care. Much decoding of youth cultures simply does not make the effort – and often does foolish things like taking a priestly exegesis (for example, by a rock journalist) at its face value, or alternatively, offering a contextualization that is wholly gratuitous.

Let me conclude this section by giving an example of the dangers of searching the forest of symbols without such a method – or indeed any method. This is the example often used by Hebdige and other theorists of punk: the wearing of the swastika emblem. Time and time again, we are assured that although this symbol is 'on one level' intended to outrage and shock, it is *really* being employed in a meta-language: the wearers are ironically distancing themselves from the very message that the symbol is usually intended to convey. Displaying a swastika (or singing lyrics like 'Belsen was a gas') shows how symbols are stripped from their natural context, exploited for empty effect, displayed through mockery, distancing, irony, parody, inversion.

But how are we to know this? We are never told much about the 'thing': when, how, where, by whom or in what context it is worn. We do not know what, if any, difference exists between indigenous and sociological explanations. We are given no clue about how these particular actors manage the complicated business of distancing and irony. In the end, there is no basis whatsoever for choosing between this particular sort of interpretation and any others: say, that for many or most of the kids walking around with swastikas on their jackets, the dominant context is simple conformity, blind ignorance or knee-jerk racism.

Something more of an answer is needed to such questions than simply quoting Genet or Breton. Nor does it help much to have Hebdige's admission (about a similar equation) that such interpretations are not open to being tested by standard sociological procedures: 'Though it is undeniably there in the social structure, it is there as an immanence, as a submerged possibility, as an existential option; and one cannot verify an existential option scientifically – you either see it or you don't.'[37]

Well, in the swastika example, I don't. And, moreover, when Hebdige does defend this particular interpretation of punk, he does it not by any existential leap but by a good old-fashioned positivist appeal to evidence: punks, we are told, 'were not generally sympathetic to the parties of the extreme right' and showed 'widespread support for the anti-Fascist movement'.[38] These statements certainly constitute evidence, not immanence – though not particularly good evidence and going right against widespread findings about the racism and support for restrictive immigration policies among substantial sections of working-class youth.

I do not want to judge one reading against the other nor to detract from the considerable interest and value of this new decoding work. We need to be more sceptical though of the exquisite aesthetics which tell us about things being fictional and real, absent and present, caricatures and re-assertions. This language might indeed help by framing a meaning to the otherwise meaningless; but this help seems limited when we are drawn to saying about skinhead attacks on Pakistani immigrants: 'Every time the boot went in, a contradiction was concealed, glossed over or made to disappear'.[39] It seems to me – to borrow from the language of contradictions – that both a lot more and a lot less was going on. Time indeed to leave the forest of symbols; and '. . . shudder back thankfully into the light of the social day'.[40]

3. Biography / Phenomenology / Living Through

In one way or another, most of the problems in the 'resistance through rituals' framework are to be found at the theory's third level: how the subculture is actually lived out by its bearers. The nagging sense here is that these lives, selves and identities do not always coincide with what they are supposed to stand for.

What must be remembered first is that the troubles associated with stylistic and symbolic innovation are not all representative of all delinquency (let alone of all post-war British youth). Mundane day-to-day delinquency is and always has been predominantly property crime and has little to do with magic, codes or rituals. I doubt that many of the intricate preoccupations of these theorists impinge much on the lives, say, of that large (and increasing) number of juveniles in today's custodial institutions: the 11,638 sent to detention centres, 7,067 to Borstals, 7,519 to prisons in 1978.

I fear that the obvious fascination with these spectacular subcultures will draw attention away from these more enduring numbers as well as lead to quite inappropriate criticisms of other modes of explanation. This, of course, will not be entirely the fault of the theorists themselves: the Birmingham group, for example, makes it absolutely clear that they are only concerned with subcultures which have reasonably tight boundaries, distinctive shapes and cohere around specific actions or places. As they are very careful to point out, the majority of working-class youth never enter such subcultures at all: 'individuals may in their personal life careers move into one and out of one, or indeed, several subcultures. Their relations to the existing subcultures may be fleeting or permanent, marginal or central.'[41]

Despite these disavowals though, the *method* used in most of this work detracts us from answering the more traditional, but surely not altogether trivial sociological questions about these different patterns of involvement. Why should some individuals exposed to the same pressures respond one way rather than another or with different degrees of commitment? As one sympathetic criticism[42] suggests, the problem arises from *starting* with groups who are already card-carrying members of a subculture and then working backwards to uncover their class base. If the procedure is reversed and one starts from the class base, rather than the cultural responses, it becomes obvious that an identical location generates a very wide range of responses and modes of accommodation.

Thus time and time again, studies which start in a particular biographical location – school, neighbourhood, work – come up with a much looser relationship between class and style. They show, for example, the sheer ordinariness and passivity of much working-class adolescent accommodation and its similarities to, rather than dramatic breaks with, the respectable parent culture.[43] In the cultural repertoire of responses to subordination – learning how to get by, how to make the best of a bad job, how to make things thoroughly unpleasant for 'them' – symbolic innovation may not be very important.

Such studies are also needed to give a sense of the concrete – some feeling of time and space; when and how the styles and symbols fit into the daily round of home, work or school, friendship.[44] Without this, it becomes difficult, for example, to meet the same standard objection levelled against traditional subcultural theory: the assumption of overcommitment and the fact that apart from the code itself, these young people may be models of conventionality elsewhere. The intellectual pyrotechnics behind many of these theories are also too cerebral, in the sense that a remote, historically derived motivational account (such as 'recapturing community') hardly conveys the immediate emotional tone and satisfaction of the actions themselves. Indeed the action (for example, fighting or vandalism) is often completely ignored except when historicism is temporarily abandoned. A good example of this might be Corrigan's wholly believable account of the context and sequence in which trouble emerges among kids on the street corners of Sunderland: how 'doing nothing' leads to 'weird ideas' which lead to trouble. Another example would be the Robins and Cohen's account of growing up on a council estate. The sense of imprisonment running through the different biographies they collect (under the heading 'We Gotta Get Out of This Place') relates closely with their theoretical explanation of what the street groups are actually doing.

Willis stands alone in showing how that (now) abused sociological task of linking history to subjective experience can be attempted. Structure is not left floating on its own – but a commitment to ethnography need not produce a series of disembodied phenomenological snapshots. He can retain the Marxist insistence that not everything is lived out at the level of practical consciousness – a level that is a poor guide to contradictions – and refuse 'to impute to the lads individually any critique or analytic motive', but still try to show what the 'giving of labour power' actually means subjectively. The struggle against subordination is lived out in the daily round of school life, in the rituals about dress, discipline, smoking, drinking, rules.

A footnote to this section on biography should draw attention to two sets of lives that have been hidden from cultural studies and delinquency theory, old and new, over these twenty-five years: girls and blacks.

For neither of these groups, of course, should this be a footnote and in the case of girls, particularly, this is just to perpetuate the very tendency which needs combating: 'It is as if everything that relates only to us comes out in footnotes to the main text, as worthy of the odd reference. We encounter ourselves in men's cultures as by the way and peripheral.' As one analysis[45] (which starts with these words of Rowbotham's) says, the absence of girls from the subcultural literature is striking and demands explanation. The last few years have seen the beginnings of such an explanation[46] – and it certainly does not simply lie in any physical invisibility of girls from these subcultures. As I originally pointed out, 'in many ways Mod was a more female than male phenomenon' (p. 157) and much more serious attention needs to be paid to this presence as well as the more general problems of applying the subculture model to girls.

In the case of black youth, the 'physical invisibility' explanation is more plausible, at least before the beginning of the 1960s. Up till then, blacks appeared mainly as the victims of Teddy Boy attacks. From about the birth of the Mods onwards, though, the presence of youth of West Indian and then later Asian origin – both new immigrant and first generation – could hardly be ignored. Their significance has now been variously acknowledged: as historical agents in their own right and objects for the 1972–3 moral panic about mugging; in Willis's argument that much of the exclusiveness of working-class culture is defined *against* ethnic minorities (and women); and Hebdige's far-reaching suggestion that the whole of white working-class youth subcultures – from Teddy Boys to punks – can be understood as a series of mediated responses to black (American) culture and then the presence of a sizeable black community in Britain.

From a more empirical direction, Pryce's detailed ethnography of black corner kids in Bristol between 1969 and 1974 not only provides information about the previously invisible, but contributes to a general understanding of the experience of subordination.[47] His hustlers show less a cerebral and symbolic rejection of work 'values' than a direct rejection of menial work itself: an abhorrence at having to take orders from the cheeky white boss, a resentment of such affronts to his pride as a man. 'Slave labour' and 'shit work' are terms used interchangeably to mean monotonous work, white man's work. Ironically, the very prop out of which Willis's white lads build up their attachment to work – masculinity – is used by these black boys to reject the low paid sub-proletarian work they are offered.

Their situation is more precarious than their white counterparts: not only are they given equivalent or lower roles in the labour market, but have the additional 'endless pressure' caused by a fragmented family life, parents with high educational aspirations for their children, a lack of community roots and being the objects of continuing racism and discrimination. Pryce describes this endless pressure – as well as the very different responses to it. The complicated overlaps between reggae, rasta and rude boy ideologies are used both by the delinquent 'teeny bopper' group and the non-delinquent politicals to give their lives some sense of purpose. It is painfully clear that future developments – such as the vulnerability of ethnic minorities to structural unemployment – will add to these 'endless pressures', creating the potential for both a greater rage and a greater social condemnation of it.

Reaction

Following my stated intention of giving more space to 'action', I can do little more here than mention in passing the relevant recent work on societal reaction. This is hardly because I am satisfied with the way this topic is treated in the book. Certainly I gave a lot of information about how the moral panic around the Mods and Rockers was created, transmitted and sustained but the theory behind this process was somewhat undeveloped. Chapter Four – on the various sources of reaction – was perhaps too detailed, while the later attempt to suggest *why* moral panics occur, not just 'now and then' but at particular times and in particular forms, hardly gave much basis for further generalization.

Subsequent contributions to what can be said about moral panics and the like have come from a number of sources. First, the intervening years have seen much interest in the major promoters of moral panics – the mass media – and in analysing the relationships between deviance and the media. This interest initially took the form of pulling together various disparate contributions about how the mass media select and present news about deviance, what models of society are revealed in this presentation and what effects they might have, particularly in shaping the control culture.[48] There have since been a number of empirical studies in Britain – on media coverage of industrial conflict,[49] on the 1972–3 'mugging' panic[50] and on crime reporting[51] – each of which has contributed to building up media theory.[52] The mugging study – to which I will return – is particularly important in locating the media's broader ideological role in shaping and reflecting a consensual view of the world.

From a quite different direction – and in a category of its own, because no one else has seriously taken up this model – there is Ditton's ingenious refinement of deviancy amplification theory.[53] What he has done is to push the 'control leads to deviance' formula to its logical extreme, and in so doing, separated out the various forms of feedback in Wilkins' original model.

Then, and most importantly, there is *Policing the Crisis*: also the product of the Birmingham Centre and also devoted to inserting history and politics into the discourse about crime. The book stands as an important substantive contribution to charting the moral panic about mugging in 1972–3, but also makes a number of important theoretical connections and claims.

The level for explaining labelling, societal reaction or moral panic is shifted from social control agencies or cultures – or vague allusions to the 'wider society' – to the specific operation of the state. This means relating the working of the moral panic – the mobilization of public opinion, the orchestration by the media and public figures of an otherwise inchoate sense of unease – to overall political shifts. In the same way as I picked out certain features of the Mods and Rockers events as touching very deep social tensions and ambiguities, so this work shows how the themes of race, crime and youth were condensed into the image of the mugger – the violent black youth – and used to articulate major shifts in British political and economic life since the War.

The Centre's work here can only be understood as part of its overall project on Gramsci's concept of hegemony. Hegemony denotes the moment when the ruling class is able not merely to coerce its subordinates to conform, but to exercise the sort of power which wins and shapes consent, which frames alternatives and structures agendas in such a way as to appear natural. The thesis is that by the 1960s, and then more openly by the 1970s, the consent which might have previously been won was undermined. Though the dominant class retained power, its repertoire of control was weakened. Concomitantly, there occurred a shift to a more coercive rather than dominantly consensual mode of control. This shift signalled the birth of a law and order society and was evidenced in the development of a pre-emptive escalation of social control. Instead of discrete moral panics of the Mods and Rockers type, with their familiar sequence of dramatic event → public disquiet → moral enterprise → mobilization of control culture, the sequence is (in the late 1960s) speeded up by creating a general disquiet and then, by the time of the 1970s mugging campaign, radically altered. The control culture is mobilized in advance, real events being anticipated and taken to confirm and justify the need for gradual ideological repression.

It is impossible to give proper critical attention here to this formidable argument.[54] All I can do is express similar reservations as applied to the 'resistance through ritual' framework. At too many points, it seems to me, the Centre's determination to find ideological closure leads them to a premature theoretical closure. The actual material selected as proof of the slide into the crisis (newspaper editorials, statements by MPs and police chiefs) does not always add up to something of such monumental proportions. The diffuse normative concern about delinquency is, I think, more diffuse and less political than is suggested. And the assumption of a monolithic drift to repression gives little room for understanding why some objects are repressed more severely than others. This, paradoxically, is the same criticism which applied to vulgar labelling theory.

Taking Stock

To read the literature on subcultural delinquency – old and new – is a depressing business. Depressing for the same reasons given in the original rather fatalistic concluding paragraph of *Folk Devils*, but also for the sense of repetition and continuity.

I do not want to suppress the considerable theoretical differences within this literature: in no way can the language and concepts of functionalism, interactionism, Marxism, structuralism, cybernetics and semiotics simply be jumbled together. But at no important point in this heterogeneous material is there much doubt about what delinquent and troublesome youth subcultures signify: a reaction (with more or less degrees of commitment, consciousness and symbolic weight) to growing up in a class society. The rest is just commentary – a little baroque and far-fetched for some tastes, but not an arena for major dispute.

The 'tone' of the literature, though – its implied value judgements and its implied policy implications – is more diverse and more difficult to capture. In the original subcultural theories, the delinquents were neither admired nor condemned. They were the rejects of a machine which had gone wrong; with careful repair work (better schools, housing, job opportunities) the kids could be incorporated into a smoothly running non-ideological, post-industrial society. The version of liberalism which emerged in labelling theory was somewhat more sceptical of the benevolent pretensions of social democracy. The social order was more obviously up for criticism and a consequent note of suppressed admiration for the delinquents crept in. *The Who*'s tribute to the Mods – 'The Kids Are All Right' – became echoed in a type of sociology which nearly implied that everything would be all right if only the kids were left alone.

When the fully blown 'new criminology' emerged, these hidden moral and political agendas became a bit more ambiguous.[55] The revolution would produce a classless society in which, by definition, problems of subordination and domination would disappear. In the meantime, one could only admire the kids even when (and perhaps especially when) they patently were *not* all right. Thus, even the 'Refusal' which punk subculture signified, its gestures of defiance and contempt, its smiles and sneers, was something to celebrate: 'I would like to think that this Refusal is worth making, that these gestures have a meaning, that the smiles and sneers have some subversive value', and further: '. . . I have sought, in Sartre's words, to acknowledge the right of the subordinate class (the young, the black, the working class) to "make something of what is made of (them)" – to embellish, decorate, parody and wherever possible to recognize and rise above a subordinate position which was never of their own choosing.'[56]

I find myself in sympathy with such an acknowledgement and do not think it far removed from what is recorded in *Folk Devils*. The dangers of romanticism, though, are always present – particularly in the political form which seeks to elevate delinquents into the vanguard of the revolution. Now virtually every theorist I have mentioned takes considerable care to avoid this premature elevation. The creative and – in the short run – often very successful – nature of the resistance is welcomed but at the same time its limits clearly recognized. Either the kids' consciousness of their position is subordinate and 'negotiated' rather than being truly oppositional and political; or opposition is expressed in only one limited area – leisure – which is anyway the inappropriate one; or the dominant culture can recuperate itself from whatever is subversive or potentially subversive; or the implicit politics of these groups is nihilist and confused, making them open, if anything, to reactionary and fascist appeals. Here is a typical recognition of these limitations: 'In the long run no one "magically" can appropriate what in reality does not belong to them by virtue of their working place in society. The pathos and futility of fighting among rival groups of socially dispossessed youth is the best demonstration of the extent of the victory of those who really do hold the class power over them.'[57]

But – and this is perhaps a credit to political faith – there is still a strong commitment to seek and to defend any signs of inarticulate criticism or historical resistance. And consequently there is a note of regret: if only the kids could see the real enemy, if only they could be awakened to their true class interests, then they would be liberated.

And, as Pearson so honestly puts it: 'Of course it would be easier to defend hooligans if they were not so badly behaved.'[58] Such candour is rare and too much of the theory masks a curious value distortion. The subculture is observed and decoded, its creativity celebrated and its political limitations acknowledged – and then the critique of the social order constructed. But while this critique stems from a moral absolutism, the subculture itself is treated in the language of cultural relativism. Those same values of racism, sexism, chauvinism, compulsive masculinity and anti-intellectualism, the slightest traces of which are condemned in bourgeois culture, are treated with a deferential care, an exaggerated contextualization, when they appear in the subculture.

This is by no means a problem unique to this literature. Levi-Strauss has dealt in a most moving and sympathetic way with the equivalent contradictions faced by the anthropologist who is a stern cultural critic at home but a conformist abroad. The value which he attaches to 'foreign societies' (read: subcultures): '. . . is a function of his disdain for and occasionally hostility towards the customs prevailing in his own native setting. While often inclined to subversion among his own people and in revolt against traditional behaviour, the anthropologist appears respectful to the point of conservatism as soon as he is dealing with a society different from his own.'[59]

As Levi-Strauss makes clear, all this is not a simple question of bias. It raises more fundamental contradictions about what social scientists are doing. To say that each group has made choices within the range of human possibilities and that all are equally valid rescues us from a blindness to everything different (from viewing, say, working-class culture wholly in terms of bourgeois norms). But it might also lead to an eclecticism which prevents us from deploring any features of a culture. Cannibalism is the anthropologist's obvious example. The dilemma is profound – though it need not necessarily lead us into abandoning sociology altogether: 'after peering into the abyss which yawns in front of us, we may be allowed to look for a way of avoiding it.'[60]

The ways Levi-Strauss recommends include moderation, honesty and self-awareness – qualities not always present in the much *too respectful* enterprise of picking on the subcultural detritus of musical notes, hair styles, safety pins, zips and boots. We might not have to go so far in the other direction as Hunter Thompson's famous epitaph to his appreciation of the Californian Hells Angels ('. . . there was no escaping the echo of Mistah Kurtz's comment from the heart of darkness; "The horror, The horror . . . Exterminate all the brutes"'[61]) to see that we can understand without being too respectful. Much of this respect, anyway, strikes some false and condescending notes. I sometimes have a sense of working-class kids suffering an awful triple fate. First, their actual current prospects are grim enough; then their predicament is used, shaped and turned to financial profit by the same interests which created it; and then – the final irony – they find themselves patronized in the latest vocabulary imported from the Left Bank.[62]

Ultimately – because of its simplicity and its translation of the obvious truths at the core of subcultural theory into a recognizable and dignified language – I would prefer to lean on Paul Goodman's classic diatribe against American society in the fifties.[63] What he saw then was the same waste of human potential, worthlessness of jobs, emptiness of education, cynicism and lack of opportunity for worthwhile experience identified in later theories.

The social critique comes first: what it is to grow up in a society where there is nothing worthwhile. Then comes the identification (again, in exactly the same way as today's theories) of 'poor youth' as the group among whom the contradictions and absurdities of industrial society show up 'first and worst'. These kids constituted for Goodman the same surplus population later theorized about in more sophisticated ways and their plight was also the same: the pathos of being compelled to go to school in order to receive an education for a society which does not need them. School was a waste, jobs were dull, and when you were questioned on the street (like Corrigan's boys twenty years later) about what you wanted to do, there was the same terrible answer – 'nothing'.

Goodman also saw social revolution as the only solution to all this, but he did not lapse into the patronizing cultural relativism which would only analyse the working-class adolescent response in its own terms and dismiss usefulness, honour and satisfaction as mere bourgeois values. The same middle-class intellectuals who spend so much time agonizing over their own alienation, the need for meaning commitment and self-fulfilment in their own work suddenly find these values bourgeois and beneath contempt. Naturally, the working classes are right to reject them, for has not history decreed that their jobs will never be satisfying?

This specious logic can be avoided by confronting these responses more honestly; as Goodman says, 'The so-called delinquent subculture has a few flashing and charming traits, but nothing in it is viable or imitable . . . Their choices and inventions are rarely charming, usually stupid and often disastrous; we cannot expect average kids to deviate with genius.'[64] Sociologists do not like making their aesthetics and morals as open and disingenuously simple as this. But the complications of current theory share the same message as Goodman's: although the kids' behaviour might not look too good, it speaks clearly enough – it asks for what we cannot give. When the last fake safety pin is sold on the Kings Road and the first juvenile unemployment figures for the 1980s appear, the message will be just the same.

It is better to adopt the simplest explanation, even if it is not simple, even if it does not explain very much.[65]

Notes and References

1   The key texts remain A. K. Cohen, *Delinquent Boys: The Culture of the Gang* (Chicago: Free Press, 1955), R. Cloward and L. Ohlin, *Delinquency and Opportunity: A Theory of Delinquent Groups* (Chicago: Free Press, 1960) and the original application to England: D. M. Downes, *The Delinquent Solution* (London: Routledge & Kegan Paul, 1966).

2 For some interesting comments on the uneven development of theories of crime and delinquency, see P. Rock, 'The Sociology of Crime, Symbolic Interactionism and Some Problematic Qualities of Radical Criminology', in D. Downes and P. Rock (Eds), *Deviant Interpretations* (Oxford: Martin Robertson, 1979), pp. 52–84.

3 In the absence of a better classification, I shall use the term 'new subcultural theory' to cover the work emerging in Britain from about 1972 and associated primarily with the Centre for Contemporary Studies at the University of Birmingham. These are the main sources on which I have based my review; they have been produced either directly from the Centre or by those working on parallel lines: S. Hall and T. Jefferson (Eds), *Resistance Through Rituals: Youth Subcultures in Post-war Britain* (London: Hutchinson, 1976); G. Mungham and G. Pearson (Eds), *Working Class Youth Culture* (London: Routledge & Kegan Paul, 1976); P. Willis, *Learning to Labour: How Working Class Kids Get Working Class Jobs* (London: Saxon House, 1978); D. Robins and P. Cohen, *Knuckle Sandwich: Growing Up in the Working Class City* (Harmondsworth: Penguin, 1978); P. Corrigan, *Schooling the Smash Street Kids* (London: Macmillan, 1979) and D. Hebdige, *Subculture: The Meaning of Style* (London: Methuen, 1979). See also the journal *Working Papers in Cultural Studies* (from 1972 to 1979) and the regular series of stencilled papers produced by the Centre since 1972. It is impossible in this short review to do justice to the considerable diversity within this literature, but unless I single out individual voices, I will take the term 'new subcultural theory' to cover some common ground.

4 Finestone's caricature of the original American theories: H. Finestone, *Victims of Change: Juvenile Delinquents in American Society* (London: Greenwood Press, 1976).

5 Willis, op. cit. p. 119. Though less explicitly concerned with delinquency or style than the other new subcultural writings, this study, I believe, will make the most enduring contribution.

6 This version of the social formation is used most explicitly in J. Clarke and T. Jefferson, 'Working Class Youth Cultures', in Mungham and Pearson, op. cit. pp. 138–58.

7 J. Clarke *et al.*, 'Subcultures, Cultures and Classes', in Hall and Jefferson, op. cit. p. 38.

8 P. Cohen, 'Subcultural Conflict and Working Class Community', *Working Papers in Cultural Studies* 2, Spring 1972, pp. 5–52. In Cohen's later work with Robins (Robins and Cohen, op. cit.) there is an even more solid location of the chains of cultural transmission, internal division and conflict in a tough inner city area – a working-class London estate – between 1972 and 1977.

9 P. Cohen, op. cit. p. 23.

10 Willis, op. cit. pp. 12–13.

11 ibid., p. 52.

12 I. Taylor, 'Football Mad': A Speculative Sociology of Soccer Hooliganism', in E. Dunning (Ed.), *The Sociology of Sport* (London: Cass, 1971) and 'Spectator Violence around Football: The Rise and Fall of the 'Working Class weekend', *Research Papers in Physical Education* 3 (2), 1976, pp. 4–9. See also J. Clarke,

'Football and Working Class Fans: Tradition and Change', in R. Ingham *et al.*, *Football Hooliganism: The Wider Context* (London: Interaction Inprint, 1978).

13 G. Pearson, '"Paki-bashing" in a North East Lancashire Cotton Town: A Case Study and Its History', in Mungham and Pearson, op. cit. pp. 48–81, and 'In Defence of Hooliganism: Social Theory and Violence, in N. Tutt (Ed.), *Violence* (London: HMSO, 1976).

14 For a good summary of how contemporary criminologists have taken up this historical work, see G. Pearson, 'Goths and Vandals: Crime in History', *Contemporary Crises* 2 (2), April 1978, pp. 119–39.

15 Hebdige, op. cit. provides the most recent and ambitious version of this whole enterprise.

16 Not equally reciprocal in all the new writing. Willis and Corrigan, for example, hardly ever see resistance as 'symbolic' while Pearson is more ambivalent: he appears to accept (in relation to 'Paki-bashing') a displacement or scapegoating theory, but also insists that the response is real and rational.

17 An idea hardly as novel as is claimed. In Albert Cohen's original theory, the process he called 'reaction formation' was symbolic in precisely this sense. What could be more magical than 'solving' your frustration at not being able to reach a goal by inverting the value system associated with this goal? This is one of the many instances of the new theories' tendency towards 'social amnesia': the repression of previous insights in order to appear new and radical. On this general tendency, see R. Jacoby, *Social Amnesia* (London: Harvester Press, 1977), especially chapter 1. Thus the *whole* of symbolic interactionism has been repressed in this way and its potential for dealing with at least some problems of meaning and symbol been lost just because its overall politics and sociology is judged to be wrong.

18 Robins and Cohen, op. cit. p. 137.

19 J. Clarke, 'Style' in Hall and Jefferson, op. cit. p. 189.

20 Robins and Cohen, op. cit. p. 113.

21 Hebdige, op. cit. p. 18.

22 One contribution which does stress 'manufactured change' is I. Taylor and D. Wall, 'Beyond the Skinheads: Comments on the Emergence and Significance of the Glamrock Cult', in Mungham and Pearson, op. cit. pp. 105–24.

23 A brilliant evocation of this spell is to be found in the bleak Wimpies and shopping arcades of Stephen Poliakoff's plays. As John Lahr comments about Poliakoff's adolescents: 'Their roots are in England, but their dreams are somewhere between the Mississippi delta and the Hollywood hills. From junk food to rock and roll they are weighted down with borrowed cultural baggage', John Lahr, 'The Psychopath as Hero', *New Society*, 28 June 1979, pp. 780–1.

24 Hebdige, of course, does do just this – and advances the rather extreme argument that the whole shape of post-war British youth culture emerges as a dialogue with black culture. See also the fine analysis in Robins and Cohen (op. cit. pp. 96–103) of the appeal of the Bruce Lee, Kung Fu mythology to the kids on the estate.

25 Pearson, 1978, op. cit. p. 134.

26 J. Ditton, 'The Dinosaur Theory of History' (paper to be given at the British

Sociological Association Annual Conference, April 1980). I am grateful to Jason Ditton for showing me this paper and for other related comments.

27 Pearson, in Mungham and Pearson, op. cit.

28 Quoted by Isaiah Berlin, *Russian Thinkers* (London: Hogarth Press, 1978), p. 242.

29 Clarke, 'Style' in Hall and Jefferson, op. cit. p. 179.

30 Hebdige, op. cit. p. 139.

31 ibid., p. 101, p. 105.

32 ibid., p. 122.

33 ibid. and also 'Reggae, Rastas and Rudies' in Hall and Jefferson, op. cit. pp. 135–54; and C.C.C.S. Stencilled Papers, Nos 20, 21, 24 and 25.

34 Hebdige, op. cit. pp. 117–20.

35 The famous words from Baudelaire's poem, *Correspondences*. That great literary symbolizer, Malcolm Lowry, thought that he knew exactly where he was going here, but used Baudelaire's phrase to project himself into the suffering of his hero in *Under the Volcano* – who saw portents and symbols everywhere, his life wracked by a symbolizing frenzy, trying to find an occult and total correspondence between all things material and spiritual. See D. Day, *Malcolm Lowry: A Biography* (London: Oxford University Press, 1974), pp. 273–4, 317–50.

36 I have selected Victor Turner's work from the standard literature not just because of the clarity of his method here but, of course, because he too uses the Baudelaire reference: V. Turner, *The Forest of Symbols: Aspects of Ndembu Ritual* (London: Cornell University Press, 1967). See especially the first essay, 'Symbols in Ndembu Ritual', pp. 19–47.

37 Hebdige, op. cit. p. 131.

38 ibid., p. 116.

39 ibid., p. 58.

40 Turner, op. cit. p. 46.

41 Hall and Jefferson, op. cit. p. 16.

42 G. Murdock and R. McCron, 'Consciousness of Class and Consciousness of Generation', in Hall and Jefferson, op. cit. p. 205 and 'Youth and Class: The Career of a Confusion', in Mungham and Pearson, op. cit. p. 25.

43 See, for example, Mungham's ethnography of commercial dance hall culture 'Youth in Pursuit of Itself' in Mungham and Pearson, op. cit. pp. 82–104. And, from outside sociology, the snapshots of youth in a Northern England cotton town in J. Seabrook, *City Close-Up* (Harmondsworth: Penguin, 1973).

44 Parker's ethnography of 'the Boys' in the Roundhouse area of Liverpool is an excellent example of how this can be done: H. Parker, *The View From The Boys* (Newton Abbott: David & Charles, 1974) and 'Boys Will Be Men: Brief Adolescence in a Down Town Neighbourhood', in Mungham and Pearson, op. cit. pp. 27–47. This is one of the few studies which gives any sense of the passage of time.

45 A. McRobbie and J. Garber, 'Girls and Subcultures: An Exploration', in Hall and Jefferson, op. cit. pp. 223–30.

46 For example, in C. Smart, *Women, Crime and Criminology* (London: Routledge, 1976) and M. Millman, 'She Did it All for Love' in M. Millman and R. Kanter (Eds), *Another Voice* (New York: Anchor Books, 1975).

47   K. Pryce, *Endless Pressure: A Study of West Indian Life Styles in Bristol* (Harmonds-worth: Penguin, 1979).

48   S. Cohen and J. Young (Eds), *The Manufacture of News: Deviance, Social Problems and the Mass Media* (London: Constable, 1973).

49   Glasgow University Media Group, *Bad News* (London: Routledge & Kegan Paul, 1976).

50   S. Hall *et al., Policing The Crisis: Mugging, the State and Law and Order* (London: Macmillan, 1978).

51   S. Chibnall, *Law and Order News* (London: Tavistock, 1977).

52   See, for example, S. Hall, 'Culture, the Media and the "Ideological Effect"' in J. Curran *et al.* (Eds), *Mass Communication and Society* (London: Arnold, 1977).

53   J. Ditton, *Controlology: Beyond the New Criminology* (London: Macmillan, 1979).

54   Or to the rest of what is really three books: a substantive analysis of the mugging panic, an interpretation of the connections between politics and delinquency among black youth in Britain, and the first serious attempt to relate ideologies of crime control to a theory of the state.

55   See S. Cohen, 'Guilt, Justice and Tolerance: Some Old Concepts for a New Criminology', in Downes and Rock, op. cit. pp. 17–51.

56   Hebdige, op. cit. pp. 3, 138–9.

57   Robins and Cohen, op. cit. p. 151.

58   Pearson, 1976, op. cit. p. 216.

59   C. Levi Strauss, *Tristes Tropiques* (Harmondsworth: Penguin, 1976), p. 502. I cannot do justice here to his wonderful chapter 'A Little Glass of Rum', pp. 501–15.

60   ibid., p. 506.

61   H. S. Thompson, *Hells Angels* (Harmondsworth: Penguin, 1967), p. 284.

62   Which is then repulped for the cultural supermarket; note, for example, this review (of Hebdige's book) in *Time Out*: 'He dissects the nihilism expressed in the zips and buckles of a Sex jacket, and digs deep into the subversive commodity fetishism of the original mods who turned their short hair and suits against the straight culture from which they had appropriated them', *Time Out*, 31 August 1979, p. 59. There might be nothing 'wrong' with these words, but why do they leave one with such a heavy heart?

63   P. Goodman, *Growing Up Absurd: Problems of Youth in the Organized Society* (New York: Random House, 1960).

64   ibid., p. 191, p. 13.

65   S. Beckett, *Malone Dies* (Paris: Olympia Press, 1959), p. 248.

1 Deviance and Moral Panics

see film on youtube w/ Ted

Societies appear to be subject, every now and then, to periods of moral panic. A condition, episode, person or group of persons emerges to become defined as a threat to societal values and interests; its nature is presented in a stylized and stereotypical fashion by the mass media; the moral barricades are manned by editors, bishops, politicians and other right-thinking people; socially accredited experts pronounce their diagnoses and solutions; ways of coping are evolved or (more often) resorted to; the condition then disappears, submerges or deteriorates and becomes more visible. Sometimes the object of the panic is quite novel and at other times it is something which has been in existence long enough, but suddenly appears in the limelight. Sometimes the panic passes over and is forgotten, except in folklore and collective memory; at other times it has more serious and long-lasting repercussions and might produce such changes as those in legal and social policy or even in the way the society conceives itself.

One of the most recurrent types of moral panic in Britain since the war has been associated with the emergence of various forms of youth culture (originally almost exclusively working class, but often recently middle class or student based) whose behaviour is deviant or delinquent. To a greater or lesser degree, these cultures have been associated with violence. The Teddy Boys, the Mods and Rockers, the Hells Angels, the skinheads and the hippies have all been phenomena of this kind. There have been parallel reactions to the drug problem, student militancy, political demonstrations, football hooliganism, vandalism of various kinds and crime and violence in general. But groups such as the Teddy Boys and the Mods and Rockers have been distinctive in being identified not just in terms of particular events (such as demonstrations) or particular disapproved forms of behaviour (such as drug-taking or violence) but as distinguishable social types. In the gallery of types that society erects to show its members which roles should be avoided and which should be emulated, these groups have occupied a constant position as folk devils: visible reminders of what we should not be. The identities of such social types are public property and these particular adolescent groups have symbolized – both in what they were and how they were reacted to – much of the social change which has taken place in Britain over the last twenty years.

In this book, I want to use a detailed case study of the Mods and Rockers phenomenon – which covered most of the 1960s – to illustrate some of the more intrinsic features in the emergence of such collective episodes of juvenile deviance and the moral panics they both generate and rely upon for their growth. The Mods and Rockers are one of the many sets of figures through which the sixties in Britain will be remembered. A decade is not just a chronological span but a period measured by its association with particular fads, fashions, crazes, styles or – in a less ephemeral way – a certain spirit or *kulturgeist*. A term such as 'the twenties' is enough to evoke the cultural shape of that period, and although we are too close to the sixties for such explicit understandings to emerge already, this is not for want of trying from our instant cultural historians. In the cultural snap albums of the decade which have already been collected[1] the Mods and Rockers stand alongside the Profumo affair, the Great Train Robbery, the Krays, the Richardsons, the Beatles, the Rolling Stones, the Bishop of Woolwich, *Private Eye*, David Frost, Carnaby Street, The Moors murders, the emergence of Powellism, the Rhodesian affair, as the types and scenes of the sixties.

At the beginning of the decade, the term 'Modernist' referred simply to a style of dress; the term 'Rocker' was hardly known outside the small groups which identified themselves this way. Five years later, a newspaper editor was to refer to the Mods and Rockers incidents as 'without parallel in English history' and troop reinforcements were rumoured to have been sent to quell possible widespread disturbances. Now, another five years later, these groups have all but disappeared from the public consciousness, remaining only in collective memory as folk devils of the past, to whom current horrors can be compared. The rise and fall of the Mods and Rockers contained all the elements from which one might generalize about folk devils and moral panics. And unlike the previous decade which had only produced the Teddy Boys, these years witnessed rapid oscillation from one such devil to another: the Mod, the Rocker, the Greaser, the student militant, the drug fiend, the vandal, the soccer hooligan, the hippy, the skinhead.

Neither moral panics nor social types have received much systematic attention in sociology. In the case of moral panics, the two most relevant frameworks come from the sociology of law and social problems and the sociology of collective behaviour. Sociologists such as Becker[2] and Gusfield[3] have taken the cases of the Marijuana Tax Act and the Prohibition laws respectively to show how public concern about a particular condition is generated, a 'symbolic crusade' mounted, which with publicity and the actions of certain interest groups, results in what Becker calls *moral enterprise*: '. . . the creation of a new fragment of the moral constitution of society.'[4] Elsewhere[5] Becker uses the same analysis to deal with the evolution of social problems as a whole. The field of collective behaviour provides another relevant orientation to the study of moral panics. There are detailed accounts of cases of mass hysteria, delusion and panics, and also a body of studies on how societies cope with the sudden threat or disorder caused by physical disasters.

The study of social types can also be located in the field of collective behaviour, not so much though in such 'extreme' forms as riots or crowds, but in the general orientation to this field by the symbolic interactionists such as Blumer and Turner.[6] In this line of theory, explicit attention has been paid to social types by Klapp,[7] but although he considers how such types as the hero, the villain and the fool serve as role models for a society, his main concern seems to be in classifying the various sub-types within these groups (for example, the renegade, the parasite, the corrupter, as villain roles) and listing names of those persons Americans see as exemplifying these roles. He does not consider how such typing occurs in the first place and he is preoccupied with showing his approval for the processes by which social consensus is facilitated by identifying with the hero types and hating the villain types.

The major contribution to the study of the social typing process itself comes from the interactionist or transactional approach to deviance. The focus here is on how society labels rule-breakers as belonging to certain deviant groups and how, once the person is thus type cast, his acts are interpreted in terms of the status to which he has been assigned. It is to this body of theory that we must turn for our major orientation to the study of both moral panics and social types.

The Transactional Approach to Deviance

The sociological study of crime, delinquency, drug-taking, mental illness and other forms of socially deviant or problematic behaviour has, in the last decade, undergone a radical reorientation. This reorientation is part of what might be called the *sceptical* revolution in criminology and the sociology of deviance.[8] The older tradition was *canonical* in the sense that it saw the concepts it worked with as authoritative, standard, accepted, given and unquestionable. The new tradition is sceptical in the sense that when it sees terms like 'deviant', it asks 'deviant to whom?' or 'deviant from what?'; when told that something is a social problem, it asks 'problematic to whom?'; when certain conditions or behaviour are described as dysfunctional, embarrassing, threatening or dangerous, it asks 'says who?' and 'why?'. In other words, these concepts and descriptions are not assumed to have a taken-for-granted status.

The empirical existence of forms of behaviour labelled as deviant and the fact that persons might consciously and intentionally decide to be deviant, should not lead us to assume that deviance is the intrinsic property of an act nor a quality possessed by an actor. Becker's formulation on the transactional nature of deviance has now been quoted verbatim so often that it has virtually acquired its own canonical status:

> . . . deviance is created by society. I do not mean this in the way that it is ordinarily understood, in which the causes of deviance are located in the social situation of the deviant or in 'social factors' which prompt his action. I mean, rather, that *social groups create deviance by making the rules whose infraction constitutes deviance* and by applying those rules to particular persons and labelling them as outsiders. From this point of view, deviance is *not* a quality of the act the person commits, but rather a consequence of the application by others of rules and sanctions to an 'offender'. The deviant is one to whom the label has successfully been applied; deviant behaviour is behaviour that people so label.[9]

What this means is that the student of deviance must question and not take for granted the labelling by society or certain powerful groups in society of certain behaviour as deviant or problematic. The transactionalists' importance has been not simply to restate the sociological truism that the judgement of deviance is ultimately one that is relative to a particular group, but in trying to spell out the implication of this for research and theory. They have suggested that in addition to the stock set of *behavioural* questions which the public asks about deviance and which the researcher obligingly tries to answer (why did they do it? what sort of people are they? how do we stop them doing it again?) there are at least three *definitional* questions: why does a particular rule, the infraction of which constitutes deviance, exist at all? What are the processes and procedures involved in identifying someone as a deviant and applying the rule to him? What are the effects and consequences of this application, both for society and the individual?

Sceptical theorists have been misinterpreted as going only so far as putting these definitional questions and moreover as implying that the behavioural questions are unimportant. While it is true that they have pointed to the dead ends which the behavioural questions have reached (do we really know what distinguishes a deviant from a non-deviant?), what they say has positive implications for studying these questions as well. Thus, they see deviance in terms of a process of becoming – movements of doubt, commitment, sidetracking, guilt – rather than the possession of fixed traits and characteristics. This is true even for those forms of deviance usually seen to be most 'locked in' the person: 'No one,' as Laing says, 'has schizophrenia like having a cold.'[10] The meaning and interpretation which the deviant gives to his own acts are seen as crucial and so is the fact that these actions are often similar to socially approved forms of behaviour.[11]

The transactional perspective does not imply that innocent persons are arbitrarily selected to play deviant roles or that harmless conditions are wilfully inflated into social problems. Nor does it imply that a person labelled as deviant has to accept this identity: being caught and publicly labelled is just one crucial contingency which *may* stabilize a deviant career and sustain it over time. Much of the work of these writers has been concerned with the problematic nature of societal response to deviance and the way such responses affect the behaviour. This may be studied at a face-to-face level (for example, what effect does it have on a pupil to be told by his teacher that he is a 'yob who should never be at a decent school like this'?) or at a broader societal level (for example, how is the 'drug problem' actually created and shaped by particular social and legal policies?).

The most unequivocal attempt to understand the nature and effect of the societal reaction to deviance is to be found in the writings of Lemert.[12] He makes an important distinction, for example, between primary and secondary deviation. Primary deviation – which may arise from a variety of causes – refers to behaviour which, although it may be troublesome to the individual, does not produce symbolic reorganization at the level of self-conception. Secondary deviation occurs when the individual employs his deviance, or a role based upon it, as a means of defence, attack or adjustment to the problems created by the societal reaction to it. The societal reaction is thus conceived as the 'effective' rather than 'original' cause of deviance: deviance becomes significant when it is subjectively shaped into an active role which becomes the basis for assigning social status. Primary deviation has only marginal implications for social status and self-conception as long as it remains symptomatic, situational, rationalized or in some way 'normalized' as an acceptable and normal variation.

Lemert was very much aware that the transition from primary to secondary deviation was a complicated process. Why the societal reaction occurs and what form it takes are dependent on factors such as the amount and visibility of the deviance, while the effect of the reaction is dependent on numerous contingencies and is itself only one contingency in the development of a deviant career. Thus the link between the reaction and the individual's incorporation of this into his self-identity is by no means inevitable; the deviant label, in other words, does not always 'take'. The individual might be able to ignore or rationalize the label or only pretend to comply. This type of face-to-face sequence, though, is just one part of the picture: more important are the symbolic and unintended consequences of social control as a whole. Deviance in a sense emerges and is stabilized as an artefact of social control; because of this, Lemert can state that '. . . older sociology tended to rest heavily upon the idea that deviance leads to social control. I have come to believe that the reverse idea, i.e. social control leads to deviance, is equally tenable and the potentially richer premise for studying deviance in modern society.'[13]

It is partly towards showing the tenability and richness of this premise that this book is directed. My emphasis though, is more on the logically prior task of analysing the nature of a particular set of reactions rather than demonstrating conclusively what their effects might have been. How were the Mods and Rockers identified, labelled and controlled? What stages or processes did this reaction go through? Why did the reaction take its particular forms? What – to use Lemert's words again – were the 'mythologies, stigma, stereotypes, patterns of exploitation, accommodation, segregation and methods of control (which) spring up and crystallize in the interaction between the deviants and the rest of society'?[14]

There are many strategies – not mutually incompatible – for studying such reactions. One might take a sample of public opinion and survey its attitudes to the particular form of deviance in question. One might record reactions in a face-to-face context; for example, how persons respond to what they see as homosexual advances.[15] One might study the operations and beliefs of particular control agencies such as the police or the courts. Or, drawing on all these sources, one might construct an ethnography and history of reactions to a particular condition or form of behaviour. This is particularly suitable for forms of deviance or problems seen as new, sensational or in some other way particularly threatening. Thus 'crime waves' in seventeenth century Massachusetts,[16] marijuana smoking in America during the 1930s,[17] the Teddy Boy phenomenon in Britain during the 1950s[18] and drug-taking in the Notting Hill area of London during the 1960s[19] have all been studied in this way. These reactions were all associated with some form of moral panic and it is in the tradition of studies such as these that the Mods and Rockers will be considered. Before introducing this particular case, however, I want to justify concentrating on one especially important carrier and producer of moral panics, namely, the mass media.

Deviance and the Mass Media

A crucial dimension for understanding the reaction to deviance both by the public as a whole and by agents of social control, is the nature of the information that is received about the behaviour in question. Each society possesses a set of ideas about what causes deviation – is it due, say, to sickness or to wilful perversity? – and a set of images of who constitutes the typical deviant – is he an innocent lad being led astray, or is he a psychopathic thug? – and these conceptions shape what is done about the behaviour. In industrial societies, the body of information from which such ideas are built, is invariably received at second hand. That is, it arrives already processed by the mass media and this means that the information has been subject to alternative definitions of what constitutes 'news' and how it should be gathered and presented. The information is further structured by the various commercial and political constraints in which newspapers, radio and television operate.

The student of moral enterprise cannot but pay particular attention to the role of the mass media in defining and shaping social problems. The media have long operated as agents of moral indignation in their own right: even if they are not self-consciously engaged in crusading or muck-raking, their very reporting of certain 'facts' can be sufficient to generate concern, anxiety, indignation or panic. When such feelings coincide with a perception that particular values need to be protected, the preconditions for new rule creation or social problem definition are present. Of course, the outcome might not be as definite as the actual creation of new rules or the more rigid enforcement of existing ones. What might result is the sort of symbolic process which Gusfield describes in his conception of 'moral passage': there is a change in the public designation of deviance.[20] In his example, the problem drinker changes from 'repentant' to 'enemy' to 'sick'. Something like the opposite might be happening in the public designation of producers and consumers of pornography: they have changed from isolated, pathetic – if not sick – creatures in grubby macks to groups of ruthless exploiters out to undermine the nation's morals.

Less concretely, the media might leave behind a diffuse feeling of anxiety about the situation: 'something should be done about it', 'where will it end?'

or 'this sort of thing can't go on for ever'. Such vague feelings are crucial in laying the ground for further enterprise, and Young has shown how, in the case of drug-taking, the media play on the normative concerns of the public and by thrusting certain moral directives into the universe of discourse, can create social problems suddenly and dramatically.[21] This potential is consciously exploited by those whom Becker calls 'moral entrepreneurs' to aid them in their attempt to win public support.

The mass media, in fact, devote a great deal of space to deviance: sensational crimes, scandals, bizarre happenings and strange goings on. The more dramatic confrontations between deviance and control in manhunts, trials and punishments are recurring objects of attention. As Erikson notes, 'a considerable portion of what we call "news" is devoted to reports about deviant behaviour and its consequences'.[22] This is not just for entertainment or to fulfil some psychological need for either identification or vicarious punishment. Such 'news' as Erikson and others have argued, is a main source of information about the normative contours of a society. It informs us about right and wrong, about the boundaries beyond which one should not venture and about the shapes that the devil can assume. The gallery of folk types – heroes and saints, as well as fools, villains and devils – is publicized not just in oral-tradition and face-to-face contact but to much larger audiences and with much greater dramatic resources.

Much of this study will be devoted to understanding the role of the mass media in creating moral panics and folk devils. A potentially useful link between these two notions – and one that places central stress on the mass media – is the process of deviation amplification as described by Wilkins.[23] The key variable in this attempt to understand how the societal reaction may in fact *increase* rather than decrease or keep in check the amount of deviance, is the nature of the information about deviance. As I pointed out earlier, this information characteristically is not received at first hand, it tends to be processed in such a form that the action or actors concerned are pictured in a highly stereotypical way. We react to an episode of, say, sexual deviance, drug-taking or violence in terms of our information about that particular class of phenomenon (how typical is it), our tolerance level for that type of behaviour and our direct experience – which in a segregated urban society is often nil. Wilkins describes – in highly mechanistic language derived from cybernetic theory – a typical reaction sequence which might take place at this point, one which has a spiralling or snowballing effect.

An initial act of deviance, or normative diversity (for example, in dress) is defined as being worthy of attention and is responded to punitively. The deviant or group of deviants is segregated or isolated and this operates to alienate them from conventional society. They perceive themselves as more deviant, group themselves with others in a similar position, and this leads to more deviance. This, in turn, exposes the group to further punitive sanctions and other forceful action by the conformists – and the system starts going round again. There is no assumption in this model that amplification *has* to occur: in the same way – as I pointed out earlier – that there is no automatic transition from primary to secondary deviation or to the incorporation of deviant labels. The system or the actor can and does react in quite opposite directions. What one is merely drawing attention to is a set of sequential typifications: under X conditions, A will be followed by A1, A2, etc. All these links have to be explained – as Wilkins does not do – in terms of other generalizations. For example, it is more likely that if the deviant group is vulnerable and its actions highly visible, it will be forced to take on its identities from structurally and ideologically more powerful groups. Such generalizations and an attempt to specify various specialized modes of amplification or alternatives to the process have been spelt out by Young[24] in the case of drug-taking. I intend using this model here simply as one viable way in which the 'social control leads to deviation' chain can be conceptualized and also because of its particular emphasis upon the 'information about deviance' variable and its dependence on the mass media.

The Case of the Mods and Rockers

I have already given some indication of the general framework which I think suitable for the study of moral panics and folk devils. Further perspectives suggest themselves because of the special characteristics of the Mods and Rockers phenomenon, as compared with, say, the rise of student militancy or the appearance of underground newspaper editors on obscenity charges. The first and most obvious one derives from the literature on subcultural delinquency. This would provide the structural setting for explaining the Mods and Rockers phenomenon as a form of adolescent deviance among working-class youth in Britain. Downes's variant of subcultural theory is most relevant and I would substantially agree with his remarks (in the preface of his book) about the Mods and Rockers events intervening between writing and the book going to press: 'No mention is made of these occurrences in what follows, largely because – in the absence of evidence to the contrary – I take them to corroborate, rather than negate, the main sociological argument of the book.'[25] At various points in these chapters, the relevance of subcultural theory will be commented on, although my stress on the definitional rather than behavioural questions precludes an extended analysis along these lines.

Another less obvious orientation derives from the field of collective behaviour. I have already suggested that social types can be seen as the products of the same processes that go into the creation of symbolic collective styles in fashion, dress and public identities. The Mods and Rockers, though, were initially registered in the public consciousness not just as the appearance of new social types, but as actors in a particular episode of collective behaviour. The phenomenon took its subsequent shape in terms of these episodes: the regular series of disturbances which took place at English seaside resorts between 1964 and 1966. The public image of these folk devils was invariably tied up to a number of highly visual scenarios associated with their appearance: youths chasing across the beach, brandishing deckchairs over their heads, running along the pavements, riding on scooters or bikes down the streets, sleeping on the beaches and so on.

Each of these episodes – as I will describe – contained all the elements of the classic crowd situation which has long been the prototype for the study of collective behaviour. Crowds, riots, mobs and disturbances on occasions ranging from pop concerts to political demonstrations have all been seen in a similar way to *The Crowd* described by Le Bon in 1896. Later formulations by Tarde, Freud, McDougall and F. H. Allport made little lasting contribution and often just elaborated on Le Bon's contagion hypothesis. A more useful recent theory – for all its deficiencies from a sociological viewpoint – is Smelser's 'value added schema'.[26] In the sequence he suggests, each of the following determinants of collective behaviour must appear: (i) structural conduciveness; (ii) structural strain; (iii) growth and spread of a generalized belief; (iv) precipitating factors; (v) mobilization of the participants for action; (vi) operation of social control.

Structural conduciveness creates conditions of permissiveness under which collective behaviour is seen as legitimate. Together with structural strain (e.g. economic deprivation, population invasion) this factor creates the opening for race riots, sects, panics and other examples of collective behaviour. In the case of the Mods and Rockers, conduciveness and strain correspond to the structural sources of strain posited in subcultural theory: anomie, status frustration, blocked leisure opportunities and so on. The growth and spread of a generalized belief is important because the situation of strain must be made meaningful to the potential participants. For the most part these generalized beliefs are spread through the mass media. I have already indicated the importance of media imagery for studying deviance as a whole; in dealing with crowd behaviour, this importance is heightened because of the ways in which such phenomena develop and spread. As will be shown, sociological and social psychological work on mass hysteria, delusions and rumours are of direct relevance here.

Precipitating factors are specific events which might confirm a generalized belief, initiate strain or redefine conduciveness. Like the other factors in Smelser's schema, it is not a determinant of anything in itself – for example, a fight will not start a race riot unless it occurs in or is interpreted as an 'explosive situation'. While not spelling out in detail the precipitating factors in the Mods and Rockers events, I will show how the social reaction contributed to the definition and creation of these factors. Mobilization of participants for action again refers to a sequence present in the Mods and Rockers events which will only be dealt with in terms of the other determinants.

It is Smelser's sixth determinant – the operation of social control – which, together with the generalized belief factors, will concern us most. This factor, which 'in certain respects . . . arches over all others'[27] refers to the counter forces set up by society to prevent and inhibit the previous determinants: 'Once an episode of collective behaviour has appeared, its duration and severity are determined by the response of the agencies of social control.'[28] So from a somewhat different theoretical perspective – Parsonian functionalism – Smelser attaches the same crucial importance to the social control factors stressed in the transactional model.

A special – and at first sight somewhat esoteric – area of collective behaviour which is of peculiar relevance, is the field known as 'disaster research'.[29] This consists of a body of findings about the social and psychological impact of disasters, particularly physical disasters such as hurricanes, tornadoes and floods but also man-made disasters such as bombing attacks. Theoretical models have also been produced, and Merton argues that the study of disasters can extend sociological theory beyond the confines of the immediate subject-matter. Disaster situations can be looked at as strategic research sites for theory-building: 'Conditions of collective stress bring out in bold relief aspects of social systems that are not as readily visible in the stressful conditions of everyday life.'[30] The value of disaster studies is that by compressing social processes into a brief time span, a disaster makes usually private behaviour, public and immediate and therefore more amenable to study.[31]

I came across the writings in this field towards the end of carrying out the Mods and Rockers research and was immediately struck by the parallels between what I was then beginning to think of as 'moral panics' and the reactions to physical disasters. Disaster researchers have constructed one of the few models in sociology for considering the reaction of the social system to something stressful, disturbing or threatening. The happenings at Brighton, Clacton or Margate clearly were not disasters in the same category of events as earthquakes or floods; the differences are too obvious to have to spell out. Nevertheless, there *were* resemblances, and definitions of 'disaster' are so inconsistent and broad, that the Mods and Rockers events could almost fit them. Elements in such definitions include: whole or part of a community must be affected, a large segment of the community must be confronted with actual or potential danger, there must be loss of cherished values and material objects resulting in death or injury or destruction to property.

In addition, many workers in the field claim that research should not be restricted to actual disasters – a potential disaster may be just as disruptive as the actual event. Studies of reactions to hoaxes and false alarms show disaster behaviour in the absence of objective danger. More important, as will be shown in detail, a large segment of the community reacted to the Mods and Rockers events as if a disaster had occurred: 'It is the perception of threat and not its actual existence that is important.'[32]

The work of disaster researchers that struck me as most useful when I got to the stage of writing up my own material on the Mods and Rockers was the sequential model that they have developed to describe the phases of a typical disaster. The following is the sort of sequence that has been distinguished:[33]

1. *Warning*: during which arises, mistakenly or not, some apprehensions based on conditions out of which danger may arise. The warning must be coded to be understood and impressive enough to overcome resistance to the belief that current tranquillity can be upset.

2. *Threat*: during which people are exposed to communication from others, or to signs from the approaching disaster itself indicating specific imminent danger. This phase begins with the perception of some change, but as with the first phase, may be absent or truncated in the case of sudden disaster.

3. *Impact*: during which the disaster strikes and the immediate unorganized response to the death, injury or destruction takes place.

4. *Inventory*: during which those exposed to the disaster begin to form a preliminary picture of what has happened and of their own condition.

5. *Rescue*: during which the activities are geared to immediate help for the survivors. As well as people in the impact area helping each other, the suprasystem begins to send aid.

6. *Remedy*: during which more deliberate and formal activities are undertaken towards relieving the affected. The suprasystem takes over the functions the emergency system cannot perform.

7. *Recovery*: during which, for an extended period, the community either recovers its former equilibrium or achieves a stable adaptation to the changes which the disaster may have brought about.

Some of these stages have no exact parallels in the Mods and Rockers case, but a condensed version of this sequence (*Warning* to cover phases 1 and 2; then *Impact*; then *Inventory*; and *Reaction* to cover phases 5, 6 and 7) provides a useful analogue. If one compares this to deviancy models such as amplification, there are obvious and crucial differences. For disasters, the sequence has been empirically established; in the various attempts to conceptualize the reactions to deviance this is by no means the case. In addition, the transitions within the amplification model or from primary to secondary deviation are supposed to be consequential (i.e. causal) and not merely sequential. In disaster research, moreover, it has been shown how the form each phase takes is affected by the characteristics of the previous stage: thus, the scale of the remedy operation is affected by the degree of identification with the victim. This sort of uniformity has not been shown in deviance.

The nature of the reaction to the event is important in different ways. In the case of disaster, the social system responds in order to help the victims and to evolve methods to mitigate the effects of further disasters (e.g. by early warning systems). The disaster itself occurs independently of this reaction. In regard to deviance, however, the reaction is seen as partly causative. The on-the-spot reaction to an act determines whether it is classified as deviant at all, and the way in which the act is reported and labelled also determines the form of the subsequent deviation; this is not the case with a disaster. To express the difference in another way, while the disaster sequence is linear and constant – in each disaster the warning is followed by the impact which is followed by the reaction – deviance models are circular and amplifying: the impact (deviance) is followed by a reaction which has the effect of increasing the subsequent warning and impact, setting up a feedback system. It is precisely because the Mods and Rockers phenomenon was both a generalized type of deviance and also manifested itself as a series of discrete events, that both models are relevant. While a single event can be meaningfully described in terms of the disaster analogue (warning–impact–reaction), each event can be seen as creating the potential for a reaction which, among other possible consequences, might cause further acts of deviance.

Let me now return to the original aims of the study and conclude this introductory chapter by outlining the plan of the book. My focus is on the genesis and development of the moral panic and social typing associated with the Mods and Rockers phenomenon. In transactional terminology: what was the nature and effect of the societal reaction to this particular form of deviance? This entails looking at the ways in which the behaviour was perceived and conceptualized, whether there was a unitary or a divergent set of images, the modes through which these images were transmitted and the ways in which agents of social control reacted. The behavioural questions (how did the Mods and Rockers styles emerge? Why did some young people more or less identified with these groups behave in the way they did?) will be considered, but they are the background questions. The variable of societal reaction is the focus of attention.

Very few studies have been made with this focus and the term 'reaction' has become reified, covering a wide range of interpretations. Does 'reaction' mean what is *done* about the deviance in question, or merely what is *thought* about it? And how does one study something as nebulous as this, when the 'thing' being reacted to covers juvenile delinquency, a manifestation of youth culture, a social type and a series of specific events? Using criteria determined by my theoretical interests rather than by how concepts can best be 'operationalized', I decided to study reaction at three levels, in each case using a range of possible sources. The first was the initial on-the-spot reaction, which I studied mainly through observation, participant observation and the type of informal interviewing used in community studies. The second was the organized reaction of the system of social control, information about which I obtained from observation, interviews and the analysis of published material. The third level was the transmission and diffusion of the reaction in the mass media. A detailed description of the research methods and sources of material is given in the Appendix.

To remain faithful to the theoretical orientation of the study, my argument will be presented in terms of a typical reaction sequence. That is to say, instead of describing the deviation in some detail and then considering the reaction, I will start off with the minimum possible account of the deviation, then deal with the reaction and then, finally, return to consider the interplay between deviation and reaction. In terms of the disaster analogue this means starting off with the inventory, moving on to other phases of the reaction and then returning to the warning and impact. The book divides into three parts: the first (and major) part traces the development and reverberation of the societal reaction, particularly as reflected in the mass media and the actions of the organized system of social control. This consists of three chapters: the *Inventory*; the *Opinion and Attitude Themes* and the *Rescue and Remedy Phases*. The second part of the book looks at the effects of the reaction and the third locates the growth of the folk devils and the moral panic in historical and structural terms.

Organizing the book in this way means that in the first part, the Mods and Rockers are hardly going to appear as 'real, live people' at all. They will be seen through the eyes of the societal reaction and in this reaction they tend to appear as disembodied objects, Rorshach blots on to which reactions are projected. In using this type of presentation, I do not want to imply that these reactions – although they do involve elements of fantasy and selective misperception – are irrational nor that the Mods and Rockers were not real people, with particular structural origins, values, aims and interests. Neither were they creatures pushed and pulled by the forces of the societal reaction without being able to react back. I am presenting the argument in this way for effect, only allowing the Mods and Rockers to come to life when their supposed identities had been presented for public consumption.

2 The Inventory

I have already said that I will be paying less attention to the actors than to the audience. Now – before analysing the first stages of the reaction – I want to say something about the typical stage and set on which the Mods and Rockers dramas took place. Of course, such distinctions between 'audience', 'actor' and 'stage' are partly artificial because the dramatalurgical analogy on which they are based *is* only an analogy. As the Mods and Rockers drama ran its course, the whole script changed and the reaction of each successive audience altered the nature of the stage. Certain things remained constant, though, and it is worth noting some of the more distinctive characteristics of the setting in so far as they affected the actions that took place.

Such scene-setting is rarely indulged in by sociologists. They have concentrated on global categories such as crime and delinquency and have analysed these phenomena nomothetically in an attempt to derive general laws and relationships. Ideographic accounts of specific events or places have been left to journalists or historians, and are used, if at all, for illustrative purposes only. In terms of the canons of conventional sociological practice this might be legitimate, but it has meant that information on peculiar manifestations of these global categories has not been gathered in any theoretically meaningful terms. Thus, in regard to gang delinquency or collective juvenile violence, there are a number of theories at a fairly high level together with intricate descriptions of the interpersonal processes within the groups. But there are few naturalistic accounts: of what it is like to grow up in a ghetto or a housing estate, of being at an outdoor pop concert, of taking part in a rock-and-roll riot in the fifties.[1] A surprising amount of theorization in such fields as gang delinquency and race riots rests on second-hand or heavily biased sources.

The relevant setting in the Mods and Rockers case, was the English Bank Holiday by the sea and all that is associated with this ritual. A journalist who wrote that '. . . perhaps it is not taking things too far to look for an explanation (of the disturbances) in the character of the British weekend by the sea'[2] was only slightly overstating the importance of such situational elements. This setting has not changed much since that particular Whitsun day described thirty years ago by Graham Greene in *Brighton Rock*.[3] Hale had been in Brighton for three hours:

> He leant against the rail near the Palace Pier and showed his face to the crowd as it uncoiled endlessly past him, like a twisted piece of wire, two by two, each with an air of sober and determined gaiety. They had stood all the way from Victoria in crowded carriages, they would have to wait in queues for lunch, at midnight half asleep they would rock back in trains an hour late to the cramped streets and the closed pubs and the weary walk home . . . With immense labour and immense patience they extracted from the long day the grain of pleasure: this sun, this music, the rattle of the miniature cars, the ghost trains diving between the grinning skeletons under the Aquarium promenade, the sticks of Brighton rock, the paper sailors' caps.

On the same Aquarium promenade during Whitsum 1965 I interviewed two pensioners from South London who had been coming to Brighton most of their Bank Holidays for thirty years. They spoke of the changes which were visible to anyone: people looked better off, there were fewer day-trippers and coaches, there were fewer young married couples ('all gone to the Costa Brava'), things were more expensive and – of course – there were more young people to be seen. The young were highly visible: on scooters, motor-bikes, packing the trains, hitching down on the roads from London, lying about the beaches, camping on the cliffs. But otherwise, to these old people, things had not changed much. They did not mention it, but perhaps there was one change 'for the better' compared to Greene's Brighton: there was little of the air of menace that surrounded the razor gangs and the race-course battles of the twenties and thirties.

The scene of the first Mods and Rockers event, the one that was to set the pattern for all the others and give the phenomenon its distinctive shape, was not Brighton, but Clacton, a small holiday resort on the east coast of England. It has never been as affluent and popular as Brighton and has traditionally become the gathering place for the tougher adolescents from the East End and the north-eastern suburbs of London. Like Great Yarmouth, its nearest neighbour to become a scene for later Mods and Rockers events, its range of facilities and amusements for young people is strictly limited.

Easter 1964 was worse than usual. It was cold and wet, and in fact Easter Sunday was the coldest for eighty years. The shopkeepers and stall owners were irritated by the lack of business and the young people had their own boredom and irritation fanned by rumours of café owners and barmen refusing to serve some of them. A few groups started scuffling on the pavements and throwing stones at each other. The Mods and Rockers factions – a division initially based on clothing and life styles, later rigidified, but at that time not fully established – started separating out. Those on bikes and scooters roared up and down, windows were broken, some beach huts were wrecked and one boy fired a starting pistol in the air. The vast number of people crowding into the streets, the noise, everyone's general irritation and the actions of an unprepared and undermanned police force had the effect of making the two days unpleasant, oppressive and sometimes frightening. In terms of the model, this was the initial deviation or impact.

Immediately after a physical disaster there is a period of relatively unorganized response. This is followed by the inventory phase during which those exposed to the disaster take stock of what has happened and of their own condition. In this period, rumours and ambiguous perceptions become the basis for interpreting the situation. Immediately after the Aberfan coal-tip disaster, for example, there were rumours about the tip having been seen moving the night before and previous warnings having been ignored. These reports were to form the basis of later accusations of negligence against the National Coal Board, and the negligence theme then became assimilated into more deep-rooted attitudes, for example, about indifference by the central Government to Welsh interests. In the next chapter I will examine such long-term opinions, attitudes and interests.

I am concerned here with the way in which the situation was initially interpreted and presented by the mass media, because it is in this form that most people receive their pictures of both deviance and disasters. Reactions take place on the basis of these processed or coded images: people become indignant or angry, formulate theories and plans, make speeches, write letters to the newspapers. The media presentation or inventory of the Mods and Rockers events is crucial in determining the later stages of the reaction.

On the Monday morning following the initial incidents at Clacton, every national newspaper, with the exception of *The Times* (fifth lead on main news page) carried a leading report on the subject. The headlines are self-descriptive: 'Day of Terror by Scooter Groups' (*Daily Telegraph*), 'Youngsters

Beat Up Town – 97 Leather Jacket Arrests' (*Daily Express*), 'Wild Ones Invade Seaside – 97 Arrests' (*Daily Mirror*). The next lot of incidents received similar coverage on the Tuesday and editorials began to appear, together with reports that the Home Secretary was 'being urged' (it was not usually specified exactly by *whom*) to hold an inquiry or to take firm action. Feature articles then appeared highlighting interviews with Mods and Rockers. Straight reporting gave way to theories especially about motivation: the mob was described as 'exhilarated', 'drunk with notoriety', 'hell-bent for destruction', etc. Reports of the incidents themselves were followed by accounts of police and court activity and local reaction. The press coverage of each series of incidents showed a similar sequence.

Overseas coverage was extensive throughout; particularly in America, Canada, Australia, South Africa and the Continent. The *New York Times* and *New York Herald Tribune* carried large photos, after Whitsun, of two girls fighting. Belgian papers captioned their photos 'West Side Story on English Coast'.

It is difficult to assess conclusively the accuracy of these early reports. Even if each incident could have been observed, a physical impossibility, one could never check the veracity of, say, an interview. In many cases, one 'knows' that the interview must be, partly at least, journalistic fabrication because it is too stereotypical to be true, but this is far from objective proof. Nevertheless, on the basis of those incidents that were observed, interviews with people who were present at others (local reporters, photographers, deckchair attendants, etc.) and a careful check on internal consistency, some estimate of the main distortions can be made. Checks with the local press are particularly revealing. Not only are the reports more detailed and specific, but they avoid statements like 'all the dance halls near the seafront were smashed' when every local resident knows that there is only one dance hall near the front.

The media inventory of each initial incident will be analysed under three headings: (i) Exaggeration and Distortion; (ii) Prediction; (iii) Symbolization.

Exaggeration and Distortion

Writing when the Mods and Rockers phenomenon was passing its peak, a journalist recalls that a few days after the initial event at Clacton, the Assistant Editor of the *Daily Mirror* admitted in conversation that the affair had been 'a little over-reported'.[4] It is this 'over-reporting' that I am interested in here.

The major type of distortion in the inventory lay in exaggerating grossly the seriousness of the events, in terms of criteria such as the number taking part, the number involved in violence and the amount and effects of any damage or violence. Such distortion took place primarily in terms of the mode and style of presentation characteristic of most crime reporting: the sensational headlines, the melodramatic vocabulary and the deliberate heightening of those elements in the story considered as news. The regular use of phrases such as 'riot', 'orgy of destruction', 'battle', 'attack', 'siege', 'beat up the town' and 'screaming mob' left an image of a besieged town from which innocent holidaymakers were fleeing to escape a marauding mob.

During Whitsun 1964 even the local papers in Brighton referred to 'deserted beaches' and 'elderly holidaymakers' trying to escape the 'screaming teenagers'. One had to scan the rest of the paper or be present on the spot to know that on the day referred to (Monday, 18 May) the beaches were deserted because the weather was particularly bad. The 'holidaymakers' that *were* present were there to watch the Mods and Rockers. Although at other times (for example, August 1964 at Hastings) there was intimidation, there was very little of this in the Brighton incident referred to. In the 1965 and 1966 incidents, there was even less intimidation, yet the incidents were ritualistically reported in the same way, using the same metaphors, headlines and vocabulary.

The full flavour of such reports is captured in the following lines from the *Daily Express* (19 May 1964): 'There was Dad asleep in a deckchair and Mum making sandcastles with the children, when the 1964 boys took over the beaches at Margate and Brighton yesterday and smeared the traditional postcard scene with blood and violence.'

This type of 'over-reporting' is, of course, not peculiar to the Mods and Rockers. It is characteristic not just of crime reporting as a whole but mass media inventories of such events as political protests, racial disturbances and so on. What Knopf[5] calls the 'shotgun approach' to such subjects – the front page build up, the splashy pictures, the boxscores of the latest riot news – has become accepted in journalism. So accepted in fact, that the media and their audiences have lost even a tenuous hold on the meaning of the words they use. How is a town 'beaten up' or 'besieged'? How many shop windows have to be broken for an 'orgy of destruction' to have taken place? When can one – even metaphorically – talk of scenes being 'smeared with blood and violence'? Commenting on the way the term 'riot' is used to cover *both* an incident resulting in 43 deaths, 7,000 arrests and $45 million in property damage *and* one in which three people broke a shop window, Knopf remarks: 'The continued media use of the term contributes to an emotionally charged climate in which the public tends to view every event as an "incident", every incident as a "disturbance" and every disturbance as a "riot".'[6]

The sources of over-reporting lay not just in such abuses of language. There was a frequent use of misleading headlines, particularly headlines which were discrepant with the actual story: thus a headline 'violence' might announce a story which, in fact, reports that *no* violence occurred. Then there were more subtle and often unconscious journalistic practices: the use of the generic plural (if a boat was overturned, reports read 'boats were overturned') and the technique, well known to war correspondents, of reporting the same incident twice to look like two different incidents.

Another source of distortion lay in the publication, usually in good faith, of reports which were later to receive quite a different perspective by fresh evidence. The repetition of obviously false stories, despite known confirmation of this, is a familiar finding in studies of the role of the press in spreading mass hysteria.[7] An important example in the Mods and Rockers inventory was the frequently used '£75 cheque story'. It was widely reported that a boy had told the Margate magistrates that he would pay the £75 fine imposed on him with a cheque. This story was true enough; what few papers bothered to publish and what they all knew was that the boy's offer was a pathetic gesture of bravado. He admitted three days later that not only did he not have the £75 but did not even have a bank account and had never signed a cheque in his life. As long as four years after this, though, the story was still being repeated and was quoted to me at a magistrates' conference in 1968 to illustrate the image of the Mods and Rockers as affluent hordes whom 'fines couldn't touch'.

This story had some factual basis, even though its real meaning was lost. At other times, stories of organization, leadership and particular incidents of violence and vandalism were based on little more than unconfirmed rumour. These stories are important because – as I will show in detail – they enter into the consciousness and shape the societal reaction at later stages. It is worth quoting at length a particularly vivid example from the media coverage of an American incident:

> In York, Pa., in mid-July, 1968, . . . incidents of rock- and bottle-throwing were reported. Towards the end of the disturbance UPI in Harrisburg asked a stringer to get something on the situation. A photographer took a picture of a motorcyclist with an ammunition belt around his waist and a rifle strapped across his back. A small object dangled from the rifle. On July 18, the picture reached the nation's press. The *Washington Post* said: 'ARMED RIDER – Unidentified motorcyclist drives through heart of York, Pa., Negro district, which was quiet for the first time in six days of sporadic disorders.' The *Baltimore Sun* used the same picture and a

similar caption: 'QUIET BUT . . . An unidentified motorcycle rider armed with a rifle and carrying a belt of ammunition, was among those in the heart of York, Pa., Negro district last night. The area was quiet for the first time in six days.'

The implication of this photograph was clear: the 'armed rider' was a sniper. But since when do snipers travel openly in daylight completely armed? Also, isn't there something incongruous about photographing a sniper, presumably 'on his way to work' when according to the caption, the city 'was quiet'? Actually, the 'armed rider' was a sixteen-year-old boy who happened to be fond of hunting groundhogs – a skill he had learned as a small boy from his father. On July 16, as was his custom, the young man had put on his ammo belt and strapped a rifle across his back, letting a hunting licence dangle so that all would know he was hunting animals, not people. Off he went on his motorcycle headed for the woods, the fields, the groundhogs – and the place reserved for him in the nation's press.[8]

Moving from the form to the content of the inventory, a detailed analysis reveals that much of the image of the deviation presented was, in Lemert's term, putative: '. . . that portion of the societal definition of the deviant which has no foundation in his objective behaviour.'[9] The following is a composite of the mass media inventory:

> Gangs of Mods and Rockers from the suburbs of London invaded, on motor-bikes and scooters, a number of seaside resorts. These were afflu-ent young people, from all social classes. They came down deliberately to cause trouble by behaving aggressively towards visitors, local residents and the police. They attacked innocent holidaymakers and destroyed a great deal of public property. This cost the resorts large sums of money in repairing the damage and a further loss of trade through potential visitors being scared to come down.

The evidence for the ten elements in this composite picture is summarized below:

1. *Gangs* – There was no evidence of any structured gangs. The groups were loose collectivities or crowds within which there was occasionally some more structured grouping based on territorial loyalty, e.g. 'The Walthamstow Boys'.

2. *Mods and Rockers* – Initially at least, the groups were not polarized along the Mod–Rocker dimension. At Clacton, for example, the rivalry (already in existence for many years) between on the one hand those from London and on the other locals and youths from the surrounding counties, was a much more significant dimension. The Mod–Rocker polarization was institutionalized later and partly as a consequence of the initial publicity. In addition, throughout the whole life of the phenomenon, many of the young people coming down to the resorts did not identify with either group.

3. *Invasion from London* – Although the bulk of day-trippers, young and old, were from London, this was simply the traditional Bank Holiday pattern. Not all offenders were from London; many were either local residents or came from neighbouring towns or villages. This was particularly true of the Rockers who, in Clacton and Great Yarmouth, came mainly from East Anglian villages. The origins of fifty-four youths, on whom information was obtainable, out of the sixty-four charged at Hastings (August 1964) was as follows: London or Middlesex suburbs – twenty; Welwyn Garden City – four; small towns in Kent – nine; Sussex – seven; Essex – four; and Surrey – ten.

4. *Motor-bikes and Scooters* – At every event the majority of young people present came down by train or coach or hitched. The motor-bike or scooter owners were always a minority; albeit a noisy minority that easily gave the impression of ubiquity.

5. *Affluence* – There is no clear-cut information here of the type that could be obtained from a random sample of the crowd. Work on the Brighton Archway Ventures and all information from other sources suggest that the young people coming down were not particularly well off. Certainly for those charged in the courts, there is no basis for the affluence image. The average take home pay in Barker and Little's Margate sample was £11 per week.[10]* The original Clacton offenders had on them an average of 15s. for the whole Bank Holiday weekend. The best off was a window-cleaner earning £15 a week, but more typical were a market assistant earning £7 10s. od. and a 17-year-old office boy earning £5 14s. od.

6. *Classless* – Indices such as accent and area of residence, gathered from court reports and observation, suggest that both the crowds and the offenders were predominantly working class. In the Barker–Little sample, the typical Rocker was an unskilled manual worker, the typical Mod a semi-skilled manual worker. All but two had left school at 15. At Clacton, out of the

* This research sample will be referred to subsequently as the 'Barker–Little sample'.

twenty-four charged, twenty-three had left school at 15, and twenty-two had been to secondary moderns. All were unskilled; there were no apprentices or anyone receiving any kind of training.

7.   *Deliberate intent* – The bulk of young people present at the resorts came down not so much to make trouble as in the hope that there would be some trouble to watch. Their very presence, their readiness to be drawn into a situation of trouble and the sheer accretion of relatively trivial incidents were found inconvenient and offensive; but if there really had been great numbers deliberately intent on causing trouble, then much more trouble would have resulted. I will make this point clearer when analysing the impact. The proportion of those whom the police would term 'troublemakers' was always small. This hard core was more evident at Clacton than at any of the subsequent events: twenty-three out of the twenty-four charged (ninety-seven were originally arrested) had previous convictions.

8.   *Violence and Vandalism* – Acts of violence and vandalism are the most tangible manifestations of what the press and public regard as hooliganism. These acts were therefore played up rather than the less melodramatic effect of the Mods and Rockers which was being a nuisance and inconvenience to many adults. In fact, the total amount of serious violence and vandalism was not great. Only about one tenth of the Clacton offenders was charged with offences involving violence. At Margate, Whitsun 1964, supposedly one of the most violent events – the one which provoked the *Daily Express* 'blood and violence' report – there was little more recorded violence than two stabbings and the dropping of a man on to a flower bed. At Hastings, August 1964, out of forty-four found guilty, there were three cases of assaulting the police. At Brighton, Easter 1965, out of seventy arrests there were seven for assault. Even if the definition of violence were broadened to include obstruction and the use of threatening behaviour, the targets were rarely 'innocent holiday-makers', but members of a rival group, or, more often, the police. The number of recorded cases of malicious damage to property was also small; less than 10 per cent of all cases charged in the courts. The typical offence throughout was obstructing the police or the use of threatening behaviour. In Clacton, although hardly any newspapers mentioned this, a number of the twenty-four were charged with 'non-hooligan'-type offences: stealing half a pint of petrol, attempting to steal drinks from a vending machine and 'obtaining credit to the amount of 7*d*. by means of fraud other than false pretences' (an ice-cream).

9.   *Cost of damage* – The court figures for malicious damage admittedly underestimate the extent of vandalism because much of this goes undetected. Nevertheless, an examination of the figures given for the cost of the damage

Table 1 Cost of Damage to Four Resorts: Easter and Whitsun, 1964

Place	Date	No. of arrests	Estimated cost of damage
Clacton	Easter, 1964	97	£513
Bournemouth	Whitsun, 1964	56	£100
Brighton	Whitsun, 1964	76	£400
Margate	Whitsun, 1964	64	£250

Source: Estimates by local authorities quoted in local press.

suggests that this was not as excessive as reported. Table 1 shows the cost of damage at the first four events.

It must be remembered also that a certain amount of damage to local authority property takes place every Bank Holiday. According to the Deputy Publicity Manager of Margate,[11] for example, the number of deckchairs broken (fifty) was not much greater than on an ordinary Bank Holiday weekend; there were also more chairs out on Whit Sunday than ever before.

10. *Loss of trade* – The press, particularly the local press, laid great emphasis on the financial loss the resorts had suffered and would suffer on account of the Mods and Rockers through cancelled holidays, less use of facilities, loss of trade in shops, restaurants and hotels. The evidence for any such loss is at best dubious. Under the heading 'Those Wild Ones Are To Blame Again', the Brighton *Evening Argus* quoted figures after Whitsun 1964 to show that, compared with the previous Whitsun, the number of deckchairs hired had dropped by 8,000 and the number using the swimming pool by 1,500. But the number using the miniature railway increased by 2,000, as did the number of users of the putting green. These figures make sense when one knows that on the day referred to, the temperature had dropped by 14°F. and it had been raining the night before. This is the main reason why there was less use of deckchairs and the swimming pool. In Hastings, August 1964, despite a big scare-publicity build up, the number of visitors coming down by train increased by 6,000 over the previous year.[12] Newspapers often quoted 'loss of trade' estimates by landlords, hotel keepers and local authority officials, but invariably, final figures of damage fell below the first estimates. These revised figures, however, came too late to have any news value.

Although there were cases of people being scared away by reports of the disturbances, the overall effect was the opposite. The Margate publicity department had a letter from a travel agent in Ireland saying that the events had 'put Margate on the map'. Leaving aside the additional young people thcmselves attracted by the publicity – they would not be defined as commercial assets – many adults as well came down to watch the fun. I was often asked, on the way down from Brighton station, 'Where are the Mods and Rockers today?', and near the beaches, parents could be seen holding children on their shoulders to get a better view of the proceedings. In an interview with a reporter during which I was present, a man said, 'My wife and I came down with our son (aged 18) to see what all this fun is at the seaside on Bank Holidays' (*Evening Argus*, 30 May 1964). By 1965 the happenings were part of the scene – the pier, the whelks, the Mods and Rockers could all be taken in on a day trip.

Prediction

There is another element in the inventory which needs to be discussed separately because it assumes a special importance in later stages. This is the implicit assumption, present in virtually every report, that what had happened was inevitably going to happen again. Few assumed that the events were transient occurrences; the only questions were where the Mods and Rockers would strike next and what could be done about it. As will be suggested, these predictions played the role of the classical self-fulfilling prophecy. Unlike the case of natural disasters where the absence of predictions can be disastrous, with social phenomena such as deviance, it is the presence of predictions that can be 'disastrous'.

The predictions in the inventory period took the form of reported state-ments from local figures such as tradesmen, councillors and police spokesmen about what should be done 'next time' or of immediate precautions they had taken. More important, youths were asked in TV interviews about their plans for the next Bank Holiday and interviews were printed with either a Mod or a Rocker threatening revenge 'next time'. The following are extracts from two such interviews: 'Southend and places won't let us in any more. It will get difficult here and so next year we'll probably go to Ramsgate or Hastings' (*Daily Express*, 30 March 1964). 'It could have been better – the weather spoiled it a bit. Wait until next Whitsun. Now that will be a real giggle' (*Daily Mirror*, 31 March 1964).

Where predictions were not fulfilled, a story could still be found by reporting non-events. So, for example, when attention was switched to East Anglian resorts in 1966, the *East Anglian Daily Times* (30 May 1966) headed a report on a play attended by a group of long-haired youths 'Fears When Ton-up Boys Walked in Groundless'. Reporters and photographers were often sent on the basis of false tip-offs to events that did not materialize. In W 1965, a *Daily Mirror* report from Hastings, where nothing at all happen headed 'Hastings – Without Them'. In Whitsun 1966 there was a report (*Daily Mirror*, 30 May 1966) on how policemen on a 'Mods and Rockers patrol' in Clacton could only use their specially provided walkie-talkies to help two lost little boys. Again, headlines often created the impression that something had happened: the *Evening Argus* (30 May 1966) used the subheading 'Violence' to report that 'in Brighton there was no violence in spite of the crowds of teenagers on the beach'.

These non-event stories and other distortions springing from the prediction theme, are part of the broader tendency which I will discuss later whereby discrepancies between expectations and reality are resolved by emphasizing those new elements which confirm expectations and playing down those which are contradictory. Commenting on this tendency in their analysis of the media coverage of the October 1968 Vietnam war demonstrations, Halloran *et al.*[13] draw attention to a technique often employed in the Mods and Rockers inventory, '. . . a phrase or sentence describing in highly emotive terms either the expectation of violence or an isolated incident of violence, is followed by a completely contradictory sentence describing the actual situation'.

The cumulative effect of such reports was to establish predictions whose truth was guaranteed by the way in which the event, non-event or pseudo-event it referred to was reported.

Symbolization

Communication, and especially the mass communication of stereotypes, depends on the symbolic power of words and images. Neutral words such as place-names can be made to symbolize complex ideas and emotions; for example, Pearl Harbor, Hiroshima, Dallas and Aberfan. A similar process occurred in the Mods and Rockers inventory: these words themselves and a word such as 'Clacton' acquired symbolic powers. It became meaningful to say 'we don't want another Clacton here' or 'you can see he's one of those Mod types'.

There appear to be three processes in such symbolization: a word (Mod) becomes symbolic of a certain status (delinquent or deviant); objects (hairstyle, clothing) symbolize the word; the objects themselves become symbolic of the status (and the emotions attached to the status). The cumulative effect of these three processes as they appeared in the inventory was that the terms Mods and Rockers were torn from any previously neutral contexts (for example, the denotation of different consumer styles) and acquired wholly negative meanings. The identical effect is described by Turner and Surace[14] in their classic study of the Zoot Suit riots* and by Rock and myself in tracing how the Edwardian dress style became transformed into the Teddy Boy folk devil.[15]

In their case study, Turner and Surace refer to this process as the creation of 'unambiguously unfavourable symbols'. Newspaper headlines and inter-personal communication following the initial incidents in Los Angeles, reiterated the phobia and hatred towards Mexican American youth. References to this group were made in such a way as to strip key symbols (differences in fashion, life style and entertainment) from their favourable or neutral connotations until they came to evoke unambiguously unfavourable feelings. Content analysis showed a switch in the references to Mexicans to the 'Zooter theme', which identified this particular clothing style as the 'badge of delinquency' and coupled such references with mention of zoot-suiter attacks and orgies. Invariably the zooter was identified with the generalized Mexican group. In the same way, the Mod and Rocker status traits were, in later stages of the reaction, to wash off on the generalized adolescent group. Their 'badge of delinquency' emerged as symbols, such as the fur-collared anorak and the scooter, which became sufficient in themselves to stimulate hostile and punitive reactions.†

Symbols and labels eventually acquire their own descriptive and explanatory potential. Thus – to take examples from an earlier folk devil – the label 'Teddy Boy' became a general term of abuse (for example, John Osborne being described as 'an intellectual Teddy Boy'); the devil was seen as a distinct type of personality (drugs were announced to soothe Teddy Boys and make them co-operative for treatment, statements made such as 'some of these soldiers here are just Teddy Boys in army uniform') and the symbols were seen as changing the person ('he was never in trouble before he bought an Edwardian suit'; 'since my son bought this thing a year ago his personality has changed').

---

* These riots took place in Los Angeles in 1943. Sailors indiscriminately beat up Mexicans and the 'zoot suit' – the long coat and trousers pegged at the cuffs worn by boys with long, greased hair – became the symbol around which the rioters rallied. In the decade preceding the riots, the treatment of Mexicans in the media gradually became less favourable and the concept of 'zoot-suiter' had been built up as a negative symbol, associated with all sorts of crime and deviance. See Turner and Surace.

† During the inventory period, scooter owners and manufacturers frequently complained about the bad publicity that they were getting. After Clacton, the general secretaries of the Vespa and Lambretta Scooter Clubs issued a statement dissociating their clubs from the disturbances.

Such symbolization is partly the consequence of the same standard mass communication processes which give rise to exaggeration and distortion. Thus, for example, misleading and inappropriate headlines were used to create unambiguously negative symbols where the actual event did not warrant this at all or at least was ambiguous. Accounts of certain events in Whitsun 1964, for example, were coupled with a report of a 'Mod' falling to his death from a cliff outside Brighton. Similarly, in August 1964 there were headlines 'Mod Dead In Sea'. In neither case had these deaths anything to do with the disturbances; they were both pure accidents. A reading of the headlines only, or of early reports not mentioning police statements about the accidents, might have led to a misleading connection. This sort of effect reached its bizarre heights in a headline in the *Dublin Evening Press* (18 May 1964) 'Terror Comes to English Resorts. Mutilated Mod Dead In Park'. The 'mutilated Mod' was, in fact, a man between 21 and 25 wearing a 'mod jacket'(?) who was found stabbed on the Saturday morning (the day *before* the incidents at the resorts) in a Birmingham park.*

Another highly effective technique of symbolization was the use of dramatized and ritualistic interviews with 'representative members' of either group. The *Daily Mirror* (31 March 1964) had 'Mick The Wild One' on 'Why I Hurled That Chisel' and another boy who said, 'I take pep pills. Everybody does here.' The *Daily Herald* (18 May 1964) quoted one boy clutching his injured head as the police bundled him into a van saying, 'Carry on with the plan'; another said, 'We're not through yet. We're here for the holiday and we're staying. Margate will wish it was Clacton when we're finished.' The *Evening Standard* (19 May 1964) found 'The Baron' who hated 'Mods and Wogs' and said, 'I like fighting . . . I have been fighting all my life.' The *Daily Mirror* (8 May 1964) found a new angle with 'The Girls Who Follow The Wild Ones Into Battle' and who said about fighting: '. . . it gives you a kick, a thrill, it makes you feel all funny inside. You get butterflies in your stomach and you want the boys to go on and on . . . It's hard luck on the people who get in their way, but you can't do anything about that.'

It is difficult to establish how authentic these interviews are. In some cases they ring so patently absurd a note that they cannot be an accurate transcription of what was actually said; the *Daily Telegraph* (31 March 1964), for example,

---

* Newspapers farthest away from the source invariably carried the greatest distortions and inaccuracies. The *Glasgow Daily Record and Mail* (20 May 1964), for example, described Mods as being dressed in short-jacketed suits, with bell bottoms, high boots, bowler or top hats and carrying rolled-up umbrellas.

carried an interview with a Rocker who said, 'We are known as the Rockers and are much more with it.' If any group had a 'with-it' self-image and would even contemplate using such a term, it certainly was not the Rockers. It would be fair to describe these interviews and reports as being composite, not necessarily in the sense of being wilfully faked, but as being influenced by the reporter's (or sub-editor's) conception of how anyone labelled as a thug or a hooligan *should* speak, dress and act. This effect may have occasionally been heightened by a certain gullibility about the fantasies of self-styled gang leaders.[16]

Through symbolization, plus the other types of exaggeration and distortion, images are made much sharper than reality. There is no reason to assume that photographs or television reports are any more 'objective'. In a study of the different perceptions experienced by TV viewers and on-the-spot spectators of another crowd situation (MacArthur Day in Chicago), it was shown how the reporting was distorted by the selection of items to fit into already existing expectations.[17] A sharpening up process occurs, producing emotionally toned symbols which eventually acquire their own momentum. Thus the dissemination of overwhelming public support in favour of MacArthur '. . . gathered force as it was incorporated into political strategy, picked up by other media, entered into gossip and thus came to overshadow immediate reality as it might have been recorded by an observer on the scene'.[18]

In this study, observers recorded how their expectations of political enthusiasm and wild mass involvement were completely unfulfilled. Through close-ups and a particular style of commentary ('the most enthusiastic crowd ever in our city . . . you can feel the tenseness in the air . . . you can hear the crowd roar') television structured the whole event to convey emotions non-existent to the participants. This effect explains why many spectators at the Mods and Rockers events found them a slight let-down after the mass media publicity. As Boorstin remarks in discussing the effects of television and colour photography: 'Verisimilitude took on a new meaning . . . The Grand Canyon itself became a disappointing reproduction of the Kodachrome original.'[19]

The Inventory as Manufactured News

The cumulative effects of the inventory can be summarized as follows: (i) the putative deviation had been assigned from which further stereotyping, myth making and labelling could proceed; (ii) the expectation was created that this form of deviation would certainly recur; (iii) a wholly negative symbolization in regard to the Mods and Rockers and objects associated with them had been created; (iv) all the elements in the situation had been made clear enough to allow for full-scale demonology and hagiology to develop: the information had been made available for placing the Mods and Rockers in the gallery of contemporary folk devils.

Why do these sorts of inventories result? Are they in any sense 'inevitable'? What are the reasons for bias, exaggeration and distortion? To make sense of questions such as these, one must understand that the inventory is not, of course, a simple sort of stock-taking into which some errors might accidentally creep from time to time. Built into the very nature of deviance, inventories in modern society are elements of fantasy, selective misperception and the deliberate creation of news. The inventory is not reflective stock-taking but manufactured news.

Before pursuing this notion, let me mention some of the more 'genuine' errors. On one level, much exaggeration and distortion arose simply from the ambiguous and confused nature of the situation. It is notoriously difficult in a crowd setting to estimate the numbers present and some of the over-estimates were probably no more than would have occurred after events such as political demonstrations, religious rallies, pop concerts or sporting fixtures. The confusion was heightened by the presence of so many reporters and photographers: their very presence could be interpreted as 'evidence' that something massive and important was happening.

As I will show when analysing the setting in more detail, it was a problem for everyone present – police, spectators, participants, newsmen – to actually know what was happening at any one time. In such situations, the gullibility effect is less significant than a general susceptibility to all sorts of rumours. Clark and Barker's case study of a participant in a race riot shows this effect very clearly,[20] and in disaster research prospective interviewers are warned, 'People who have discussed their experiences with others in the community can rapidly assimilate inaccurate versions of the disaster. These group versions may quickly come to be accepted by a large segment of the population.'[21]

Important as such errors may be in the short run, they cannot explain the more intrinsic features of deviance inventories: processes such as symbolization and prediction, the direction of the distortions rather than the simple fact of their occurrence, the decision to report the deviance in the first place and to continue to report it in a particular way. Studies of moral panics associated with the Mods and Rockers and other forms of deviance, as well as detailed research on the mass communication process itself (such as that by Halloran and his colleagues) indicate that two interrelated factors determine the presentation of deviance inventories: the first is the institutionalized need to create news and the second is the selective and inferential structure of the news-making process.

The mass media operate with certain definitions of what is newsworthy. It is not that instruction manuals exist telling newsmen that certain subjects (drugs, sex, violence) will appeal to the public or that certain groups (youth, immigrants) should be continually exposed to scrutiny. Rather, there are built-in factors, ranging from the individual newsman's intuitive hunch about what constitutes a 'good story', through precepts such as 'give the public what it wants' to structured ideological biases, which predispose the media to make a certain event into news.

The weekend of the Clacton event was particularly dull from a news point of view. Nothing particularly noteworthy happened nationally or inter-nationally. The fact that the event was given such prominence must be due partly at least to the absence of alternative news. The behaviour itself was not particularly new or startling. Disturbances of various sorts – variously called 'hooliganism', 'rowdyism' or 'gang fights' occurred frequently throughout the late fifties and early sixties in coastal resorts favoured by working-class adolescents. In 1958, for example, Southend Police had to appeal for outside support after rival groups had fought battles on the pier. In Whitley Bay, Blackpool and other northern resorts there were disturbances and fighting often more severe than any of the early Mods and Rockers episodes. For years British holidaymakers on day trips or weekend excursions to such European coastal resorts as Calais and Ostend have been involved in considerable violence and vandalism. In Ostend, from the beginning of the sixties, there was a period of the year referred to as the 'English season' during which holidaymakers and members of amateur football clubs caused considerable damage and trouble, rarely reported in the British press. The Mods and Rockers didn't become news because they were new; they were presented as new to justify their creation as news.

It would be facile to explain the creation of the inventory purely in terms of it being 'good news'; the point is simply that there was room for a story at that initial weekend and that its selection was not entirely due to its intrinsic properties. Labelling theorists have drawn attention to the complex nature of the screening and coding process whereby certain forms of rule-breaking are picked out for attention, and in Chapter 6 I will deal with the historical and structural features which opened this particular behaviour to the type of reaction it did receive. These are features which relate to social control as a whole and not just the media. The media reflected the real conflict of interests that existed at various levels: for example between local residents and police on the one hand and the Mods and Rockers on the other. In such situations the media adjudicate between competing definitions of the situation, and as these definitions are made in a hierarchical context – agents of social control are more likely to be believed than deviants – it is clear which definition will win out in an ambiguous and shifting situation.[22]

Once the subject of the story is fixed, its subsequent shape is determined by certain recurrent processes of news manufacture. Halloran *et al.* refer to the development of an *inferential structure*: this is not intentional bias nor simple selection by expectation, but '. . . a process of simplification and interpretation which structures the meaning given to the story around its original news value'.[23] The conceptual framework they use to locate this process – and one that is equally applicable to the Mods and Rockers – is Boorstin's notion of the *event as news*. That is to say, the question of 'is it news' becomes as important as 'is it real?' The argument simply is that:

> . . . events will be selected for news reporting in terms of their fit or consonance with pre-existing images – the news of the event will confirm earlier ideas. The more unclear the news item and the more uncertain or doubtful the newsman is in how to report it, the more likely it is to be reported in a general framework that has been already established.[24]

It is only when the outlines of such general frameworks have been discerned, that one can understand processes such as symbolization, prediction, the reporting of non-events and the whole style of presentation. The predictability of the inventory is crucial. So constant were the images, so stylized was the mode of reporting, so limited was the range of emotions and values played on, that it would have been perfectly simple for anyone who had studied the Mods and Rockers coverage to predict with some accuracy the reports of all later variations on the theme of depraved youth: skinheads, football hooligans, hippies, drug-takers, pop festivals, the Oz trial.

In Michael Frayn's delightful fantasy *The Tin Men*, the Newspaper Department of the William Morris Institute of Automation Research tries to show that 'in theory a digital computer could be programmed to produce a perfectly satisfactory daily newspaper with all the variety and news sense of the hand made article'. Once this idea was exploited commercially, 'The stylization of the modern newspaper would be complete. Its last residual connection with the raw, messy, offendable real world would have been broken.'[25] The Department's example is 'Child Told Dress Unsuitable by Teacher':

V. Satis. Basic plot entirely invariable. Variables confined to three. (1) Clothing objected to (high heels/petticoat/frilly knickers). (2) Whether child also smokes and/or uses lipstick. (3) Whether child alleged by parents to be humiliated by having offending clothing inspected before whole school. Frequency of publication: once every nine days.

The Department's other examples include 'Paralysed Girl Determined to Dance Again', 'I Plan to Give Away My Baby, Says Mother-to-be' and 'They Are Calling It the Street of Shame'. One could have also fed into the computer 'Youngsters/Youths/Wild Ones/Scooter Boys/Hells Angels, Invade/Beat Up/Wreck, Town/Cinema/Football Match/Pop Festival'.

This is not to imply that all these images are fictitious; after all, children *are* told that their dress is unsuitable by teachers, paralysed girls *might* be determined to dance again, collective episodes of adolescent violence and vandalism take place often enough. As one analysis of press distortions in reporting American racial violence (in the direction of exaggerating supposedly new elements of planning, organization sniping and leadership) concludes: 'Unwittingly or not, the press has been constructing a scenario on armed uprisings. The story line of this scenario is not totally removed from reality. There *have* been a few shoot-outs with the police, and a handful may have been planned. But no wave of uprisings and no set pattern of murderous conflict have developed – at least not yet.'[26]

One cannot, of course, leave the analysis of 'general frameworks', 'scenarios', 'inferential structures' and 'selective misperception' at the social psychological level. One must understand the bases of the selection in terms of more long-term values and interests; before doing this, however, we must see how the perceptual basis of the inventory was developed by means of more permanent opinions and attitudes. This is the question taken up in the next chapter.

3   Reaction: Opinion and Attitude Themes

The relationship between one's perception of a social object and one's attitude towards it is a complex one. In simplest terms, at least two sequences occur: one perceives and selects according to certain orientations already in existence and then, what is perceived is shaped and absorbed into more enduring clusters of attitudes. These processes, of course, merge into each other, but it is more the second one that this chapter is concerned with: how the images in the inventory were crystallized into more organized opinions and attitudes. These opinion and attitude themes correspond roughly to what Smelser calls generalized belief systems: the cognitive beliefs or delusions transmitted by the mass media and assimilated in terms of audience predispositions.[1]

Once the initial impact has passed over, the societal reaction to any sudden event, particularly if it is perceived as a dislocation of the social structure or a threat to cherished values, is an attempt to make sense of what happened. People talk less about the event itself and more about the implications of it. This sequence could be observed, for example, in the mass media and public reaction to the sudden and unusual event of the shooting of three policemen in London in 1966: speculations about the shooting itself and a presentation of the images of the actors involved (the inventory) were replaced by discussions of the 'issues': restoration of the death penalty, arming of policemen, the nature of violence in society. The combination of this sequence with a constellation of other events such as the spectacular uncovering of the activities of organized criminal gangs, laid the foundation at the time for a moral panic about violent crime. An almost identical constellation repeated itself in 1971 with the Blackpool police shooting and the outbursts from senior Scotland Yard officers about 'our streets not being safe to walk in'.

Similarly, research on the mass media response to the Kennedy assassination showed the transition from initial reporting to the need for interpretation.

People had to make sense of what may be considered an absurd accident. They wanted an explanation of the causes of the murder, a positive meaning to be given to the situation and a reassurance that the nation would come through the crisis without harm.[2] All these things the mass media provide by reducing the ambiguity created by cultural strain and uncertainty. In the case of mass delusions, a significant stage in the diffusion of the hysterical belief is the attempt by commentators to restructure and make sense of an ambiguous situation. In such situations theories arise to explain what cannot be seen as random events. An outbreak of windshield pitting, for example, is explained as vandalism, meteoric dust, sand-flea eggs hatching in the glass, air pollution, radioactive fallout, etc.[3]

Many of these theories and the themes to be discussed below are based on no more than the sorts of rumours present in mass delusions and serve partly the same function: the reduction of ambiguity. Although the rumours, themes and beliefs derive mainly from the mass media, they later encounter reinforcement or resistance in a group setting. The individual is exposed to a barrage of information and interpretation during which his ideas change or crystallize: 'Over time these group formulated and group supported interpretations tend to override or replace individual idiosyncratic ones. They become part of the group myth, the collection of common opinions to which the member generally conforms.'[4] These collective themes reverberate through the social system, creating the conditions on which subsequent stages are built.

This description, of course, oversimplifies the communication process by assuming a unitary set of values into which the themes are absorbed like a pool of water absorbing the ripples from a dropped stone. The communication flow is much more complicated, and information is accepted or rejected and finally coded in terms of a plurality of needs, values, membership and reference groups.

I will consider some of these differences later; at this stage I want to present in ideal–typical categories the opinion and attitude themes about the Mods and Rockers as they appeared in the mass media and other public forms. These themes derive from all the opinion statements by the media (editorials, articles, cartoons), in the media (letters, quotations from speeches, statements, sermons, etc.) and in other public arenas such as parliamentary and council debates. What follows is by no means a catalogue of all types of opinions that were expressed; some were too idiosyncratic and bizarre to classify. These are just the themes which emerged with sufficient regularity to justify thinking that they were fairly widespread and would have some effect on public opinion as a whole.

The themes are classified into three categories: (i) *Orientation*: the emotional and intellectual standpoint from which the deviance is evaluated; (ii) *Images*: opinions about the nature of the deviants and their behaviour; (iii) *Causation*: opinions about the causes of the behaviour. (The set of opinions dealing with solutions or methods of handling the behaviour will be dealt with when considering the societal control culture.) These categories are not entirely exclusive; a statement such as 'it's because they've got too much money', belongs to both the Images and Causation categories.

Orientation

Disaster – As pointed out when considering the disaster model, the behaviour was often perceived as if it were a disaster, and this is, in fact, an orientation which endured through later opinion statements. As a direct result of the inventory, the psychological impact and social significance of the Mods and Rockers were perceived to be of disastrous proportions.

The natural disaster analogy was often explicitly drawn, perhaps nowhere more clearly than by Mr David James, the MP for Brighton Kemptown, during the second reading of the Malicious Damage Bill:

> I was not in Brighton during the weekend to which references have been made, but I arrived there later to find a sense of horror and outrage felt by the people who live there. It was almost as if one had been to a city which, at least emotionally, had been recently hit by an earthquake and as if all the conventions and values of life had been completely flouted. This was deeply felt.[5]

In a previous debate, the MP for the constituency in which Great Yarmouth falls, hoped that the town '. . . will never suffer the ravages which Clacton suffered',[6] while another MP referred to '. . . the delinquent youth who sacked Clacton'.[7] Similar analogies were used in editorials after Whitsun 1964: 'Goths by the sea' (*Evening Standard*, 18 May); 'the marauding army of Vikings going through Europe massacring and plundering, living by slaughter and rapacity' (*The Star*, Sheffield, 18 May); 'mutated locusts wreaking untold havoc on the land' (*Time and Tide*, 21 May), etc. The disaster analogy is, of course, particularly well suited to describing the reactions of idyllic rural areas and places such as the Isle of Wight on being subjected to pop festivals and similar happenings.

Most statements emphasized the threat to life and property, particularly the latter, and the picture of a town being 'wrecked' was reinforced by quoting rumours about resorts armour plating their deckchairs and insurance companies offering policies to the resorts to cover them against losses incurred through Mods and Rockers as well as normal storm damage. But it was clear throughout that it was not only property that was being threatened, but 'all the conventions and values of life'. As the *Birmingham Post* (19 May 1964) put it, drawing on Churchill's 'We will fight them on the beaches' speech: the external enemies of 1940 had been replaced on our own shores in 1964 by internal enemies who 'bring about disintegration of a nation's character'.

In the same way as most disasters are determined by impersonal, inexorable forces against which human action has little effect, an irrational, unreachable element was seen in the Mods' and Rockers' behaviour. A widely quoted article in *Police Review* spoke about the 'frightening' realization that when law and order — which is based on nothing more than individual restraint — is loosened, 'violence can surge and flame like a forest fire'. It could be compared with the football riot in Peru: 'a disallowed goal and over 300 dead before sanity could be restored. Clacton, Margate and Lima have one element in common — restraint normal to civilised society was thrown aside.'[8] This orientation to crowd behaviour is identical to Le Bon's original conception of the mob as possessing the irrationality and ferocity of primitive beings.

Reaction from abroad sounded even more like reaction to a disaster. Italian papers forecast a tourist rush from English holidaymakers scared to go to their own resorts. At least two English MPs returned prematurely from Continental holidays to survey the damage in their stricken constituencies. The Chairman of the Clacton UDC had phone calls from Paris and Washington asking about conditions in the town.

Prophecy of Doom — As a result of the prediction element in the inventory, the deviance was not only magnified, but seen as certain to recur and, moreover, likely to get worse. The tone of some opinion statements was that of Old Testament prophets predicting certain doom and then following with exhortations about what could be done to avert the doom. So, after Whitsun, 1964, Mr Harold Gurden, MP, who had before the event successfully moved a resolution calling for intensified measures to control hooliganism, stated: 'The latest incidents reinforce what I said and the warning I gave. This thing has got worse and will get worse until we take some steps' (*The Times*, 20 May 1964).

Besides conforming to self-fulfilling prophecies, such statements illustrate Becker's point about the unique dilemma of the moral entrepreneur who has to defend the success of his methods and at the same time contend that the problem is getting worse.[9]

It's Not So Much What Happened — A variant of the previous two themes is the type of opinion that attempts to put the behaviour 'in perspective' by perceiving that the reports *were* exaggerated. It is not the behaviour itself which is disturbing but fantasies about what could have happened or what could still happen. Ominous visions are conjured up about what the behaviour might be leading to: mass civil disobedience, Nazi youth movements, Nuremberg rallies and mob rule.

It's Not Only This — If the previous theme looked behind what happened, this one looks all around it. Through a process of free association, statements conveyed that the problem is not just the Mods and Rockers but a whole pattern in which pregnant schoolgirls, CND marches, beatniks, long hair, contraceptives in slot machines, purple hearts and smashing up telephone kiosks were all inextricably intertwined. One must orient oneself not just to an incident, a type of behaviour or even a type of person, but to a whole spectrum of problems and aberrations.

The type of associated deviance varied: other deviance of a similar type (hooliganism, vandalism, violence), deviance of other types (drug-taking, promiscuity) or other more general social trends. The point of the association was determined by attitudinal or ideological variables: so the *New Statesman* was worried by other youths being exploited by the 'hucksters of music and sex' and the *Tribune* by other 'educational rejects'.

Associations were not only made with adolescent problems: 'The society which produces the Margate and Ramsgate neurotic adolescents is also producing a neurotic middle age which cannot sleep and a neurotic old age which fills our mental hospitals.'[10] The invariably high figures for road deaths over Bank Holidays made other associations inevitable. Under headings such as 'Madness in the Sun', 'The Bank Holiday of Shame' and 'The Destroyers', it was made clear that bad drivers and bad teenagers could be seen as functionally equivalent. The *Daily Mail* (19 May 1964) imagined people saying, 'It's a lovely holiday — let's go out and smash something. Or kill someone. Or kill ourselves.' While admitting that drivers are more murderous and roads offer the bigger danger, the *Mail* thought there was little to choose between the 'mad variety' of wild ones on the roads and on the beaches.

Images

Spurious Attribution — The tendency towards spurious attribution on which the putative deviation is built, stems directly from the inventory. This tendency is not only present in 'popular' statements but in more informed attitudes and also, as Matza has convincingly suggested, in the image of the delinquent held by contemporary criminologists. In all cases, the function of the spurious attribution is the same: to support a particular theory or course of action.

The initial stage in the labelling process was the use of emotive symbols such as 'hooligans', 'thugs' and 'wild ones'. Via the inventory, these terms entered the mythology to provide a composite stigma attributable to persons performing certain acts, wearing certain clothes or belonging to a certain social status, that of the adolescent. Such composites are of an all-purpose sort, with a hard core of stable attributes (irresponsibility, immaturity, arrogance, lack of respect for authority) surrounded by fringe attributes varied more or less logically according to the deviance in question. So, in the famous 1971 Oz trial, the youthful pornographers were awarded the hard-core attributes plus such specialized ones as moral depravity and sexual perversity.[11] It would be quite feasible to get the digital computer from *The Tin Men* to programme a few basic composite stigma stories.

Perhaps the first public catalogue of the auxiliary status traits attributed to the Mods and Rockers was made by Mr Thomas Holdcroft, the prosecutor at the first Clacton trial. In his speech, he listed the following traits: no views at all on any serious subject; an inflated idea of their own importance in society; immature, irresponsible; arrogant; lacking in any regard for the law, for the officers of the law, for the comfort and safety of other persons and for the property of others. This composite was captured in the term 'wild ones', which, however, was soon to be replaced in the mythology by the term used by the Margate magistrate, Dr Simpson: 'Sawdust Caesars'. The 'Sawdust Caesars' speech – to be discussed in detail later – made a tremendous impact: over 70 per cent of the immediate post-Margate statements used the term or its variations ('vermin' and 'ratpack'). Although less successful in passing into the mythology, other labels coined in editorials were equally picturesque: 'ill conditioned odious louts' (*Daily Express*); 'retarded vain young hot-blooded paycocks' (*Daily Sketch*); 'grubby hordes of louts and sluts' (*Daily Telegraph*); 'with their flick knives, their innumerable boring emotional complexes, their vicious thuggishness which is not cunning but a more bovine stupidity; their ape-like reactions to the world around them and their pseudo bravery born of the spurious comfort of being in a mob . . .' (*Evening Standard*).

Not all attribution was so emotive: '. . . likely to be timid and shifty, backward, apathetic, ungregarious and notably inarticulate. Individually he will probably not seem particularly vicious. He is nearly always unattractive' (Lucille Iremonger in the *Daily Telegraph*). Intellectual opinion produced appropriately intellectual, but otherwise just as spurious attributes: 'a new Outsider without Mr Colin Wilson's brains or the beatniks' blended flamboyance or stoicism . . . rarely intelligent . . . rarely individualistic . . . inadequate . . . under-developed' (*Guardian*).

In a series of one hundred randomly chosen opinion statements (post-Whitsun, 1964) the following descriptive nouns were used: louts (5), thugs (5), savages (2), ruffians, maniacs, hooligans, hoodlums, yobbos, brats, human wolves, lemmings, rowdies, apes, misfits and morons. Descriptive traits included: neurotic, sick or unstable (5), show-off or exhibitionist (4), violent (4), cowardly (4), aimless or rudderless (4), half-baked, immature (3), precocious (2), dirty, unwashed (2), slick, slickly dressed (2), foolish or slow-witted (2), cynical, inarticulate. The attributes of *boredom* and *affluence* were mentioned so often as to warrant discussion as separate themes.

Another type of spurious attribution is guilt by association; all teenagers going down to the resorts were attributed with the same guilt, and hence putative deviation, as those who actually caused damage or injury. Many opinion statements, for example, drew attention to the role of girls in egging on their boy friends; a letter in the *Evening Standard* (21 May 1964) claimed that the major stimulus to violence came from '. . . the oversexed, squalid, wishful little concubines who hang about on these occasions, secure in the knowledge that retribution will not fall upon them'. This sort of attribution was supported by inventory interviews of the 'Girls Who Follow The Wild Ones Into Battle' type, although traits other than enjoyment of violence were more consistently attributed to girls; particularly promiscuity and drug-taking. These themes became more prominent after August 1965 when there were press reports, based on remarks made by the commander of the Margate police division, that parents summoned to the police station were shocked to find '. . . that their daughters have been sleeping around with youths carrying the recognised weekend kit, purple hearts and contraceptives' (*Daily Telegraph*, 31 August 1965).*

The process of spurious attribution is not, of course, random. The audience has existing stereotypes of other folk devils to draw upon and, as with racial stereotyping, there is a readily available composite image which the new picture can be grafted on to. The emergent composite draws heavily on folklore elements such as the Teddy Boys, the James Dean–Marlon Brando complex, *West Side Story* gangs and so on. As with racial stereotypes there is no necessary logical connection between the components; they are often

---

* Not for the first time, the only two national papers to use this sort of story were the *Telegraph* and the *Daily Sketch*.

self-contradictory.[12] Thus Jews are intrusive, but also exclusive; Negroes are lazy and inert, but also aggressive and pushing; Mods are dirty and scruffy, but also slickly dressed; they are aggressive and inflated with their own strength and importance, but they are also cowardly. An image rationalizes a particular explanation or course of action; if an opposite image is perceived as being more appropriate to this end, then it is easily invoked. Such images are even mobile enough to be held simultaneously, as in a *Daily Mail* headline: 'They're Pin Neat, Lively and Clean, But A Rat Pack'.

Affluent Youth – The £75 Cheque – Attitudes and opinions are often bolstered up by legends and myths. The uncivilized nature of immigrants is illustrated by the story of empty tins of cat meat found in dustbins of Indian restaurants. Teenage sexual promiscuity is illustrated by the story of schools where girls who have lost their virginity wear a badge.

Perhaps the most recurrent of the Mods and Rockers stories was the one about the boy who said he would sign a cheque for a £75 fine (see p. 21). Although it took some time to circulate, this story was still being quoted as long as four years after the 'event'. The affluence theme is one of the most powerful and persuasive components in the Mods and Rockers image, based as it is on the more general stereotype of teenage affluence and serving itself as a rationalization for the widely held belief that 'fines won't hurt them'. Even if the mythical elements in the £75 cheque story and its variants were exposed, this attitude theme would persist.

Although the term 'classless' appeared both in the inventory and occasionally in subsequent stages, it was apparent that the dominant image was not of a group actually drawn randomly from all social classes. This was the 'new, new rich'.

Divide and Rule – Generals, captains of sports teams and gang leaders are all aware of the mechanism whereby attack on one's own side is deflected by exploiting grievances or jealousies among the enemy. Similarly, the adult community, faced with an apparent attack on its most sacred institution (property) and the most sacred guardians of this institution (the police) reacts, if not consciously, by overemphasizing differences among the enemy. The thought that violence might be directed towards oneself and, worse still, might be attributable to defects in one's own society, was neutralized by over-emphasizing the gang rivalry between the Mods and Rockers. This tendency may again be traced back to reports of the 'warring-gangs-clash-again' type and is attributable less to conscious and malicious policy than to the fact that the 'warring gang' image is the easiest way for the ignorant observer to explain such a senseless and ambiguous crowd situation:

. . . what in fact may be a confused situation involving miscellaneous youths with marginal membership and varied motives is too often defined by observers as a case of two highly mechanized and organized gang groups battling each other over territory. They project organization onto the gang and membership status onto a fellow curiosity seeker.[13]

This effect was compounded by the later commercial exploitation of the Mods and Rockers division. The apotheosis of the Divide and Rule theme was the suggestion that the problem could be solved by letting the two groups fight it out in a park or sports field.

Hot-blooded Youth or Lunatic Fringe — The themes discussed so far have not been threatened by counter themes, but in answering the question: 'how representative are the Mods and Rockers of young people in Britain as a whole?', we find two apparently contradictory opinions.

On the one hand, there is the recurrent ascription to the *whole* adolescent age group of a number of stereotypical traits. As Friedenberg suggests, the tendency of adults to see adolescence, delinquency and aggressive sexuality as functionally equivalent, creates the composite status of what he calls a 'hot-blooded minority'.[14] Thus the entire age group and particularly the visible representations of teenage culture are endowed with the spurious deviation of the folk devils they have spawned. Partly because the teenage culture is less pervasive in Britain than it is in America, this type of identification was incomplete: distinctions *are* made between delinquents and the rest.

When moral panics like these reach their peak, though, such distinctions become blurred and the public is more receptive to general reflections on the 'state of youth'. On the basis of the 'It's Not Only This' theme, disturbing images are conjured up: all young people are going to the dogs, there is an adolescent malaise, this is just the top of the iceberg. Educationalists talked about 'letting our teenagers down' and invariably the 'Boredom' and 'Affluence' themes referred to the whole age group. Articles were headed 'Facing the Facts About Youth', 'What's Wrong With Young People Today' or (as in foreign papers) 'British Youth in Revolt'. Numerical estimates are difficult to make but somewhere near a half of the opinion statements expressed this theme. As usual, the popular press provided an archetypal statement:

For years now we've been leaning over backwards to accommodate the teenagers. Accepting meekly on the radio and television it is THEIR music which monopolizes the air. That in our shops it is THEIR fads which will dictate our dress styles . . . we have watched them patiently through the wilder excesses of their ban the bomb marches. Smiled indulgently as they've wrecked our cinemas during their rock and roll films . . . But when they start dragging elderly women around the streets . . . etc. (*Glasgow Sunday Mail*, 24 May 1964)

To counteract this theme, however, the great majority of opinion statements reflected what might be called the 'Lunatic Fringe' theme. The Mods and Rockers were perceived as an entirely unrepresentative minority of young people: most young people are decent and conforming, and the Mods and Rockers were giving them a bad name. The Lunatic Fringe theme occurs in most editorials and public utterances of MPs, youth leaders and other self-styled experts who pontificated after the events. It pervaded the debate on the second reading of the Malicious Damage Bill:

> The Bill has been provoked by the irresponsible behaviour of a small section of young people, and I emphasise again that it is an extremely small section. (Charles Morrison, MP)

> . . . one cannot really judge the moral standard of our youth by the behaviour of those eccentrics who produced the hooliganism at the seaside resorts which resulted in the introduction of the Bill. (Eric Fletcher, MP)[15]

In the strong form of this theme, the 'rest' are seen as not only conforming and decent but positively saintly. The Chancellor of the Exchequer (Mr Maudling) thought the Mods and Rockers untypical of 'this serious, intelligent and excellent generation', and according to one paper:

> There are two kinds of youth in Britain today. There are those who are winning the admiration of the world by their courageous and disciplined service in arduous mountain, jungle or desert territory – in Cyprus, on the Yemen border, in Borneo. And there are the Mods and Rockers, with their flick knives . . . etc. (*Evening Standard*, 18 June 1964)

In the 110 opinion statements from public figures, there were 40 explicit references to this theme.

At first glance, the 'Hot-blooded Youth' and 'Lunatic Fringe' themes would appear to be incompatible; one can *either* say that the whole younger generation is going from bad to worse and that the Mods and Rockers merely exemplify this trend, *or* that the younger generation are as good or better than any other and that the Mods and Rockers are the exceptions to the rule. It should be comparatively simple then to calculate which view is more widely held. In fact this is not so. As with stereotyping and labelling as a whole – and as cognitive dissonance theory makes clear – attitudinal logic is not necessarily logical. A logical explanation for the two themes appearing simultaneously – as they often did – might run like this: 'I know that in the pure statistical sense, the number involved in this sort of thing must be a minute proportion of the whole age group, yet so many things that young people get up to today disturb me ("It's Not Only This") and who knows what this sort of thing will lead to ("It's Not So Much What Happened")? So I can't help thinking that this is evidence of a much deeper malaise affecting youth in general.'

In practice, of course, such an argument is hardly necessary; the paradox is only apparent. In the same way as the first theme is part of the more general short circuit function of labelling and stereotyping, the Lunatic Fringe theme also has an important function: to reassure the adult community that all is well, they can rest secure in the knowledge that not the whole generation is against them. When the theme was repeated in the courts (as it often was, in the form of statements by police, counsel and magistrates about how well-behaved the majority of young people had been in contrast to the offenders) one can see its other function in ensuring that the denounced person is made to look fully deserving of his punishment by contrast to the ideal counter-conception. This is one of Garfinkel's conditions for a successful status degradation ceremony:

> The witnesses must appreciate the characteristics of the typed person and event by referring the type to a dialectical counterpart. Ideally, the witnesses should not be able to contemplate the features of the denounced person without reference to the counter-conception, as the profanity of an occurrence or a desire or a character trait, for example, is clarified by the references it bears to its opposite, the sacred.[16]

Moral panics depend on the generation of diffuse normative concerns, while the successful creation of folk devils rests on their stereotypical portrayal as atypical actors against a background that is overtypical.*

---

* I am indebted to Jock Young for this notion of levels of typicality which he uses in his analysis of the mass media imagery of drug-takers.

Causation

A Sign Of The Times – From the 'It's Not Only This' orientation, we would expect that the behaviour was seen not as the sickness itself but as a symptom of something much deeper. Although the image of the actor is predominantly a free-will rather than a deterministic one, the behaviour is seen as related to a contemporary social malaise. The predominant explanation is in social rather than psychological terms. This seems to reflect an impatience with psychological explanations which are equated with a 'soft' line; even the 'bad' or broken home explanation was hardly ever used.[17] Another consequence of seeing the behaviour as an inevitable result of the way society is going, is that situational factors are played down.

The Mods and Rockers were seen, then, as 'holding up a mirror to the kind of society we are' (*Scotsman*, 8 June 1964). The aspects of the social malaise most commonly mentioned were: the decline in religious beliefs, the absence of a sense of purpose, the influence of the do-gooders' approach and the coddling by the welfare state. These factors are all part of a general swing; in fact, the 'swing of the pendulum' was the most frequently used metaphor: there had been a reaction to the strict discipline of the Victorians, but when society sees what has happened (i.e. the Mods and Rockers), the pendulum will swing back again.

Although the pendulum argument tends to be associated with a particular ideology – reactionary or conservative – its global, 'Sign of the Times orientation is shared with moral crusades from other positions. Thus where the *Daily Telegraph* railed against 'our modern welfare society', writers in *Tribune* complained of 'a society sick with repressed violence' and concluded that 'There is something rotten in the state of Britain and the recent hooliganism at Clacton is only one manifestation of it' (*Tribune*, 10 April 1964).

It's Like A Disease – One of the most misleading and misconceived analogies in regard to explaining delinquency is the attempt to compare it to a disease.[18] People are somehow 'infected' by delinquency, which 'spreads' from person to person, so one has to 'cure' the 'disease'. In regard to hooliganism, with its distinguishing feature of large public gatherings, this sort of analogy is used even more often and can be propped up with popular versions of mass-hysteria theory. Many observers likened the Mods and Rockers to a spreading social disease. *The Guardian* talked about an 'ailment' to be 'cured' and in Dr Simpson's memorable phrase, some were '. . . infected with this vicious virus'. One of the most vocal proponents of this theory was Mr W. R. Rees-Davies, the MP for the constituency which includes Margate:

It spreads like a disease. If we want to stop it, we have to be able to get rid of those children from the school, and quickly . . . We must immediately get rid of the bad children so that they cannot infect the good.[19] You must weed this type out . . . put them in a special school so that the others won't be infected . . . it's a contagious germ.[20]

Cabalism – In this theme, the behaviour which was to a large degree unorganized, spontaneous and situational, is seen as having been well planned in advance as part of some sort of conspiratorial plot.

In their attempt to explain the finding from the polls after the Kennedy assassination that the majority believed that Oswald did not act alone, Sheatsley and Feldman call this belief 'cabalism'.[21] Leaving aside the possibility that this belief might be true (a possibility they do not admit), their interpretation of this tendency has interesting parallels with the Mods and Rockers case: 'Rather than indicating widespread paranoia and demonstrating the consequences of extremist propaganda [sic] . . . in many cases cabalism provides the most easily understandable and acceptable explanation.' People who were reluctant to use other explanations could, by assuming conspiracy, remove some of the capriciousness from the situation.

The same tendency towards conspiratorial mythology is evident in reactions to phenomena such as racial disturbances,[22] student demonstrations and – to cite an example closer to the Mods and Rockers case – riots and disturbances at recreational or sporting events:

> Several reports of disturbances attributed careful pre-planning to a small cadre of dedicated instigators, who allegedly circulated rumours before the event and selected targets on the scene. Actual proof of 'planning' however, as opposed to mere repetition of common rumours, is difficult to obtain.[23]

With the Mods and Rockers, the strong form of the cabalism theme consisted of assertions that the events were masterminded, perhaps by a super gang with headquarters in some café on the M1. The weaker form of the theme merely asserted the role of leaders; a tightly knit core of criminally motivated youths (to paraphrase a cabalistic explanation of another crisis, the seamen's strike in 1966), who led a gullible mob into a planned battle. The *Daily Telegraph* talked about 'destructive riots which are carefully organized and planned in advance . . . the police underestimated the degree of organized malice'.

Such themes can be traced back to the inventory interviews with self-styled gang leaders and also reports of secret meetings by 'top-level' policemen and Home Office officials to consider 'strategy for the next attack'. The 'fight against crime' metaphor lends itself to the counter image of the fight against law and order.

Boredom – Boredom was the most frequently used single causal concept in regard to the Mods and Rockers. It evoked, however, two types of themes.

The first blames society, in particular the schools, youth clubs and churches, for having failed to provide young people with interests, opportunities, creative outlets or a sense of purpose. In a widely publicized sermon, the Bishop of Southwell asked young people to 'forgive the older generation that has too often failed to engage your energies'. Boredom is seen not only as a plausible cause but it is related to defects in the social structure. The application of opportunity theory to leisure goals may be seen as a sociologically sophisticated version of this theme.[24]

The other boredom theme points to the increased opportunities available to the present younger generation not even dreamt of by today's adults, and concludes that if anything like boredom does exist, it is a defect in the psychological make-up of young people themselves. They suffer, as the Margate Entertainment Manager put it, from 'chronic restlessness'. If they have to look for kicks outside what society has munificently provided for them, it is because of their own greed, hedonism and ungratefulness: 'I will not myself accept the proposition that hooliganism is an indictment of society at large. It is purely an indictment of those who cannot think of anything better to do in the most beautiful and varied country in the world.'[25]

In this view, boredom is dismissed as a 'fashionable excuse' or a 'fancy theory': '. . . laziness, selfishness and lust are still the important causes.'[26] There is in this theme a note of hurt and bewilderment, which echoes the eternal parental reproach: 'after all we've done for you . . .'. The strong form of this theme actually asserts that the cause of the behaviour is that 'we've given them too much'.

Of the opinion statements that mentioned boredom, about 35 per cent endorsed the 'not enough opportunities' theme, the rest the 'opportunities not taken' theme. Despite the ideological gap between these orientations, they tend to provide a common rationale for solutions of the 'give them an outlet and a sense of purpose' variety, whether these take the form of 'put them in the army' or 'build a better youth service'. The boredom theme also implies for some a 'looking for kicks' image, which gives the behaviour a wanton and deliberate aura. This might lead to the rejection of positivist-type explanations even among those predisposed to accept psychological or sociological determinism. They concede that while delinquency in general might be affected by broken homes, lack of opportunity and in some senses might be problem-solving behaviour, the Mods and Rockers were simply ungrateful hedonists, out for kicks. This explanation is more consonant with the more persistent folklore elements characteristic of such social types.

Differential Reaction

Clearly the societal reaction – even that portion of it reflected in the mass media – is not homogeneous. One cannot assume that the inventory images and the themes discussed in this chapter, diffused outwards to be absorbed symmetrically by all of society. Standard research on mass media influences indicates how complicated and uneven this flow is, and basic questions need to be asked about the representativeness of these images and themes and whether significant differences exist in terms of age, sex, social class, region, political affiliation and so on. The already processed images of deviance are further coded and absorbed in terms of a plurality of interests, positions and values.

In the absence of a full-scale public opinion type survey, these questions cannot be satisfactorily answered. They are important enough, however, to attempt, and using the limited data available – mainly from the Northview sample and Brighton sample – some of the more striking differences as well as instances where expected differences did not materialize, will be indicated.

1. *Mass Media and Public* – The first, and perhaps most striking difference is that between the mass media and the various types of public opinion. For most dimensions of this comparison, the mass media responses to the Mods and Rockers were more extreme and stereotypical than any of the samples of public opinion surveyed. This is not to say that the mass media images were not absorbed and were not the dominant ones to shape the reaction, but rather that the public coded these images in such a way as to tone down their more extreme implications. In this sense, the public could be said to be better informed about the phenomenon than the media or the moral entrepreneurs whom the media quoted.*

---

* Research on some other forms of deviance has pointed to a similar tendency. One analysis of mass media reports on mental illness showed that they present ideas further removed from the opinions of experts than the opinions held by the 'average man'.[27]

While the initial orientation of the media to the Mods and Rockers was in terms of the threat and disaster theme, just less than 50 per cent of the Northview sample responded in these terms. The others either saw the behaviour as a limited problem or else, in the case of about 15 per cent, immediately reacted by blaming the press for exaggerating the phenomenon. Similarly, in the Brighton sample 55.8 per cent saw what was happening in purely negative terms, although only half of these used threatening adjectives ('disgusting', 'horrible', 'terrible') and the rest, terms like 'annoying'. The remaining 46.2 per cent were indifferent or puzzled.

In regard to the prediction factor in the inventory, while the media were sure that the Mods and Rockers would continue, both the Northview and Brighton samples were less certain. Of the Northview sample 42.5 per cent thought that the phenomenon would die out and that it was just a passing phase or fashion; 15 per cent thought it would continue unless it was dealt with severely and 22.5 per cent thought that it would inevitably continue:

> It's part of our present day set up (*Doctor*).

> It won't die out as long as there are enough yobs with money who thrive on publicity (*Social Worker*).

> You can expect it every weekend now – it will go on just like the marchers (*Councillor*).

The rest of the sample did not know whether the Mods and Rockers would continue. The Brighton sample was evenly divided: 38.4 per cent thought that the behaviour would continue unless something was done; 33.8 per cent thought that it was just a passing phase; and 29.8 per cent didn't know. Some of this uncertainty in the two samples reflects the fact that the questions were asked at a fairly late stage in the development of the phenomenon, when there already were objective signs of its decrease in significance. Nevertheless, even at this stage, the media were ritualistically using the images of prediction and inevitable disaster.

Asked to describe what sort of young person was involved in the Mods and Rockers events, both samples used somewhat less clear-cut images and stereotypes than the mass media. Leaving aside the special images (for example, from the 'Sawdust Caesars' speech) the spurious attribution in the mass media centred around the stereotype of the affluent yob. The dominant picture was of adolescents drawn from the traditional 'delinquent classes', but with plenty of money to spend, riding expensive motor-cycles and more than ever predisposed to senseless violence. In the Brighton sample, 47.7 per cent thought that these were 'ordinary kids', just out for fun, 33.9 per cent thought they were just typical delinquents. An almost identical proportion – 32.3 per cent – of the Northview sample thought that the Mods and Rockers were just the same as any other delinquents; the added elements were the gang, the uniform, the motor-bikes: all the components of the Hells Angel type of image. 12.8 per cent thought that only the ring leaders were the hard-core delinquent types; the rest just tagged along for kicks. 43.6 per cent did not think that the Mods and Rockers were of the delinquent type: either because they came from a broader cross-section of the population or because they had no real criminal intent and were just out for kicks. A further 11.3 per cent were undecided about this. In regard to social class composition, the mass media images were again slightly sharper: in the Brighton sample 30 per cent thought that the Mods and Rockers were working class and from secondary moderns, 15 per cent were unsure and 55 per cent thought they were affluent and from all social classes.

Another way of looking at the image is to see in what ways – if any – the Mods and Rockers were thought to constitute an entirely new phenomenon. A new type of deviance is usually seen as more threatening than something which has been coped with in the past and the media tended to stress the supposedly new elements in the situation: more violence, more mass hysteria and a higher level of organized gang warfare. Very few of the Brighton sample saw these as new features; only four (6.1 per cent) thought that there was more violence. About 30 per cent thought that what was happening was simply the old folk devils (spivs, Teddy Boys) under a new name, while the largest group (56.9 per cent) thought that the new feature was the evidence of greater affluence and mobility. Slightly more of the Northview sample (33.1 per cent) thought that the behaviour itself was quite new:

> . . . there used to be hooliganism before, sheer devilment, just to annoy others . . . but there was nothing vicious: this is the new element, this pure thuggery. (*Headmaster*)

15.1 per cent thought that the only new elements were greater affluence and mobility and a further 37.6 per cent thought that there was nothing new in the behaviour: what had happened was that the old actors had moved on to a new stage, the Teddy Boys had come out of the Elephant and Castle and were getting more publicity than ever:

> In Poplar now, life is probably peaceful and quiet over the Bank Holidays. (*Headmaster*)

> Instead of half a dozen louts in one place, you have them all together in Clacton. (*Youth Worker*)

> Instead of fighting it out on Clapham Common or a bomb site, they go down to the resorts. (*Youth Worker*)

One frequently expressed version of this picture is the image of a basic pool of deviants, who keep reappearing in new guises; as one Northview youth leader put it: '. . . now that the Aldermaston marches are finished, you have all these kids running about with nothing to do.' Such images may be just as misleading as the stereotype of greater violence, hysteria and organization – or even more so – but they are not as threatening.

It appeared also that the type of stigmatization used by the press – the branding of the Mods and Rockers as new folk devils – was not always agreed to by the public. Asked about their feelings if their own son or brother went down to one of the resorts with a group of Mods or Rockers, most of the Brighton sample (about 70 per cent) thought that they wouldn't mind or that they wouldn't be sure how they would respond. Twelve per cent would not let him go down in the first place, and the remaining 18 per cent would have punished him if they found out afterwards. The Northview sample – in roles such as employers, teachers and youth leaders – were somewhat more likely to let their knowledge about a boy's participation in the Mods and Rockers activities carry over into their other dealings with them. Four (3 per cent) would not continue to employ him, eleven (8.2 per cent) would be suspicious and watchful about his other activities and a further 41.4 per cent would talk to him, try to understand his behaviour and dissuade him from further involvement. Only 16.5 per cent said that they wouldn't do anything and that the boy's personal life would not be their concern. These responses obviously varied according to occupational groups: headmasters stressing how the boy's action could harm the reputation of the school and employers, such as solicitors, tending to say that a boy who was a hooligan couldn't be trusted.

The Northview sample was asked specifically about their opinions on the way the press and television had covered the Mods and Rockers phenomenon. Their responses were overwhelmingly critical, if not hostile, towards the mass media: 40.5 per cent felt that the media had exaggerated and blown the whole thing up, and a further 41.3 per cent actually attributed responsibility to media publicity for part of what had happened. Only 4.5 per cent (six respondents) thought that the media had been accurate and were just carrying out their duty to report the facts. The remaining 13.5 per cent had no opinion about the media coverage. Over 80 per cent, then, were explicitly critical of the role of the media.

I have drawn attention to the public awareness of media exaggeration and distortion and the existence of some differences between public and media opinions only to emphasize the different ways in which images are coded and the operation of some sort of 'credibility gap' in the mass communication process. These are standard findings in the field of mass communication, and should not be thought in any way exceptional. The differences between the public and the media were not always very large and might have been smaller if the public samples were more representative: in one case (Northview) the respondents were better – and sometimes professionally – informed about the type of phenomenon in question, and in the other case (Brighton) the respondents were actually observing the situation at first hand, and therefore had evidence before their eyes to contradict some of the more gross mass media distortions. There is little doubt that the mainstream of reaction expressed in the mass media – putative deviance, punitiveness, the creation of new folk devils – entered into the public imagery and it certainly, as I will show in the next chapter, formed the basis of control measures.

2. *Young and Old* – Superficially one might expect that age differences in the reaction would be very noticeable: older people being more punitive and less able to identify with the deviant group. Neither sample is representative enough – particularly of the younger age group – to fully support this expectation, although the findings are in the predicted direction. Only 23.3 per cent of the younger age group in Northview (20–39) saw the behaviour as a threat, compared to about 55 per cent of the older groups. The younger age respondents were also more likely than the others to blame the press for exaggeration and distortion. In the Brighton sample, there was a tendency for the oldest respondents (over 60) to be more hostile and punitive than the youngest (under 24) but, on the other hand, the middle-aged respondents were less hostile than the youngest.

Other sources suggest that age differences are not as straightforward as might be expected and that young persons were by no means immune from absorbing the mass media imagery or responding punitively. The effect of the 'Lunatic Fringe' theme might, in fact, have been to alienate the rest of the young people even more from the Mods and Rockers. Respectable youth organizations were always quick to denounce the deviants as being totally unrepresentative of young people in Britain and to dissociate their members from what had happened. Letters along these lines were frequently published, and sentiments such as the following from an article in the 'Teen and Twenty Page' of the *Brighton and Hove Herald* (23 May 1964) were common: 'Just what sort of corkscrew mind finds enjoyment from such a twisted activity as smashing up shop windows, car windows, scooters and such? It's almost unbelievable, isn't it?'

A content analysis of essays on the Mods and Rockers written by twenty-five third- and fourth-form pupils in a school in the East End of London, shows not only how fully the media images were absorbed but also how little identification with the Mods and Rockers there was in a group which by social class, age and geographical position should have shown some identification. None of the writers saw themselves as potential Mods or Rockers (despite the current stereotype which saw all youth as divided along these lines) and the behaviour was quite alien to them: 'they' were seen as 'absolutely stupid', 'a childish crowd', 'all a load of idiots'. The behaviour was rarely excused:

> Some people excuse the Mods and Rockers by saying that they are discontented and bored. I think that this is just a 'front', for an awful lot of other teenagers manage to find something else to do than this senseless fighting.

> Although some people think that inadequate recreation facilities are an excuse for vandalism and destruction, I think there is none except stupidity and being unconcerned with the respect that should be given to other people's and the public's property.

About a third of the group did see boredom as a justifiable reason, or mentioned factors such as the desire for publicity, provocation by the police or adult condemnation of teenagers. Of the solutions suggested for the problem, seven were 'soft' (more youth clubs, cut down press publicity, provide places for young people to let off steam, adults should be more tolerant), six were conventional (fines, repayment of damage) and twelve were 'hard' (using fire hoses on the crowds, tear gas, hard labour schemes, flogging, long prison sentences, banning the offenders from the town). The following are two examples from the last group:

> Instead of giving them a few months in detention centres or fining them, I think it would be better to humiliate them in some way, e.g. invite the public to see them being given six of the best across their backside with a

birch twig and then let the public pelt them with rotten fruit while they are in the stocks set up on the beach. This might teach them a lesson . . .

I think the Mods and Rockers should not only pay for the damage, but also fix it. If they get out of hand in these seaside places the fire brigade should be brought in to soak them with water. Then they shouldn't be allowed in trains and buses. They wouldn't like to walk home to London in soaking clothes and I don't think they would do it again.

The fact that these were signed essays written as part of normal class work might have led to the expression of views thought to be more acceptable to the teacher, and as this was a grammar school these were the views of working-class 'college boys' rather than 'corner boys'. They do at least cast doubt, however, on the simplistic assumption that age differences alone will produce different reactions to such juvenile deviance as the Mods and Rockers. The way the societal reaction, and the mass media particularly, segregate the deviant and bipolarize folk devils from the rest of the community, is a stronger basis for attitude formation. During moral panics, such polarization is even more predictable.

3. *Locals and Outsiders* – It is not clear what differences one would expect between the attitudes of local residents and those living elsewhere. On the one hand, locals who were directly exposed to the situation might be more resistant to some of the distortions presented in the mass media. On the other hand, they would be more affected by any negative consequences of the behaviour (such as loss of trade, damage to the town's image) and therefore might respond more punitively.

Neither of these effects was observable in a particularly clear-cut fashion and perhaps they balanced each other out. Local people I spoke to did tend to be more realistic than the press, the Northview sample and other outsiders in their perception of what had actually happened. This difference, however, was not much in evidence in the reaction of local magistrates, press and moral entrepreneurs. The moral entrepreneurs particularly overestimated the amount of support and sympathy they would get from local residents. On the other hand, those local residents who did see the problem as directly affecting their lives, were very extreme and punitive in their reactions. In the Brighton sample, 62.5 per cent of local residents characterized what was happening as 'terrible' or 'annoying' compared to 45.5 per cent of outsiders who used these terms. The threat to commercial interests was obviously a more real one to locals. To this must be added the presence in towns such as

Hastings, Eastbourne and Margate of a large number of retired and elderly persons to whom the behaviour was especially alien and frightening.

4. *Male and Female* – A general impression from various sources is that females were more intolerant than males. In the Brighton sample a larger proportion of the females (35.4 per cent) expressed initial disgust than the males (11.8 per cent). They were also more likely to want the police to use tougher measures and all eight of the sample who were in favour of using corporal punishment were women. The women were twice as likely than the men to name 'lack of parental control and discipline' as the cause of the Mods and Rockers phenomenon. There were no great differences on any of the other questions and the tendency for females to be more punitive in regard to deviance would need to be supported from other sources.

5. *Social Class* – Some more general remarks will be made later on the relevance of social class variables. The survey data alone showed very few significant social class differences, especially in terms of initial reaction and general orientation to the events. There was a slight tendency for working-class respondents to explain the behaviour in terms of 'lack of parental control' while middle-class respondents were more likely to invoke the 'looking for kicks' image as a causative explanation.

6. *Political Affiliation* – There was a tendency in the Brighton sample for the Conservative voters to be more likely to use the 'disgusting' or 'annoying' categories (64.3 per cent) compared to 38.7 per cent among the Labour voters. Conservatives were also more likely to want the police to be tougher and to favour the use of Detention Centres.

I must repeat that any generalizations from this data about public reactions as a whole, should be made with caution. In concentrating on the ways in which moral panics are transmitted through the mass media and reflected in the responses of the social control system, I have not dealt adequately – as future research should do – with the patterning of such reactions in the wider society.

Modes and Models of Explanation

From the inventory through to the opinion and attitude themes, one can trace the features by which the Mods and Rockers were identified as deviants of a particular type and placed in their appropriate position in the gallery of folk devils. Of course, moral panics are not intellectual exercises whereby correct labels are decided upon, in the same way, for example, as the doctor fits symptoms into diagnostic categories or the botanist classifies his specimens.

The point is that the process of identifying deviance, necessarily involves a conception of its nature. The deviant is assigned to a role or social type, shared perspectives develop through which he and his behaviour are visualized and explained, motives are imputed, causal patterns are searched for and the behaviour is grouped with other behaviour thought to be of the same order.

This imagery is an integral part of the identification process: the labels are not invented after the deviation. The labellers — and the ones I have concentrated on are the mass media — have a ready-made stock of images to draw upon. Once the initial identification has taken place, the labels are further elaborated: the drug addict, for example, may be fitted into the mythology of the dope fiend and seen to be dirty, degenerate, lazy and untrustworthy. The primary label, in other words, evokes secondary images, some of which are purely descriptive, some of which contain explicit moral judgements and some of which contain prescriptions about how to handle the behaviour.

Thus, what Lemert calls the *societal control culture* '. . . the laws, procedures, programs and organizations which in the name of a collectivity help, rehabilitate, punish or otherwise manipulate deviants'[28] contains not just official institutions and personnel but also typical modes and models of understanding and explaining the deviance. The fact that such models are seldom coherently articulated should not lead us to assume their absence and to interpret images such as those surrounding the Mods and Rockers as if they had a random relationship to each other. These images are part of what Berger and Luckman refer to as the 'conceptual machinery that accounts for the deviant condition', and as such, perform a basic function in justifying a particular view of the world: '. . . the deviant's conduct threatens the societal reality as such, putting into question its taken-for-granted cognitive and normative . . . operating procedures.'[29] The devil has to be given a particular shape to know what virtues are being asserted. Thus, the senseless and meaningless image which is the dominant one attributed to vandalism, affirms the value of utilitarian, rational action. People in our society do things for certain accredited motives; behaviour such as vandalism which appears not to be motivated in this way, cannot be tolerated and is nihilated by describing it as senseless. The only way to make sense of vandalism is to assume that it does not make sense; any other definition would be threatening.

I will later analyse some of the functions of the conceptual machinery presented to account for the Mods and Rockers and consider the forces that shaped its content. The basic mode of explanation, one that is applied to most forms of deviance, was expressed in terms of a consensual model of society. Most people are seen to share common values, to agree on what is damaging, threatening or deviant, and to be able to recognize these values and their violations when they occur. At times of moral panic, societies are more open than usual to appeals to this consensus: 'No decent person can stand for this sort of thing.' The deviant is seen as having stepped across a boundary which at other times is none too clear.

When this model is taken for granted, the apparent inconsistencies in the inventory and the opinion and attitude themes are reconcilable. From either side of the ideological spectrum, for example, one can subscribe to the Hot-blooded Youth and Sign of the Times themes – or various other notions postulating a widespread social malaise – and identify the deviant group in Lunatic Fringe terms. After all, the deviants were like animals, affected by some sort of disease or the gullible victims of unscrupulous ringleaders. Primitive theories of crowd behaviour (individuals losing their control because of the mob situation) could be invited to supplement the picture of under-socialized beings, continually searching for excitement through violence.

The model is not only flat and one-dimensional, but it is totally lacking in any historical depth. This is a direct consequence of the standard mass media coverage of deviance and dissent.[30] Symbolization and the presentation of the 'facts' in the most simplified and melodramatic manner possible leave little room for interpretation, the presentation of competing perspectives on the same event or information which would allow the audience to see the event in context.

The dominant societal models for explaining deviance need careful consideration by the sociologist, not only because of their intrinsic interest or because they afford him the opportunity to expose their more naïve and absurd bases but also because such models form the basis of social policy and the societal control culture. These conceptions, images and stereotypes affect how and at what point the deviant is fed into the social control apparatus. If the sexual offender is seen as sick, then one attempts to cure rather than punish him; if the typical shoplifter is seen as the 'harmless little old woman' or the 'kleptomaniac', then this group will be less subject to formal legal sanctions. An integral part of the conceptual machinery then, is the body of justifications and rationalizations for acting in a particular way towards the deviant. The actual way the control system did operate and was influenced by the beliefs transmitted by the mass media is the subject of the next chapter.

4 Reaction: The Rescue and Remedy Phases

This chapter is concerned with 'reaction' not in the sense of what was thought about the Mods and Rockers but what was done about them or what was thought should be done about them. My central focus is on the organized system of social control and the way it responded in terms of certain images of the deviant group and, in turn, helped to create the images that maintained these folk devils. While using the terminology from disaster to cover this whole phase of the moral panic, I will use three further categories to cover the responses: (i) Sensitization; (ii) the Societal Control Culture; (iii) Exploitation.

Sensitization

Any item of news thrust into the individual's consciousness has the effect of increasing the awareness of items of a similar nature which he might otherwise have ignored. Psychological cues are provided to register and act upon previously neutral stimuli. This is the phenomenon of sensitization which, in the case of deviance, entails the reinterpretation of neutral or ambiguous stimuli as potentially or actually deviant.

Sensitization is a form of the simplest type of generalized belief system, hysteria, which '. . . transforms an ambiguous situation into an absolutely potent generalized threat'.[1] Ambiguity, which gives rise to anxiety, is eliminated by structuring the situation to make it more predictable. On this basis, anxiety, say, about an unidentified flying object, can be reduced by defining the object as a flying saucer and then assimilating similar phenomena into this cognitive framework. Sensitization to deviance rests on a more complicated belief system because it involves not only redefinition but also the assignment of blame and the direction of control measures towards a specific agent thought to be responsible. This corresponds to Smelser's 'hostile belief'. So, in such examples as the zoot suit riots, the 'weeks immediately preceding the riots saw an increase in suspicion and negative symbolization and the emergence of hysterical and hostile beliefs about the Mexicans' responsibility for various community troubles.[2]

The first sign of sensitization following initial reports was that more notice was taken of any type of rule breaking that looked like hooliganism and, moreover, that these actions were invariably classified as part of the Mods and Rockers phenomenon. In the days following the first two or three major happenings, newspapers carried reports of similar incidents from widely scattered localities. In the week after Margate (Whitsun, 1964), for example, incidents were reported from several London suburbs and Nottingham, Bromley, Windsor, Coventry, Waltham Cross, Kingston, Blackpool and Bristol. This build-up of reports has its exact parallel in the initial stages of mass hysteria. In Johnson's famous study of how a small American town was affected by a 'Phantom Anaesthetist' scare, the first signs of hysteria were calls reporting gassing symptoms or prowlers after an initial story (headed 'Anaesthetic Prowler on the Loose') of a woman supposedly having been gassed.[3] The police found nothing, but within a few days dozens of reports came in, elaborate precautionary measures were taken and there was intense police and public activity to apprehend the Phantom Anaesthetist. An identical build-up is described in a 1954 study in Seattle, Washington following initial reports about car windshields being damaged[4] and in another study in Taipei after reports that children had been slashed by razor blades or similar weapons.[5]

Many of the hooliganism incidents reported after the inventory were 'real' enough – having been partly stimulated by the type of publicity which made many young people easily provoked and on the look-out for trouble. The point is that whether or not the incidents happened, public sensitization of the sort that occurs in mass hysteria, determined the way they were reported and, indeed, whether they were reported at all. The following is one such incident:

> On the 20th May, 1964, two days after Margate, 23 youths appeared in West Ham Magistrates Court, charged with using insulting behaviour. The boys had apparently swarmed over the pavement pushing each other and shouting after they had come out of a dance hall in Forest Gate the night before. The police tried to disperse them after there had been a lot of horseplay. The *Evening News* (20/5/64) under the heading '23 Mod Crowd Youths Fines' noted that the boys wore Mod clothes and reported the chairman of the bench saying, 'You must all know that this sort of thing cannot be allowed to go on.'

The first point to make about the report is that without sensitization, this sort of incident might not have been interpreted as being part of the Mods and Rockers phenomenon; it might have been written off by spectators and policemen alike as 'horseplay' or another 'dance hall brawl'. A manifestation of public sensitization was the number of false alarms received by the police. In Stamford Hill, for example, the police stated after answering a false alarm, 'People are a bit jumpy after the trouble on the coast.' The low threshold at which the public became 'jumpy' enough to call the police was paralleled by increased police vigilance, partly in response to public pressure. In Skegness, for example, following relatively minor incidents on a Saturday night, during which the police arrested four youths and intervened in a dance hall fight, reinforcements were sent for on the Sunday. According to the local paper, it was clear that this action was taken because of threats of 'Clacton and Margate trouble'; the reinforcements '. . . enabled the police to put on the biggest show of strength that Skegness has known. And it did the trick' (*Lincolnshire Standard*, 22 May 1964). A similar event occurred at Woking, where fears of a Mods and Rockers battle at the fair spread around the town. Acting on these rumours and a request from the fair's proprietor, the police patrolled the fair and kept in radio contact with reserves. There was no trouble at all (*Woking News and Mail*, 29 May 1964). Later in the month, on police advice, a big road scooter rally in Battersea Park was called off to avoid Mods and Rockers hooliganism.

It is apparent from many reports, that the police and courts' actions were consciously affected by the original incidents. This is less clear in the West Ham magistrate's remarks, but in a number of other cases the reference was more explicit. In Blackburn, for example, the Police Superintendent, prosecuting two youths charged with using threatening behaviour (they had been in a crowd of twenty flicking rubber bands at passers-by), said in court:

> This case is an example of the type of behaviour that has been experienced in many parts of the country during the last few weeks and it has been slowly affecting Blackburn. We shall not tolerate this behaviour. The police will do everything within their power to stamp it out. (*Lancashire Evening Telegraph*, 29 May 1964)

As might be expected, such sensitization was more obvious in the resorts themselves, even outside the Bank Holiday period. The week after Whitsun, 1964, the police in Brighton stopped a coachload of young people and ordered it out of town. Magistrates, especially in Brighton and Hastings, made it clear in their pronouncements from the bench that they would regard hooliganism and related offences as manifestations of the Mods and Rockers phenomenon. As such, this type of deviance would be reacted to in terms of the inventory images and subsequent opinion themes.

The other significant point arising from the Forest Gate incident, is the type of headline given to the report. Invariably other incidents received similar treatment: 'Mods and Rockers Strike Again', 'More Teenage Violence', etc. It is inconceivable that this type of symbolization could have been used without the inventory build-up and it is also unlikely that these reports would have been given the prominence that they were given. Throughout this period, the press, itself sensitized to signs of deviance, was the main mechanism for transmitting the sensitization to others.

It did this, not only by reporting and reinterpreting hooliganism-type events but, as in the inventory period, creating stories out of non-events. So, for example, after Whitsun, 1964, the *East Essex Gazette* (Clacton) carried the headline 'Thugs Stay Away from N.E. Essex' and many other similar 'all quiet here' stories were printed. Another type of non-story was the reporting of an incident together with denials by local figures, such as Chief Constables, that the incident had anything to do with the Mods and Rockers.

These negative stories have the same cue effect towards the deviant symbols as the positive stories. Sensitization occurs because symbols are given a new meaning; disaster studies show how in sudden disasters, or where the precipitating agent is unknown, warning cues are assimilated within the normal frame of reference – the roaring sound of a tornado is interpreted as a train, or the sound of water in a sudden flood is interpreted as a running faucet.[6] Such cues are not missed when the population is sensitized to them, and in fact the tendency then is to over-react. During moral panics and in situations of physical threat, one 'doesn't take a chance' or is 'rather safe than sorry'.

In the same way as first-hand experience, word of mouth or folklore teach a community to recognize the sign of a tornado, so did the media create an awareness of what signs would signify this particular threat and what actions were called for. Media reports during this period not only used but elaborated on the previous symbolization. Incidents in the days immediately following a Bank Holiday, for example, were invariably reported as 'revenge battles'. These usually had nothing to do with the original incidents and were merely 'ordinary' hooliganism events being reinterpreted. Another type of assimilation of news into the mainstream of the belief system was shown by a *Daily Telegraph* report (18 May 1964) about the drowning of three boys from an overturned punt at Reading. The headline read 'Mods and Rockers See Three Drown'. In fact, although youths identified as Mods and Rockers were present on the river bank, they were just as peaceful as the hundreds of other holidaymakers with them. The owner of the punt specifically stated (in an interview in the *Daily Mail*) that the boys who hired the punt were 'not the Mod and Rocker type'.

Right through the sequence then, each incident is taken as confirming the general theme. Turner and Surace describe the identical process:

> Once established, the zooter theme assured its own magnification. What previously would have been reported as an adolescent gang attack would now be presented as a zoot-suit attack. Weapons found on apprehended youths were now interpreted as the building up of arms collections in preparation for zoot-suit violence.[7]

In summary, the effects of sensitization appear to have been: (i) greater notice being taken of signs of hooliganism, (ii) reclassification of such events as being Mods and Rockers activities, (iii) crystallization of the symbolization process started in the inventory. The crucial issue is not whether the incidents were 'real' or not, but the process of their reinterpretation. The line between this process and pure delusion is not easy to draw. Although both the Phantom Anaesthetist and the Phantom Slasher were demonstrably psychogenic phenomena, they started off with real events, which had to be reacted to in a particular way. 'Mrs A.' who started off the Mattoon incident actually had a mild hysterical attack, but the crucial point was her dramatic interpretation of her symptoms which aroused press interest. As the news spread, similar symptoms were reported, more exciting stories were written and the 'affair snowballed'.[8] Jacobs notes the identical effect in his Taipei study: reports of slashings were '. . . both a product of and helped to intensify the hyper-suggestibility and hysteria so characteristic of the affair'.[9]

This snowballing effect is identical to deviance amplification, and is characteristic of moral panics at their height. One does not want to make too much of this analogy, because the Mods and Rockers after all were not imaginary phantoms, but the parallels in the diffusion of the belief systems are remarkably close. For one thing, in both phenomena, the dominant vehicles for diffusion are the mass media. Even the sequence of reporting described in mass delusion studies had exact parallels in the Mods and Rockers reports: for example, when the actual incidents tailed off, the papers held the excitement alive with other types of reports (non-stories, opinion statements, descriptions of local reaction). Features on the resorts described the feeling of relief that it was all over, mingled with apprehension that more might come: 'Giving A

Collective Sigh of Relief', 'Margate Is Quiet, But Licking Its Battle Scars', 'A Town In Fear – What Can Be Done To Stop More Fights?' Compare these quotes with a Mattoon paper during the equivalent phase: 'Mattoon's "mad anaesthetist" apparently took a respite . . . and while many terror-stricken people were somewhat relieved, they were inclined to hold their breath and wondered when and where he might strike next.'[10] Several attacks were reported on the night of that item.

There is a further type of sensitization worth noting: what may be termed the 'widening of the net' effect. A characteristic of hysteria is that the 'wrong' stimulus is chosen as the object of attack or fear. This process may be observed during the protracted manhunt following sensational crimes or jailbreaks: in the wave of hysteria all sorts of innocent people or actions are labelled as suspicious. Thus, during the much publicized 1971 manhunt for the alleged Blackpool police killer, Sewell, numerous suspects were 'spotted' and brought in for questioning by the police.* In his pioneering study of a case of moral enterprise – the passing of the sexual psychopath laws – Sutherland noted the fear aroused during the manhunt for a violent sexual offender: 'Timid old men were pulled off streetcars and taken to police stations . . . and every grandfather was subject to suspicion.'[11]

When the general cueing effect produced by sensitization is combined with the type of free association in the 'It's Not Only This' theme, the result is that a number of other deviants are drawn into the same sensitizing net. In the phase after the inventory, other targets became more visible and, hence, candidates for social control. These targets are not, of course, chosen randomly but from groups already structurally vulnerable to social control.

One such target was the practice of sleeping rough on the beaches which is usually tacitly condoned in seaside resorts. During the summer holidays after the hooliganism publicity, however, towns like Brighton and Margate began to take a stricter line towards this activity. In Brighton, in August 1965, the police rounded up 15-year-old girls sleeping on the beach and took them to the police station. No charges were made, but parents were contacted to come and fetch their daughters. This was '. . . part of the town's new policy to make parents responsible for their daughters' safety' (*Evening Standard*, 30 August 1965). The *Daily Mirror* (31 August 1965) referred approvingly to the 'morals patrols'. Other groups caught in the net were more puzzling; for example,

---

* This process is, of course, facilitated by the invariable publication of Identikit compositions, out-of-date photos and artists' impressions.

all teenage weekend campers were banned from a camping ground outside Brighton. This type of teenager perhaps shares nothing more with the Mods and Rockers than the status of being adolescent.

The most important targets affected by sensitization, though, were the beatniks. Immediately after Clacton, there were rumours in Hastings about a plan to spray the caves near the town with a strong-smelling chemical to make them uninhabitable by beatniks. In November 1965 the Bournemouth Private Hotel and Guest Houses Association campaigned to ban beatniks from the town, and a similar resolution was passed by the Great Yarmouth Hotel and Guest House Association. This resolution made it clear that no differentiation was to be made between the Mods and Rockers and the beatniks, they all had the same symbols: '. . . these people . . . are easily identified by their unkempt locks, their bedrolls, their scooters and motor-cycles, etc.'

To talk about this widening of the net does not imply that, before the Mods and Rockers, these resorts welcomed beatniks with open arms. In many cases, though, there did exist an uneasy tolerance, particularly by the police who are well aware of the distinction between the beatnik and the potential 'hooligan'. This was traditionally the situation in Brighton, where only a few weeks before Clacton, the Chief Constable was quoted as saying about the beatniks, 'They are no nuisance at all.'[12] Clacton and subsequent events decreased the local tolerance quotient and opened the door to the moral entrepreneurs. The *Brighton and Hove Gazette* (5 May 1964) warned about the danger of letting the beatniks sleep on the beach and cause damage during the summer. It quoted protests from traders and advocated having powerful floodlights turned on the beaches. At various times during 1964, local councillors suggested hosing the beatniks off the beach or waking them up with searchlights on their faces at 5 a.m. A local MP called for a total ban on beach sleeping.

On the whole, the police resisted such pressures, holding the view that the beatniks were neither harming anyone nor breaking any particularly important rules. One result of sensitization though, was, in some instances, to narrow the gap between the moral crusaders and the rule enforcers. And in areas far away from the scenes of the Mods and Rockers events – for example, in Devon and Cornwall – the phenomenon was used to justify new control measures against beatniks, beach sleepers and others.

The Societal Control Culture

Sensitization is merely one mechanism involved in the amplification of deviance. Although the official agents of social control were just as susceptible as the public to this mechanism and, in fact, by their own actions also magnified the deviance, we have to consider their role in the reaction stage quite separately. Theirs is not the pristine, relatively unorganized response to on-the-spot deviance but an organized reaction in terms of institutionalized norms and procedures. The social control agents correspond to the organizations responsible in the rescue and remedy phases for dealing with the consequences of disaster; the police, medical services, welfare organizations, etc. The sum total of the organized reaction to deviance constitutes Lemert's 'societal control culture' ('. . . the laws, procedures, programs and organizations which in the name of a collectivity help, rehabilitate, punish or otherwise manipulate deviants').[13]

The aim of this section is to describe some common elements of the control culture that developed around the Mods and Rockers. In response to what pressures did it operate? How was it affected by previous stages in the sequence? How did the established agents of control adapt to the deviance and what new forms of control were developed? These questions will be answered by distinguishing firstly three common elements in the control culture: diffusion, escalation and innovation. Then the reaction of three main types of social control will be described in detail: (i) the police; (ii) the courts; and (iii) informal action at the local level, particularly in the form of 'action groups' directed at forming an exclusive control culture.

1. *Common Elements*

(i) *Diffusion* – The first most visible feature of the control culture was its gradual diffusion from the area where the deviant behaviour made its immediate impact. This feature is analogous to the way in which the social system copes with disaster in the rescue and remedy phases: the emergency rescue system on the spot is eventually supplemented or replaced by agents from the suprasystem (e.g. national or even international organizations). Similarly, in cases of mass hysteria the scare is felt far beyond its immediate victims. The involvement of control agencies such as the police might move from local to regional to national levels, a 'state of emergency' might be declared or a public inquiry constituted.

In response to the Mods and Rockers, involvement diffused (not, of course, in a straight line), from the local police force, to collaboration with neighbouring forces, to regional collaboration, to co-ordinating activity at Scotland Yard and the Home Office and to the involvement of Parliament and the legislature. In this process, a number of other agents were drawn into the control system; for example, RAF planes were used for airlifts of police and AA and RAC patrols helped by warning the police of any build-up of motor-bike or scooter traffic on roads leading to the resorts. Transport police on railway lines leading to the resorts were alerted and at later stages directly involved in control operations by turning back 'potential troublemakers' before they reached their destinations.

(ii) *Escalation* – It was not only the number of control agents that was extended, but the whole scope and intensity of the control culture. A crucial determinant of this escalation process is the generalized belief system that emerges from the inventory. It is this belief system which serves to legitimate the action of control agents and which is eventually assimilated into the existent mythology of the control culture. The exaggeration and negative symbolization provided the immediate legitimation: if one is dealing with a group which is vicious, destructive, causing the community a financial loss and repudiating its cherished values, then one is justified in responding punitively. To quote again from the zoot suit riots study: the new symbols provided the sanction to regard Mexicans as no longer associated with a favourable theme, but '. . . evoked only the picture of persons outside the normative order, devoid of morals themselves and consequently not entitled to fair play and due process'.[14]

If one conceives of the situation as catastrophic and moreover thinks it will happen again, get worse and probably spread (Disaster – Prophecy of Doom – It's Not So Much What Happened – It's Like A Disease), then one is justified in taking elaborate and excessive precautionary measures. This sort of relationship between belief systems and social control is illustrated nicely in social policies towards drug addiction:

> If the addiction problem can be inflated to the proportion of a national menace, then, in terms of the doctrine of clear and present danger, one is justified in calling for ever-harsher punishments, the invocation of more restrictive measures and more restrictions on the rights of individuals.[15]

It was in terms of the 'doctrine of clear and present danger' that the control agents operated and it was the logic of their own definition of the situation which forced them to escalate the measures they took and proposed to take to deal with the problem. This orientation is reflected in the opinion statements where the phrases that most frequently appear are 'tighten up', 'take strong measures', 'don't let it get out of hand', etc. The dominant themes were retribution and deterrence, together with the protection of society which was given a special legitimation by invoking the image of those who had to be protected: innocent holidaymakers, old people, mums and dads, little children building sand castles and honest tradesmen.

(iii) *Innovation* — The final common feature of the control culture was that it was not only extended in degree but also in kind, by the actual or suggested introduction of new methods of control. This reaction corresponds to 'innovation' in Cohen's adaptation of Merton's typology to conceptualize responses to deviance.[16] To Cohen, innovation as a response mechanism denotes the disregard of institutionalized limits on the choice of means, e.g. McCarthyism or use of third degree. I would include this aspect, but also the type of innovation that is open to control agents and not to deviants — to change or propose to change the institutionalized limits themselves through legislative means.

The reaction of the control culture was innovatory in the sense that the range of control measures was found wanting: both in the way it was implemented and its content. Any changes or proposed changes were again legitimated by invoking the belief system. If, for example, one is dealing with an affluent horde of scooter riders, then 'fines won't touch them' and one has to propose innovatory measures such as confiscation of scooters or forced labour camps. The same beliefs which justify escalation, may also justify the innovation (in Cohen's sense) which is involved in the suspension of certain principles governing individual liberty, justice and fair play. Those police and court practices — discussed later — which involved such suspension or were merely novel, were at first regarded with suspicion, or dismissed as being over-reactions. They eventually became accepted and routinized: various Council vans converted into police squad cars became no longer a novelty in Brighton.

The Margate opinion statements were analysed to determine the extent to which the mass media reflected the innovatory response. The results are presented in Table 2. Although the non-specific solutions are more difficult to classify, a fairly large proportion of them are innovatory in the sense that they call for a tightening up of existing measures rather than just an efficient implementation of them. As for the specific measures, nearly all were innovatory to some extent, but more particularly the largest single category: the demand to give more powers to the police.

The true innovators either listed several solutions in different permutations or else spelt out their plans in intricate detail. They tended to be innovators in Cohen's sense. The following are four such solutions, representative of the various degrees of sophistication in this reaction:[17]

1. Ban the wearing of Mod clothes, issue a 'get your hair cut' order (a law to be passed to keep men's hair reasonably short), let it be known that mob

Table 2 Opinion Statements on Solutions to the Mods and Rockers Problem

Number of Statements Discussing Solutions	300
Number not proposing specific solutions	160
Number proposing specific solutions	140

Non-Specific Solutions:

% 'Hard' (stiff sentences, clamp down hard, more discipline, tighten up, etc.)	81%
% 'Soft' (strengthen home life, build up citizenship, creative outlets, etc.)	19%

Specific Solutions (Single most important solution proposed in each statement):

More powers to police (road blocks, tear gas, dogs, commando equipment, fire hoses, etc.)	28%
Corporal punishment	14%
Longer prison or detention centre sentences	9%
Heavy fines or compensation	9%
National Service	9%
Non-military National Service (building roads, digging the Channel tunnel, etc.)	8%
Disqualify from driving or confiscate bikes	7%
Cut out all publicity	7%
Attendance centre type schemes (especially work in public, like mending deckchairs)	3%
Others	6%

violence will be dealt with more strongly – especially by the use of hose pipes, birching and hard work on the land.

2. Use fire hoses, repayment of damage and probation orders with special conditions forbidding 'yobs' to ride motor vehicles or travel more than six miles from home, forbid 'each convicted yob' to associate with others convicted, forbid them to drink, to leave home on the next Bank Holiday or to stay out after 9 p.m.

3. Further power to be given to the police by using road blocks to intercept troublemakers; an extension of the Vagrancy Act to deal with beach sleepers; the greater use of remand in custody as a punishment ('Seven days inside and the hated compulsory bath, can have a salutory effect on the young hooligans with no previous convictions'); police dogs; detention centres; attendance centres; the publishing of names and addresses of juveniles found guilty of the Margate type of offence.

4. Because of the ambiguities involved in defining 'unlawful assembly intended to provoke a breach of the peace', the common law should be changed to prevent hooliganism. Power should be given to the police, whenever they find it necessary, 'to stop a gang travelling on road vehicles on the basis that it constitutes unlawful assembly, to confiscate the vehicles without compensation, leaving the members of the gang the burden of proving that they were an innocuous cycling club'.

Tables 3 and 4 show the extent to which innovatory responses occurred in groups drawn from the public – the Brighton and Northview samples respectively.

Support for innovatory proposals was particularly clear in the Northview sample. The principle of restitution was the dominant one; not simply through financial reparation but by supporting the 'work scheme' idea: this involved visible restitution (repairing broken windows or sweeping the streets) organized along paramilitary lines. Other work that was suggested included cleaning hospitals, observing in casualty wards and taking spastic children on holidays. One respondent (a headmaster) suggested that the offenders should be taken on naval exercises to see how tough they are . . . 'if they have the courage, it will make them into men'. The confiscation of bikes or licences was also a consciously applied innovatory principle, and one magistrate went further in suggesting that the offenders should be given hammers to smash up their own bikes: 'a childish action should be met with a similar punishment'.

Table 3 Brighton Sample: Single Most Favoured Solution to the Mods and Rockers Problem

Solution	Number	Percentage
On-the-spot measures such as fire hoses; 'instant justice'; more powers to the police	15	23.1
Detention centres	14	21.5
Fines, compensation	13	20.0
Army, National Service	9	13.8
Corporal punishment	8	12.3
Others, don't know	6	9.2
	65	99.9

Table 4 Northview Sample: Judgements on Appropriate Punishments for the Mods and Rockers

Punishment	Average Weight*	Rank Order
Full repayment	1.45	1
Work scheme	2.00	2
Heavy fines	2.33	3
Detention centre	2.34	4
Confiscate licences	2.67	5
Confiscate vehicles	2.84	6
Punish parents	2.97	7
Corporal punishment	3.20	8
Borstal	3.25	9
Probation	3.40	10
Army	3.50	11

Scale		
	Very much in favour	1
	In favour	2
	Undecided	3
	Against	4
	Strongly against	5

2. The Control Agents

(i) *The Police* – As society's officially designated agents of civil power, the police play a crucial role in the labelling process, both in the immediate reaction to deviance, as well as the ongoing reaction in later stages of the sequence. Their immediate definitions of the situation will be described when analysing the impact phase.

At this stage, police action may be conceived as part of the control and sensitization processes. The police had to react to any perceived threat to law and order in terms of their perception of their allocated social role. Sensitization may have operated indirectly in that the police were spurred to action not so much out of conviction but to satisfy the public that they were doing their job properly. This normal effect was heightened by the peculiar pressures to protect the town's image that are exerted on holiday resort police forces by civic and commercial interests. This factor is particularly operative in the holiday season. To these pressures must be added the on-the-spot factors such as strain caused by undermanning, lack of sleep and inadequate specialized training in crowd control. These situational pressures and difficulties, together with an assimilation of the inventory images, created the type of cultural and structural pre-conditions which must be spelt out before studying the initial social reaction.

The elements of diffusion, escalation and innovation can all be distinguished in the police reaction. In the first place, the preparations for each Bank Holiday weekend became increasingly complex and sophisticated. At the initial incident in Clacton, the police were almost totally unprepared but in the course of the amplification process, an organization and set of practices were built up specifically geared to Bank Holiday hooliganism. Police action in this respect was often highly ritualistic. Even when it was clear that the behaviour was dying out, the operations were mounted on the same scale.

The simplest response of the police to their definition of the situation and the pressures placed on them, was to implement the 'show of force' principle and to increase the sheer number of officers on duty. It became standard practice to cancel police leave for the Bank Holiday weekend. In Brighton, Whitsun 1964, the total amount paid out in police overtime was £2,000 – four times the cost of the Clacton damage before the holiday began. At the next weekend, August 1964, bringing reinforcements by air from the Metropolitan area and feeding them cost Hastings £3,000. Table 5 shows the overtime cost to Brighton over the next four Bank Holidays.

Not only was leave cancelled for the local force, but reinforcements were used from neighbouring forces and the network of co-operation was extended to Scotland Yard. In August 1964, by calling on the Metropolitan Police 'Sky Squad' and neighbouring forces, the Chief Constable of Hastings trebled the

Table 5 Police Overtime Costs, Brighton, Easter 1965–Easter 1966

Bank Holiday		Cost of Police Overtime
Easter 1965		£5,600
Whitsun 1965		£3,700
August 1965		£2,700
Easter 1966		£5,000
	Total	£17,000
Minus £1,000 normally spent on overtime each Bank Holiday		£4,000
	Extra cost	£13,000

(Information supplied by the Chairman of the Watch Committee at meeting of Brighton Council, 28 April 1966.)

existing police strength on the spot. Before Whitsun 1965, plans were made at the Home Office to use the RAF to fly reinforcements. Increase in numbers was accompanied by an increase in the range of equipment used. At a fairly early stage wider use was made of truncheons by some forces and others introduced police dogs and police horses. Brighton pioneered the conversion of vehicles borrowed from civil defence, water, public health and education departments, into police vans with two-way radios. Other forces, such as Clacton, favoured walkie-talkie communication.

Although each local force had their own specific variations, most used similar control tactics, at first on an *ad hoc* basis and later as considered policy. These tactics included:

(i) Keeping 'suspicious'-looking youths, who might cause trouble, pinned into one spot, usually on the beach.

(ii) Keeping crowds on the pavements moving along in order to avoid any obstruction.

(iii) Keeping certain previously designated 'trouble spots' free of likely looking Mods or Rockers.

(iv) Immediate arrest of actual troublemakers.

(v) Harassment of potential troublemakers, e.g. by stopping scooter riders to produce their licences or confiscating studded belts as dangerous weapons.

(vi) Separating the Mods and Rockers, preferably by breaking them up into small groups.

(vii) Rounding up certain groups and giving them 'free lifts' to the roads leading out of town or to the railway station.

Given the highly charged emotional atmosphere at the time and police antagonism towards the Mods and Rockers, these policies or their variants produced responses that could be classified as innovatory. Forced by their own definitions, the police adopted practices involving a suspension of principles such as neutral enforcement of justice and the respect for individual liberty. Such abuses of power included the unnecessary involvement of the public in the crowd control tactics. Holidaymakers, adults and youths alike, found themselves caught up in the overzealous application of these tactics – stopped if they were walking too fast, moved along if they were walking too slow, planted on to the beach when they wanted to go elsewhere, their protests not only ignored but putting them under threat of arrest.

Most harassment was reserved for the young people who could be identified through the process of symbolization. Clothing styles, hair-styles and scooters were made grounds for regarding someone as a legitimate target for social control and in a crowd situation such symbols tended to blur. The practice of keeping certain previously designated trouble spots clear was certainly innovatory. A group congregating in such a spot, even if this was a bus shelter and they were sheltering from the rain, would risk arrest if they refused to move. The position is not analogous to, say, a certain spot being temporarily designated as a no-parking area; the assumption here is that the motorist would have somewhere else to park. The Brighton police apparently assumed that the only alternative would be to 'get out of town'. In certain cases, purely on the basis of symbolization, young people were in fact forced out of town – either by being given 'free lifts', or by being turned away from the station.

Harassment was usually more subtle than straightforward expulsion. This particularly took the form of stopping scooters to examine the driver's licence or the machine's roadworthiness. Such practices can be interpreted as either the ascription of secondary status traits (anyone who drives around dressed like that must be driving illegally) and hence providing an excuse to pin a charge, or simply to make things so unpleasant and inconvenient for the scooter-boys that they would move away.

In Brighton, Easter 1966, some teams of uniformed police officers kept up continuous patrols, stopping groups of teenagers, lining them up and searching them for drugs or weapons. Working on the widening-of-the-net principle, those sleeping in cars, under deckchairs and boats were woken, searched and ordered to move on. Some were taken to the police station and made to strip. The drug scare at that time provided an easy rationalization for this; the *Daily Sketch* (12 April 1966) quoted a 'police spokesman' as saying: 'It is impossible to search them thoroughly without taking them to the police station and making them strip.' In fact, only one drug charge was made.

Between 5.30 and 6.00 a.m. on Whit Monday, 1966, the Brighton police were observed using a particularly innovatory technique – they would place 'No Waiting' signs in front of cars at that time legally parked, wake the occupants up and point to the sign outside the car and tell them to move off. A prominent citizen of Brighton with whom I was observing this practice, humorously referred to it as 'knocking up cars'. When asked what the police did if the youths in the car objected, he replied, 'Well, we can always knock them off for obstruction.'

Much publicity was given to a special technique perfected by the Southend police. It was even quoted by a Chief Judge of the United States Court of Appeal in addressing the Chicago Crime Commission on the need for the police to get broader powers of search and seizure:

You may have heard how the constables of Southend, England, deal with the teenage hooligans known as 'Mods' and 'Rockers' when they visit that seaside resort. Chief Constable McConnach says: 'Anything which reduces their egos is a good thing. I do not encourage any policeman to arrest them. The thing to do is to deal with them on the spot – we take away their belts. We have a wonderful collection of leather belts. They complain that they cannot keep their trousers up, but that is their problem entirely.'[18]*

It is clear that besides the innovatory component, these sorts of techniques also involve the control agents in 'the dramatization of evil'.[19] Deviants must not only be labelled but also be seen to be labelled; they must be involved in some sort of ceremony of public degradation. The public and visible nature of this event is essential if the deviant's transition to folk devil status is to be successfully managed. This staging requirement fits in well with the common police belief that a good way to deal with adolescents, particularly in crowd situations, is to 'show them up' or 'deflate their egos'. Formal as well as folk punishments involving public ridicule have been a feature of most systems of social control.

At the initial incident at Clacton, the police provided a striking example of this public dramatization. Following an incident in which twenty to thirty youths were refused service at a cafeteria, the police frogmarched two youths to the police station, with about one hundred others following behind, jeering and shouting. At 7.30 on the last evening of the Whitsun 1964 weekend, the Brighton police rounded up all the Mods and Rockers in the vicinity of the beach and marched them in a cordon through the streets to the station. This 'sullen army' (*Evening Argus*, 19 May 1964) was watched along the route by a crowd of onlookers. They were then escorted on to the train. Care was taken that no one would turn back from the first station out of Brighton: any young person with long hair or jeans had to convince the police that he lived in Brighton or Hove before being allowed out of the station. Successful symbolization provided the basis for these – and other – innovatory and dramatizing measures and ensured their support.

---

* In 1970 Southend police were still using the same technique, this time to cope with skinheads. The bootlaces, belts and braces of 'likely looking troublemakers' were confiscated and local shopkeepers were 'requested' not to sell replacements to young people. Leaving aside its dubious legal status, there is no evidence that this tactic has the slightest deterrent effect. It says much for the persistence of the Southend police that it continues to be used and widely supported.

Such extensions or abuses of police power might be regarded by some as marginal and legitimate. Others were more serious, including allegations of wrongful arrest. In the Barker–Little sample, twenty out of the thirty-four codable answers to the question 'Why did the police arrest you?' involved charges of arbitrary arrest. These boys claimed that they had either been doing nothing or moving away from trouble when arrested. Even allowing for what is thought of as the typical delinquent response of self-righteousness, this is a fairly high proportion. The following case is typical:

> The boy claimed that he had been playing 'childish games' on the beach with other Mods and came off the beach with a piece of wood which he had been kicking about on the sand. He tossed it on a pile of rubbish by the steps. 'A policeman said: "Pick that up laddie" and like a fool I did. He arrested me and I was charged with carrying an offensive weapon.' The boy saw that, faced with an apparent riot, the police needed to arrest somebody to deter others. He pleaded guilty in court because he thought it would be best to get it over with and was fined £75 for this and threatening behaviour (his first offence).

I personally observed three similar incidents and, in addition, friends and relatives of other boys were contacted who had stories of wrongful arrest. One such story concerned a boy who had volunteered to go along with the police as a witness after two friends had been arrested for throwing stones. On arrival at the police station, despite protests, he was arrested and charged as well. Somewhat more substantial evidence is contained in a report prepared for the National Council of Civil Liberties on the incidents at Brighton, Easter 1965. This was the highwater mark of police over-reaction. Over 110 arrests were made, the vast majority of them for offences directly or indirectly provoked by the police activity, i.e. obstruction or using threatening behaviour. There were very few cases involving damage, personal violence or drugs. There was only one offensive weapon charge: a boy carrying a steel-toothed comb.*

---

* I was informed from unofficial sources that the police had been reprimanded after the weekend for being too enthusiastic. This might have been in response to a report in *The Times* critical of the police, the high number of appeals involving allegations of wrongful arrest and the publicity generated by the NCCL. In any event there appeared to be a change in policy by Whitsun, when, although there were just as many police present, they were considerably less active.

Nine separate allegations of wrongful arrest were made in letters to the NCCL.* These came from independent sources and there is no apparent collusion. It was difficult to follow up all these cases, but at least three resulted in successful appeal. (In at least another fifteen cases, not known to the NCCL, there were successful appeals for wrongful arrest or disproportionately high sentences.) All these letters made the same general complaint: that the police had decided in advance to take strong measures or to arrest a certain quota and had thus made arbitrary arrests before any offence was committed or provoked offences to be committed. The following are extracts from two such letters:

> . . . a friend came up and greeted us perhaps a little louder than he should have, and was pulled aside by a police sergeant and reprimanded for doing so. While waiting for him, my friends and I were told to 'move on' by a police officer who, as he said this, pushed my friend Dave. He replied to this statement that he was waiting for our friend who was still talking to the police sergeant. The policeman then said the same thing again, still pushing Dave. 'Move on.' My friend Dave replied that he was moving on, which of course he was. The policeman told my friend not to give him any lip, my friend then asked what he had said to be lippy, the policeman then shoved my friend against a beacon by a zebra crossing saying that he had told him to move on and he was to get across there; my friend was just about to go across the crossing when a car pulled out in front of him, stopping him from crossing; the car was only there for a few seconds and within that time the policeman said to Dave, 'I told you to move, you're under arrest . . .' A police van pulled up and my friend was literally thrown into the van. (Letter from C.F.)

> I was overtaken by a group of Rockers (25 or 30) who were walking along the pavement chanting 'Digadig – Dig' and generally behaving in a manner which I understand would be likely to frighten some people. I was not part of this group. I was not chanting, shouting or in any way behaving in a manner which did or could have frightened anyone or led to any breach of the peace . . . my friend and I were merely walking to catch the train. Just as the Rockers had passed us a police van drew alongside the kerb and

---

* The original copies of these letters and other documents were studied. Initials only are used, and other identifying information altered in all quotations from these sources.

police jumped out of the van. I distinctly heard one policeman say: 'He will do.' I was grabbed, punched in the mouth and bundled into a police van. I offered no resistance nor did I give any abuse – I was much too surprised at the unexpected turn of events to say or do anything. (Statement from T.M.)

T.M. and his friend, P.W., arrested at the same time, were found guilty after being remanded in custody for ten days. Later both had their appeals allowed at Brighton Quarter Sessions, one of them being awarded costs.

These reports also indicate another aspect of police activity – corresponding more closely to Cohen's 'innovation' – the unnecessary use of force. The police often used violence in handling crowd situations, e.g. by pushing and tripping young people from behind as they moved them. Force was particularly used in making arrests even when the offender had not struggled or resisted. A freelance photographer (J.G.) trying to photograph such an incident had his camera smashed and after complaining and refusing to move away, was arrested. The court was told that he was 'leading a mob of screaming teenagers across the beach' and he was charged with obstructing a constable whom he claims not to have seen till after his arrest.

Such specific claims are difficult to substantiate; observation in Brighton over that weekend, though, bears out the fact that such violence was not uncommon:

> Outside the aquarium, about a dozen Mods were brought up from the beach following an incident. The police formed a rough chain across the pavement leading to the van. As each boy was shoved into the van he got a cuff on the head from at least three policemen in the line. I also saw a sergeant kicking two boys as they were hurled into the van.
>
> (*Notes*, Brighton, Easter Monday, 1965, 11.30 a.m.)

A number of further allegations were made, either in the NCCL letters or to myself, involving abuses which could not be substantiated by observation as they did not occur in public. I can only say that these allegations of police misconduct after arrest were internally consistent. A repeated complaint was of the use of force in the police van – three boys writing to the NCCL claimed that they had been punched, kicked or held face downwards on the floor during the ride to the station. Every letter complained about the conditions in custody in the Brighton Police Station. Most were placed in overcrowded communal cells, together with the usual weekend drunks, from time of arrest up to anything like three days.*

They were refused water or washing facilities and in one case (T.M.) given only two bread and tea meals in the twenty-seven hours between his arrest and his removal to Lewes Prison to be remanded in custody. Another boy claimed to have been given only bread and marge for forty-eight hours. All the boys, including one with a kidney complaint, whose father's representations about this were ignored by the Chief Constable and Magistrates Clerk, had to sleep on the concrete floor. Six separate allegations were made that the police had beaten up some of the boys in the cells. The nephew, wife and mother of a 22-year-old man arrested for letting down the tyres of a police van claimed to have witnessed police brutality in the station when they visited him. Another complaint, made in three letters and repeated by some of the boys in the Barker–Little sample, was that the police coerced boys into pleading guilty: 'A policeman came three times to the bars . . . and made the statement that those who pleaded guilty would be dealt with sooner and more leniently, while those who pleaded not guilty would be held at least a week in remand' (letter from J.G.).

It should be stressed that such allegations represented very much a minority view. One of the most unambiguous of public attitudes – and one that was fed back to reinforce the actions of the police – was of support and admiration for the police. The foundation for this attitude was laid in inventory reports about 'How the Police Won the Battle of Brighton'. These reports polarized the images of the good, brave policemen with the evil, cowardly mob. The *Daily Mirror* (19 May 1964), for example, reported on how two hundred Mods advancing on the Margate Town Hall were routed by one brave policeman. In fact, the Mods were milling around, rather than advancing and there were at least four policemen. But the counter-conceptions had to be stressed between 'The Hoodlums and the Real Heroes'; the police, self-controlled and patient, had to meet a provocative jeering mob, hundreds of whom were '. . . turned away by a handful of men in blue'.†

---

* The Brighton police denied a NCCL charge that sixty youths had shared a cell. Because of lack of space 'they were put in the cell corridor' (*Guardian*, 28 April 1965).

† This sort of imagery is identical to that used in covering crowd clashes between political demonstrators and the police: 'Police Win Battle of Grosvenor Square', 'The Day the Police Were Wonderful', 'Fringe Fanatics Foiled at Big Demonstration: What the Bullies Faced', etc. For a detailed analysis of the media portrayal of the police in one such case, the 1968 Vietnam demonstrations in London, see Halloran *et al.*[20]

These images were definitely absorbed by the public. Of the total number of post-Margate opinion statements, less than 1 per cent were critical of the police (mentioning, for example, their provocative tactics or their hyper-sensitivity to leather jackets or long hair). The rest only had praise for the police, or went further to make the familiar charge that the policeman's hands were tied and that he should be given more powers. In the Brighton sample, 43 (i.e. 66.2 per cent) agreed with the methods used by the police, a further 13 (20 per cent) thought that the police should have been tougher and only 9 (13.8 per cent) criticized the police for being unfair or provocative.

Additional signs of public support for the police could be seen in the courts, where prolonged applause from the public benches followed statements by the Chairman complimenting the police. The same reaction occurred during parliamentary debates. Letters to local papers in the resorts were mainly in praise of the police, 'this gallant bulwark of society' (*Brighton and Hove Herald*, 23 March 1964). The *Hastings and St Leonards Observer* (8 August 1964) published fifteen letters about the Mods and Rockers: thirteen expressed gratitude to the police, one did not mention them and one writer complained about his son and daughter being unjustifiably harassed by the police. This last letter resulted in ten letters in the next issue denouncing the writer's attitude and accusing him of being emotional, unbalanced and waging a private vendetta against the police. These letters again expressed gratitude to the policeman '. . . and his allies [sic] the magistrates'. One writer said: 'If I had a thousand pounds, I would give it to the police. What would we do without them?', and another called for money to be sent to the Police Convalescent Home '. . . as tangible appreciation for the police winning the Battle of Hastings, 1964'. Such calls did not go unheeded: besides the hundreds of letters sent to them directly, the Brighton police received over £100 for the Police Benevolent Fund and, according to a local journalist, were embarrassed by the sheer volume of congratulations that poured in.

(ii) *The Courts* – Whereas police decisions and procedures leave unknown the number of deviants not labelled and processed, court decisions and procedures enable the next stage of the system to be more precisely observed. One can record in quantifiable terms the proportions who are processed and sent on to the next stage and one can also 'measure' this decision in terms of the severity of the sentence.

The high points in escalation were the sentences given at Whitsun, 1965 (Brighton). In keeping with the control agent's dilemma, any quiet weekend after these sentences was claimed as proof of their deterrent value and any trouble was either played down or used to justify the need for increased and still harsher penalties. Comparable figures for each incident unfortunately could not be located because the hearings were not always reported in full, and, in the case of sentences passed after remand or bail, not reported at all as the interest had by then died down. Attempts to obtain fuller figures from official sources were not successful. Tables 6 and 7 summarize the available information for the first of these two incidents.

In the case of Brighton, Easter 1965, so many were arrested (between 110 and 120) and the situation in the two sittings of the court so confusing, that estimates of the numbers actually charged ranged from 70 to 110. Of the actual charges it is only clear that the greatest number were for 'Wilfully Obstructing the Police in the Execution of Their Duty' or 'Use of Threatening Behaviour whereby a Breach of the Peace was Likely to be Occasioned'. These two accounted for nearly three-quarters of all sentences. Others included assaulting the police (about seven) unlawful possession of drugs (five) and a few each of malicious damage, obscene language and stone-throwing. Because virtually every offender was remanded in custody, it is difficult to trace all subsequent sentences. It is only clear that greater use was made of the detention centre – a trend throughout the period – and fines were increased. These cases supplied the greatest proportion of successful appeals; in one case the Recorder substituted a £25 fine for a sentence of three months in a

Table 6 Court Action – Margate, Whitsun 1964

Charges		Sentences	
Threatening behaviour or threatening words	37	Conditional discharge	1
Threatening behaviour plus offensive weapon	3	£25 fine	1
Offensive weapon	5	£50 fine	30
		£75 fine	6
Malicious damage or wilful damage	–	Detention centre (3 months)	6
Assault plus offensive weapon	1	Detention centre (6 months)	1
Assaulting police	–		
Obstructing police	–	Jail (3 months)	1
	–		–
	46		46

(Note: Because of incomplete information it is impossible to match the offences with the sentences.)

Table 7 Court Action – Hastings, August 1964

Charges	Sentences		
Threatening behaviour	Case dismissed*	1	
Abusive behaviour	Conditional discharge	1	
	£10 fine	1	
	£20 fine	3	
	£25 fine	2	
	Detention centre (3 months)	13	
	Detention centre (3 months) + £50 fine	2	
		—	23
Malicious damage	Detention centre (2 months)	1	
Wilful damage	Detention centre (3 months)	2	
	Detention centre (4 months)	1	
		—	4
Obstructing police	£10 fine	1	
	£20 fine	4	
		—	5
Offensive weapon	Detention centre (3 months)	1	
	Detention centre (6 months)	4	
		—	5
Assaulting police	Detention centre (6 months)	2	
	Prison (3 months)	1	
		—	3
			40

* All except this case bound over for £25 to keep the peace for two years.

detention centre because it was a first offence. The press reported very few of the successful appeals.

The use of the remand in custody by the Brighton magistrates at Easter 1965 warrants special attention as this was a consciously applied innovatory principle. It was clear that the magistrates were using their power to remand as a 'form of extra-legal punishment',* in order to provide the youths with a short taste of imprisonment.

* Editorial comment in the *Observer* (25 April 1965). A senior magistrate in the Northview sample claimed that word had gone round the magistrate's clerks at the time to make greater use of the remand in custody; he commented himself: 'Although it is not strictly legal and is rather naughty, a remand in custody for more than a week is a good idea.' A recent study has shown the general haphazard and inadequate bases for magistrates' decisions to remand defendants on bail or in custody.[21]

The grounds on which bail can be refused, especially for juveniles, are fairly limited, but it was quite apparent that these grounds were not being applied to individual cases and that bail was refused as a matter of principle. The Chairman of the Magistrates, Mr H. Cushnie, was widely quoted as saying that bail would not be entertained at all, no matter what surety was offered.* While most newspaper reports of the court proceedings quoted the magistrates' reason for remand as being 'in order to enable the police to make enquiries', this, in fact, was not the reason given in court when bail was opposed. Inspector W. Tapsall, prosecuting, said that his opposition was, firstly, on the grounds that if the boys were allowed to go free on bail justice would not be done and, secondly, that the public must be protected. The first of these grounds is not a legal one and the second not easily justified. Often on the basis of no other evidence than the reading of the charges, a boy who had done nothing more than refuse to 'move along' would be certified as an 'unruly person'. The result was that many relatively minor cases, including those involving juveniles, were remanded in custody in prison for up to three weeks. In one case two juveniles, eventually fined £5 each for obstruction, spent eleven days in Lewes Prison.

The punitive and arbitrary use of remand was illustrated in one case where the accused, after already being remanded in custody once for eleven days, was again refused bail and 'sentenced' to a further week in custody. A few minutes later he was taken back to the court and informed that the constable whom he was alleged to have obstructed, was going on leave, so the 'sentence' would be reduced to four days to enable the case to be heard before the constable's holiday. Few knew the procedure for appealing against being remanded, and in one case referred to the NCCL, a boy (D.H.), who did know the procedure, was refused a form to apply to the Judge-in-Chambers for bail. This is a serious allegation in view of the fact that a test case brought by the Council on behalf of a 16-year-old boy resulted in his immediate release from prison on bail.

There were a number of other unusual actions by the courts. In two cases (Hastings, August 1964 and Brighton, Easter 1965) there were rulings by the magistrates that the names of all juveniles be published. The Hastings Chairman (Mr A. G. Coote) also ordered in certain cases that fingerprints should be taken. The Brighton Chairman (Mr Pascoe) announced that warrants would

---

* At Whitsun 1964 the Brighton magistrates in fact granted bail to a 17-year-old arrested for insulting behaviour. The amount of bail was £1,250.

be issued for the arrest of any father who failed to attend the court. In at least one case a father who was not notified of the date of the hearings was subjected to the indignity of his name being published as being 'too busy' to attend his son's hearing. Parents who were present at the preliminary hearings were often rudely addressed by the magistrate or clerk, not allowed to say what they wanted to, and their offers to stand bail were, of course, refused. It was hard for some of the parents to escape the conclusion that their attendance too was a form of 'extra-legal punishment'.

The court actions – and those of the other control agents – must be seen as the logical result of the way the control culture had defined the situation. The logic of this definition – a product of, and in turn a determinant of the inventory images and attitudes – left the magistrates in no doubt about their role: they had to clamp down hard, make an example of these offenders and deter others. This type of logic imposed by the assimilation of a belief system is not, of course, unknown in the history of criminal trials. The immediate parallel that suggests itself is the Teddy Boy phenomenon of the 1950s; control agents then acted in ways identical to their reaction to the Mods and Rockers a decade later. Tony Parker, in his account of the trial of Michael Davies, has described vividly how Davies was sentenced '. . . not so much for what he might have done, as for being a symbol of something which the contemporary public found abhorrent and threatening to their stable way of life'; the build-up of prejudicial and melodramatic headlines ('Edwardian Suits – Dance-Music – and a Dagger') meant that not only Davies's alleged offence was on trial, '. . . but everything about him, and all he had the misfortune to represent'.[22] The boy stabbed to death on Clapham Common was a symbol of what the public had expected the Teddy Boys to be capable.

The Davies case was an extreme example. The hundreds of routine Mods and Rockers offences processed by the courts displayed some of the more subtle facets of the complicated relationship between belief systems and the operation of social control. One might quote the case of 'Peter Jones' to show the use of situational logic and, subsequently, the deviant's social background, in justifying control measures. Jones was sentenced to three months in a detention centre for using threatening behaviour in Brighton on Whit Monday, 1965. He had thrown a make-up case (?) at a group of Rockers being chased by Mods. On appeal, his counsel said that Jones had passed six 'O levels' and wanted to sit for three more. He had never been in trouble before and was shocked at his first contact with the law. A letter was read from his headmistress saying what a disgrace it was that a school prefect and house captain with an example to show, had shown it this way. The Deputy Recorder allowed the appeal because, although the detention centre would give Jones a chance to study, he would not get the same facilities as at school. The sentence was altered to a conditional discharge. Nevertheless, maintained the Recorder, the magistrates were absolutely right in taking the line that they did in the circumstances at the time. They had to have regard to the deterrent effect on others. Those who did not have the advantage of Jones's background were seen as justifiable offerings on the altar of general deterrence.

The extent to which action was influenced by the generalized belief system rather than judgments on the individual offender on the one hand or generalized principles of sentencing on the other, can perhaps best be indicated by quoting some pronouncements by magistrates in giving their judgments. The following extracts are all by the Chairman of the Hastings Bench, Mr A. G. Coote, at Whitsun 1964;[23] they are representative of other pronouncements at the time:

> In considering the penalties to be imposed, we must take into account *the overall effect* on the innocent citizens of and visitors to the Borough. Though some of the offences committed by individuals may not *in themselves* seem all that serious, they form *part and parcel* of a *cumulative series* of events which ruined the pleasure of thousands* and adversely affected the business of traders. The Hastings Bench has always taken a stern view of violent and disorderly conduct and we do not propose to alter that attitude. In pursuance of that policy we shall impose in these cases penalties – in many cases the maximum – which will punish the offenders and will effectively deter other law breakers.

> We shall find that because of *the prevalence of this type of occurrence* and the necessity of condign punishment we must send you to prison.

> Your conduct is *of the kind* we are determined to end in this borough. (Emphasis added.)

These sorts of statements are comprehensible in terms of the dramatization element in the societal control culture. This element is illustrated with particular vividness in the court, the perfect stage for acting out society's ceremonies of status degradation. These are encounters in which each side

---

* One of the Hastings magistrates was evidently one of these 'thousands'. During the hearing he revealed that he was in a crowd which had retreated into Woolworths for safety during an incident.

knows its lines, and, as Erikson comments on a church trial during Puritan times 'when the whole affair is seen as a ceremony and not a test of guilt, as a demonstration rather than an enquiry, its accents and rhythms are easier to understand'.[24] This ceremony not only publicly labels the deviant but functions to stir up moral indignation to a still higher pitch.

The ritualism of the Mods and Rockers' courts was emphasized by the atmosphere in which the proceedings took place. Invariably the preliminary hearings were arranged at times when courts do not usually sit: Bank Holidays, Sundays and, in one case, until midnight. Extra drama was sometimes provided by the use of special buildings. These arrangements were made – and publicly announced – as long as two weeks before the Bank Holiday as if to give notice of the impending ceremony. In Margate, the court was surrounded by a 'horde of screaming teenagers', the doors were guarded by a strong force of police and another twelve policemen mingled with the crowds in the public gallery. The courts were invariably crowded and in the case of Brighton at least, where I observed a number of hearings, it was apparent that many spectators attended in the spirit of a gladiatorial display. After an 'interim statement' made by the Chairman at one sitting, the crowd broke out into spontaneous applause. Sentences, particularly when accompanied by homilies, were often greeted by loud clapping. The question of guilt or innocence did not take up much time, and the resemblance of the proceedings to a mock trial was brought home to those relatives who claimed that the police had told them before the trial to bring along enough money for the fines. The monotony of the ritual hearings with the repeated certification of the offender as an 'unruly person' was livened only by audience participation and the occasional screams, scuffles and bangings from the cells below.

The magistrates themselves acted out their role in meaningless exchanges with witnesses or relatives and outbursts of ritual hostility towards the offender. Parents were often informed too late to be present at the hearings and when they were there, they were subjected to the following type of questioning:

Chairman: Did you know that your son was in Brighton?
Father: Yes.
Chairman: Did you know that he was in the Automat?
Father: No.

This exchange was greeted by gasps of surprise in the audience and 'I told you so' looks between the magistrates, the implication clearly being that the father was somehow responsible for his son's supposed offence and should have known, although sixty miles away at the time, of his son's presence in the Automat. Most direct hostility was reserved for the offenders, as in the following encounter between the Chairman and a 17-year-old boy, fined £20 for obstructing the police:

Chairman: Various police forces were trying to avoid something dreadful happening and were forced to keep you on the move.
Defendant: We were trying to get home.
Chairman: It was a pity you came here in the first place.
Defendant: Yes, it was.

This dramatization of deviance, so important in creating the polarization effect, was illustrated nowhere more clearly than in the public pronouncements of the Margate magistrate, Dr George Simpson, at Whitsun 1964. Perhaps never before have the *obiter dicta* of a local magistrate been so widely quoted and it was only in the Oz trial six years later that a judge – Michael Argyle – received the same treatment and for exactly the same reasons.

Virtually every court report quoted Dr Simpson's 'Sawdust Caesars' speech in full and his terminology significantly influenced the mass media symbolization and the process of spurious attribution. His phrases were widely used as headlines: '"Sawdust Caesars hunt in pack," says magistrate'; '"Clamp down on Mods and Rockers – A Vicious Virus," says J.P.' 'Town Hits Back on Rat Pack Hooligans', etc.

Any ambiguity and any unanswered questions about the nature of the deviance and the deviant's confrontation with social control were resolved by Dr Simpson's verbal structuring of the situation; as a commentator on the press pointed out: '. . . by Tuesday, papers were being influenced not by what happened, or even what their own reporters were telling them had happened, but by what Dr Simpson said had happened' (*Spectator*, 22 May 1964).

The melodramatic atmosphere already having been created, Dr Simpson opened the show by issuing a warning that any interruption or disturbance would be most rigorously dealt with. What noise there was, added to the drama: the crowds outside, and the audible reaction to the scale of the fines including cries from the boys' girl-friends and even gasps of surprise from policemen on hearing that boys they had arrested for threatening behaviour, had been given £50 or £75 fines. The first of the forty-four youths to come before the court was a 22-year-old from London who pleaded guilty to using threatening behaviour.[25] It is worth quoting in full the message he received because it was really meant for a much wider audience:

It is not likely that the air of this town has ever been polluted by the hordes of hooligans, male and female, such as we have seen this weekend and of whom you are an example.

These long-haired, mentally unstable, petty little hoodlums, these sawdust Caesars who can only find courage like rats, in hunting in packs, came to Margate with the avowed intent of interfering with the life and property of its inhabitants.

Insofar as the law gives us power, this court will not fail to use the prescribed penalties. It will, perhaps, discourage you and others of your kidney who are infected with this vicious virus, that you will go to prison for three months.

The following are a few of Dr Simpson's further comments:

'It's a pity that you didn't stick to your knitting' (to a 19-year-old knitting worker fined £50 for carrying an offensive weapon).

'Margate will not tolerate louts like you' (to an 18-year-old, given six months in a detention centre).

To a 19-year-old plumber's mate accused of carrying a roll of newspaper with coins in the middle as an offensive weapon: 'I don't suppose you were using this newspaper to further your literary aspirations.'
Defendant: 'I'm sorry. I don't understand.'
Simpson: 'Never mind, you'll understand what I'm going to say now: £50.'

'Perhaps your school will consider a framed reproduction of your conviction' (to a 17-year-old grammar school boy fined £75 for possessing an offensive weapon and using threatening behaviour).

On the second day of the hearings: 'It would appear that you have not benefited from yesterday's proceedings. We listened to these paltry excuses and there is no doubt that you were a part of the dregs of these vermin who infested the town yesterday and the day before, and we think the penalty must be appropriate.'

'It is strange to see this procession of miserable specimens, so different from the strutting hooligans of yesterday.'

The follow-up to this ceremony was the inflation of Dr Simpson into a folk hero: he personalized the forces of good against which the forces of evil were massed. Like all such folk heroes, he, single-handed – 'a small man in a light grey suit' (*Daily Express*, 19 May 1964) – had overcome sheer brute strength. 'The Quiet Man Who Rocks the Thugs', had his personality, career and views on various social issues presented to the public. He told reporters that he realized from the beginning that he was dealing not just with a local fracas but with something that had become a national problem. It had reached 'colossal national proportions' (Disaster); he was aware of a 'general pattern of deliberate viciousness' (It's Not Only This), scooters and motor-bikes were 'almost in the nature of offensive weapons' and he wished he had the power to deprive hooligans of their means of transport (Innovation).

His justice was not that of the impersonal, faceless representative of social control. Like Batman saving Gotham City, he had saved his own town, where he had lived 'as a beloved local family doctor for twenty-four years'. On the Sunday night before the hearings, he had, according to the *Daily Mail* (19 May 1964), toured Margate with his wife to see the gangs. His wife described what they saw:

> We saw for ourselves how tired the policemen looked. We have lived in Margate for twenty-four years and last night was dreadful. The town was full of dirty grubby teenagers. It must not be allowed to happen again . . . I think my husband did the right thing. These people have got to be taught a lesson.

On the day after the hearings, many newspapers carried photographs of Dr Simpson, quietly strolling along the deserted Margate beaches, 'surveying the Whitsun battleground', and contemplating how nice it was 'to be able to walk along here again without fear of being molested' (*Daily Express*, 20 May 1964). At the same time as he rejoiced in the problem having been dealt with satisfactorily – 'I think I taught them a lesson in court on Monday' – he had to remind society that the problem was still there: 'it may take more than one dose of nasty medicine to persuade these thugs that this behaviour does not pay.'

3. *Towards an Exclusive Control Culture*

The courts and the police, as officially designated agents of social control, had to operate in terms of a socially sanctioned role. They could not opt out of this role; they had to take some action. Their action was also limited to rule enforcement, rather than the creation of new rules. The fact that these limits were often exceeded, is attributable not to their absence, but to the perceived innovatory aspects of the behaviour itself, sensitization, symbolization and the whole belief system. Rationalizations such as 'new situations need new remedies' account for those elements exclusively directed at the particular deviance being controlled.

It would, however, be an incomplete analysis of the control culture to look only at the official control agents. Social control is much broader in scope, including as it does informal mechanisms such as public opinion on the one hand, and highly formalized institutions of the state on the other. I described the reaction to the Mods and Rockers as diffusing from the relatively unorganized on-the-spot reaction of the local community (the pristine form of the social reaction in the amplification model) to an increasing involvement of other individuals and groups. Such diffusion produces a generalized belief system – mythologies, stigmas, stereotypes – but it also produces or tries to produce new methods of control. The informal societal reaction can be extended and formalized, the ultimate formalization being achieved when new laws are actually created.

This section will be concerned with the ways in which the local reaction moved towards the creation of an exclusive control culture with methods – as well as a belief system – specifically directed towards the Mods and Rockers. This movement embodies many of the typical features of the whole moral panic, the same features that have been documented in analyses of rule creation and social problem formation. Cases of the former – the abolition of slavery, the prohibition movement, the passing of the Marijuana Tax Act, the creation of the sexual psychopath laws – and of the latter – the drug problem, the pornography problem, the pollution problem – have suggested the operation of a certain more or less fixed sequence. This starts off with the perception by some people of a condition which is trouble-making, difficult, dangerous or threatening and requiring action: 'something should be done about it'. A specific rule is deduced from the general value which is felt should be protected or upheld, and, if appropriate, a method of control is suggested.

Early students of social problems envisaged a somewhat rigid sequence from awareness to policy determination to reform or control.[26] As with the amplification model, such formulations assume too mechanistic a flow, without recognizing that, say, unqualified rejection is not the only reaction to deviance and that the transition from one stage to another has to be explained. Even less deterministic models, however, have to take into account certain universal conditions, of which I would like to suggest at least three: *legitimating values, enterprise* and *power*.

Values must always be present to legitimate what Becker calls 'blowing the whistle': that is, enforcing existing rules or attempting to enforce new rules. (His analogy of blowing a whistle is in some respects unfortunate in that it implies that an essential property of the referee – impartiality – is present. In the game of deviance this is hardly so: society is the referee and the other side at the same time.) In his own research on the Marijuana Tax Act Becker analyses the legitimating values of humanitarianism, the Protestant ethic particularly of self-control and the disapproval of action aimed solely at achieving ecstasy.[27] The presence, alone, of such values does not guarantee successful rule creation or social problem definition; there must also be enterprise: someone takes the initiative on the basis of interest and uses publicity techniques to gain the support of the organizations that count. Finally, this 'someone' must either be in a position of power himself or must have access to and be able to convince such powerful institutions as the mass media, legal and scientific bodies and political authorities.

Once such conditions can be met, the general appeals – 'all right thinking persons would deplore . . .', 'we cannot tolerate . . .' – must be applied to the particular case in question. The appeal must be supported by a belief system – the inventory images, the opinion themes – which conveys the message that the phenomenon is indeed the appropriate target for action. Often, crusades and appeals are justified on the basis of deviation which is wholly or partly putative. Thus, for example, Sutherland shows that all the propositions on which the sexual psychopath laws are based are demonstrably false or at least questionable.[28] Putative deviation has similarly been documented in areas such as drug addiction.[29]

In regard to the Mods and Rockers, there was a process whereby members of the public, acting as informal control agents, brought pressure to bear for rule creation; that is, they referred their 'local' problem to the legislature. It is significant that the action took this form rather than merely pressing for more efficient action by the control agents. In sudden unexpected forms of deviance, the institutionalized agencies are often thrown off balance and any deficiencies they have become obvious. They are sometimes themselves blamed for the deviance: this is a common reaction following political assassinations which expose inadequacies in security arrangements. In the case of the Mods and Rockers, though, there was widespread support for the police and the courts; it was believed that they were doing their job as best they could but were handicapped by being given insufficient powers or by having to deal with a problem that was really the government's. Blame and responsibility were thus shifted upward in the hierarchy.

Students of natural disasters have noted a similar scapegoating process: those involved in the disaster are usually exonerated – 'they only did their job' – and government figures become targets for attack and protest in a situation for which they had no conceivable direct responsibility.[30] Similarly, 'non-natural' disasters, such as the Ibrox Park incident during which spectators were crushed to death after a football match, have to be defined as part of a national problem, in this case spectator safety and crowd control at sporting fixtures. I would suggest, in fact, that this pyramidical conception of blame and responsibility, together with a parallel belief system which sees the phenomenon in question as being only the visible tip of a more broadly based condition (It's Not Only This) are further prerequisites for successful moral enterprise.

The whole process in which informal agents stepped in and attempted to institutionalize new control methods is analogous to the process in a disaster whereby the emergency or therapeutic social system refers the problem to the 'suprasystem' or 'restorative social system'. The crude responses of the emergency social system meet the immediate needs for food, shelter and rescue in a disaster in the same way as the police and courts met the immediate problems presented to the community by the Mods and Rockers: the identification and labelling of the deviants, the protection of person and property, the handing out of retribution. The slower responding organizations of the suprasystem then come into action; with the diffusion of news, the disaster (depending on its nature and the type of inventory that is made about it) may be defined as a national problem. There follow public meetings, inquiries, petitions and, as in the case of rule creation, the demand is made that emergency systems be given more power or that the suprasystem take over.

The first step is to see how those immediately affected defined the problem. Clearly, hooliganism is not a 'crime without a victim' and the development of exclusive control measures depends, in part, on how the victims articulated the way they had been affected. As could be expected from the orientation themes, the initial reaction by the victims in the local community was to define what happened as disastrous. In fact, it was the initial reaction of self-styled spokesmen of the seaside resorts which did so much to arouse the panic and subsequent sensitization. The pattern was set after Clacton, with the various panic statements made to the press: 'I've seen riots in South America, but this was almost mob rule' (Mr J. Malthouse, the manager of a seafront hotel); 'Clacton would be one gigantic wreckage tonight except for our fine British bobbies' (Councillor E. Payne, Chairman of the resort's publicity council). Similar statements were made after the subsequent events. 'We were on the very edge of a total riot. Only a little more hysteria next time and it will be quite beyond control. And at the moment there is nothing that can really stop a next time happening' (Mr A. Webb, President of the Brighton Hotels Association). This sort of reaction was played up by the press: Brighton was 'a town seething with anger and resentment' (*Evening Argus*, 18 May 1964); Margate was 'a town in fear . . . hopelessness . . . and bubbling anger' (*Evening Standard*, 19 May 1964) and the owner of a café 'damaged in the riots' pleaded with the reporter not to publish his name: 'They will come back and smash up my shop. I want no more trouble. Go away.'

Some local people evidently translated their fears into action; there were rumours after Clacton and every other event, of vigilante squads being formed by local tradesmen to protect their property. After Easter 1964, although there was only a very minor incident in Margate, some local residents there were sufficiently sensitized by the Clacton build-up, to start preparations for the summer. Amusement caterers armed themselves with children's baseball bats, and the manager of a seafront coffee club wanted every establishment to have a doorman armed with a tear-gas missile to keep the gangs away.

It is difficult to judge how representative this sort of reaction was. Clearly, newspaper reports exaggerated the intensity of the feeling and the vigilantes and tear-gassers were very much in the minority. Only a small number of tradesmen were personally affected by the disturbances; most only heard about them at second hand. Nevertheless, in seaside resorts depending almost wholly on summer visitors, the fear of loss of trade was a very real one and in such avenues of community opinion as editorials and letters in the local press, council debates and public speeches (e.g. on school prize-giving days), a genuine anxiety was reflected. One precondition for the development of exclusive control culture was therefore present: the definition by certain people of the situation as inimical to their interests and that something should be done about it.

It is important to be clear about the nature of these interests because it is the perception of what interests are to be protected that shapes the subsequent campaigns for rule creation. In the last analysis the 'interests' may derive from what Ranulf referred to as 'the disinterested tendency to inflict punishment',[31] but more immediately, interests were presented in purely financial terms. The campaigns for action were based on appeals to commercial interest and the leading figures behind these campaigns were often leaders of commercial and business organizations. Chambers of Commerce and Hotel and Guest House Associations were among the most prominent pressure groups, and the Council intervention was based on protecting the town's holiday trade, its 'good image'. The commercial interest can be seen operating in the sequence of statements made by these individuals and organizations: the first reaction was to panic, but as soon as it was realized that this might, in fact, operate against the towns' interest by creating further panic (not only sociologists know of self-fulfilling prophecies) early statements were modified and local figures objected that press reports had been exaggerated. Thus the Mayor of Margate complained:

> I consider that the whole affair has been badly mishandled in that nation-wide publicity has been given to the activities of a comparatively few witless hooligans. Had they been ignored and even if they are ignored from now on these louts will be cut down to size and their minor disturbances will be dealt with locally in a proper manner. Can it now be agreed to let local people deal with local events?

The commercial interest gave the demands a peculiar form: 'If this happens again, people won't come here on holiday; we must get rid of the Mods and Rockers either by driving them out, or by not letting them in in the first place; we don't care where they go – let them go and wreck up Margate (or Hastings, or Brighton, or Eastbourne) as long as they don't come here.' These demands echo the sanction of banishment used in tribal and other simpler communities, the same primal in-group aggression towards the deviant enshrined in our folklore by Westerns in which the outlaw is 'ridden out of town'.

At this point there appears a contradiction within the demands. Although many local people were, like the Mayor of Margate, dismayed with the publicity, rather than 'seething with fear and anger', they knew that nothing would be done if the problem were defined in purely local terms. To create rules, a problem must not only be conceptualized in mass-appeal terms, it must also be defined in such a way that it is seen as the legitimate responsibility of the suprasystem. In other words, it is not enough to 'let local people deal with local events'; the event had to be magnified to national proportions and the responsibility for it shifted upwards. So after the initial Clacton event there were immediate calls for Home Office inquiries and 'the Government', 'do-gooders' or 'reformers' were made scapegoats.

This shifting upwards of responsibility has, in fact, its own commercial motive. Because the 'looking for kicks' image was so prevalent, it was realized that to define the problem in purely parochial terms would reflect on the resort's facilities. Whereas outside opinion interpreted 'boredom' in a broader sense, local people thought in terms of on-the-spot boredom and were anxious to dispel any ideas that a lack of recreational facilities in the resort could have caused the trouble: 'There's plenty to do in X; if they were bored it's not our fault.'

Given the presence of such preconditions for successful role creation as problem awareness, the recognition of specific legitimating values, self-interest and the beginnings of a pyramidical conception of responsibility and causation, what form did the local demands take? The first type of demands were not for specific policies, but were rather undifferentiated appeals for assistance. Calls were made for Home Office inquiries, for the laws to be 'tightened up', for the courts and the police to be given 'more powers'. A statement by the Chairman of the Hastings Bench is typical of such vague generalized appeals:

> . . . the three justices sitting today are unanimous in their view that it is now time for Parliament to consider what measures shall be adopted to crush this form of mass hooliganism, which is now patently repetitive at holiday times. If nothing is done, thousands of innocent people will continue to suffer fear, injury and damage to property.

A similar generalized build-up took place in editorials, letters to the press and in statements by local MPs. At an early stage some specific policy proposals were also made, and these increased under the impact of sensitization and the crystallization of opinions. Thus out of twenty-three letters printed in the *Evening Argus* in the four days after Whitsun 1964, seven specifically proposed corporal punishment.

The disaster analogy was often made explicit in the suggestion that the government should be given emergency powers, such as setting up of road blocks at the main entrance to target towns 'and turning back . . . any scooters, motor vehicles or larger vehicles on which doubtful looking teenagers were travelling . . . Entry by rail could also be restricted . . . we did these things successfully during the war' (Editorial, *Hastings & St Leonards Observer*, 8 September 1964). The vigilante-type solutions also appeared – as in the examples from Margate quoted earlier – and in such proposals as those of a Brighton restaurant proprietor in 1964, who wanted to arm with cudgels a thousand of Brighton's 'decent young people', and send them to 'beat the hell out of these Mods and Rockers' (*Evening Argus*, 18 May 1964).

The next stage was the attempts by organizations to formalize policy statements. In some cases, abortive action groups were formed. This is the stage at which resolutions are passed, petitions signed and deputations sent. After Whitsun, 1965, the Great Yarmouth Hotels and Guest Houses Association called for the banning of Mods, Rockers and beatniks:

> We cannot believe that it is not possible . . . to find some legal way of putting this town completely out of bounds to these people . . . We call upon all other trade associations and persons who hope to continue to carry on their business in Great Yarmouth to join us and demand that some positive action is taken as the time for compromise is past. (*Caterer and Hotel Keeper*, 1 July 1965)

In August 1965 sixty Margate traders called for new legislation in a petition which was sent to the Chamber of Commerce and passed on to the MP. In September, a meeting of the Brighton LVA supported a proposal for protest action by Brighton traders against light penalties imposed on hooligans. A committee member, who was also on the Chamber of Commerce, intended to ask the next Chamber meeting to make representations to the watch committee and local MPs. At the same time in Margate, the Isle of Thanet LVA. decided to press local police to receive a deputation and one member stated: 'It's time that the business people of the town did something about this. Let's try to protect ourselves. Every licensee should urge his customers to sign a petition so that we can get a law passed to ensure that anybody found sleeping out at night will be prosecuted on sight' (*Morning Advertiser*, 4 September 1965).

A feature of appeals at this stage is that the opinion and attitude themes are articulated more clearly and the proposals show all the inventory elements and the subsequent sensitization. An example of this is the net-widening effect in the call to ban beatniks and beach sleepers as well as Mods and Rockers, and in campaigns in seaside resorts against hooliganism at other times of the year.[32]

This type of agitation for the establishment of an exclusive control policy was not confined to local organizations. At a fairly early stage, those individuals whose opinions are invariably quoted by the mass media on 'youth problems' proclaimed their solutions: vicars, youth workers, probation officers, marriage counsellors, psychiatrists, headmasters, disc jockeys and respectable pop stars ('They Are Just Louts,' says Dreamer Freddie, *Daily Mirror*, 23 May 1964). Speeches were made at conferences, church services, prize-giving days and passing-out parades. These pronouncements, together with the whole media bombardment, helped to create a separate control culture in the sense of spreading the mythologies and stereotypes, but they did not directly lead to exclusive control policies. The demands made were too vague, not addressed to anyone in particular and not made by organized pressure groups with much power. There were one or two exceptions to this. For example, at the annual general meeting of the Magistrates Association in October 1964, the following resolution was debated:

That in view of the recent troubles between gangs of young people, this Association urges the Home Secretary to introduce further legislation, possibly by the extension of the principle of the Attendance Centre, whereby these delinquents are not only punished but the punishment is such as to direct their energies into productive channels for the benefit of the community.

After considerable discussion the resolution was defeated by 103 votes to 84; although another resolution which seems to have been directed at the Mods and Rockers was carried:

That this Association urges the provision of powers whereby disqualification from holding a licence or confiscation of the vehicle could be ordered in certain cases where a motor vehicle is used for the furtherance of crime or for certain breaches of the peace.[33]

At a certain ill-defined point, some of the sporadic campaigns and appeals became formalized into fully fledged action groups. Even granting the overall paucity of the literature on rule and social problem creation, very little attention has been given to the nature of action groups that have operated in such areas as the control of drugs, prostitution, homosexuality, pornography and obscenity. In the latter case, for example, the work of such groups as Mrs Mary Whitehouse's National Viewers' and Listeners' Association, the Clean Up TV Campaign, the Longford Committee and the Festival of Light, cry out for attention in terms of the sociology of moral enterprise.

From another perspective, such action groups can be seen as germinal social movements. They meet most of the formal criteria spelt out in the literature on such movements,[34] although they are difficult to classify in terms of its typologies. The action groups correspond closely to what Smelser calls 'norm-oriented movements' and are preceded by and undertaken in the name of 'norm-oriented beliefs',[35] that is, the mythology presented in the inventory and crystallized in later stages. All of Smelser's value-laden stages were present before the action groups were formed: strain (deviance); anxiety; an identification of the agents responsible; a generalized belief that control was inadequate; a belief that the trouble can be cured by reorganizing the normative structure itself ('there ought to be a law'); and, finally, the formulation of specific proposals to punish, control or destroy the agent. In content as well as development, the Mods and Rockers action groups shared an important characteristic with crusading social movements: the advocation of programmes entailing the rigorous implementation of folk prescriptions such as better law enforcements and stiffer penalties.[36]

I shall describe two groups which arose wholly in response to the Mods and Rockers disturbances. Although these groups gathered a great deal of momentum, they left behind them almost no organizational residue, few of their policies were implemented and they failed in producing any direct legal change. Nevertheless, their activities are of considerable interest both in terms of illustrating the belief system and reaction built around the Mods and Rockers, and in highlighting some more general features of moral panics, moral enterprise and the sociology of law enforcement.

The Seatown* Council Group was only in the most rudimentary sense a group at all. In April 1966 twelve senior Aldermen and Councillors tabled a motion urging the Council to press the government to create an enforced work scheme for convicted Mods and Rockers. The motion received wide publicity, under such headings as 'Make the Rockers Dig' and 'Hard Labour Plan For The Rowdy Mods'. The exact text was as follows:

> That despite the unceasing efforts of the police and notwithstanding the imposition of heavy fines on offenders or even their being sentenced to periods of detention, Public Holidays continue to be characterised in seaside resorts and other places by disturbances created by bands of so-called Mods and Rockers, to the disturbance of residents and visitors, to the diversion of the Police from other duties and to the excessive strain upon them and the undoubted detriment of the resorts concerned.
>
> Accordingly this Council Resolves:
>
> That H.M. Government be urged to take steps to legislate that these offenders might be sentenced to periods of enforced work for the public benefit and to make the necessary arrangements therefor.
>
> It is further resolved:
>
> That copies of the foregoing resolution be forwarded to the local Members of Parliament, the Association of Municipal Corporations and the British Resorts Association with requests that they give their full support.

The scheme was elaborated in press statements by one of the main signatories of the motion, Alderman F., who had in mind the formation of a

---

* I have used the names 'Seatown' and later 'Beachside' to disguise the identities of the two resorts whose action groups I studied.

Labour Corps, run on similar lines to an Army glasshouse. The youngsters 'should be given a short haircut, strict discipline and made to work on the roads or other national projects'.

Immediately after the motion was announced, I contacted Alderman F. who referred me to the other major figure behind the motion, Alderman K., who in the next four months, through letters, discussions and a questionnaire, was my main source of information about the group. At the time of the motion being tabled, Alderman K. was Chairman of the Watch Committee. He is also a journalist who, for many years, had contributed a regular feature on the Bank Holiday for a local newspaper.

The motion was debated two months later, by which time there were seventeen signatures. It was carried by a clear majority: approximately forty in favour and ten against, with about twenty abstentions (mostly from the minority Labour group). The following were the main arguments behind this attempt to achieve normative change.[37]

The central justification for any action would be to put an end to behaviour that was causing Seatown a loss of trade and was damaging its image. The action then, would be purely on the basis of rational self-interest. To some this self-interest involved another dimension: '. . . our moral obligation to protect and honour the name of Seatown,' and the problem was perceived on a wider screen (It's Not Only This):

> Of course the incidents in Seatown and other places are clear indications of more serious trouble. This is largely concerned with the obvious attitude of some young people that they must be allowed to do exactly as they wish and must not be restrained in any way however annoying their conduct may be to others.[38]
>
> Seaside towns are not for thugs but for good family people who want to enjoy themselves in peace and happiness. But from Blackpool to St Ives this is not possible today.

The appeal for action was often highly personalized: 'If those who oppose the motion had any relative injured by these thugs, they would be taking a different position.' Individual cases were used to support the appeal, as, for example, a story quoted in the debate by Alderman F., about a honeymoon couple in Seatown being pushed around by a group of thugs: the husband couldn't defend himself because of their sheer numbers:

> His wife was in tears and he was trembling with rage when he saw me. 'Alderman,' he said, 'I can't tell you what an indignity I've suffered on my

honeymoon. A bride of a week and I didn't have the courage to defend her. For the rest of our lives our memories of our honeymoon will be marred by that experience.'[39]

The next step was to define the problem in such a way that legislative action was the only suitable solution. The police and courts had not defaulted in their duties, but their weapons were inadequate to deal with an entirely new problem. The novelty of the problem was consistently stressed: the greater numbers and the greater mobility which demanded deterrence on a new scale and above all the greater affluence which made fines anachronistic and ineffectual. What was needed was a period of discipline directed to turning out better citizens and, as the only existing institutions which do this – the detention centres – were costly and in short supply, something new must be devised. The Labour Camp scheme was the logical answer imposed by this definition of the situation.

In the course of the debate most of the popular arguments against this position were raised: the troublemakers were only a small hard core and one shouldn't be driven into panic measures which might affect the gullible ones who were simply following the crowd; this sort of problem has existed before; all had been done to meet the problem – particularly by the police – and the law properly enforced was enough; the problem was, in fact, already diminishing; the type of legislation proposed would be retrograde, panic legislation 'which would put the clock back 100 years' and was '. . . the thin end of the wedge leading to enforced labour camps'; that if Seatown should do anything, it should be to attract all sections of the community: these youngsters should be welcomed to Seatown so that they could see it as 'a place to be looked after, not to give trouble in'. These counter arguments received little support in the debate.

The extent to which the motion was supported locally is difficult to gauge in the absence of a reliable measure of public opinion. Alderman F. claimed to have received 108 letters about the plan; only two not in favour. Alderman K. also claimed wide local support:

Apart from this particular issue there is overwhelming support from the local press and the vast majority of those who have written to the Press supporting much stronger action to deal with the grave nuisance of these completely anti-social hooligans. Seatown has no sympathy at all for the modern 'head shrinking' approach to this grave problem.

Although such claims might be accurate in regard to the official media of public opinion and the professional moral entrepreneurs, my own evidence suggests that public opinion gravitated away from the extremes at both ends ('Clamp down, keep them out' and 'Welcome them') and took up an indeterminate position somewhere between apathy and the punitive extreme. In any event, the proposal left behind little sustained interest either among its formulators or the wider public and was not incorporated in any legislation. The group did, however, contribute to and to some extent institutionalize the already hostile atmosphere in the town towards young people, and its supporters were instrumental in denying facilities to an experimental youth project in Seatown.

The other action group I would like to consider met with roughly the same fate although it had more immediate impact, was more diverse in its aims and methods and set up a much more formal organizational framework. It is also of particular interest in providing an insight into the characteristics of an exemplary, if extreme, moral entrepreneur. This action group is the 'Beachside' Safeguard Committee.

Beachside had experienced the Mods and Rockers disturbances since their earliest beginnings in 1964. The resort was particularly affected in 1965 when the usual concern was voiced by Councillors and local newspapers. None of these protests was carried very far though, and it was only after incidents at Easter 1966 that any organized community action was taken. These incidents themselves were not very different from previous Bank Holidays, nor were many more arrests made. The moral enterprise of one individual – whom I shall call 'Geoffrey Blake' – was the new element in the situation. Although the following account of the action group draws upon a number of sources, the picture of Blake's own involvement derives entirely from a series of interviews with him during 1966.

Blake, the proprietor of a small private hotel near the seafront, had long felt that 'something should be done'. The Easter disturbances were the last straw; during and immediately after the weekend, he discussed his views with a friend, also a hotel owner. He decided that the best thing to do would be to call a public meeting. He had some experience in public relations and knew that this was the best way to get publicity. From the beginning, the campaign was run with a certain professionalism.

Letters were written 'on behalf of a group of private citizens' to various public figures and bodies inviting them to a public meeting to try to find 'a severe and final deterrent'; people were 'being frightened by these ignorant louts'. Letters went to the MP for Beachside, the Chief Constable, the Town

Clerk, the Clerk to the Magistrates and the Secretary of the Beachside Hotel Association. An advert was printed in the local paper calling the public to a meeting to discuss the 'scourge of the Mods and Rockers'. Blake obtained full national publicity, and before the meeting in April four national papers carried stories of the campaign. In the subsequent few weeks he gave two radio and four TV interviews, and claimed to have received 'about eighty' letters of support and 'numerous' phone calls from all over the country. All these sources congratulated him on his action as a public-spirited citizen, offered him various suggestions and wished him good luck 'with the cause'.

The meeting was attended by some four hundred members of the public and about the same number, according to Blake, had to be turned away. No official council representative attended. The meeting's chairman, elected from the floor (Beachside's Conservative MP for fifteen years until the previous election) said that he was 'astonished at what can only be called the virtual boycott of the meeting by leading citizens'. Blake attributed the council's boycott to their 'typical burying their heads in the sand attitude . . . they are right out of touch'. More realistically (in view of their subsequent co-operation) the eventual chairman of the Safeguard Committee, Mr 'Hale', attributed the council's boycott to their antagonism towards Blake's methods.[40] They resented his usurpation of their duties and his implication that they had failed to grasp the urgency of the problem.

The meeting discussed procedural questions, considered what sort of organization should be set up, and listened to concrete suggestions about what to do with the Mods and Rockers. The most favoured suggestion was reintroduction of the birch; other suggestions were: more severe fines, conscription and stopping the youths before they came into the town. In Blake's words 'it was generally waving the stick at them'.

The main outcome of the meeting was the formation of the Safeguard Committee aimed at putting the enterprise on a representative and organized basis. Its brief was to press civic leaders to inform the Home Secretary of the local demand for action: he should be pressed to 'restore law and order to this ancient County Borough'. The meeting also wanted to deplore the adverse publicity which had blown the matter up. The Committee consisted of some thirty members representing various local organizations: Chamber of Trade; Chamber of Commerce; Hotel and Guest House Association; Licensed Victuallers Association; Hotel and Restaurants Association; Ratepayers Association; Taxi Association; Motor Coach Association; Townswomen's Guild; Fruiterer's Guild; Newsagents Association; Amusement Parks Association, etc.

The Committee was broken down into a deputation of four under the chairmanship of Hale, a local businessman. The other members were Blake himself, a representative of the Chamber of Commerce and a representative of the Licensed Victuallers Association (an ex-policeman).

The deputation met a group of council officials: the Mayor, the Deputy Mayor, the Chairman and Deputy Chairman of the Watch Committee, the Town Clerk, the Deputy Town Clerk and the Chief Constable. The local paper reported that 'both sides drew a veil over the talks' (*'Beachside Mail'*, 20 May 1966) and no statements were made. Hale confirmed that the meeting was secret, but revealed that the police and corporation had given them a sympathetic hearing and had promised co-operation. The deputation in turn had conceded that their methods – particularly in calling a public meeting – were mistaken in appearing to put the council on trial.* Hints were made that among the plans considered was the use of helicopters to bring reinforcements and the application of strong-arm methods by the police to break up the gangs. Forms were obtained from the Chief Constable for the enrolment of fifty special constables to help the police during the approaching Whitsun weekend.

It is difficult to trace the history of the group beyond this stage. Whitsun was remarkably quiet in Beachside. It is extremely unlikely that this was due to the presence of special constables; the fact was that there were very few young people present at all to make any trouble.† Inquiries could not establish how many special constables were on duty, if any. If the young people were kept out of town by some other ingenious scheme, this was not generally known and, in any event, was either unsuccessful or not used in August when, in fact, there were considerable disturbances in the town. The Committee appears to have disintegrated, leaving behind, though, a fair impact on local opinion and having directly influenced policy at least temporarily. It is possible that the police and council would have acted without the Safeguard Committee but the Committee and all the publicity generated by Blake probably precipitated some action.

What sorts of individuals are the moving forces behind such action groups? Becker distinguished two species of moral entrepreneurs – rule enforcers (control agents) and rule creators. The prototype of the rule creator is the

---

* It is extremely unlikely that Blake himself made this concession; his whole enterprise was based on the perception that the authorities *had* failed.

† During a conversation with Blake over this weekend, he apologized that I had to travel all the way to Beachside and not see any trouble. Moral entrepreneurs have some interest in the continuation of the deviance they object to in order to justify their own actions.

moral crusader or crusading reformer; he is the man who, with an absolute ethic, sets out to eradicate the evil which disturbs him. Although Becker noted that not all supporters of moral crusades are so pure and single-minded in their motives, he did not describe these other types.

Supporters of the Mods and Rockers action groups may be divided into the genuine crusaders and the pragmatists. The crusader is moved by righteous indignation as well as self-interest. Unlike the pragmatist, he sees the action as a 'cause' or a 'mission' and he sees the enterprise as continuing even after the short-term goals are achieved. Indeed, objective evidence means little to him; as Smelser notes of norm-oriented beliefs in general: if evil occurs, it is as predicted, if not, plans were changed because of trickery.[41]

Typically also, the crusader sees beyond the immediate problem and locates it in a much wider context. Although individuals like Alderman K. showed some of these characteristics, it was Geoffrey Blake who clearly exemplified them all.

I would not want to claim that the following profile of Blake – drawn directly from interview notes – is typical of supporters or even crusaders. At the same time, Blake was 'representative' in the sense of personifying so many elements of the belief system about the Mods and Rockers.

Personal Information: Aged 40; working-class parents. On leaving school, served an apprenticeship; was active in the Union which he now thinks has 'gone to the dogs' since being absorbed into the bigger trade-union structure; the unions have got too powerful: 'It's another sign of the masses taking over, you lose your sense of identity in the bigger organization.' Navy during the war. Interested in music and entered into show business through jobs such as press agent and publicity manager. Eventually managed a famous pop star. Knows 'everything about the publicity world' and is cynical about it: 'there's nothing they won't do to get money. You can give me all this crap about the press and TV having a duty to the public, but really there's only one thing they're after and that's a good story to sell.' Bought the hotel 2½ years previously because he couldn't stand the pace of life in London; he wanted to slow down. Fond of Beachside and wouldn't go anywhere else in this country but wouldn't mind going to New Zealand or America. Sees himself as a candidate for emigration 'because of the way things here are going'.

Perception of the Problem: On the surface, he stresses that the protection of commercial interests is his main motive. He claims there is objective evidence for the incidents having affected the town's holiday trade: one sixty-bedroom hotel had only two bookings over Easter, his own bookings went down and he knows of other cancellations. A sea-front novelty shop which normally does £1,000 of business, took only £40. People 'had been terrorized by the mobs. In my hotel people were staying in the whole day; they were too terrified to move about . . . £4,000 has been lost through cancellations. In the fifteen weeks of the peak season, we have about 7,000 people per week down here. It's a family resort and they are the ones who are scared away. Must we lose these thousands of people and our living because of fifteen hundred to three thousand ignorant louts? And if we lose a thousand "innocent" Mods and Rockers, so what? . . . What we're trying to do in Beachside is to protect our safety and our town. All traders have to live and this is my home; they are therefore depriving me of my living. This is the most blatant misuse and abuse, what the trade unions would regard as the most serious crime possible: depriving a man of his living.'

It is clear, though, that Blake had other motives and orientations. 'It's not just the commercial questions; it's also a humiliation. I mean, that we should have to stand by and not be able to do anything.' The problem was not just Beachside's: 'It's not just our problem, it's a national problem and that's why I'm willing to give you all the information I can. Perhaps our experience will be able to help others . . . These hooligans are not just hooligans in Beachside, they're hooligans at home as well, during the week and not just Bank Holidays.' It was not just a question of damage or violence: '. . . authority was getting into disrespect. It was being blatantly refuted . . . this is like a disease running rife, if it goes unchecked, there's no knowing where it will end . . . This is mob rule and it must be brought to heel; you've got to start stemming the flood before it's too late . . . We must make some stand.'

Individual action had to be taken, because the 'powers that be' had failed to see the urgency of the problem. 'It's an immediate problem and therefore you have to take immediate steps – it's like road accidents: if you clamp a 15 m.p.h. speed limit everywhere, road deaths will immediately go down, it's as simple as that . . . You must look at it like this: there's a break in the dike and therefore you've got an immediate problem: how to stop up the dike. It's just this that the authorities don't see. It's no good sticking your head in the sand and putting across a high moral tone. This might pay off in ten years time, but it's no good *now*. You might be making things better for 1976, but it won't help in 1966. It's not that I don't think of these deeper implications . . . It's like a drowning man; he doesn't want to invest in a life boat . . . I know that to do your type of research properly it will take ten years to find things out, but what use is that to us now? . . . You need an emergency law, something like the Emergency Tax.'

How specifically had the official agents failed? 'The council have been blatantly inactive . . . They don't want to get their hands dirty. The police could aid us, but if you ask me, the Chief Constables are just concerned with keeping their crime rates down so they don't want many arrests; their heads are in the sand, just like anybody at Whitehall. Do you remember that film "Carlton-Browne of the F.O."? . . . they file something away and pretend it doesn't exist . . . they didn't even use the reserves over Easter. Mind you, the policemen themselves are doing great jobs, but their hands are tied. They're the ones who wear the handcuffs today, not the criminals . . . in the same way as the church has lost its power, so has the policeman.

'You've got to have the right line of authority to deal with this sort of thing – ripping up cinema seats. But if the police try to use their authority, you get cries about a "police state". This is just crap.'

The courts are also found wanting: 'There was this case last month of the Recorder commuting a six-month detention centre sentence to a fine . . . and then I heard a rumour that the £50 fine was not allowed because it was too difficult to collect . . . people don't see the need for a radical solution to a radical problem. Look at something like kicking a policeman in the face – you know what the sentence here for that was? A £2 fine.'

What sort of solution? Any solution had to be applied urgently and it had to be drastic. 'A serious problem demands a serious solution. Many solutions we have suggested have met with the cry about "protecting citizens' rights". They say we are taking civil liberty; but what about the terror they strike in others so you can't walk along the front safely? No sane man will attack someone and just beat him into the ground. You *have* to deal strongly with this lot.'

He favours most ideas put forward at the public meeting; above all, any method should affect the offender personally. 'Anything that's personal must work. That's why I'm sure that bringing back the birch will work; it must work. Take the Isle of Man; they used the birch when they had this trouble and as far as I know, none of those thugs ever went back. It's the only way: something personal, something that will hurt. It also doesn't cost the ratepayers much and it's also immediate and decisive and not long drawn out. Look, if you read in the paper "Two boys were birched at Beachside today", that's it, isn't it? It's not "Severe fines were imposed following incidents a week ago" which is then followed by an appeal!'

Blake also favoured schemes to exclude the Mods and Rockers from the town in the first place: 'Why not stop them before they come in? After all, an Englishman's home is his castle, and we're trying to protect our castle . . . I'd like to see them totally banned from Beachside . . . It would be quite easy: you just have to station a few policemen on the two bridges and roads leading into town. Yes, banning them would be just the job; I wouldn't mind if we had something like the Chateau D'If to send them to.'

Another effective means of punishment would be public ridicule: 'They should be exposed to public ridicule. This is what the Vicar suggested. He would like to see the pillory used; this would really work. They want to do things in public, therefore they should be ridiculed in public.'

Other innovatory ideas were '. . . to form some groups of citizens to go round inspecting things. If they saw anyone giving trouble, they could jump out of their car and clamp a heavy ball and chain on these thugs' feet, so heavy they couldn't walk. This would soon put a stop to it . . . or you could get hold of a corporation dustcart with a cage, put the thugs into this and drive them round the town.'

There were also suggestions to improve law enforcement by the police: 'Why was the Unlawful Assembly Law not put into action? A court could be set up in any public building and the court could then ban these people, take them to the town boundaries. Look it up in "Moriarty's Police Law" – the Riot Act, Unlawful Assembly, Breach of Peace – it's all there . . . the Police tried to keep them moving, but this isn't enough. They just moved up and down the front terrorizing people. Large police patrols with dogs would be just the thing. You see, dogs will bite immediately and you can't argue back to a dog. A bite or two and that's it.'

These and other measures should be applied to all the youths involved. 'It's all very well talking about getting the ringleaders, but I don't think this will get you anywhere. OK the German thing was caused by their leaders, but first you had to shoot the soldiers, didn't you? *Then* you get the leaders.'

His general viewpoint on punishment is that 'the public must know that their wrongs are being judged severely. It's like this dog here; if I tell him to jump down, he knows what will happen to him if he doesn't listen. And the same with my little boy; people do things if there's proper authority behind what they're told.

'You'll always have crime, I know that; people will chance anything, they'll chance their life even. But look at these Great Train Robbery sentences: thirty years: now if somebody's about to steal a 3/6 Post Office book, he'll think about those thirty years before he does anything. Or take the abolition of hanging. You blokes say that you can show statistics to prove that hanging doesn't make any difference; well I don't know if it does good in *general*. But if it saves ten out of 200 that's enough, isn't it? . . . All the world is busy turning the other cheek, but there are some things you have to rebuff . . . I like the idea of these road gangs in Finland: my brother came back from a holiday there and told me how they get them all on the road gangs; traffic offenders and all. They say there is much less crime there now. Or take Saudi Arabia, where they cut off a hand for theft; that must be effective! . . . You see, what the brains of the country are forgetting is what *we* feel like. They have to try and do something; the government is so damn inactive that they don't care for the people, they don't bear them in mind.'

Perception of Causes: Immediate factors were important, for example, the publicity and the influence of the mob: 'The mass hysteria gets them; you see bank clerks dressed up as Mods. They do things they wouldn't do by themselves.' But there are fundamental, long-term causes: 'Basically, I think it all stems from boredom. Boredom, plus the affluent society, this is the basic problem. If they had to work they would have no time for all this . . . there's too much done for them and therefore they've got time and money on their hands. The automation and everything must make them bored with life; craftsmanship is gone, everything is mass produced. And they just have to switch on the TV to be entertained. You've got to keep them away from all sorts of temptation, just like the cows you keep away with an electric fence . . . What else do they have to do except sign on at the Labour? They don't even have to do it twice a week now. This is a national problem; if Labour gets back again, this country will go to complete economic ruin, and then they'll have to work, won't they? It might be a good thing from this point of view.

'We've got to deal with it severely now, but this doesn't mean that I don't see the roots of the trouble; which is that we've let them down. It's neglect by their parents, that's what it is, a sheer lack of interest. There's no sense of authority any more; at home there's too much familiarity with "mum" and "dad" and this leads to contempt of all authority . . . There's no respect any more for law and order. It's really a question of the masses taking over. You have some Four Star hotels in Beachside, in the old days you had to be somebody to get in there, now anyone can go, there's no more respect . . . All this business about giving them a vote at eighteen. What ideas do they have at eighteen? You'll be having a Mod as Prime Minister next. It's mass rule like the masses of the Chinese; it's going to get just the same here with no birth control being used . . . There is too much emphasis on the mass; you have all these coloured people coming in here. Well, I don't want to live with them, Japs or anyone else. They've got their own places; Ghana, Palestine, these places have got home rule now, so these people should go back to their origins. But MPs are too concerned with national issues to see these things; they don't see that people in their own constituencies don't want, for example, to live with immigrants . . . The power of the trade unions is another thing, they now rule the world; the mass is ruled by the mass . . . Public opinion? Well, the way public opinion works is like this: the intelligent people think about something, then the less intelligent, then the even less intelligent, and then the voters! I'm going to live in the jungle if the country goes on like this; we're going back, I'm sure of that. It's nothing but mob rule; for the mob is ruling and Trafalgar Square is their rebel headquarters.

'When there were troubles after the First World War, people said, "It's the aftermath of the war" and they've used the same excuse after the last war. But it's been twenty years now, so there must be other causes; though perhaps we're due for another war now . . . You can spend ten years trying to find out these deep causes, but for us it's an immediate problem; we've got to earn our livelihood.'

The profile is partly one of an archetypal moral crusader, who is fighting for a 'cause' and 'making a stand'. In this respect, Blake shares much with the more respectable crusaders of our time – the Mary Whitehouses, the Lord Longfords, the Cyril Blacks: single-mindedness, dedication, self-righteousness, a tendency to exaggerate grossly and over-simplify even more so. But in addition, the profile is familiar enough to those acquainted with the authoritarian personality syndrome and its correlates: cynicism and destructiveness, authoritarian submission, extreme punitiveness, puritanism, racial prejudice,* fear of the

---

* Blake apparently experienced little dissonance between cognition and behaviour in regard to this attitude. Some time after these interviews, he received national publicity again, this time for asking a West Indian guest to leave his hotel. Blake announced that his policy was not to accept coloured or foreign guests. This incident was one of the first of its kind

masses and projection. I must repeat that I am not suggesting that this constellation of attitudes typifies moral panics in general or will always be found in the control culture dealing with such folk devils as the Mods and Rockers. The central role, though, played by individuals such as Blake in cases of moral enterprise needs to be studied; this implies looking at the type of society in which such attitudes originate and which subsequently allocates to the individuals who embody them, key parts in its ceremonies of social control.

I will conclude this section by considering how much of this agitation and action group activity permeated through to bodies such as the legislature to which the appeals were ultimately addressed. At the most elementary level, individual MPs clearly took an immediate and considerable interest in disturbances in their own constituencies. Their appeals were similar to those of others in calling for the suprasystem to take over or augment emergency system arrangements. Immediately after Clacton, the MP for Harwich urged stiffer penalties and said that he would welcome an opportunity to discuss the matter with the Home Secretary. He assured local traders and hoteliers that their commercial interests would be protected and that the hooliganism would not happen again. He specifically proposed to increase the penalty for malicious damage exceeding £20, to a prison sentence of up to five years. At the same time, the Home Secretary called for reports on the outbreaks and other MPs made generalized appeals: 'Jail These Wild Ones – Call by M.P.s' (*Daily Mirror*, 1 April 1964).

As the events built up, appeals became more specific, more influenced by the belief system, and articulated in a more formalized framework. After Whitsun 1964, full reports from the affected areas were sent to the Home Secretary and arrangements were made for a joint meeting of Chief Constables. One MP forecast that the wave of hooliganism could become a general election issue and tabled a series of questions, including a suggestion that the police should be given new powers to act against those who incite their companions to violence, without being actually involved themselves. Other MPs announced that they intended calling for a return of corporal punishment for hooliganism. A Brighton MP came to London after watching the weekend events to put questions to the Prime Minister. His idea was to revive the type of National Service Act which sent Bevin Boys to work in the mines and other types of national non-military service. There should also be 'reconditioning

referred to the Race Relations Board and was used as the test case to establish whether anti-discrimination legislation applied to private hotels.

centres' like those run by the Ministry of Labour in the days of pre-war unemployment. The boys could be drafted into building projects, and become the equivalent of the Foreign Legion. If necessary, this labour could be used for building the Channel Tunnel. This MP had a private meeting with the Home Secretary in which plans were proposed to establish police reinforcements in camps on the South Downs during Bank Holiday weekends. Forces ready to move at a moment's notice could be drafted from London. Although this might have occurred without the MP's intervention, this policy was put into practice by the next Bank Holiday.

After the initial events of 1964, the subject of the Mods and Rockers directly or indirectly entered into Parliament in the following sequence:

31 March: Drugs (Prevention of Misuse) Bill published.

8 April; House of Lords: Earl of Arran tables resolution calling for the raising of the minimum driving licence age for certain vehicles from 16 to 19 '. . . in view of the invasion of Clacton by young motor cyclists on Easter Sunday and the consistently heavy casualty rates among the youngest age groups.'

15 April; House of Commons: Mr Frank Taylor tables resolution 'That this House in the light of the deplorable and continual increase in juvenile delinquency and in particular the recent regrettable events in Clacton urges the Secretary of State for Home Department to give urgent and serious consideration to the need for young hooligans to be given such financial and physical punishment as will provide an effective deterrent.'

27 April; House of Commons: Two hour debate on Mr Gurden's notion, 'Juvenile Delinquency and Hooliganism'.

4 June; House of Commons: 'Seaside Resorts (Hooliganism)': statement by the Home Secretary.

4 June; House of Lords: 'Hooliganism and Increased Penalties' (statement by Home Secretary read).

23 June; House of Commons: Malicious Damage Bill, Second Reading.

2 July; House of Commons: Malicious Damage Bill, Third Reading.

The Drugs (Prevention of Misuse) Bill was obviously conceived and drafted well before the Clacton event a few days earlier. The Bill, nevertheless, was presented by the mass media *as if* it were a result of what had happened at

Clacton and, moreover, its supporters justified it by employing images from the Mods and Rockers inventory.

Clacton, in fact, provided one of the first big scares about drug use among juveniles. Press headlines such as 'Purple Heart Happy Hoodlums' and 'Drug Crazed Youths' were fairly common and concern was expressed that there was a causal connection between pep pills and hooliganism. A local MP wrote: 'One of the difficulties was that these young people had taken purple hearts . . . there was undoubtedly a man selling purple hearts along the front at the time and it was felt that very strong action should be taken against him.'[42]

There was little evidence of much drug usage at Clacton; there is even less evidence of any causal connection between hooliganism and the use of amphetamines.* The result of all the publicity, however, was massive support for what *The Times* (31 March 1964) called 'hastily constructed legislation' and *The Economist* (4 April 1964) 'a singularly ill-conceived bill'. Whatever else it was, the Bill (which aimed to reduce peddling by increasing the penalties for possession to fines of up to £200 and/or six months in prison) was not effective; the next three years saw a rapid increase in the amount of drug usage in seaside towns. There was an apparently random relationship between policy and problem in the sense that a patently ineffective policy was supported, partly at least, for the 'wrong' reasons, whereas, when the 'right' reasons presented themselves, no policy was forthcoming.

The first actual parliamentary debate on the Mods and Rockers took place a month after Clacton. The debate was on a motion, from Mr Harold Gurden, noting '. . . with concern the continuing increase in juvenile crime and outbreaks of hooliganism among young people' and calling for more intensive measures to deal with the problem. The context of this motion was clear: 'I use the word hooliganism, as implying vandalism in the context of the recent events at Clacton, where, I was glad to learn today, the courts have imposed heavy fines on those concerned.'[43]

There was nothing in this two-hour debate – from which I have quoted extracts in Chapter 3 – to suggest that MPs were in any way immune from

---

* A research report[44] on the association between amphetamines and general delinquency does in fact quote a case of a boy who took large dosages at both the Clacton and Brighton events in 1964. There is no evidence, though, that such a pattern is typical; in any event, the amphetamine users in the research sample were not any more likely to have committed violent crimes than the non-users. The authors' conclusion that any relationship between delinquency and drug-taking is parallel rather than causative is borne out by observation at the resorts.

absorbing the inventory images. In the course of this long debate, though, the seaside incidents were mentioned explicitly only five times and the term 'Mods and Rockers' not at all. Apparently, there had not yet been time for symbolization to take its full effect. Two months later, during the second reading of the Malicious Damage Bill, the images had crystallized; twelve of the sixteen Members spoke about the seaside resort events and seven specifically referred to 'Mods and Rockers'. All other symbols were also more sharply drawn.

At times of moral panic, politicians in office, even though one might expect them on the basis of their personal records to be full of moral indignation, often act to 'calm things down' and minimize the problem. Thus it was with the Home Secretary, Mr Henry Brooke, the only participant in the first debate who expressed an awareness of the exaggerations and distortions.

> Some of the reports of what happened at Clacton over the Easter weekend were greatly exaggerated . . . At Clacton more than 1,000 young people came by one means or another, apparently with little money on them, intending to sleep wherever they could find some form of shelter. The weather was bad over the Easter weekend and there was little or nothing to do. They became bored, tempers flared and a certain amount of fighting broke out. There was nothing like a riot or gang warfare. Clacton was not sacked.[45]

He went on to note that acts of assault, theft or malicious damage were isolated and committed by a small group of individuals. After the Whitsun events, he made a formal statement in response to nine specific questions that had been tabled. The statement again noted that the numbers involved were not large, paid tribute to the work of the police, endorsed the salutary deterrent effect of sharp sentences and, while rejecting suggestions for giving the courts more powers (such as confiscation of vehicles and corporal punishment), proposed to deal with malicious damage.[46]

The decision to focus on malicious damage is interesting in view of the fact that in the earlier debate, the Home Secretary had specifically stated that the penalties for dealing with vandalism were entirely adequate and he did not see the need for changes in the law. A few weeks later, under the immediate influence of the Whitsun inventory, he announced that he would ask Parliament to widen and strengthen the powers of the courts. The Malicious Damage Bill was introduced soon afterwards and became effective on 31 July.[47]

It was clear from the Home Secretary's original statement and the subsequent debate on the second reading that, while the Act was obviously to

apply to vandalism in general, it was an emergency measure directed specifically at the Mods and Rockers. As such it may be seen as a normative
formalization by the control culture, and the Act was justified by MPs and
others almost wholly by appeal to the belief system. It would be a severe
deterrent against violence and vandalism; it would 're-establish and reinforce
the principle of personal responsibility';[48] it recognized the affluence of the
potential offenders: 'We must not forget that many of these youngsters are
the sons and daughters of comparatively well-to-do people. All that is necessary
in their case once they are fined is to get their parents to pay the fine so that
their little darlings can go free. There is no punishment for these youngsters
at all.'[49]

The measures were exclusively hailed as direct reprisals against the Mods
and Rockers: 'Brooke Hits Hooligans in the Pocket', 'Brooke Rocks the
Rockers', 'New Move to Stamp Out Mod Violence', etc. The specificity of the
Act was shown in Mr Brooke's own statement: 'I hope that, with the help of
the House, it [the Act] will be in operation before the August Bank Holiday.'[50]

This statement underlines the ritualistic element in the Bill which, even
on admission of its supporters, proposed fairly modest changes. In fact,
the legislative changes took place in direct response to the demands to the
suprasystem for 'something to be done – and soon'. As the Home Secretary
stated:

> I want the Bill also to be a reassurance to the long-suffering public. They
> were long-suffering at these holiday places, for many of them had their
> Whitsun holidays or their Whitsun trade spoiled by these young fools. I
> want to reassure them by showing them that the Government means
> business.

This reassurance was a true ritualistic response to deviance in the sense that
Cohen intended: '. . . affirmations and gestures of indignation by means of
which one aligns oneself symbolically with the angels, without having to take
up cudgels against the devil.'[51] Whatever the 'devil' was in the seaside resorts,
it was not primarily vandalism. Parliament was not simply being misled by
inventory exaggeration of the amount of vandalism; the two Members
representing seaside resorts who spoke during the debate, went out of their way
to inform the House that, in fact, there was very little damage done: 'in the main
the Bill deals only with damage, there was practically no damage done in
Brighton';[52] 'I know that Brighton, which is a much bigger place, had all the
damage and we had relatively little, with much talk and not very much harm.'[53]

The explanation for directing exclusive normative control against what was really putative deviation, lies in the nature of vandalism as the most visible manifestation of the phenomenon and the one most calculated to evoke social condemnation.[54] To align oneself symbolically with the angels, one had to pick on an easy target; the fact that the target hardly existed was irrelevant; it could be, and already had been, defined.

To summarize this long section on the control culture: the official reaction to the Mods and Rockers was mediated by a belief system and in turn generated a set of beliefs to rationalize the control methods used. The methods and beliefs were supplemented by the not altogether successful attempts by unofficial agents to create an exclusive control culture. A few rules were created – mostly ritualistic in nature and not evidently effective – and these survived beyond the period of their initial usage. More to the point, the whole amalgam of the societal reaction survived its origins in the form of mythologies and stereotypes about the folk devils it had partly created.

The burden of my analysis in the next chapter will be to show that the reaction did not have its intended or anticipated effect, but, in fact, increased or amplified the deviance. Before going on to this, one further element in the reaction to deviance, exploitation, needs some attention.

The Exploitative Culture

Without defining precisely what he meant, Lemert drew attention to the phenomenon of *deviance exploitation*.[55] His examples of the special exploitative culture which surrounds deviants were confined mainly to direct exploitation on the basis of the deviant's marginal status or aspirations to normality. Thus, the physically deformed, the aged, widows, the mentally ill, members of minority groups, ex-convicts, are preyed upon by fraudulent individuals and organizations, offering patent medicines, faith cures, youth restorers, skin lighteners and other treatments or services. Not all exploitation is so crude though; there is also what Lemert called 'the socioeconomic symbiosis between criminal and non-criminal groups'.[56] This refers to the direct or indirect profit derived from crime by persons such as bankers, criminal lawyers, corrupt policemen, court officials and lawyers involved in 'fixes'.

I will categorize these types of exploitation (to which Lemert and Goffman tend to confine their remarks) as *commercial exploitation*. There is another exploitative pattern, though, in the use of the deviant in communication, particularly public, to defend or announce an ideology, for example, religious or political. The latter is illustrated in Erikson's study of the early Puritans' reactions to various forms of religious deviance.[57] This pattern is exploitative in the sense that the deviant is being used for societally defined ends without any regard to the consequences of this on the deviant himself. I will refer to this type as *ideological exploitation*. Another type, which may contain both ideological and commercial elements, is the exploitation of the deviant as an object of amusement or ridicule. The historical case of hunchbacks being used as court jesters has its contemporary variants in the practice of exhibiting those with more bizarre physical deformities at circuses and fairgrounds.

The commercial exploitation of folk devils such as the Mods and Rockers is obviously linked with the general market in teenage consumer goods. While the stereotype of the scheming millionaires who 'exploit' innocent teenagers into buying clothes and records against their will is grossly oversimplified, it is nevertheless clear that the market is quick to seize a peg on which to display its products. (A well-known non-commercial salesman, Billy Graham, promised, before his 1966 visit to London, to preach on the theme 'Mods and Rockers for Christ'.)

The Mods and Rockers division was ready-made for such exploitation, and commercial interests were able to widen this division by exaggerating consumer style differences between the two groups. Special Mod boutiques, dance halls and discotheques were opened, a book was published called *Dances for Mods and Rockers*, and in at least one large dance hall in South London, a white-painted line was drawn in the middle of the floor to separate the Mods and Rockers. Consumer goods were advertised using the group images; some of the very shops in Brighton which had protested about loss of trade caused by the disturbances were selling 'The Latest Mod Sunglasses'. Clubs and coffee bars in seaside resorts were advertised as 'The Top Mod Spot of the South' or 'The Mods' Own Club'.

This type of symbiotic relationship between the condemners and the condemned, the 'normal' and the 'deviant', was shown nowhere more clearly than in the mass media treatment of the Mod–Rocker differences. The *Daily Mail* quiz 'Are You A Mod or Rocker?', published immediately after Clacton, was only the most notorious example of this. The whole inventory phase may be seen as an exploitation or manipulation of symbols by the mass media; even symbols at times must be seen to stand for some real event, person or idea, and if these did not manifest themselves, then they had to be manufactured.

Seaside resorts were invariably full of journalists and photographers, waiting for something to happen, and stories, poses and interviews would be extracted from the all too willing performers. One journalist recalls being sent, in response to a cable from an American magazine, to photograph Mods in

Piccadilly at five o'clock on a Sunday morning, only to find a team from *Paris Match* and a full film unit already on the spot. 'Mod hunting,' as he remarks, 'was at that time a respectable, almost crowded subprofession of journalism.'[58] The fact that those who were hunted were willing performers, does not make the pattern any less exploitative; presumably hunchbacks were not always unwilling to perform the jester role. A boy persuaded by a photographer to pose kicking a telephone kiosk, is in a real sense being used. It is clear that people who denounce deviance may at the same time have a vested interest in seeing deviance perpetuated, at least temporarily, until the phenomenon loses its 'sales value'.*

Ideological exploitation involves a similar ambivalence in the sense that the exploiter 'gains' from his denunciation of deviance and would 'lose' if the deviance proved, in fact, to be less real and less of a problem than is functional for his ideology. This type of exploitation occurs as part of the sensitization process as it involves the use of the Mods and Rockers symbols in previously neutral contexts. At annual meetings of Chambers of Commerce, Boy Scout and Air Training Corps ceremonies, school prize-givings, mayoral inaugurations and in numerous other public contexts, the Mods and Rockers symbols were used to make an ideological point. Audiences were told what to do to prevent themselves or others from becoming Mods and Rockers or were congratulated on not already being Mods and Rockers. The events and their symbolic connotations were used to justify previous positions or support new ones:

> The men in the B.B.C. who feed violence, lust, aimlessness and cynicism into millions of homes nightly must squarely consider their responsibility.

> One of the main reasons for what happened is the present Government's attitude to working-class adolescents as fair game for blatant exploitation by commercial interests.

> . . . consider now the effect of TV violence in relation to happenings at Brighton and Margate and use your great power to help provide an answer.

---

* Social scientists are clearly not immune from this sort of involvement with their subject matter. The researcher who, in spite of himself, hopes that the phenomenon will take a particular form in order to prove his theories or give him some other more ideological satisfaction, is only the more obvious example of this and I cannot claim that I always viewed the Mods and Rockers without any such involvement. When the object of study is deviance, there is the risk of other sorts of involvement. As one researcher[59] notes: 'Many criminologists have an intense (and perhaps vicarious) personal interest in the criminal exploits of their subjects. Many are intrigued voyeurs of the criminal world.'

The true criminals are the maladministrators of this country, an inadequate educational system, lack of decent housing and all the amenities that make a decent citizen.[60]

Exploitation was often for more specific ends: the President of the National Association of Chief Educational Welfare Officers called for more officers to be recruited: 'The matter is urgent if we wish to avoid these Clacton and Brighton affairs spreading into other parts of the country.' Similarly a Marriage Guidance Council called for volunteers to run group discussions for young people. Numerous youth clubs called for more funds to build up facilities which would prevent the Mods and Rockers 'disease' from spreading. All such appeals, which, of course, negatively polarized the Mods and Rockers even further, were made in terms of interest group perspectives (particularly useful for political parties as 1964 was election year). The fact that the deviance was reacted to in terms of such perspectives, and that the Mods and Rockers were all things to all people, was shown in those instances where the Mods and Rockers, instead of being denounced, were welcomed for ideological reasons. So, for example, some of the Provos and members of the Destruction in Art movement hailed the Mods and Rockers as the *avant-garde* of the anarchist revolution. On his arrival in London, the Provo leader, Bernard de Vries, was optimistic about the spread of the movement in Britain and was sure that if the Mods and Rockers were given opportunities for demonstrations and happenings, they would turn pacifist.[61]

Like other aspects of the societal reaction, the exploitative culture both reflects and – as the next chapter considers – creates the amplification of deviance. What I have suggested in this chapter is that, in addition to the ordinary deviation amplification sequence (initial deviance, societal reaction, increase in deviance, increase in reaction, etc.), a similar process is at work within the reaction itself. This is indicated, during the moral panic, by the presence within the control culture of such features as sensitization, diffusion, escalation, dramatization and exploitation. These were parasitic on each other, as were the different groups of reactors: for example, the media reacting not so much to the deviance, but to what the magistrates said the deviance was. Thus, almost independent of the deviance, the reactors amplified the situation. One of the flows that can be visualized runs something like this:

(i) *Initial deviance* leading to:
(ii) the *inventory* and (iii) *sensitization* which feed back on each other so as to produce:

(iv) an *over-estimation* of the deviance which leads to:

(v) an *escalation* in the control culture.

Such escalation (in addition to feeding back on the other reaction stages, for example, by proving that the deviance *is* threatening enough to require all this effort) affects the way in which the deviance itself develops, the subject of the next chapter.

5 On the Beaches: The Warning and the Impact

This is the point at which to return to the 'impact phase', the original scene of each event, and observe something of the interaction between the various audiences and actors involved. How was the stage set? How were the crowd scenes (there were few leading roles) played out? How did the various elements in the societal reaction – media, control agents – influence what was happening?

After this chapter, the disaster sequence will have to be abandoned and the dramatalurgical analogy will also have nearly exhausted its utility. What have been visualized as audiences and actors will have to be analysed as occupants of particular positions – young, old, middle class, working class – in a particular society, England – at a particular time, the 1960s. But for the time being the dramatalurgical analogy is far from played out; indeed, more than at any other point in the narrative is it justified to use the language of the theatre to describe what was happening. In a real sense, being on the beaches was being on stage.

Setting the Stage: The Warning Phase

For a very obvious reason, disaster researchers have devoted considerable attention to studying the warning phase: reactions to warnings are crucial in determining the effects of the disaster. Research has concentrated on the stages in the psychological reaction to threat, paying particular attention to the defence and coping mechanisms which inhibit a realistic assessment of the approaching disaster.[1] The culmination of a sequence involving recognition and validation of the appropriate cues, the expression of emotional responses such as fear and anxiety and a definition of the alternative actions available in the situation, may be disbelief or distortion (the danger will occur later than expected, it will be worse elsewhere). The eventual outcome depends on factors such as set or anxiety level ('if a person is "set" to expect a disaster a minor suggestion will raise the probabilities of occurrence in his mind considerably so that reaction to the disaster, whether it is imminent or not, is precipitated'[2]) and familiarity with similar situations.

While parallel processes developed in the warning before each Mods and Rockers event, a crucial difference was that there were very few of the factors tending to produce denial, disbelief, defence and other such end-products described in disaster research. There was little warning before the initial Clacton event, but the inventory build-up and reaction to this and subsequent events was such that the widely disseminated warnings and threats were generally believed. Few were predisposed to erect the elaborate defence mechanisms that are used, for example, to discount the possibility of nuclear warfare. The inventory, particularly the prediction factor, was crucial in building up a reaction to deviance identical to the sensitization which occurs in an 'effective' disaster warning:

> If a threat cannot be denied, there is likely to be an increased sensitization to the danger, so that cues to danger result in overreaction and emotional and sometimes precipitous behaviour. Where threat cannot be dis-counted, aggressive and projective behaviours begin to develop and scapegoating, polarising of antagonists, and other hate and fear situations are generated.[3]

The analogy between the warning phase of a natural disaster and a situation close to the Mods and Rockers disturbances is also used by Thompson in his description of the tension in a resort prior to an expected Hells Angels invasion: 'As the weekend began, the atmosphere at Bass Lake was reminiscent of a Kansas hamlet preparing for a tornado.'[4]

Such elements could be observed throughout the whole sequence of the reaction to the Mods and Rockers, and they were condensed and concertinaed before each single event. As such, they were part of the general sensitization process already described, but two further unfolding features of the warning phase need to be noted. The first is the tendency for the warning system to become more complicated and formalized and to start earlier; the second is the increasingly unreal and ritualistic nature of the system as evidenced by the number of false alarms and warnings out of proportion to the imminent threat.

Initially, the warning system operated only locally and was confined to certain seaside resorts on the south coast. Although there was nothing intrinsic in the Clacton event to expect that it would be repeated, the way it was reacted to made the threat of a repeat performance very real to the other resorts. It needed only one interview with a Rocker who said (or who was quoted as saying) 'Next time Brighton will get it' to increase the threat. The atmosphere of expectation and apprehension before the Bank Holiday immediately after Clacton can be gauged from the local press at the time.

A few days before Whitsun, a Brighton paper carried a story headed: 'Rioting Rockers Plan Raid on Brighton Soon' (*Evening Argus*, 13 May 1964). It was claimed that a number of seaside towns had been warned by letter and anonymous phone calls that they would be targets for the next Mods and Rockers 'invasion'. Details were given of police preparations ('we will crack down on them immediately') and on the Saturday, there was another report 'Seaside Towns Ready for Trouble' in which it was disclosed that police leave had been cancelled in Brighton, Eastbourne and other resorts. At about the same time an editorial in another Brighton paper (*Brighton and Hove Gazette*, 15 May 1964) carried a warning about '. . . the riot-raising Rockers who, rumour has it, have it in mind to do a Clacton on Brighton'. In case the action properties of this warning cue had not been assimilated by the public, readers were urged: '. . . if they see signs of a "little Clacton" brewing, they should give the police their active support in reporting it.' This type of warning is equivalent to inhabitants of a flood area being told to evacuate when sirens sound; but while their evacuation would *reduce* the effects of the disaster, the Brighton inhabitants, sensitized to report signs of a 'little Clacton' would, in fact, *create* deviance in something like the original sense suggested in the transactional approach. This is the paradox intrinsic in moral panics.

Warnings in Margate at that time were more specific as there had been minor incidents there over Easter. The build-up in the *Isle of Thanet Gazette* in April and May, with articles such as 'Put Them in the Stocks', and stories of local vigilantes, leaves little doubt that the Mods and Rockers were expected. As early as 3 April an editorial noted that the Easter hooliganism '. . . can be construed as a foretaste of the type of behaviour which will be rife on our seafronts during the coming holiday season, unless swift and effective action is taken right now . . .'.

After the second wave of incidents confirmed expectations, warnings became articulated at a much broader level. The national press and other sources of public opinion made it clear that the Mods and Rockers were now an institutionalized threat to seaside resorts. Symbolization made the cues for recognizing incipient deviance ('little Clactons') much easier to pick up.

Warnings were sounded earlier and the threat was expressed in terms of certainty and not probability. So, by August 1965, the *Evening Standard* (27 August 1965) carried a prominent report describing police preparations and quoted a police spokesman about leave being cancelled '. . . as a precaution against the *usual* riots between rival teenage gangs' (emphasis added).

As the societal control culture moved towards diffusion, escalation and innovation, so did the warning system become more formalized and bureaucratized. Shortly before August Bank Holiday, 1964, the Home Office Airborne Police Scheme to fly reinforcements in RAF Transport Command, was publicized. A local paper, in a report headed 'Town Is Ready For All Comers' announced that besides elaborate police preparations, special arrangements had been made to open the Town Hall courtroom over the weekend. (*Hastings and St Leonards Observer*, 1 April 1965). These were not only warnings but stage-setting ceremonies: there was no doubt that the show would take place, one just had to make sure that the folk devils and their denouncers would have the appropriate arenas for their performance.

Certain Chief Constables institutionalized the practice of formal press conferences to explain preparations. Elaborate plans were made well in advance and national institutions such as the Home Office began to take a co-ordinating role. These 'secret' plans were judiciously leaked well before the expected event ostensibly to warn the Mods and Rockers what was in store for them, but also to reassure the public that something was being done. A week before Easter 1965, the *Sunday Telegraph* (11 April 1965) carried a detailed report of a Home Office conference the previous week attended by the Commissioner of Police and Chief Constables from all forces in southern England which might be affected. At the same time in Clacton, arrangements were made to station a squad on the main road junction on the outskirts of the town to transmit warnings to a seafront patrol equipped with walkie-talkie sets. In 1966 an even more sophisticated warning system was set up. The Chief Constable of Hastings revealed at a conference of senior police officers at Leicester University that a secret network of plain-clothes police and informers were operating in clubs and coffee bars.[5] Agents who had infiltrated the ranks of Mods were passing information direct to Scotland Yard and had apparently noticed a sinister development – the rise of self-appointed mob leaders. According to the Chief Constable, danger signs of this advanced planning could have been noticed well in advance at football riots and the organized interruption of political meetings during the General Election. The police now had their own early warning system to detect such signs: 'These people will not be able to get together without our knowing something about it beforehand.'*

As in the cases of mass delusion described previously, the situation was ambiguous enough to allow for a number of false alarms to occur. Unfulfilled expectations, however, did not lead to a breakdown in the warning system or the erection of psychological defences against threat; if things did not happen, this could be explained in terms of the effectiveness of the deterrent ('they know we won't stand for them in X') or a change in the invasion plan. When public interest in the Mods and Rockers died down, and there was consequently less need for such rationalizations, the warnings became less publicized – despite the fact that the behaviour itself had not considerably changed its pattern. The deviance was now a regular occurrence, so there was no need for formal warnings. One merely had to consult a calendar to find out the date of the next show.

The Crowd Scenes

What happened and what was the atmosphere during the impact phase of a typical incident? The first feature to be noted was that in every instance, the young people present constituted a crowd or series of interlocking crowds, rather than a group (or gang) or even less, two highly structured opposing groups (or gangs). In terms of the organizational criteria used by sociologists to define such phenomena,[6] the collectivities were at the least defined ends of the continua, and were far removed from the image of cohesive gangs presented in the inventory. Leadership was more spontaneous, actions were more momentary and less premeditated, emotions were more transitory, organization was weaker and goals were less clearly defined than most descriptions of the incidents using the 'warring gangs' image, lead one to believe.

Neither could the crowds be characterized in terms of the classic stereotypes of crowd or mob mentality. There was little of the initial psychological homogeneity which is supposed to characterize such groupings, and there was a considerable range in background and motivation. Homogeneity developed only through continued interaction and even at the peaks of crowd activity

---

* See Withey's remarks about 'overreaction' and emotional behaviour. One might speculate that such fantasies about planning (cabalism) and spies infiltrating coffee bars, provided control agents with a satisfaction analogous to gang-leaders' fantasies about gang life.

there were very diverse patterns of participation. These were not like revolutionary crowds or lynch mobs, but, on the whole, a series of passive and uncertain groups waiting to be entertained.

Passivity and expectancy were the dominant moods, and the context – the ritual Bank Holiday weekend by the sea – was one of leisure and entertainment. Brighton, Clacton, Margate, Southend – whatever the differences between them – share common characteristics on these occasions: a certain shabbiness, the overstrained and overpriced commercial facilities, a strange sensation of crowds moving almost randomly around you, and the all-pervasive smell of onions, hot dogs and fish and chips, the sense of cheapness and somehow having been cheated.[7]

But while Graham Greene was right in detecting a certain desperate air in the search for pleasure at these times, such moods are balanced by the positive exaltation produced by being away from home, from responsibilities, from routine.[8] For the kids coming down to the resorts during those heady years of the mid-sixties, the weekend was an event, a happening, a ceremony which, in some senses, was affirmative. This was where the action was. It was the action of consumption which Goffman talks about when describing the 'fancy milling' process in such crowd settings:

> . . . mere presence in a large, slightly packed gathering of revelling persons can bring not only the excitement that crowds generate, but also the uncertainty of not quite knowing what might happen next, the possibility of flirtations, which can themselves lead to relationship formation, and the lively experience of being an elbow away from someone who does manage to find real action in the crowd.[9]

Such generalized processes have to be put in their specific cultural setting and seen at a particular time in history: the point at which a whole new generation was beginning to define just simply *being present in a crowd* as an event. The pop concert, the love-in, the happening and (most appropriately named of all) the be-in, could be events even if, and perhaps especially if, nothing at all happened. One was just with others. The only structure was that brought to the event by its participants.

Now while the Mods and Rockers scenes were every bit as unstructured as this, most of the crowd – with the exception of the constant beatnik population and the hippies and flower children of the later years – had not quite reached the cultural sophistication by which non-action is defined as action. Their aim was excitement, but for most of the time nothing happened and so the dominant feelings were boredom, listlessness, ennui, a sense of drifting aim-lessness and lack of any specific plans. In these respects, of course, the kids were not much different from most adults on holiday at any time. But this mood was missed by the outsider because it clearly was incongruent with the folk devil image.

The following conversation, overheard between two 15-year-old girls huddled together on a windswept Brighton beach, conveys something of this tone:

First Girl: What's the time?
Second Girl: Three o'clock.
First: Blimey, we don't have to sit around here for another three hours, do we?
Second: We could get a train before.
First: Well, but you never know.

(*Notes*, Easter Sunday, 1966)

Let me quote two further examples, one from the notes of a youth worker on the Archways project, the other from a journalist:

> I asked them why they had come down. Many didn't know, but from later conversation, I gathered it was to pick up girls. Some came because they went to Clacton last year and Margate the year before; some came because everyone else was coming. I asked them where they had planned to sleep. Few had planned anything; they'd expected to find a spot on the beach. Few had considered cold weather or rain. Some had come without even a blanket . . . The general impression I formed of what they actually did in Brighton was rather hazy. 'Nothing', was the usual response. They seemed to wander about rather aimlessly; they were bored and cold . . .[10]

> I asked an Eltham boy whether he was enjoying himself. 'Not really.' Why did he come then, when this was all he knew he could find? 'There's nothing doing in London.' But what is there doing anywhere that you'd like to do? 'Well, if you put it like that, there isn't.'[11]

There are two significant points to be made about such reports. The first is the total and almost cynical awareness by the kids of what their situation was: a boy who said to me, 'Well, we're bored at home, so it's a change to come down here and be bored at Brighton,' was being more than a little serious. Then, there was the apparent lack of understanding by outside observers as to why such feelings were dominant at all. These feelings can make sense as I will suggest in the next chapter, in terms of the discontinuities in leisure values stressed in Downes's theory of fringe working-class delinquency.

This boredom was accompanied, though, by the perpetual hope (which, under the impact of the inventory and the subsequent societal reaction, became a more conscious expectation) that something would happen; after all, 'you never know'. A conversation with an Archways volunteer (who had misinterpreted the situation from his own middle-class perspective) conveys this expectancy:

Volunteer: Was Brighton what you expected?
Fifteen-year-old Mod: Well, I didn't expect anything, I don't think.
Volunteer: No?
Mod: Well, you know, I just thought I'd see what was happening, and if things turned out right, then we'd have a ball, wouldn't we?

It is clear in the context that for 'things to turn out right' would mean that there would be trouble or excitement: fights between Mods and Rockers, baiting of the police, throwing girls into the sea, 'buying up some pills', or 'finding a bird'. If these things happened, one could 'have a ball'; there was no specific plan in coming down other than to take part in or (more likely) to watch any sign of fun.

Trouble, excitement, action (or in the later skinhead version 'aggravation'), was built into the crowd scenes. There were not just the common elements described in other reviews of disturbances at sporting and recreational events[12] – an influx of outsiders into a small town or amusement centre, their high visibility in terms of interests, age group and overt symbols such as dress – but a particular sequence of societal reactions which created new scenarios to play out. Increasingly, the action became more ritualistic and predictable. While only a quarter of the Barker–Little sample (at the beginning of 1964) admitted to going to Margate expecting trouble, all of them expected trouble at the subsequent weekend's gatherings. As trouble became defined as institutionalized, the hope that something would happen became a definite expectancy.

The inventory reporting can be seen as having a reinforcing effect on already existing tendencies to expect and look forward to trouble. Constant repetition of the violence and vandalism images and reports about preparations for the next 'invasion' generated an atmosphere in which something *had* to happen. With the exception of those 'troublemakers' who, like Matza's positivist delinquents, nearly corresponded to their stereotype, the young people coming down constituted a massive audience. Usually this was an audience at a non-event, but the non-event had to be made into an event in order to justify the journey and the predefinitions of what the situation would be. Whatever little initial homogeneity there was in the crowd, could be attributed to this expectancy factor, as reinforced by the societal reaction. A group of boys walking down the beach could get caught up in a nexus of mutual misunderstandings; *ego* thinking that *alter* will perform a certain role and expect the same of him, while at the same time *alter* perceives *ego* in identical terms and both perceive that the publicly defined situation was making demands on them.[13]

Once a dominant perception is established the tendency is to assimilate all subsequent happenings to it. It is in this context that one must view the relatively trivial incidents which attracted attention and sometimes triggered off trouble. Through the process of sensitization, incidents which would not have been defined as unusual or worthy of attention during a normal Bank Holiday weekend, acquired a new meaning.

> Two boys stopped to watch a very drunk old tramp dancing about on the beach. They started throwing pennies at his feet. Within 45 seconds there were at least 100 people gathered round and in 60 seconds the police were there. I turned my back on the crowd to watch the spectators gathering on the promenade above and by the time I turned back, two policemen were leading a boy away from the crowd.
>
> (*Notes*, Brighton, Easter, 1965)

Other similar precipitating, or potentially precipitating, incidents were road accidents, a Rocker walking past a group of Mods, a group of youths being refused service in a bar or café and scooter riders being stopped to produce their licences. Where incidents did not occur 'naturally' they had to be created. The following is what I mean by a more natural type of incident – natural in the sense of having a culturally understood precipitant and sequence:

> . . . The boys (from Ealing mainly) were in the dance suite in a body of about 35 people. They were obviously creating a disturbance because a bouncer told one of the group to leave. The boy obviously took exception to being singled out and so pulled a gun from out of his pocket and threatened the bouncer with it. Apparently the bouncer had said, 'Go on, then, pull the trigger' to which the youth replied, 'I haven't any fucking

bullets.' The gun was a toy cap gun. The youth was then in the position of having his bluff called and was defenceless. Obviously, loss of face was involved in this as well. His friends realized this and created a tremendous uproar in the dance suite to make sure that they did keep the upper hand. There was a bloody fight and the police and ambulance were called.[14]

Often though the sequence was more contrived, and while malice or damage might have been the end result, the initial step was less likely to be maliciously inspired, than in Matza and Sykes's term 'manufactured excitement'. Crowd members, usually younger ones, could be seen self-consciously and deliberately trying to attract attention with ploys such as throwing stones at a paper policeman's helmet floating on the sea, ducking girls into the water, ganging up to bump someone on the dodgem cars, riding on the children's merry-go-round, jumping from the pier with an open umbrella held aloft. These were the events out of which trouble could come. More often than not the crowd would not respond; when it did so it would act momentarily and then return to just simply waiting around. One might see a hundred kids milling around, some of them throwing stones, others shouting and then suddenly moving on together as if nothing had happened.

The air of expectancy generated in these incidents is very similar to the 'milling process'[15] observed in crowds gathering around a road accident or similar event. One finds not just a restless, excited physical movement, but a process of communication in which individuals try to restructure an ambiguous situation by seeking cues in the reaction of others. It is this type of restructuring which marks the next crucial stage: without it, a concentrated and even excited crowd would have soon disintegrated. A socially sanctioned meaning was given to the situation by seeing others act and through the development of rumours.[16] In the milling process, individuals become more sensitized to each other and a common emotional tone develops, mediated by the type of circular reinforcement described earlier. In such ambiguous situations, rumours should be viewed not as forms of distorted or pathological communication: they make sociological sense as co-operative improvisations, attempts to reach a meaningful collective interpretation of what happened by pooling available resources.

Rumour, then, substitutes for news when institutional channels fail. Compared to news, it is low in formalization and this element – as Shibutani suggests – is inversely related to collective excitement. The suggestibility and behavioural contagion reported in certain crowd situations are again not pathological processes, but are forms of reciprocal reinforcement of emotional responses which provide the channels and controls for rumours to develop.[17] A rapid dissemination of mood and content via rumours, constricts the range of alternative responses and the intensity of non-inhibited responses increases. One is sensitized to concentrate on particular targets, shutting other considerations out. In constructing rumours, only those items consonant with the mood are selected. The participants seek a justification for their action and the rumours provide the 'facts' to sanction what the crowd wanted to do anyway.[18]

This analysis applies equally to the spread of definitions to the control agents and the mass media during the reaction phases. In the present context, the point is that the content of the shared definition that emerged in the crowd about what was happening, owed much to this reaction. The mass media provided the images and stereotypes with which ambiguous situations could be restructured; a stone-throwing incident might not have progressed beyond the milling stage if there were no readily available collective images to give meaning to the activity. These images provide the basis for rumours about 'random' events; so, an incident in which a girl was carried on a stretcher to an ambulance was variously explained by the crowd gathering round as 'this bloke with her must have knifed her', 'too many pills if you ask me', 'these Rockers' birds just drink all the time'.

Different versions of such events are circulated and eventually assimilated into one theme that receives collective sanction. Each link in the chain of assimilation involves preconceptions derived from sources such as the mass media; without publicity about 'stabbings on the beach' or 'drug orgies' the rumours about the girl being carried to the ambulance would have assumed an entirely different form.

The form and content of the rumours are important because they serve to validate a particular course of action: the deviant, as well as the control agent, uses collective imagery (which may be objectively false) to justify action. This type of process is paralleled in the genesis of other types of violent outbreaks such as race riots. The sequence includes: (i) murmurs of unrest before the outbreak; (ii) the spread of specifically threatening rumours ('something is going to happen tonight'); (iii) the precipitating spark (which may itself be an inflammatory rumour, for example, of police brutality); and (iv) fantastic rumours spread during the disturbance (for example, of murder by the other side) which are used to justify violence.

The following are examples of these four types of rumours during the impact phase: (i) 'I heard a bloke say the cops at Southend are really getting tough this Easter'; (ii) 'There's going to be trouble on the pier tonight when these Rockers get there'; (iii) 'Let's go – there's a big fight at the station'; (iv) 'There were thirty of them beating up one of our blokes.' In Clacton, the specific rumours circulating were those alleging hostility from the 'other side': in this case, local residents. There was a story of a group being refused breakfast at a café, and another about an old woman stopping three boys in the street and shouting abuse at them about their clothes. In later incidents, numerous rumours spread to reinforce the Mods–Rockers barrier ('The Mods are wearing lipstick this time', 'You can smell the grease on those Rockers; they never wash'). Later on, stories of police brutality and intimidation were particularly common ('They beat this bloke up in the cells'). One legend circulating in Brighton in Easter 1965, was about a drunken out-of-uniform policeman brawling with some boys in a café; they didn't know that he was a policeman and when he was getting the worst of the fight he screamed a 'signal' and his friends arrived to arrest most of the boys there.

The truth of such rumours is not at issue: the point is that they can be traced to certain elements in the societal reaction and they serve both to validate a mood and course of action, and to solidify a diverse crowd into a homogeneous mob. The rapidly fluctuating content of the rumours also illustrates a significant aspect of the Mods and Rockers phenomenon: the way in which the targets chosen for hostile action changed under the impact of the belief system.

In the first place, if, during any one event, an object of hostility became inaccessible, or rumours were spread of new targets, a satisfactory substitute would be accepted. If there were no Rockers in sight, the Mods would quite happily turn on the beatniks; in the course of one morning, the target could rapidly change from Rockers, to beatniks, to police, depending on the mood of the crowd, rumours of victimization or actual police interference. In the second place, the dominant target throughout the whole sequence changed: in Clacton, the enemy was Clacton (the shopkeepers, the weather, the lack of facilities); in Margate and Brighton, at Whitsun (under the impact of the war-ring gangs image), the enemy was the Rockers; later on (under the impact of the control culture), the enemy became the police.

Implicit in the analysis so far is a recognition of the importance of symbolization. This process provided a short-circuited definition of the situation whereby deviants and control agents used culturally sanctioned signs and symbols to justify or validate perceptions or actions. The inventory symbols prepared the crowd for action because shared images and objects contribute to uniform action: if a dance hall becomes defined as 'The Top Mod Spot of the South', then the defence of it against invading Rockers takes on a symbolic significance. Symbols such as clothing, hair-style, linguistic innovations and other stylistic attributes also create a sense of group cohesion. A crucial stage in the emergence of folk devils, is the point in the moral panic when such symbols become recognized (initially, in an exaggerated and distorted way), elaborated on and then diffused. Stigmatization and other negative sanctions then become easier to apply and the chance of triggering off an amplification sequence – through facilitating identification and solidarity within the group – is multiplied.

In the rapidly shifting crowd situation and the heightened emotional atmosphere, the slightest cue or sign could become a significant symbol. The following are some examples of symbolization and sensitization during the impact period:

> A young journalist, who was trying to get into the Margate courtroom, was shown to the cells instead of the Press Bench because he had fairly long hair and was wearing jeans. 'You look just like them,' he was told.
>
> *(Interview* with P.B., 19 November 1964)

> Wearing a white shirt and tie with a conventional sportscoat, I was walking with a group of Mods down the promenade which had temporarily been made a 'one-way'. After we were moved along by the police, I turned round and together with a number of others started walking back the wrong way. Although I was pushed once, the police were not as abusive to me as to the others; the boys on either side of me were bodily turned around and pushed in the other direction.
>
> *(Notes*, Brighton, Easter, 1965)

> Wearing a pair of old jeans and an army-type anorak, I had a hamburger and a cup of tea in a café. Not having any change, I gave the waitress a £5 note and being in a hurry started walking towards the cash desk. I heard the manager angrily say, 'Hasn't he got anything else?', but as soon as he saw me approaching he smiled nervously and said, 'Oh, I was going to argue until I saw you.'
>
> *(Notes*, Brighton, Easter, 1966)

> A boy accidentally fell to his death over the cliffs at Saltdean (Brighton) during the night. When his friends woke up and missed him, one went across to the houses on the other side of the road to phone the police. 'But,' he told a reporter, 'they wouldn't open their doors at first. They thought we were out for trouble; you know what it is.'
>
> *(Evening Argus*, 18 May 1964)

So far, this dissection of the crowd scenes has remained in the context of generalizations about crowd and collective behaviour and some particular links suggested by the transactional approach. The wider backdrop remains the development of the Mods and Rockers phenomenon as a whole but, for the moment, we will remain in the theatre.

The Audience

A more direct influence on the behaviour than the belief system was the presence of spectators during the impact period. If the mass media can be said to have created a metaphorical audience, one may also talk of a literal audience: the adults who lined the beaches and promenades to watch the battle being enacted before them. As early as Whitsun 1964, one local paper (*Brighton and Hove Herald*, 23 May 1964) carried a photo of a man in a crowd of boys swinging deckchairs, holding his child above his head to get a better view of the proceedings. Crowds of adults were always conspicuous at each stage of an event: milling around any sign of potential excitement, watching fights, making a path through which arrested boys could be bundled into the police van, crowding the public benches of the courts. If it cannot be said that they came down with the specific intention of watching the Mods and Rockers, certainly – at least when the phenomenon reached its peak – they regarded the troubles as part of the scene, and were subject to the same hope and expectancy as the boys and girls themselves. When the events tailed off in 1966 and there was little of a show to be seen, the gaping spectators were even more noticeable. Old hands could be seen pointing out the scene of previous campaigns: 'You should have seen it last year, love,' 'Remember they were throwing all those deckchairs from up there?'

It is difficult to generalize about the motives which brought the spectators to the scene. The simplest explanation is that they came because there was nothing to do or else – when the young people were present in such great numbers that they occupied much of the available space – because they were forced to watch. One did not get the impression, though, that there were many unwilling spectators. Sheer curiosity accounted for a large element of the motivation. This is analogous to the phenomenon of 'mass convergence' observed in disaster studies: the public flock to the scene of the disaster not so much to help, but to stare compulsively at the damage and rescue work. One might, in addition, speculate along conventional psychoanalytical lines, that the adults watching in fascinated horror were gaining some vicarious satisfaction from the sight of aggressive or sexually suggestive behaviour.

A more convincing sociological explanation is that the Mods and Rockers events were viewed as a ceremony. This was a modern morality play,* in which good (the police and the courts) met evil (the aggressive delinquent). Like all morality plays – or bull fights, which the atmosphere often resembled – there was little doubt about which side would win: the devil's place was known in advance. This type of morality image was sedulously cultivated by the mass media in the interest of consensus, and the audience reaction showed that the image was absorbed. The passive fascination (which might correspond to the psychoanalytical 'vicarious satisfaction' and the aficionado's admiration for the brave bull) was livened only when the forces of good triumphed. On a number of occasions spectators were observed cheering the police when they made an arrest and when boys were bundled into a police van, the type of remark one heard was 'that'll teach them a lesson', or 'put them in Lewes for a few nights, that'll show them'. In the courts there was applause from the public benches when the Chairman praised the police.

Whatever the reason for the spectators' presence and involvement, it is as important to observe their *effect* on the behaviour during the impact, remembering that just about everyone present – including the Mods and Rockers – played the spectator role at one time or another. One direct effect of the numbers of spectators was, in fact, to hinder the police in performing their duties of crowd control. The more important effect of the audience, though, was more subtle in that its very presence provided an encouragement to deviance. The audience is part of the crowd, and even if it may disapprove, it makes the crowd larger numerically and increases the expression of strength and support for what is being done. Turner and Killian quote the Southern Commission on the Study of Lynchings to show that the spectators often constituted a source of protection for the very elements of which they might disapprove.[19] In the presence of an audience, the more active members of the crowd become committed to a line of action, because to back down would be to lose face. A passive audience may also have unwittingly contributed to creating what F. H. Allport originally termed 'the impression of universality' whereby the crowd member loses some responsibility through assuming that

* A team of researchers studying football hooliganism have noted a similar element in these public confrontations between policemen and deviants '. . . Spectators seemed to adopt the attitude that the scenes were comparable to those shown at old-fashioned music halls where villains and heroes were booed and cheered in a ritualized manner.'[20] There is a crucial difference, though, between these situations: at football matches it is often the police who are the villains, at the resorts it was always the Mods and Rockers.

'everybody is doing it'. Exaggeration – by observers and participants – of the numbers involved, only heightens this effect.

In the case of violence, as Westley suggests,[21] the presence of others can lead to a direct escalation. In each type of violence he analyses – by mob members, concentration camp guards and police – the violators have a symbiotic relationship to a supportive audience. The police, because of public support for the use of violence against criminals and other non-persons such as the insane, can use an audience to legitimate illegal forms of violence. Escalation occurs when there is a combination of a group willing to use violence and an audience to which it plays and will encourage it and give it moral support. For the crowd the presence of spectators and cameras might have decreased inhibitions about provoking the police. The kids were one up in a situation which called for some restraint on the part of the police and they knew that the police image would suffer if unnecessary violence was observed by the audience.

The Mass Media

This is the point at which to analyse the more explicit on-the-spot role of the mass media which, as we have seen, operated from the outset in reinforcing and giving shape to the crowd's sense of expectancy and in providing the content of rumours and shared definitions with which ambiguous situations were restructured. Although popular commentators on the Mods and Rockers often blamed 'publicity' for what happened (and the press responded with indignant editorials about its 'duty' to publish the 'facts'), the term 'publicity' was used in a somewhat restricted sense. It either referred to the publicity immediately before the event (during the warning phase), which advertised the disturbances and pin-pointed the resorts where they would take place, or to the supposed gratification young people derived from the exposure to publicity during the event.

The first of these factors operated in the gross sense of publicizing the event in such a way that it might look attractive, but it is unlikely to have directly influenced the choice of target: asked where they got the idea from (of going to Margate), 82.3 per cent of the Barker–Little sample mentioned friends as their source, only 2.9 per cent mentioned newspapers and 2.9 per cent television. Only a handful I spoke to at any stage said that anything in the press or television *initially* decided them on a particular resort. The media more likely reinforced rather than initiated rumours already current. There were certain exceptions, though, when during the weekend a sensational report or

TV interview might have directly attracted new crowds. One notorious BBC interview in which two Rockers said that reinforcements would be arriving was followed by a sudden influx of both Mods and Rockers, large numbers of whom might have been attracted by the excitement the interview promised.

There were also signs of direct publicity-seeking behaviour in the sense that on-the-spot attention from journalists, reporters and photographers was a stimulus to action. The following account is by one of the boys in the Barker–Little sample: 'By the railway station a cameraman asked, "Give us a wave". So me and a group ran about and waved some flags we bought. My picture was in the paper. We were pleased; anybody would be.'

If one is in a group of twenty, being stared at by hundreds of adults and being pointed at by two or three cameras, the temptation to do something – even if only to shout an obscenity, make a rude gesture or throw a stone – is very great and made greater by the knowledge that one's actions will be recorded for others to see. There is a tendency for the participant in such situations to exaggerate the extent of his involvement and to look for some recognition of it. Thus at every weekend, young people could be observed at newspaper kiosks buying each edition of the evening paper as it appeared and scanning it for news of disturbances. The exploitative element in this feedback is reflected in the rumours – which, at least in one case, I am certain were firmly based – that press photographers were asking suitably attired young males to pose kicking in a window or telephone kiosk.

The cumulative effects of the mass media, though, were at the same time more subtle and more potent than simply giving the events pre-publicity or gratifying the participants' need for attention. Through a complex process that is not yet fully understood by students of mass communication, the mere reporting of one event has, under certain circumstances, the effect of triggering off events of a similar order. This effect is much easier to understand and is better documented in regard to the spread of crazes, fashions, fads and other forms of collective behaviour, such as mass delusion or hysteria, than in cases of deviance. The main reason why this process has been misunderstood in regard to deviance – particularly collective and novel forms – is that too much attention has been placed on the supposed direct effects (imitation, attention, gratification, identification) on the deviants, rather than the effects on the control system and culture and hence (via such processes as amplification) on the deviance.

The simple triggering-off or suggestibility type effects can be seen even in apparently individual forms of deviance such as suicide. A particularly vivid example is the spread in self-immolation as a form of suicide following the report in 1963 of a Vietnamese monk burning himself to death as an act of political protest. This is a form of suicide almost completely unknown in the West; in the period 1960–63, there was only one such case in England, yet in 1963, there were three and in 1964, nine. A similar progression in numbers occurred in America.[22] In this case, the contagious or imitative effect was in the technique rather than the motivation behind the act. Cases where the motive as well as the technique is stimulated by mass communication, might be the spread of prison riots, prison escapes and racial and political riots. A particularly well-documented example is the Swastika Epidemic of 1959–60. The contagion effect could be clearly shown in plotting the curve of the epidemic.[23]

An example closer to the Mods and Rockers is the spread during the fifties of the Teddy Boy riots and similar phenomena elsewhere in Europe. Most commentators on these events acknowledged the role of publicity in stimulating imitative or competitive forms of behaviour[24] and some studies have been made on the mass media coverage of such events.[25] At the same time, though, blame was put on 'publicity' in the restricted sense and there was little awareness of the complex ways in which mass communication operates before, during and after each 'impact'. The causative nature of mass communication – in the whole context of the societal reaction to such phenomena – is still usually misunderstood.

The common element in all these diverse examples of the amplification of violence is that an adequate medium of communication must be present for spreading the hostile belief and mobilizing potential participants. The mass communication of the news of one outbreak is a condition of structural conduciveness for the development of a hostile belief which, in turn, has to sensitize the 'new' crowd (or individual deviant) to incipient or actual action and lower the threshold of readiness by providing readily identifiable symbols. The possibility that the mere reporting of one event might have a triggering and eventually amplifying effect, has been apparent to many observers of contemporary crowd violence. This recognition lies behind suggestions to consciously use the media to achieve aims of crowd control.[26]

The triggering-off, sensitization and other such effects of mass communication described so far, deal with the way in which the likelihood of deviant behaviour during the impact was increased: one almost *had* to attempt to see or take part in trouble. The inventory and subsequent opinion themes, though, also affected the *form* and *content* of the behaviour. The societal reaction not only increases the deviant's chance of acting at all, it also provides him with his lines and stage directions.

The crucial effect here is the way in which deviant behaviour is shaped by the normative expectations of how people in that particular deviant role should act. Much of the Mods and Rockers behaviour can be conceptualized in terms of a role-playing model. Posing for photos, chanting slogans, making warlike gestures, fantasizing about super-gangs, wearing distinctive insignia, making a mock raid on an ice-cream van, whistling at girls, jeering at the 'other side': all these acts of 'hooliganism' may be seen as analogous to the impersonation of mental illness resorted to by those defined as mentally ill. The actor incorporates aspects of the type cast role into his self concept and when the deviant role is public – as hooliganism is by definition – and the deviants are in a situation of heightened suggestibility, then this incorporation is often more conscious and deliberate than in those types of 'private' deviance such as mental illness, homosexuality and drug-taking, to which transactionalist writers have applied such concepts.

New recruits might search for and positively try to exemplify the values and imagery portrayed in the stereotypes. The media created some sort of diversionary side-show in which all could seek their appropriate parts. The young people on the beaches knew very well that they had been type cast as folk devils and they saw themselves as targets for abuse. When the audiences, TV cameras and police started lining themselves up, the metaphor of role-playing becomes no longer a metaphor, but the real thing. One acute observer at the live TV coverage of the Mod Ball at Wembley (a week after the initial Clacton event) described a girl in front of the cameras worshipping a hair salvaged off Mick Jagger's trousers, as being like a man acting drunk when he is hardly tipsy, 'acting out this adoration. She sees she is being watched, grins sheepishly and then laughs outright.'[27]

In the present context, the importance of the role-playing perspective is that the content of the type cast role was present in the inventory and crystallized more explicitly in the process of spurious attribution or labelling. This is not to say that a new one to one link between the labelling and the behaviour was formed. For one thing, the type cast hooligan role was known to the potential actors before the deviance even began; like the labellers themselves, they could draw upon an existent folklore and mythology. The point, however, was that the normative element in the role was reinforced by the societal reaction: although the actors might already have been familiar with the lines and the stage direction, they were now confirmed in their roles. In the same way as the 'chronic' schizophrenic begins to approximate closer to the schizophrenic role, so did the Mods and Rockers phenomenon take on every time an increasingly ritualistic and stereotypical character.

Although the hooligan role was ready made and had only to be confirmed by the labelling process, there were other elements in the behaviour which could be directly traced to the societal reaction. The first of these was the way in which the gap between the Mods and Rockers became increasingly wider and obvious. Although (as I will show in the next chapter) the Mods and Rockers represent two different consumer styles – the Mods the more glossy fashion-conscious teenager, the Rockers the tougher, reactionary tradition – the antagonism between the two groups was not initially very marked. Despite their real differences in life styles – visible in symbols such as the Mods' scooters and the Rockers' motor-bikes – the groups had a great deal in common, particularly their working-class membership. There was, initially at least, nothing like the gang rivalry that is supposed to characterize the type of violent conflict gang enshrined in folklore by the 'Sharks' and 'Jets' of *West Side Story*. Indeed, one could not justifiably talk of 'gangs' at all in any meaningful sociological sense. The only structured grouping one could find in the early crowds was based on slight territorial loyalty and it was tenuous enough to be broken up in the crowd situation.

Constant repetition of the warring gangs' image, however, had the effect of giving these loose collectivities a structure they never possessed and a mythology with which to justify the structure. This image was disseminated in the inventory, reinforced through the symbolization process, repeated in the 'Divide and Rule' and 'Cabalism' themes, used to advantage in the form of commercial exploitation and repeated during the warning phase. Even if these images were not directly absorbed by the actors, they were used to justify control tactics, which, as we shall see, still further structured the groups and hardened the barriers between them.

The mass media – and the ideological exploitation of deviance – also reinforced another type of polarization: between the Mods and Rockers on the one hand, and the whole adult community on the other. If one is seen as the 'enemy' in the 'war against crime', it is not difficult to respond in similar spirit: one 'rejects the rejectors' and 'condemns the condemners'. The specialized effect of the Lunatic Fringe theme, is to segregate and label those involved by emphasizing their difference from the majority. A striking parallel from a similar form of deviance was the labelling by the motor-cycling 'Establishment' of riders identified with the Hells Angels image as the 'one per cent who cause all the trouble': the term 'one percenter' was then used by the groups as an honorific epithet, reinforcing their commitment.[28]

The Control Agents

The police – the main control agents operating during the impact period – had two types of effect on the behaviour; the one immediate and the other more sustained. The immediate effect of police policy and action was to create deviance – not only in the sense of provoking the more labile members of the crowd into losing their tempers but in Becker's sense of making the rules whose infraction constituted deviance. The types of control tactics adopted by the police under the impact of sensitization and symbolization involved a certain arbitrary element. The practice, for example, of designating certain areas in advance as 'trouble spots' meant that youths with the appropriate symbols could be moved along even if they were causing no apparent harm. In one case in the Brighton court, a constable from Eastbourne, who had been helping the local force, gave evidence that he had seen a number of youths standing under a bus shelter; they were not doing anything, but he 'had heard that this was a trouble spot' and had told them to move away. Not all moved away quickly enough and one was arrested. 'If you allow him to get away with what he did,' the constable told the court, 'and not move when the police told him to, then others would be free to come down. It was necessary in the public's interest that these youths should not shelter from the rain in this particular shelter.'

The police (and the courts) acted on the assumption that certain forms of behaviour, although not criminal in themselves, were, under the particular circumstances, so situationally improper* as to call for official action. It must be emphasized that the majority of arrests throughout were for offences which are both potentially provocable and involve considerable police discretion. This means that the sheer number of charges could give a distorted picture of the disturbances. In Brighton, Whitsun, 1965, for example, there was little serious trouble: the weather (there was hail and sleet) had sent people home early and the Chief Constable even issued an official statement that most young people had been well behaved and the police were in control. But 'in control' meant making a large number of discretionary arrests; from late Saturday to Monday there were over 110 arrests. These were not clear-cut offences, such as possessing an offensive weapon or assault, but charges which required highly

---

* The notion of situational impropriety is derived from Goffman; his discussions of attitudes to 'lolling' and 'loitering' are particularly apposite to the situation on the beaches where the police appeared to be given a license to move people along who were doing nothing; one had to appear purposeful.[29]

subjective definitions of what constituted 'obstruction', 'abusive', 'threatening', 'insulting', 'disorderly' or 'unruly' behaviour. These terms could only acquire an objective and reified status through the acceptance of situational logic which, in turn, was based on the belief system. The following are examples of this situational logic; the first two are from statements by the Inspector prosecuting in the Brighton court, the second two are from Hastings:

In a case of wilful obstruction: 'In the circumstances which operated in Brighton at the time, it can be seen that what the boys did was likely to provoke a breach of the peace.'

In a case of using threatening behaviour: 'We will allege that he was one of nine or ten Rockers chanting "We want blood" and we would also allege that in these particular circumstances in Brighton at the time he should be classified as unruly and we will oppose bail on these grounds.'

An 18-year-old girl was at the back of a crowd which was being moved. She refused to move quickly and turned round to her side where the constable was walking and said, 'Don't push me, you . . . copper; I will report you.' The prosecutor commented: 'This is a case where in ordinary circumstances the police would shrug the thing off, but in an inflammable situation of this nature, silly little girls like this could cause a great deal of trouble.'

In one of the few cases that were actually dismissed in Hastings (August 1964) on the grounds of insufficient evidence, a boy, P.G., was charged with abusive behaviour. According to the evidence, a constable had seen a large group of 'unruly youths' walking along obstructing the road. Along with other officers, the constable moved one part of the group along the promenade. P.G. was one of the group and the constable heard him jeer at another officer and make personal observations including the remark, 'Look at freckles.' This sort of remark 'might not have been taken much notice of in normal circumstances, but because of the inflammatory nature of the occasion, it assumed much greater proportions. Things could snowball very rapidly.'

The last two cases, together with personal observation of similar incidents, bear out Becker's point that a great deal of enforcement activity is devoted not to the enforcement of the rules, but getting respect from the people the enforcer deals with: 'This means that one may be labelled as a deviant, not because he has actually broken a rule, but because he has shown disrespect to the enforcer of the rule.'[30] This factor assumed a particular significance at the seaside resorts, where police were hypersensitive to being exposed to public ridicule. In view of the audience watching their actions, this feeling was understandable. No matador wants to be laughed at.

The more sustained effects of police action were less visible, but, in terms of the amplification model, as important. These effects were to increase the deviance by unwittingly solidifying the amorphous crowd forces into more viable groups for engaging in violence and by further polarizing the deviants against the community.

These sorts of effects are well known to students of gang behaviour. The early Chicago sociologists – particularly Thrasher and Tannenbaum – documented the ways in which attack, opposition or attempted suppression increase the group's cohesion. According to Thrasher, such attack was virtually a necessary prerequisite for any embryonic street group to become a gang. More recently, Yablonsky has shown the same effects and they have also been documented in the general literature on crowd control in political, racial and other types of disturbances.

The crowd situation offers, *par excellence*, the opportunity for police intervention to have the unintended effect of solidifying the opposition. Such solidification and polarization takes place not simply in the face of attack, but attack that is perceived as harsh, indiscriminate and unfair. Even if the attack was not like this, the ambiguity of the crowd situation offered the maximum possible opportunity for rumours of such police action to spread. In the same way that the Mods and Rockers were perceived symbolically and stereotypically by the police, the police too were perceived by the crowd as the 'enemy'. Here was a Punch and Judy show, with each side having a partially false perspective on the other and each acting in order to justify this perspective.

It was not just a question, though, of a nexus of mutual misunderstandings; the police did objectively act in such a way as to increase solidification and polarization. In the first place, their control tactics were based on the assumption that the young people present were either divided into two homogeneous groups, Mods and Rockers (the Divide and Rule theme) or constituted a single homogeneous mass. Both these assumptions were false. By emphasizing the Mods and Rockers' difference (e.g. by preventing the two groups from coming into proximity) the police might have widened the gulf between the groups. In one particular case (not in a seaside resort) the police, under full publicity, attempted to call two groups together for a peace treaty.* By seeing the crowd as a homogeneous mass, to be controlled on the basis of the visible stigmata of dress, a greater sense of cohesion develops. If subject to indiscriminate harassment or even if only witnessing the innovatory use of violence by the police, the more marginal and passive sections of the crowd could quite easily develop a sense of resentment and grievance. This could be the first step towards a sense of identity and common purpose with the real or imagined hard core of the crowd, with 'police brutality' as a convenient rallying point.

It should be noted that feelings of persecution were particularly acute among the Rockers, who were observably discriminated against by the police. This group was more visible than the amorphous Mod crowds and also occupied in the public mind the traditional 'yobbo' status. Their existent minority group status *vis-à-vis* the Mods and their sense of fighting a rearguard battle against the new emancipated teenagers, was reinforced by the police who naturally enough found it easier to identify a minority group. The literature on crowd control points to this type of partiality as being particularly provocative and police are usually impressed with the necessity to avoid entering into issues that move the crowd.

Another source of solidification stemmed from the fact that the opposition was largely ineffectual. From the initial incident at Clacton, the police were faced with a new situation for which there had been little precedent. Unlike the Metropolitan Police, the police forces of small seaside resorts have little or no experience in handling potentially violent crowd situations such as political demonstrations. The tactics of crowd control emerged on an *ad hoc* basis and were necessarily over-influenced by false perceptions of the situation and the highly charged emotional atmosphere. This meant that hallowed strategies such as 'the show of force', which most manuals on crowd control advocate in such situations, were not properly implemented. Either the 'force' was not strong enough, or had a comic opera aspect (e.g. the use of converted public health vehicles as patrol vans), or police action was often hesitant instead of quick and decisive, or action went beyond the show of force to the actual use of force. In the face of control that was manifestly inadequate to deal with the crowd if it did, in fact, become a viable violent mob, the crowd could easily

---

* Yablonsky comments on a similar peace treaty: 'The meeting gave a degree of official recognition to the illegal activity of a disorganized connection of neighbourhood youth. Moreover the treaty may have structured a loosely developed conflict. The meeting confirmed the fact that there was trouble brewing between rival groups. Now two "gangs" had a war truce.'[31]

develop a sense of its potential power. If one hundred Mods are chasing a handful of Rockers across the beach, the sight of a handful of policemen in turn pursuing the Mods can only appear somewhat ludicrous and undignified. It only needed one unfortunate policeman's helmet to fall off for the situation to move very far from a successful show of force.

The third source of solidification and polarization was the effect of dramatization. Although, by definition, a show of force has to be publicly demonstrated if it is to have a deterrent effect, it need not be overdramatized. The dramatic techniques described earlier, such as frogmarching two youths to the police station or marching a group through the streets, could only have the effect that Tannenbaum intended in his phrase 'the dramatization of evil'. These techniques effectively polarize the forces of good and evil and solidify by creating the sense of resentment, which is a natural reaction to being exposed to public ridicule. If such effects are combined with a sense of persecution, the whole situation could take on a mythical, chimerical meaning. The activist Mod or Rocker (real or imaginary) could, like Shellow and Roemer's 'Hells Angels' function not only as vicarious exemplars of behaviour that some young people might fantasy but also act as legendary champions who will rescue the persecuted; they quote one motor-cyclist witnessing police harassment: 'Just wait till the Hells Angels hear about this when they come in tomorrow. They'll come down and tear this place apart.'[32]

That this type of polarization did, in fact, occur, can be seen in the changing attitudes towards the police. In the first series of events, the crowd, with a few exceptions, maintained fairly good-humoured relations with the police. 'Attacks' on the police were usually disrespectful gestures, such as knocking off helmets. As the moral panic progressed, though, the lines hardened and relationships between the crowd and the police deteriorated. In Brighton, August 1965, a policeman attempting to arrest the apparent leader of a group of one hundred Mods charging across the beach, was immediately stoned and when he lost his helmet in a scuffle, it was pounced upon and used as a football. In Great Yarmouth at Easter, 1966, four policemen were assaulted and one of them kicked about the head. The following incidents illustrate the strained atmosphere and the way in which hostility to authority became generalized:

> A policeman walked quite peacefully between two rows of boys near the aquarium. Some of them started whistling the Z-car theme and one shouted out 'Sprachen the Deutsch constable?'

> A boy was throwing stones outside a shop under the archway. The owner

came out and shouted at him: 'If you come down here you must behave.' The boy retorted (not quite loud enough for the man to hear): 'Or else you'll get your fuckin' army on to us.'

(*Notes*, Brighton, Easter, 1966)

The role of the courts in the control culture can be seen as reinforcing the tendency towards solidification and polarization. The sentences were seen as not only sanctioning police action, but as being intrinsically harsh and unfair: this was the overwhelming response among the boys in the Barker–Little sample. The use of the remand in custody as a punitive measure was a particularly widely felt grievance. The dramatization effect achieved by the magistrates' pronouncements left little doubt – certainly among the offenders' friends and relatives waiting in the foyer of the Brighton court – that the magistrates were using their powers for ritual reasons: they were denouncing deviance by making an example of the offender. Such denunciations – combined with the widely held view that the police had been arresting on a 'quota' system – led readily enough to feelings of resentment and martyrdom.

It should be noted throughout that the amplificatory effects of the control culture were fed back into the mass media, which further exaggerated them, thus producing another link in the sequence. If the policemen did not see themselves as 'the brave men in blue' fighting the evil mob, nor the magistrates themselves as society's chosen mouthpieces for denouncing evil, these polarizations were made on their behalf by others.

Summary

Before providing a brief summary of this chapter, two footnotes should be added to my argument about the unintended effects of the societal reaction.

The first relates to the supposed 'inevitability' of the societal reaction. While it is true that each stage of the reaction appears to be a logical product of the prior one, the deviance amplification model is a typical rather than an inevitable sequence. There are no overwhelming technical reasons why it should not be broken or at least re-routed at various points, for example, by creating alternative modes of presenting the news. Even direct intervention by control agents could be different and not produce all the effects I have suggested. Thus – to take examples on an admittedly small scale – one might compare the Mods and Rockers' events with a similar situation where disturbances were, in fact, prevented. Shellow and Roemer have described a case of threatened Hells Angels' disturbances and the polarization of crowds of motor-cyclists arriving at a resort for Labour Day weekend motor-cycle races.[33] They outline three conditions under which exuberance and rowdiness lead to rioting:

(i) Recreational, service and control facilities 'flooded' by overwhelming numbers of visitors, who were then left at loose ends, ready for any kind of 'action'.

(ii) Ineffectual, often provocative, attempts at control and expression of authority by police or officials.

(iii) Development of a sense of group solidarity among members of the crowd.

All these three conditions were present during a typical impact period; in the American resort, polarization was partly, at least, prevented by an educational programme aimed at impressing three facts on the police:

(i) that motor-cyclists are not essentially different from other citizens and need not be treated as a breed apart;

(ii) that motor-cyclists are not a homogeneous class but come in a variety of shapes and sizes; some innocuous, some potentially troublesome;

(iii) that indiscriminate, harsh treatment of all motor-cyclists would confirm the latter's sense of persecution, increase group solidarity among them, and go far towards creating the very polarization we wished to avoid.

For reasons that are not technical, it is unlikely that such methods will be tried very often* nor, of course, are they likely to be successful ways of preventing primary deviation. They need consideration, though, in the light of assertions that there is something fixed and inevitable in the way deviance of the sort in question might be controlled.

The second footnote – a theoretically more important one – is that I have tended to consider only the negative or unintended consequences of law enforcement and social control. This should not be taken to mean that police and court action had no deterrent effect or that a certain amount of violence

---

* Shellow and Roemer also make recommendations which might well apply to British sea-side resorts about improving the recreational facilities in order to prevent the milling that precedes crowd disturbances. The Brighton Archways Ventures might be viewed as an attempt in this direction. Another attempt to control a juvenile crowd disturbance, this time by deliberately exploiting the ambiguous nature of the crowd situation, is described in W. Buikhuisen, 'Research on Teenage Riots', *Sociologia Neerlandica* 4 (Winter, 1966–7), pp. 1–21.

and vandalism was not contained or prevented. A problem, though – as in evaluating all types of social control – is that it is by no means clear what constitutes successful law enforcement, either in its deterrent or preventive aspects. Many claims for such success are difficult to evaluate. For an example of 'deterrence' one may take the fact that some 65 per cent of the boys in the Barker–Little sample said that they would not get mixed up in that sort of thing again and most gave the punishment, and fear of worse, as the reason. Most also believed, though, that they would be the only ones deterred, and even individual deterrence was limited by the fact that each event tended to attract crowds from specific geographical areas; only four of the Margate group had been at Clacton. Their own friends certainly weren't deterred by the punishment: they either thought of it as a joke or, at worst, thought that the mistake had been to get caught.

For an example of 'prevention' we may look at Clacton, Easter, 1965, where, in response to local pressure to avoid a repetition of the previous year's incidents, the police took elaborate precautions including the use of walkie-talkies and the deliberate policy of making things miserable for all scooter riders entering the town. There were virtually no arrests and it was claimed that the show of force had worked. In fact, though, the 1964 incident was quite isolated as far as Clacton was concerned, Margate and the south coast resorts always being more popular with the Mods. The very few Mods who might have set out for Clacton in Easter 1965, were possibly stopped by the weather which, if anything, was worse than the previous year. The best one can say, then, for these two claims of successful 'deterrence' and 'prevention' respectively, is that the evidence is ambiguous.

In the final chapter, the broader implications of these footnotes will be related to the whole question of de-amplification and how the growth of moral panics and social types ever becomes arrested.

In summary, the societal reaction may be thought to have affected the nature, extent and development of the deviant behaviour during the impact phase in the following ways:

1   The societal reaction in general and the inventory in particular:
    (a) reinforced and magnified a predisposition to expect trouble: 'something's going to happen';
    (b) provided the content for rumours and the milling process, thereby structuring the 'something' into potential or actual deviance; such rumours and images facilitated deviance by solidifying the crowd and validating its moods and actions;

    (c) created a set of culturally identifiable symbols which further structured the situation and legitimized action.

2   The presence of an audience gave encouragement to deviance and helped escalate violence.

3   The mass media in general:

    (a) operated to publicize the events;

    (b) led to direct publicity-seeking behaviour;

    (c) created a triggering-off or contagion effect, whereby the hostile belief was spread and the participants mobilized for action;

    (d) provided the content for deviant role-playing behaviour by transmitting the stereotypical expectations of how persons in the particular deviant roles should act;

    (e) together with the commercial exploitation, magnified the Mods–Rockers dichotomy and gave the groups a greater structure and common ethos than they originally possessed;

    (f) together with the ideological exploitation, polarized the deviants further against the community.

4   The agents of control:

    (a) 'created' deviance by applying situational logic to law enforcement;

    (b) because control was unfair, indiscriminate, ineffectual, based on spurious attribution and overdramatized – or perceived in these terms – repeated the effects of 3 (e) and (f), thus solidifying an amorphous crowd into a more unified, hostile and polarized collectivity.

6 Contexts and Backgrounds: Youth in the Sixties

It is no less difficult to untangle the reasons for the societal reaction to a form of deviance or social problem than it is to understand why the behaviour or condition is there in the first place. In this concluding chapter, I would like to suggest some of the reasons for the reactions to the Mods and Rockers and place these in the specific historical and cultural context in which the phenomenon developed. The crucial question to ask is not the simple transactional one of why the behaviour was seen as deviant at all – the answer to this is fairly obvious – but why the reaction took the particular form and intensity it did at the particular time. What was it that prompted the control culture's responses, the Margate magistrate's remarks, the indignation of people like Blake or a Brighton newspaper editor's description of the incidents as 'without parallel in English history'?

Models such as that of deviation amplification are incomplete unless set in the context of such questions. So far, in a series of somewhat mixed metaphors, we have viewed the objects of the moral panic as Rorschach blots, folk devils, actors on a stage, images flickering on a screen. This was, after all, how they appeared to society: as processed images. But both the images and the way they were reacted to were socially created and – without making any metaphysical assumptions about the 'true' reality – we must look for the real social contexts of this creation. The central indictment of the way the mass media handles such areas as deviance, social problems and politics, is precisely that no such alternative explanatory frameworks are presented. It is not just a matter of bias, unreliability or unfairness but the use of stereotypical modes of presentation and frameworks such as that of the 'event of news', which virtually deny the possibility of the consumer obtaining a serious perspective on the underlying social content of what is being reported.

This one-dimensionality is a feature not just of the media but of some sociological theories of deviance. A common enough criticism of transactional theories is that they play down the original sources of the behaviour which is being reacted to, thus giving an asymmetrical picture of the transaction. My present criticism is that it is the reaction itself which is often left unexplained. Models such as deviation amplification deal well enough with what happens in the machine (the feedback and snowballing effects during the reaction sequence) but inadequately with why the initial reaction takes place and even less adequately with why the whole sequence itself might come to an end. For these problems we have to look outside the machine and outside the theatre.

The Emergence of the Mods and Rockers

The twin themes of affluence and youth – the second essentially subordinate to the first – have dominated most analyses of post-war social change in Britain. In the popular rhetoric, they have appeared under the Macmillan 'Never Had It So Good' slogan, in the sociological version, under the guise of the embourgeoisement debate. Any analysis, for example, of the way in which the mass media over this period attempted to interpret and make political sense of what was happening, would have to understand the whole theme of the changing styles of life which followed in the wake of 'affluence'. Specifically, one would have to focus on the myth of the classless teenage culture and how this was perpetuated by the mass media. Youth – even when, and perhaps especially when, it was being troublesome – was initially the supreme, the most glamorous and the most newsworthy manifestation of the affluence theme. Justifiably, an important study of the popular press during the period 1935–65 uses the youth theme as a metaphor for social change.[1]

Before the war, the major spending power lay with the over twenties. No age group emerged – in terms of fashion or symbolic allegiance – in a self-conscious attempt at isolation from the dominant culture. In the years between 1945 and 1950 the grounds for change were laid by a constellation of economic and demographic variables. There was a large unmarried teenage generation (between 15 and 21) whose average real wage had increased at twice the rate of the adults'. This relative economic emancipation created a group with few social ties or responsibilities and whose stage of development could not really be coped with by the nuclear working-class family.

Within a very short time, the ideal teenager was presented in consumption terms. As a reward for full production, he was to be allowed the full spectacle of commodities that the market could offer, and moreover offer and package in a way especially designed for him. This is not to say that he was simply 'exploited' or 'manipulated'; such concepts, particularly when applied to pop music, are too crude to allow for the way in which the adolescent consumer is also an active agent in creating modes of expression which reflect his cultural experience.[2]

Soon, the emerging styles became associated with deviant or publicly disapproved values. The Teddy Boys were the first youth group to mark their symbolic innovation – and it was a considerable one – with defiance, anger or gestures of separation. In exactly the way that occurred later with the Mods and Rockers, such emerging styles became indelibly confused with other phenomena. On the one hand they were confused with the general youth theme: Hot-blooded Youth, It's a Sign of the Times, Affluence . . . On the other, they were perceptually merged into day-to-day delinquency problems, the mundane troubles which make up nearly all the work of the control system and had little to do with (and never have) the headline troubles which are the stuff of moral panics. Before tracing the particular stylistic antecedents of the Mods and Rockers, some rather general account of the relationships between the youth culture and aggressive fringe delinquency is needed.[3]

The most superficial way of identifying this relationship is through the It's Not Only This and Hot-blooded Youth types of themes, that is, the assumptions that teenage culture is firstly homogeneous and, secondly, congruent with delinquent or deviant values. The argument is that in the absence of a ritualized transition to full adult status, a limbo is created characterized by conflict, uncertainty, defiance and deviance. An autonomous youth culture, embodying values insulating the group from the problems of the age transition, provides the source of such diverse forms of deviance as delinquency, student radicalism and a drug-connected dropping out. Such manifestations are seen to be exacerbated by the new affluence – as in the Affluence and Boredom themes.

This picture is considerably misleading. It ignores the ways in which adult society actively uses the whole idea of adolescence and the youth culture in particular, to neutralize any real generational conflict. The young are consigned to a self-contained world with their own preoccupations, their entrance into adult status is frustrated and they are rewarded for dependency. The teenage culture makes them into ineffectual outsiders.[4] The culture itself is not homogeneous; although its artefacts might be blandly classless, it is highly stratified along class, regional, educational and other lines. Moreover, since its creation in the fifties, a mainstream of teenage entertainment culture has been conformist in character, and conspicuous for its passivity and continuity with adult values. The first pop heroes embodied the highly conservative values involved in the success stories of being discovered and making it: thus Tommy Hicks, the merchant seaman from Bermondsey, became Tommy Steele, Harry Webb, the factory clerk from Cheshunt, became Cliff Richard, and so on.[5] This strand continued into the sixties via some of the Liverpool groups, and then Tom Jones, Lulu, Engelbert Humperdinck and others. Despite protestations to the contrary from both apologists and defenders of the pop scene, it was not just the Mums and Dads who bought these records.

There are, of course, other streams, which perhaps now have become dominant. But their links with delinquency are not the simple ones of extrapolation from message to behaviour which are usually assumed to operate. It is some of the complexities of the relationship between social class, the teenage culture and what I will call *expressive fringe delinquency*, that I would like to refer to. The focus is not on mundane day-to-day delinquency (which consists primarily of property offences) but on behaviour labelled variously as hooliganism, vandalism, rowdyism and which occurs during middle to late adolescence. More specifically, it is on those manifestations of this behaviour associated with collective symbolic styles. Such behaviour should not be explained as being *either* instrumental *or* expressive, but simultaneously as both, and it is these parallel routes to the Mods and Rockers' events that need separate consideration.

A Problem and a Solution

The instrumental route is that concentrated on by subcultural theorists of delinquency.[6] The argument is that although growing up in industrial society presents certain common problems, the structural and normative diversity of our society allows the problems to be experienced differentially, particularly across class lines, and only makes certain solutions available. A stream of working-class adolescents over the last fifteen years or so have gone through the school system without showing allegiance to its values or internalizing its aspirations. They leave their secondary moderns as soon as possible, accurately perceiving the implications for their future lives of the education they've received. As Downes says, they are not inherently disillusioned about the jobs any more than they are about education: the jobs are dull and tedious. Money becomes – quite rightly – just about the most important occupational criterion. There is a sense of personal redundancy and waste, a drifting from job to job without any real expectation of the next one being any more interesting than the previous one. As Goodman puts it, nobody asks whether jobs are worthy, dignified, useful, honourable: one grows up realizing that during one's productive years one will be spending eight hours a day doing something that is no good.

All this, it might be said, is not new: how many people do feel that their jobs are worthwhile and dignified? And, moreover, when have working-class adolescents not been left out of the conventional educational and occupational races? Over the last fifteen or so years, though, one significant new feature has appeared – the mass teenage culture – to point for some to new aspirations. One must take care not to exaggerate the universality of the culture's effects: it does not serve as a direct shaper of aspirations in the sense of creating specific desires, say, to become a pop star and, indeed, in some traditional working-class areas and whole underdeveloped regions such as the north-east of England, it has hardly permeated through at all. But from the beginning its manifestations were pervasive. The new glossy constellation, in all its guises, had no serious rival: not the traditional working-class culture, not the youth service and not political or community involvement. While the culture is superficially classless, its meaning differs across class lines. The middle-class adolescent has always had other alternatives: satisfaction through education or job, or 'constructive' solutions such as community social work, charity walks, Duke of Edinburgh-type schemes. (It is only recently that this group has been collectively involved in action that opens it to some public condemnation, for example, drug involvement and organized reaction against the regimentation of school.)

For the working-class adolescent only the town was left. And here – right from the drab cafés of the fifties to the more sophisticated entertainment arenas of the next decade – ways have been blocked. These scenes provided few opportunities for excitement, autonomy and sense of action. Either nothing at all was offered or it was dull and mediocre. He did not have enough money to participate nor the talent, luck or personal contacts to really make it. So, faced by leisure goals he could not reach, with little commitment or attachment to others, his situation contained an edge of desperation.[7] He saw himself as effect rather than cause, he was pushed around by 'them'. Rather than accept all this, rather than do nothing at all, he manufactured his own excitement, he made things happen out of nothing.

It was precisely this form which the happenings on the beaches took. This is not to read into the situation a sophistication and awareness absent in the participants themselves. The Mods in the mid-sixties were all too aware of the absurdity of both their problem and their solution. This was the charac-teristic mood I described in the last chapter: the drifting, the apparent

ss, the ever-present but somewhat desperate hope that
ld happen and, in the end, the readiness to make that something
asked the boy or girl on the street corner, the beach, the Wimpy,
amusement arcade, the pier, the disco, what they wanted to do, they would answer 'nothing'. And this answer had to be taken at its face value. All that was left was to make a gesture, to deliberately enter into risky situations where putting the boot in, throwing rocks around, dumping a girl into the sea, could be seen for what they were. Add to this volitional element the specific desires for change and freedom over the holidays, to get away from home, the romance of roughing it on the beaches or sleeping four to a bed in a grotty seafront boarding-house, finding a bird, getting some pills. One chose these things, but at the same time one was in a society whose structure had severely limited one's choice and one was in a situation where what deterministic forces there were – the lack of amenities, the action of the police, the hostility of the locals – made few other choices possible.

The Style

The first signs of all this, the first murmurings of separation later to be expressed so explicitly and vehemently by such groups as the Rolling Stones and The Who, came with the Teddy Boys. They were the first group whose style was self-created, although they were reacting not so much against 'adults' but the little that was offered in the fifties: the café, the desolate town, the pop culture of the dance halls, Locarnos and Meccas aimed at the over twenties.[8] Their style was adapted from a different social group – the Edwardian Dandy – and its exaggeration and ritualization were mirrored in the groups' activities: a certain brutality, callousness, indifference and almost stoicism.

Although it was less than most people – and certainly the press – imagined, the violence was there and it was frightening enough to provoke a moral panic.[9] There was nothing as dramatic as the Clacton incident which 'made' the Mods and Rockers, but the Teddy Boy style was also very clearly shaped by the societal reaction to its initial manifestations. The stylistic innovations were seen – and quite rightly so – as being not just ones of dress, but as heralding a new cultural contour to be taken into account in society's normative map making.

The heroes of the fifties were cast in the very American mould of the brute and the hipster: Brando and Dean being the most perfect and Presley the nearest musical equivalent. But while this type emerged from and pointed towards many more complicated streams in America, the Teddy Boy was extraordinarily simple in what he represented. It would have been difficult to predict from 'Rock Around the Clock', 'Disc Jockey Jamboree' and the rumblings that sometimes accompanied them, all the proliferation, confusion and sorting out in the youth scene during the subsequent few years.

The Mods were to emerge in what Nuttall calls the *classic* as opposed to the *romantic* idiom. The Teddy Boy style – born in what was very much the traditional working-class areas of South London – ended up (as clothing styles often do in their last dying moments) in grotesque extremes which gave way to the more 'reformed' drape suit. This was the point at which the new teenager of the end of the fifties, personified perfectly in Colin Macinnes' stylized *Absolute Beginners*,[10] really began to stake his claim. These kids were sharp and self-confident, although unsophisticated and gauche compared to their American equivalents. Even among the middle classes at the time, no type as sophisticated and hip as Sahinger's Holden Caulfield could be found. They adopted what was briefly called the 'Italianate' style of dressing, drifted into the world of Expresso bars and were drawn musically to rhythm and blues, particularly small groups, rather than the loud excesses of rock.

Some, like Nuttall, see these kids – and not the Rockers, as was popularly believed – as the real descendants of the Ted. They inherited his vanity, confidence and fussiness; they were too fastidious for the motorway caffs which at that time were attracting another stream. And it was their 'sharp dressing' which led to the modern, the modernist, the Mod. By now, the beginning of the sixties, changes were diffusing rapidly, the youth culture was being opened up to new influences and it was difficult to sort out the types. Already the art school students and college or university drop-outs were appearing on the scene, and the musical focus switched from loud rock, from the brief skiffle craze and from the older conformist ballad tradition, to indigenous groups such as the Beatles, the Kinks, the Pretty Things, the Rolling Stones. A bright hysterical ambience began concentrating in the London clubs such as the Flamingo and the Marquee. This was where the Mod era began and it had reached at least one of its peaks by 1963.

In the meantime, the Rockers were evolving. They could justifiably be seen as similar to the Teds in at least two senses: they were in many respects the *lumpen*, those who hadn't caught on to the new teenage image personified by the Mods; also, they were more outgoing and direct, closer to the butch image of earlier years. But, as Nuttall stresses, they were not just transformed Teds: they leaned towards the romantic stream in their longing for the earlier crudities of pure rock. Their transitional models – like the Italianate styles had been for the Mods – were the ton-up boys of the motorways. These boys saw the Teds becoming too respectable – a few years before the end of the decade, Teddy Boy suits were already being sold at jumble sales – and they went directly to the old American 'Wild Ones' theme: the black leather, the motor-bikes, the metal studs. Away from the city and the coffee bars, they belonged on the motorway and the transport cafés. The more legendary of the cafés, such as the Busy Bee and the Ace on the southern end of the M1 are still, more than ten years later, shrines for the faithful. 'Rockers' – the term, of course, deriving from the loyalty to early rock – was simply the name given and taken by this group.

So, leaving aside all the other significant developments on the youth scene that were beginning to tick over, by 1962–63 the Mods and Rockers division was already there. But – and this is what is missed by all commentators, however sensitive to the nuances of this division – it was *not* a division between all adolescents, nor, more importantly, was the division public knowledge in any significant sense. To the groups themselves, the gap might indeed have seemed sharp enough:

> 'Mod' meant effeminate, stuck-up, emulating the middle classes, aspiring to a competitive sophistication, snobbish, phony. 'Rocker' meant hopelessly naïve, loutish, scruffy and above all betraying: for the mods . . . wanted a good image for the rebel group, the polished sharp image that would offset the adult patronization by which this increasingly self-aware world of the adolescent might be disarmed.[11]

But such contrasting self-images were never part of the outsider's consciousness. And the wholly unequal balance between the groups by 1963 must also be understood. The Rockers were left out of the race: they were unfashionable and unglamorous just because they appeared to be more class-bound. The images of lout and yobbo which they had inherited from the Teds hardly made them marketable property. The Mods, on the other hand, made all the running and although the idiom they emerged out of was real enough, it was commercial exploitation which made them completely dominant. This was the Mod era, the manic frenzied years of all-night discos in the West End and the New Towns of southern England, the steel toothed combs, the purple hearts, the peculiar tone of near hysteria caught so perfectly by Tom Wolfe in his description of the 'kinetic trance' of 'Noonday Underground' at Tiles in Oxford Street.[12]

The life in such scenes ('Two hundred and fifty office boys, office girls, department store clerks, messengers, members of London's vast child work-force of teenagers who leave school at fifteen, pour down into this cellar, Tiles, in the middle of the day for a break')[13] was literally and metaphorically underground. On the surface, the intensity of the Mod thing was diluted, but only slightly, by commercialism: Carnaby Street, Cathy McGowan, Twiggy, transistor radios always on to Radio Caroline (opened on Easter Sunday, 1964), boutiques, the extravagant velvets, satins and colours of the more flamboyant of the early Mods. By the middle of 1964 there were at least six magazines appealing mainly to Mods, the weeklies with a circulation of about 500,000, the monthlies about 250,000. There was also *Ready, Steady, Go*, a TV programme aimed very much at the Mods, with its own magazine related to the programme and which organized the famous Mod ball in Wembley. This was the time when whole streams within schools, sometimes whole schools and even whole areas and housing estates were talked of as having 'gone Mod'.

In this rapid diffusion, the outsider could be forgiven for missing some of the less superficial changes. Unlike the commercial entrepreneurs (who saw this all along) he missed, for example, the significant emergence at this time of the working-class girl, who received her relative economic freedom much later than the male. The special market aimed at her was just beginning to reach its apex and in many ways Mod was a more female than a male phenomenon. At the Bank Holiday weekends the 15-year-old Mod girl, with her pasty, mask-like make-up, her flapping bell-bottomed trousers, her flat chest, her painted staring eyes and clutching her cheap Japanese transistor to her ear, was always the dominant sight. More pathetically and more obviously than anyone else, she had been cheated.

The public only saw those of her kind who made it or were about to make it. Like Tom Wolfe's Linda: the 17-year-old Essex girl who left school at 15 (as most of her six brothers and sisters had), starting a job as a clerk, drifting into Tiles, finding a job (at £9 10s. a week) selling shoes in the arcade next to the club, being spotted by chance and getting her photo published '– and Linda is *on the verge*, she could become a model or . . . a *figure*, a celebrity, however these things happen . . . and yet Linda doesn't give all that much of a damn about it.'[14] And there were few Lindas.

The outsider also never saw that this diffusion had produced a considerable and very rigid streaming within the Mod idiom itself. Almost from the beginning there was a distinction between the more extravagant stream, attracted to the frothy world of the boutiques, the camp, the flotsam of the art school followers. They were very different from the sterner group, with their wide jeans, old army anoraks or combat jackets, canvas shoes. These were the ones who, on their Corgis or Lambrettas, were thought to be involved in the clashes with the Rockers at the resorts. In fact, by 1964–5, the so-called Mod was hardly recognizable. Leaving aside such groups as the beats, the Rockers themselves and the Anglicized plastic flower children, youth workers at Brighton could distinguish at least between *the scooter boys* (dressed in plain but smart trousers and pullovers, plus anoraks, often trimmed with fur; usually uninterested in violence, but involved with the law in a range of driving offences); *the hard Mods* (wearing heavy boots, jeans with braces, short hair, the precursors of the Skinheads, usually prowling in large groups with the appearance of being jumpy, unsure of themselves, on the paranoic edge, heavily involved in any disturbance) and *the smooth Mods* (usually older and better off, sharply dressed, moving in small groups and usually looking for a bird).[15]

To the extent that one could distinguish any core values in this period, these were certainly values congruent with both the style that was selected and the structural problems that had to be faced. There was something more than the rejection of the work ethic which our earlier analysis of the working-class adolescent situation pointed to. These groups – as Dave Laing suggests – had no real conviction about the rationality of the division between work and play, production and consumption. They were not the occupants of the passive consumption role that society had condemned them to and then condemned them for playing: 'Because they no longer believed in the idea of work, but had to submit to the necessity of it, they were not passive consumers as their television and light ale elders were.'[16] Laing goes on to quote from an article in *Heatwave* about the 'furious consumption programme which seemed to be a grotesque parody of the aspirations of the Mods' parents'.[17] What the adult saw on *Ready, Steady, Go* and on the beaches was a stylized version of this programme. They could not see the way in which the clothes, the pills and above all the music were actively used by the kids as catalysts, and modes of expression. Quite rightly, Laing, Nuttall and other such commentators see the essence of the Mods' subversive potential not in the occasional outbursts of violence and still less in drug-taking (an activity which, in its pill form at least, mirrors the bourgeois consumer notion of how to buy solutions to problems) but in their calculated attempt to live in leisure time, not just to consume but to create themselves into Mods. The fact that such erosion of the work ethic occurs in other groups[18] does not make it less significant.

A few lines about some of the music of the time are necessary. By looking at two groups in particular – the Rolling Stones and The Who – as well as using a general stylistic analysis, one arrives at the same roads to the beaches as did theories stressing instrumental solutions. Music was much more important for the Mods than the Rockers – and also than for the Teds who had not grown up as a generation through the whole Rock explosion. If the Beatles tuned in to the ethos in its most general way – and changed as this changed – it was the Rolling Stones who were the first major liberators. As Cohn puts it in two memorable phrases: 'they stirred up a whole new mood of teen arrogance' and they were 'turning into the voice of hooliganism'.[19] The title of one song, 'Get Off My Cloud' could have been the theme of the early years of the separatist youth culture, but more specifically than the separation theme, they managed to convey so many other dominant moods. Theirs was the voice of arrogance and narcissism celebrated by the early Mods; of aggression and frustration (captured especially in 'I Can't Get No Satisfaction' – a song never referring to purely sexual frustration); of cynicism (as in 'Mother's Little Helper') and the occasional hysterical scream at being able to thwart the adult world's attempts at manipulating them. Referring back to Downes's argument, it can be seen how 'right' these moods were for what the kids wanted to use their culture for.

The Stones's background was complicated (ex-art school, Jagger an LSE dropout) and they were to move on to more complicated things, giving up the purist rhythm and blues strand. In contrast, The Who were pure and complete Mod. They came straight out of Shepherds Bush, 'one of the most major Mod citadels'[20] and they were unambiguously and uncomplicatedly representative of the new consumers. Although they were eventually managed and staged by entrepreneurs of the swinging London scene, who invariably were middle class, they explicitly stood for, sang about and understood (a gift nearly non-existent in the pop world) their origins.

They shared anger and aggression with the Stones, but there were no cynical attacks on the affluent society and there was none of Jagger's arrogance and certainty. Their dominant mood was uncertainty, the jumpiness and edginess of the hard Mods, and an almost ugly inarticulateness and tension. This started with early songs such as 'I Can't Explain' (their first record) and moved through 'Substitute' ('The simple things I say are all complicated') and reached its convulsive climax with 'My Generation', Pete Townsend's battle hymn of unresolved and unresolvable tensions, which, more than any other song, was the sound of Brighton, Margate and Clacton. Now, six years later, The Who still include this song in most of their live performances and the orgy of smashed instruments and deafening feedback with which it ends, gives the message as much as the words do:

> People try to put us down
> Just because we get around.
> Things they do look awful cold
> Hope I die before I get old.

> This is my generation, baby
> Why don't you all f-f-f-fade away
> Don't try to dig what we all say
> I'm not trying to cause a big sensation
> I'm talking about my generation.
>
> This is my generation, baby,
> My generation.

Although The Who have also moved on to some other things, this tone still remains and the stuttering anger has not become much less pronounced. In his classic *Rolling Stone* 1968 interview, quoted by Dave Laing and many others, Pete Townsend testifies to the enduring influence of the Mod experience:

> It really affected me in an incredible way because it teases me all the time, because whenever I think 'Oh you know youth today is never going to make it' I just think of that fucking gesture that happened in England. It was the closest to patriotism that I've ever felt.

This was the same gesture which my analysis of the instrumental problems of the working-class adolescent in the mid-sixties led to. So, by another route, we arrive on the beaches, the scenes where this book started. By 1964 the Rockers, as Nuttall puts it, 'seemed almost endearingly butch':[21] they were dying out, but fought with the stubborn bitterness of a group left out of the mainstream of social change. Without the publicity that was given to the initial clashes with the Mods, their weakness would have become more apparent and they would have metamorphosed into another variant of the tougher tradition. Their very nature and origins made their chances of gaining strength autonomously (for example, by attracting new recruits) virtually out of the question. Such groups are essentially self-limiting.

In a different way, the reaction also kept the Mods going. Even by 1963 the symbols had not crystallized: newspapers were still using the term 'Teddy Boy' to describe *both* groups or terms such as 'ton-up kids' to describe the Rockers; as in the early days of the Edwardians, the term 'Modernists' appeared more than anywhere else on the fashion pages. It needed a public drama to give each group its identity as folk devils. My argument in this chapter has been that although 'endogenous' factors – the youth culture, the structural position of working-class adolescents – are themselves difficult to separate from the societal reaction, such factors receive their initial importance in the creation of social types. The assignment of negative identities to these types is then dependent on the moral panic.

The Sociology of Moral Panics

Just as the Mods and Rockers did not appear from nowhere, so too must the societal reaction, the moral panic, be explained. Magistrates, leader writers and politicians do not react like laboratory creatures being presented a series of random stimuli, but in terms of positions, statuses, interests, ideologies and values. Their responsiveness to rumours, for example, is not just related to the internal dynamics of the rumour process as described earlier, but whether the rumours support their particular interests.

The foundations of this particular moral panic should be understood in terms of different levels of generality. At the lowest level, there were those peculiar to the Mods and Rockers phenomenon; at the highest, abstract principles which can be applied to the sociology of moral panics as a whole or (even more generally) to a theory of the societal reactions to deviance.

I will not reconsider here some of the lowest order processes already dealt with: how the ambiguity of the crowd situation lent itself to panic rumours, how the media created the news and images which lent the cognitive basis for the panic, how situational pressures conditioned the control culture. A higher level starting-off point must be the same as that which structured our consideration of the Mods and Rockers themselves, namely, the ways in which the affluence and youth themes were used to conceptualize the social changes of the decade.

The sixties began the confirmation of a new era in adult–youth relations. The Teddy Boys (and their European equivalents – the *halbstarke*, the *blouson noir*) were the first warnings on the horizon. What everyone had grimly prophesied had come true: high wages, the emergence of a commercial youth culture 'pandering' to young people's needs, the elevation of scruffy pop heroes into national idols (and even giving them MBEs), the 'permissive society', the 'coddling by the Welfare State' – all this had produced its inevitable results. As one magistrate expressed it to me in 1965, 'Delinquency is trying to get at too many things too easily . . . people have become more aware of the good things in life . . . we've thrown back the curtain for them too soon.'

The Mods and Rockers symbolized something far more important than what they actually did. They touched the delicate and ambivalent nerves through which post-war social change in Britain was experienced. No one wanted depressions or austerity, but messages about 'never having it so good' were ambivalent in that some people were having it too good and too quickly: 'We've thrown back the curtain for them too soon.' Resentment and jealousy were easily directed at the young, if only because of their increased spending power and sexual freedom. When this was combined with a too-open flouting of the work and leisure ethic, with violence and vandalism, and the (as yet) uncertain threats associated with drug-taking, something more than the image of a peaceful Bank Holiday at the sea was being shattered.

One might suggest that ambiguity and strain was greatest at the beginning of the sixties. The lines had not yet been clearly drawn and, indeed, the reaction was part of this drawing of the line. The period can be seen as constituting what Erikson terms a 'boundary crisis', a period in which a group's uncertainty about itself is resolved in ritualistic confrontations between the deviant and the community's official agents.[22] One does not have to make any conspiratorial assumptions about deviants being deliberately 'picked out' to clarify normative contours at times of cultural strain and ambiguity, to detect in the response to the Mods and Rockers declarations about moral boundaries, about how much diversity can be tolerated. As Erikson notes about so-called 'crime waves', they dramatize the issues at stake when boundaries are blurred and provide a forum to articulate the issues more explicitly. Two things might be happening here:

> . . . the community begins to censure forms of behaviour which have been present in the group for some time but have never attracted any particular attention before, and . . . certain people in the group who have already acquired a disposition to act deviantly move into the breach and begin to test the boundary in question.[23]

Again, the notion of 'deviantly disposed' people actually 'moving in' to test the boundary should not be taken too literally. One only has to account for some autonomous potential for defiance from young people to see how the spiral of conflict develops. The real Devil, whose shapes the early Puritans were trying to establish, was the same devil that the Mods and Rockers represented.

It should be noted that scapegoating and other types of hostility are more likely to occur in situations of maximum ambiguity. The fact that it was not very clear what the Mods and Rockers had actually done, might have increased rather than decreased the chances of an extreme reaction. Groups such as the Northview sample had a very unclear image of the behaviour, but supported fairly punitive sanctions. The message that did percolate through confirmed suspicions that little good would come from the new era. The threats posed by the Teddy Boys might now be realized and the situation was ripe for beliefs such as those expressed in the It's Not Only This theme.

As soon as the new phenomenon was named, the devil's shape could be easily identified. In this context, the ways in which the deviance was associated with a fashion style is particularly significant. Fashion changes are not always perceived simply as something novel, a desire to be different or attract attention or as fads which will ultimately die out. They might be seen as signifying something much deeper and more permanent – for example, 'the permissive society' – and historically, stylistic changes have often represented ideological commitments or movements. So, for example, the Sans Culottes in the French Revolution wore long pants instead of conventional breeches as a symbol of radicalism and the American beatnik style became identified with certain signs of disaffiliation.

Mod fashions were seen to represent some more significant departure than a mere clothing change. The glossiness of the image, the bright colours and the associated artefacts such as motor scooters, stood for everything resented about the affluent teenager. There were also new anxieties, such as the sexual confusion in clothing and hair-styles: the Mod boy with pastel-shaded trousers and the legendary make-up on his face, the girls with their short-cropped hair and sexless, flat appearance. The sheer uniformity in dress was a great factor in making the threat more apparent: the cheap mass-produced anoraks with similar colours, and the occasional small group riding their Vespas like a menacing pincer patrol, gave the appearance of greater organization than ever existed, and hence of a greater threat.

The way in which a single dramatic incident – or, at least, the reporting of this incident – served to confirm the actors' deviant identity is also important. To draw on the analogy already used, the situation was similar to that in which a natural disaster brings to the surface a condition or conflict that previously was latent. The requirement of visibility – and hooliganism is by definition public and visible – so essential for successful problem definition, was met right from the outset. Mass collective action which before was played out on a more restricted screen, now was paraded even to audiences previously insulated by geographical, age and social class barriers.

This leads on to another major reason for the form of the reaction. The behaviour was presented and perceived as something more than a delinquent brawl and the Mods and Rockers could not be classified very plausibly as the ordinary slum louts associated with such behaviour in the past. They appeared to be affluent, well clothed and groomed and, above all, highly mobile. They had moved out of the bomb-sites in the East End and the streets of the Elephant and Castle. The various forms which hooliganism had taken in the past were not of the same order. Oxbridge-type 'pranks' or 'high spirits' could be tolerated and not assigned social problem status not just because the deviants were protected by their relative power, but because such activities occurred on a relatively small scale, were self-contained and invisible. The student only became a folk devil when his actions became more political, more visible and more threatening. Grosvenor Square, the Essex troubles, the Cambridge Garden House affair, were his Clactons. Similarly, the street gangs of the slums and housing estates could, if not tolerated, simply be allocated the traditional delinquent position. This was just how you expected kids from that sort of area/home/school to behave. But now, things were literally and meta-phorically too close to home. These were not just the slum louts whom one could disown, but faintly recognizable creatures who had crawled out from under some very familiar rocks.

Allied to threats posed by the new mobility (the groups' motor-bikes and scooters were obsessively seen as important) and the wider stage on which the behaviour was now being played out, was the image of class barriers breaking down in the emergence of the teenage culture. Traditionally, the deviant role had been assigned to the lower class urban male, but the Mods and Rockers appeared to be less class tied: here were a group of impostors, reading the lines which everyone knew belonged to some other group. Even their clothes were out of place: without leather jackets they could hardly be distinguished from bank clerks. The uneasiness felt about actors who are not quite in their places can lead to greater hostility. Something done by an out-group is simply condemned and fitted into the scheme of things, but in-group deviance is embarrassing, it threatens the norms of the group and tends to blur its boundaries with the out-group.

The Mod was unique in that his actual appearance was far away from the stereotypical hooligan personified by the Teddy Boy or the Rocker. He was also nowhere near as identifiable as the beatnik or hippy. Dave Laing attributes the Mods' subversive potential to this very ordinariness. With few exceptions, their dress was neat and not obviously extreme: 'The office boys, typists and shop assistants *looked* alright, but there was something in the way they moved which adults couldn't make out.'[24] His disdain for advancement in work, his air of distance, his manifest display of ingratitude for what society had given him (this appears strongly in the Boredom and Affluence themes): these were found more unsettling than any simple conformity to the folklore image of the yob. The detection of a new element in deviance is found more disturbing than being presented with forms which society has already successfully coped with.

Such feelings were even more understandable and pronounced in places like Brighton. The town had not yet come to terms with the fact that the old type of summer visitors and day-trippers from London were no longer coming to Brighton, but spending their holidays on package trips to the Costa Brava. The respectable working-class couples in their twenties and thirties were no longer packing out the boarding-houses or spending money in the traditional avenues of entertainment which had remained basically unchanged for decades. The very old were still coming down, but a coach-load of pensioners down for the day were hardly big spenders.

It was the much younger group that was 'flooding' the place, and to them the town turned a double face. These were not the sort of people to attract to Brighton and the discouragement they faced was all too obvious. Some were refused service in cafés and pubs, chased away if they were congregating around a shop or seafront stall, even refused accommodation by the landladies of the guest-houses. On the other hand, these were the new 'affluent hordes' and there were no compunctions about exploiting them commercially, for example, by raising prices. It could be seen, though, from the Seaview and Beachside action groups, that the dominant local face was hostile and resentful: these scruffs and hooligans should not be allowed to frighten away the decent holidaymakers, the family groups (who, by this time, were tailing off anyway). There were other new menaces besides the Mods and Rockers: the long-haired Continental youths in the language schools that had sprung up on the south coast and (in Brighton) students from Sussex University who were not only offensive in appearance but partly instrumental in getting Brighton its first Labour MP for generations.

The Mods and Rockers just represented the epitome of these changes; to many local residents, as a Brighton editor put it '. . . they were something frightening and completely alien . . . they were visitors from a foreign planet and they should be banished to where they came from'. When in 1965 the new Mayor of Brighton outlined his vision of the town's future as 'a popular holiday resort where the whelk stalls and the Mods and Rockers will be a thing of the past', a local newspaper's editorial comment was 'Mods and Rockers we would gladly be without – they are a pricey pest. But whelk stalls? . . .' (*Brighton and Hove Gazette*, 4 June 1965).

It was not surprising then, that at the local level, any 'solution' not based on the policy of total exclusion met with hostility. The early voices of the Seaview and Beachside groups were echoed in the sustained campaign against schemes such as the Brighton Archways Ventures[25] and later presences such as those of beatniks and hippies in resorts like St Ives. As a Brighton Alderman said about the beatniks, 'These are people who ought not to be in Brighton and if they are unfortunately here, they ought not to be catered for in any way' (*Evening Argus*, 24 November 1967). The rhetoric of moral panics – 'We won't allow our seafront/area/town/country to be taken over by hooligans/hippies/blacks/Pakistanis' is a firmly established one.

If the Mods and Rockers had done nearly all they were supposed to have done in the way of violence, damage to property, inconveniencing and annoying others (and clearly they did a lot of these things), it does not need a very sophisticated analysis to explain why such rule-breaking was responded to punitively. But threats need not be as direct as this and one must understand that the response was as much to what they stood for as what they did. In one of the few analyses of the relationships between moral indignation and the social structure, Gusfield – looking at Prohibition and the post-Repeal periods – explains the responses of the temperance movement as symbolic solutions to conflict and the indignant reaction to loss of status.[26]

He suggests – directly following Ranulf's classic analysis[27] that moral indignation might have a disinterested quality when the transgression is solely moral and doesn't impinge upon the life and behaviour of the judge; it is a 'hostile response of the norm upholder to the norm violator where no direct personal advantage to the norm upholder is at stake'.[28] This disinterested quality might thus apply to the Bohemian, the homosexual, the drug addict, where questions of style and ways of life are at stake, but not to the political radical, whose action might threaten the structure of society nor to the delinquent who poses direct threats to property and person.

I doubt whether this distinction between 'interested' and 'disinterested' is a viable one, as it seems to imply much too narrow a conception of interest and threat. With groups such as drug-takers and hippies[29] even though little apparent physical or 'political' threat is involved, there is a direct *conflict of interests*. There is certainly a great deal at stake for the norm-upholder if he allows such action to go unpunished and his indignation has only a slight element of the disinterested about it. In the case of the Mods and Rockers, the moral panic was sustained both by the direct threats (in the narrow sense) to persons, property, commercial interests and the gross interests threatened by the violation of certain approved styles of life. Such a combination of interests can be seen clearly in the individuals like Blake. He saw physical dangers, personal disadvantages and the physical threat represented by all the youth culture was supposed to be: prematurely affluent, aggressive, permissive and challenging the ethics of sobriety and hard work. In his case (but perhaps not in all the forms of moral indignation Ranulf tries to explain this way) one might also detect the psychological element of the envy and resentment felt by the lower middle classes, supposedly the most frustrated and repressed of groups. They condemn, that is, behaviour which is secretly craved.

More fundamentally, a theory of moral panics, moral enterprise, moral crusades or moral indignation needs to relate such reactions to conflicts of interests – at community and societal levels – and the presence of power differentials which leave some groups vulnerable to such attacks. The manipulation of appropriate symbols – the process which sustains moral campaigns, panics and crusades – is made much easier when the object of attack is both highly visible and structurally weak.

Coming to an End

The one more or less explicit way in which the emergence of the Mods and Rockers as folk devils and the generation of the moral panic around this have been related to each other, is via the model of deviancy amplification. A very truncated form of how one such sequence may have run is illustrated below.

Initial Problem   (stemming from structural and cultural position of
↓   working-class adolescent)

Initial Solution   (deviant action and style)
↓

Societal Reaction   (involving elements of misperception, e.g. in
                     inventory and subsequent distortion in terms of
                     long-term values and interests)

↓

Operation of Control (sensitization, dramatization, escalation)
Culture, Exploitation
and Creation of
Stereotypes
↓

Increased deviance,
Polarization
↓

Confirmation of   (theory proved)
Stereotypes

Although it is not implausible to suggest that something like this sequence may have operated, one problem immediately apparent in any attempt to generalize too rigidly from it, is that no readily available explanation exists as to how and why the sequence ever ends. Putting the stages in some context – even as cursorily as this chapter has done – raises one defect of the amplification type of model, namely, that it is a-historical. This is paradoxical, because such processual models were put forward specifically to counteract static, canonical theories of deviance. Clearly, the use of cybernetic language such as feedback and stimuli is too automatic and mechanistic and does not allow for the range of meanings given to human action and the way in which the actor can move to shape his own passage. Both these elements can be examined if – taking the sequence merely as one typical movement in time – we try to answer the question of why it ever ended. What stopped the moral panic? Why do we still not have Mods and Rockers with us?

Looking firstly at the reaction from the public and the mass media, the answer is that there was simply a lack of interest. At no stage was there a simple one-to-one relationship between action and reaction: the Mod phenomenon developed before public attention branded it as evil, the attention continued ritualistically for a while even when the evil was subdued and finally the attention waned when other phenomena that were both new and newsworthy forced themselves into the public areas. While drugs, student militancy and hippies became the headline social problems of the later half of the sixties, 'traditional' fringe delinquency of the expressive type continued – even at seaside resorts – without much attention being paid to it. In northern resorts, less accessible places like the Isle of Sheppey or near certain cafés and roundabouts on inland roads, the same behaviour that took place in Clacton, Brighton or Margate was repeated. But the behaviour was too regular and familiar to be of note, it was not as visible as the original incidents and some of the original actors, particularly the Rockers, were leaving the stage. There were also the sorts of processes which occur in cases of mass delusion: a counter-suggestibility produced by the absurdity of some of the initial beliefs and a tailing off of interest when it was felt that 'something is being done about it'.

Like the last spurts of a craze or fashion style, the behaviour was often manifested with an exaggerated formalism. There was a conscious attempt to repeat what had been done two or three years before by actors who almost belonged to another generation. The media and the control agents sometimes seized on to this behaviour, gave it new names and attempted to elevate it to the Mods and Rockers position. In places like Skegness, Blackpool and Great

Yarmouth, the new hooligans were called by the press or control agents, 'Greasers', 'Trogs' or 'Thunderbirds'. But such casting was not successful, even when there was an attempt to make the actors look even worse than the Mods and Rockers (as they, in turn) had been made to look worse than the Teddy Boys. At the end of 1966, for example, a Police Inspector told the Great Yarmouth court that the offenders were from '. . . the roughneck types who have come hell bent on causing trouble to everybody, including the police, but also the innocent youths who are trying to enjoy themselves . . . They are not the usual Mods and Rockers.' So already, the devils of three short years before were recast into relatively benign roles in the gallery of social types exhibited in the name of social control. It took another few years before the drug-taker and the student radical – destined, one thinks, for fairly permanent occupancy – were joined in the folk devil role by a more traditional working-class representative, the Skinhead.

Internal changes within the Mod phenomenon must also be appreciated. There was a straightforward generational change in which the original actors simply matured out. In 1966 one spoke to 19-year-olds who said that they used to be Mods but now it was 'dead' and anyway cost too much. Already by 1967, the major proportion of kids in towns like Brighton did not identify with, or even mention, either of the two groups. This sort of change is familiar to students of fads, crazes and fashions: an initial period of latency where the style or action is only followed by a few, is succeeded by a period of rapid growth and diffusion. There is, then, a phase of commercialization and exploit-ation, slackening off, resistance or lack of enthusiasm, followed by stagnation and the eventual preservation of the style in nostalgic memories. In his perceptive history of the pop explosion George Melly deduces the same basic pattern: 'What starts as revolt finishes as style – as mannerism.'[30] Thus – to use Melly's examples – the Monkees were plastic Beatles, Barry McGuire a plastic Bob Dylan. The cycle mirrors the stage of the adolescent breaking from his family; once this is through, the impetus is lost. The state is one of instant obsolescence.

The years of the Mod decline were actually more complicated than Melly's 'cycle of obsolescence' explanation suggests. By 1965 there were several strands within the Mod scene and the more extravagant Mods – who were too involved in the whole rhythm and blues, camp, Carnaby Street scene to really 'need' the weekend clashes – began merging into the fashion-conscious hippies and their music began to grow closer to underground sounds.[31] The others were never distinctive enough to maintain any generational continuity. Yet another curious and unpredictable twist was to take place:

It was not until the sixties had almost drawn to a close that the cool classic English tradition reasserted itself with the skinheads, whose formalisation of labouring clothes, braces, jeans, vests, heavy boots and orphanage haircuts was the most dourly anti-romantic style yet arrived at. It was a return to the position of the ted, but in reverse. The ted was striving to surmount his working-class family. The skinheads were and are striving to form a dissident group which enjoys all the security of a working-class identity. Thus they despise the strong bourgeois element in the underground and throw their lot in with their local football team and Enoch Powell. Armed, stoic, harrying the Pakistanis exactly as the Teds harried the West Indians in the Notting Hill riots in 1958. The simple clanging of reggae, ska and rock-steady swept away all the fancy arabesques of acid rock.[32]

Using parallels from the world of art and fashion though, is not enough. When more than a sheer aesthetic revolt is at stake, when the gesture is one that speaks of disgust, apathy, boredom and a sense of one's *own* obsolescence and lack of power, then the instrumental and expressive solutions are brought together. The power of the symbols to differentiate their users from those who accept defeat, becomes deflated. The sheer increases in what was familiar, standardized and routine, instead of – as the Mod's era often was – exciting and alive, accounts for much of this deflation. There is a striking parallel in Becker's account of the decline of the Alliance Youth (the Wandervogel) in the Germany of the twenties:

> . . . the ways in which social objects, expected responses and reflected selves were defined had become relatively standard . . . it is a little hard to feel elation at its fullest intensity when thousands of others have undergone the same experience and have told all about it to everyone willing to lend an ear.[33]

It would, of course, be romantic in the extreme to talk of elation being the dominant mood of the Mods and Rockers. For much of the time any elation that a sense of action could bring, was submerged by the discomfort, unpleasantness and resentment caused by the treatment they received from nearly all the adults whom they encountered. This factor forces attention to another reason for the whole phenomenon coming to an end: the fact that social control might have its intended consequences. In the somewhat romantic eagerness of transactional theorists to point to the evil effects of social control in leading to yet more deviance, they have conveniently suppressed the possibility that potential deviants might, in fact, be frightened off or deterred by actual or threatened control measures. After being put off the train by the police before even arriving at your destination, and then being continually pushed around and harassed by the police on the streets and beaches, searched in the clubs, refused service in cafés, you might just give up in disgust. The game was simply not worth it. In a mass phenomenon such as the Mods and Rockers a form of de-amplification sets in: the amplification stops because the social distance from the deviants is made so great, that new recruits are put off from joining. The only joiners are the very young or the *lumpen* who have access to few other alternatives. These are the ones who might fight with the ferocity of a group who knows it is being left behind. In the meantime, the original hard-core might mature and grow out of deviance.

Mentioning the possibilities of de-amplification leads on to the few final comments that one is obliged – rightly, in my opinion – to make about the policy implications of the sort of sociological account so far presented. Many such implications have been implicit in my account and there is no need to spell them out again in detail. The difficulty with such sociology, though, is that different readers can draw different implications, not all of them necessarily compatible with each other. One might argue, for example, that if the *initial* manifestation of such phenomena as the Mods and Rockers (other examples might be various forms of vandalism, subcultural drug-taking, soccer hooliganism) is difficult or even impossible to prevent, one should attempt secondary prevention: for example, restraining the mass media in order to stop the first stages of amplification. Given a basic consensus – which the sociologist might not share – about the need for control or prevention, such an argument is not implausible. Nor is a common-sense view, that certain forms of deviant behaviour are best left alone on pure utilitarian grounds. That is, the cost of mounting any social control operation is just not worth it. Or else, a humanitarian liberal view could be argued: many of the punishments were harsh and unjust and should be wholeheartedly condemned.

All these – and many more – implications could be deduced from this study and ones like it. Sociologists do not have the power to stop such implications being made or acted upon, although they might offer their own perspectives on the theories which inform them. Manifestly, a view of deviance which assumes that it will disappear if one makes some minor adjustments in the way it is reacted to, does not do much justice to the nature of the phenomenon. Despite using terms such as 'panic' and analogies from the study of mass hysteria and delusion, I have not implied that the Mods and Rockers were psychogenic apparitions who would have gone away if we had simply ignored them or ingeniously invented some means of de-amplification (although this might, perhaps, have avoided much unhappiness, cost and inconvenience).

We are dealing on a large scale – and therefore the problem is infinitely more complex – with what Laing and the anti-psychiatry school are concerned with on a small scale. The argument is not that there is 'nothing there' when somebody is labelled mentally ill or that this person has no problems, but that the reaction to what is observed or inferred is fundamentally inappropriate. The initial step is one of unmasking and debunking: an intrinsic quality of the sceptical and transactional perspective on deviance. Once the real as opposed to the surface legitimations of the societal reaction are exposed, there is a possibility of undermining them and devising policies that are both more effective and more humane. The intellectual poverty and total lack of imagination in our society's response to its adolescent trouble-makers during the last twenty years, is manifest in the way this response compulsively repeats itself and fails each time to come to terms with the 'problem' that confronts it. Much is required from the sociologist of deviance who points such things out. It is not enough to say that witches should not have been burnt or that in some other society or in another century they might not have been called witches; one has to explain why and how certain people get to the stake now.

Ultimately, I am pessimistic about the chances of changing social policy in regard to such phenomena as the Mods and Rockers. More moral panics will be generated and other, as yet nameless, folk devils will be created. This is not because such developments have an inexorable inner logic, but because our society as present structured will continue to generate problems for some of its members – like working-class adolescents – and then condemn whatever solution these groups find.

Appendix: Sources of Data

The bulk of the fieldwork on the project was carried out between 1964 and 1967. The time between Easter 1964 (the date of the first Mods and Rockers event at Clacton) and September 1966 (the end of a three-year cycle of Bank Holiday weekends) is referred to as the *research period*. The following were the main sources of data used:

1. Documentary

(i) Press references to the Mods and Rockers during the whole research period. This includes all national papers (dailies and weeklies) as well as local press from the main areas involved: Brighton, Clacton, Great Yarmouth, Southend, Hastings and Margate.

Tape recordings of most national radio and television (BBC) news broadcasts over the Bank Holiday weekends during the research period.

(ii) A special collection of press cuttings covering the incidents at Margate over Whitsun 1964. These cuttings were compiled for the Margate Corporation by an agency, items being selected purely on the basis of the word 'Margate' being present. There were 724 separate items from papers dated 15 May–12 June. These include 223 editorials or columnist comments; 110 reports of speeches, interviews with public figures, etc.; 121 letters; 270 reports or features covering the incidents themselves.

(iii) Local publications of a more restricted circulation – parish newsletters, council minutes, annual reports of statutory or voluntary associations, etc.

(iv) Miscellaneous national documents such as the Hansard reports of the relevant parliamentary debates in the Commons and the Lords.

(v) Letters and reports received by the National Council of Civil Liberties alleging malpractices by police or courts during the various incidents.

(vi) Reanalysis of interview schedules used in a survey of forty-four youths convicted in the Margate magistrates court, Whitsun 1964.*

2. *Original*

(i) Two pilot questionnaires administered to a group of nineteen trainee probation officers in the preliminary stages of the study (December 1964). The first was in open-ended form and dealt with attitudes to various aspects of the Mods and Rockers – images, causes, solutions and initial reactions. The second was in the form of a ninety item Likert-scale covering responses to a hypothetical incident of hooliganism of the Mods and Rockers type. This scale was also completed by groups of teachers and WEA students.

(ii) Interviews and informal discussions in Brighton, Margate and Hastings at the end of 1964, after the first wave of incidents. Formal interviews were held with editors of all the local newspapers and various publicity department officials. Informal discussions, of the type used in the first stages of a community study, were held with informants such as hotel keepers, shop assistants, bus conductors, taxi-drivers and newspaper sellers.

(iii) Letters, some of them followed up with a personal interview and others with a postal questionnaire, were written to the MPs of the areas involved, local councillors and a range of other public figures who made statements about the Mods and Rockers and proposed plans to deal with them. In certain cases, individual plans crystallized into the more institutionalized forms, which are referred to as 'action groups'. Three such action groups were studied in detail, through prolonged contact with their main initiators – the 'Beachside' Safeguard Committee, the 'Seatown' Council Work Camp Scheme and the Brighton Archways Ventures.

(iv) In the case of the Brighton Archways Ventures, I participated as a volunteer worker over three Bank Holiday weekends. This was a Brighton based youth project, eventually financed by the Department of Education and Science and staffed by full-time social workers. It was designed to provide cheap sleeping accommodation and other help for young people coming down to Brighton and catered for all the diverse groups drifting down to the beaches: initially, more the Mods and Scooter Boys and later, the beatniks.[†]

---

* Some findings from the survey were reported in Paul Barker and Alan Little, 'The Margate Offenders: A Survey', *New Society*, 30 July 1964, pp. 6–10. I am grateful to Paul Barker for giving me access to the completed interview schedules.
† The history of the project has now been written up in three volumes – *Brighton Archways Ventures Report* (mimeo. 650 pages).

(v) Sixty-five interviews, thirty of which were tape-recorded, were carried out in Brighton over the Whitsun Bank Holiday, 1965. Members of the public standing on the promenade or pier watching the Mods and Rockers were interviewed on a quota sample basis by myself and another graduate criminology student. There were five refusals out of the original seventy approached in two days.

The following are the questions asked and the background characteristics of the sample (referred to in the book as the 'Brighton sample').

Brighton Sample (Whitsun 1965) Interview Schedule

I. Preamble

I'm from the University of London, doing a study of what people think about this sort of thing. Do you mind giving me ten minutes to answer a few questions? There are no right or wrong answers – I just want your personal opinion. If you don't mind talking into this tape-recorder, it'll save time because I won't have to write everything down. I'm not going to ask you for your name, so don't worry about what you say.

II. Question Guide

1. How do you feel about this sort of thing?
2. What do you think is the main cause of all this?
3. Do you think that this sort of thing is something new?
4. Do you think that we're going to have this sort of thing with us for a long time?
5. Do you agree with the way the police are handling this?
6. How would you like to see the ones who cause trouble handled?
   (a) on the spot
   (b) by the police
7. What would you do if your own child/brother/friend got involved in this?
8. What sort of youngsters do you think these are:
   Probe for: Local or out of town?
   Type of school?
   Social class?
   'Ordinary kids' or 'Delinquent types'?

III. Personal Information

Would you mind giving me some information about yourself, so that we can check, like Gallup Poll do, that we've got a cross section of opinion? Don't answer any of these questions if you don't want to.

Male 1		Local Resident 5	
Female 2		Out of town 6	
16–20 3		Occupation..........................	
21–24 4		....	
25–29 5		....	
30–34 6		....	
35–44 7		Labour............................... 1	
45–49 8		Conservative 2	
50–64 9		Liberal............................... 3	
65+ 10		Other................................ 4	
Married 1			
Single................................ 2			
Widowed 3			
Divorced/Separated 4			

Social Characteristics of Brighton Sample
(N = 65)

Sex	Male: 34	*Marital status*	Married: 31
	Female: 31		Single: 23
			Widowed/Divorced: 11
Age	16–20: 9		
	21–24: 9		
	25–29: 1	*Political affiliation*	
	30–34: 2		Labour: 31
	35–44: 6		Conservative: 28
	45–49: 6		Others/Don't know: 6
	50–64: 24		
	65: 8		
Place of residence	Local: 32	*Social class*	Working class: 40
	Out of Town: 33		Middle class 22
			Upper class 3

(vi) On the spot observations were made at every Bank Holiday in 1965 and 1966 in either Brighton or Great Yarmouth. The happenings themselves were observed as well as police activity and the reactions of visitors and local residents, such as shopkeepers with whom informal discussions were held. The court proceedings at Brighton were observed and recorded on three occasions. During one Bank Holiday (Brighton, Easter, 1966) the method used came closer to what sociologists unhumorously refer to as 'participant observation' in that I wore what could roughly be called Mod clothes and enjoyed the days with various groups on the beaches and the nights in the clubs.

(vii) Between summer 1965 and summer 1966, I carried out a survey of attitudes to delinquency in a London borough I called 'Northview'. The sample contained 133 'social control agents', people with key formal or informal positions in the delinquency control system or in some senses, opinion leaders in the local community. It was made up of roughly equal numbers of businessmen, councillors, doctors, headmasters, lawyers, magistrates, religious leaders, social workers and youth workers. Each member was interviewed personally, and the long list of questions (on delinquency in general, the courts, methods of prevention, etc.) contained four questions covering attitudes to the Mods and Rockers.*

(viii) Twenty-five essays written by third- and fourth-form pupils from a school in the East End of London. The essays entitled simply 'The Mods and Rockers' were set by the English teacher as part of normal course work.

---

* Full details of the sample and interview schedule can be found in S. Cohen, 'Hooligans, Vandals and the Community: Studies of Social Reaction to Juvenile Delinquency' (unpublished Ph.D. thesis, University of London, 1969).

Notes and References

Chapter 1

1 For example, Christopher Booker, *The Neophiliacs: A Study of the Revolution in the English Life in the Fifties and Sixties* (London: Collins, 1969); David Bailey and Francis Wyndham, *A Box of Pin-Ups* (London: Weidenfeld & Nicholson, 1965); Bernard Levin, *The Pendulum Years* (London: Jonathan Cape, 1970); and (in a different way) Jeff Nuttall, *Bomb Culture* (London: Paladin, 1970).
2 Howard S. Becker, *Outsiders: Studies in the Sociology of Deviance* (New York: Free Press, 1963), Chaps 7 and 8.
3 Joseph Gusfield, *Symbolic Crusade: Status Politics and the American Temperance Movement* (Urbana: University of Illinois, 1963).
4 Becker, op. cit. p. 145.
5 Howard S. Becker (Ed.), *Social Problems: A Modern Approach* (New York: John Wiley, 1966).
6 See Herbert Blumer, 'Collective Behaviour', in J. B. Gittler (Ed.), *Review of Sociology* (New York: Wiley, 1957); Ralph H. Turner, 'Collective Behaviour', in R. E. L. Farris (Ed.), *Handbook of Modern Sociology* (Chicago: Rand McNally, 1964), and Ralph H. Turner and Lewis M. Killian, *Collective Behaviour* (Englewood Cliffs, NJ: Prentice-Hall, 1957).
7 Orrin E. Klapp, *Heroes, Villains and Fools: The Changing American Character* (Englewood Cliffs, NJ: Prentice-Hall, 1962).
8 The sceptical revolution can only be understood as part of a broader reaction in the social sciences as a whole against the dominant models, images and methodology of positivism. It is obviously beyond my scope to deal here with this connection. For an account of the peculiar shape positivism took in the study of crime and deviance and of the possibilities of transcending its paradoxes, the work of David Matza is invaluable: *Delinquency and Drift* (New York: Wiley, 1964) and *Becoming Deviant* (Englewood Cliffs, NJ: Prentice-Hall, 1969).
9 Becker, *Outsiders: Studies in the Sociology of Deviance*, op. cit. p. 9.
10 R. D. Laing, *The Divided Self* (Harmondsworth: Penguin, 1965), p. 34.
11 A fuller account of these and other implications of the sceptical position is given in my Introduction and Postscript to Stanley Cohen (Ed.), *Images of Deviance*

(Harmondsworth: Penguin Books, 1971). Some examples of work influenced by this tradition can be found in that volume but more directly in Rubington and Weinberg's excellent collection of interactionist writings: Earl Rubington and Martin S. Weinberg (Eds), *Deviance: The Interactionist Perspective* (New York: Collier-Macmillan, 1968).

12 Edwin M. Lemert, *Social Pathology: A Systematic Approach to the Study of Socio-pathic Behaviour* (New York: McGraw-Hill, 1951) and *Human Deviance, Social Problems and Social Control* (Englewood Cliffs, NJ: Prentice-Hall, 1967).

13 Lemert, *Social Pathology*, op. cit.

14 ibid. p. 55.

15 See John I. Kitsuse, 'Societal Reaction to Deviant Behaviour: Problems of Theory and Method', *Social Problems* 9 (Winter 1962), pp. 247–56.

16 Kai T. Erikson, *Wayward Puritans: A Study in the Sociology of Deviance* (New York: John Wiley, 1966).

17 Becker, *Outsiders: Studies in the Sociology of Deviance*, op. cit. Chaps 7 and 8.

18 Paul Rock and Stanley Cohen, 'The Teddy Boy', in V. Bogdanor and R. Skidelsky (Eds), *The Age of Affluence: 1951–1964* (London: Macmillan, 1970).

19 Jock Young, 'The Role of the Police as Amplifiers of Deviancy, Negotiators of Reality and Translators of Fantasy: Some Aspects of our Present System of Drug Control as seen in Notting Hill', in Cohen, op. cit.

20 Joseph Gusfield, 'Moral Passage: The Symbolic Process in Public Designations of Deviance', *Social Problems* 15 (Fall 1967), pp. 175–88.

21 Young, op. cit. and *The Drug Takers: The Social Meaning of Drug-Taking* (London: Paladin, 1971).

22 Erikson, op. cit. p. 12.

23 Leslie T. Wilkins, *Social Deviance: Social Policy, Action and Research* (London: Tavistock, 1964), Chap. 4. I have made a preliminary attempt to apply this model to the Mods and Rockers in 'Mods, Rockers and the Rest: Community Reaction to Juvenile Delinquency', *Howard Journal of Penology and Crime Prevention* XII (1967), pp. 121–30.

24 Young (1971) *The Drug Takers*, op. cit.

25 David H. Downes, *The Delinquent Solution: A Study in Subcultural Theory* (London: Routledge & Kegan Paul, 1966), p. ix.

26 Neil J. Smelser, *Theory of Collective Behaviour* (London: Routledge & Kegan Paul, 1962).

27 ibid. p. 17.

28 ibid. p. 284.

29 Early journalistic accounts of disasters have given way to more sophisticated methods of data collection and theorization. The body in the USA most responsible for this development is the Disaster Research Group of the National Academy of Science, National Research Council. The most comprehensive accounts of their findings and other research are to be found in: G. W. Baker and D. W. Chapman, *Man and Society in Disaster* (New York: Basic Books, 1962) and A. H. Barton, *Social Organisation Under Stress: A Sociological Review of Disaster Studies* (Washington, DC: National Academy of Sciences, 1963). See also A. H. Barton, *Communities in Disaster* (London: Ward Lock, 1970).

30   Robert K. Merton, Introduction to Barton, *Social Organisation Under Stress*, op. cit. pp. xix–xx.
31   C. F. Fritz, 'Disaster', in R. K. Merton and R. A. Nisbet (Eds), *Contemporary Social Problems* (London: Rupert Hart-Davis, 1963), p. 654.
32   I. H. Cissin and W. B. Clark, 'The Methodological Challenge of Disaster Research', in Baker and Chapman, op. cit. p. 30.
33   From: Barton, *Social Organization Under Stress* op. cit. pp. 14–15; D. W. Chapman, 'A Brief Introduction to Contemporary Disaster Research', in Baker and Chapman, op. cit. pp. 7–22; J. G. Miller, 'A Theoretical Review of Individual and Group Psychological Reaction to Stress', in G. H. Grosser *et al.* (Eds), *The Threat of Impending Disaster: Contributions to the Psychology of Stress* (Cambridge, Massachusetts: MIT Press, 1964), pp. 24–32.

Chapter 2

1   For a more extended development of this point, see my 'Directions for Research on Adolescent Violence and Vandalism', *British Journal of Criminology*, 11 (October 1971).
2   Peter Laurie, *The Teenage Revolution* (London: Anthony Blond, 1965), p. 131.
3   Graham Greene, *Brighton Rock* (Harmondsworth: Penguin, 1965), p. 6.
4   Laurie, op. cit. p. 130.
5   Terry Ann Knopf, 'Media Myths on Violence', *Columbia Journalism Review* (Spring 1970), pp. 17–18.
6   ibid. p. 20.
7   See, for example, Norman Jacobs, 'The Phantom Slasher of Taipei: Mass Hysteria in a Non-Western Society', *Social Problems* 12 (Winter 1965), p. 322.
8   Knopf, op. cit. p. 18.
9   Edwin M. Lemert, *Social Pathology* (New York: McGraw Hill, 1951), p. 55.
10 Paul Barker and Alan Little, 'The Margate Offenders: A Survey', *New Society*, 30 July 1964. *See* Appendix.
11 Interview (23 November 1964).
12 Estimate by Hastings Stationmaster, quoted in *Hastings and St Leonards Observer* (8 August 1964).
13 James D. Halloran *et al.*, *Demonstrations and Communications: A Case Study* (Harmondsworth: Penguin Books, 1970), p. 112.
14 Ralph H. Turner and Samuel J. Surace, 'Zoot Suiters and Mexicans: Symbols in Crowd Behaviour', *American Journal of Sociology* 62 (1956), pp. 14–20.
15 Paul Rock and Stanley Cohen, 'The Teddy Boy', in V. Bogdanor and R. Skidelsky (Eds), *The Age of Affluence: 1951–1964* (London: Macmillan, 1970).
16 Yablonsky has provided numerous examples of how outside observers accept at face value the fantasies of gang leaders and members. See Lewis Yablonsky, *The Violent Gang* (New York: Free Press, 1962).
17 Kurt and Gladys Lang, 'The Unique Perspective of Television and its Effect: A Pilot Study', *American Sociological Review* 18 (February 1953), pp. 3–12. Halloran and his colleagues (op. cit.) report an identical process in their analysis of the TV coverage of the 1968 anti-Vietnam war demonstrations.

18 Lang, op. cit. p. 10.
19 Daniel J. Boorstin, *The Image* (Harmondsworth: Penguin Books, 1963), p. 25.
20 Kenneth B. Clark and James Barker, 'The Zoot Effect in Personality: A Race Riot Participant', *Journal of Abnormal and Social Psychology* 40 (1965), pp. 143–8.
21 I. H. Cissin and W. B. Clark, 'The Methodological Challenge of Disaster Research', in G. W. Baker and D. W. Chapman, *Man and Society in Disaster* (New York: Basic Books, 1962), p. 28.
22 The notion of a 'hierarchy of credibility' in regard to deviance is suggested by Howard S. Becker in his paper 'Whose Side Are We On?', *Social Problems* 14 (Winter 1967), pp. 239–67.
23 Halloran *et al.*, op. cit. pp. 215–16.
24 ibid. p. 26.
25 Michael Frayn, *The Tin Men* (London: Fontana Books, 1966), pp. 31–5.
26 Terry Ann Knopf, 'Sniping: A New Pattern of Violence?', *Transaction* (July/ August 1969), p. 29.

Chapter 3

1 Neil J. Smelser, *Theory of Collective Behaviour* (London: Routledge & Kegan Paul, 1962), Chap. 3.
2 See the various papers in Bradley S. Greenberg and Edwin B. Parker (Eds), *The Kennedy Assassination and the American Public: Social Communication in Crisis* (Stanford: Stanford University Press, 1965) particularly Parker and Greenberg, 'Newspaper Content on the Assassination Weekend', pp. 46–7, and J. D. Barker, 'Peer Group Discussion and Recovery from the Kennedy Assassination', p. 119.
3 Nahum Z. Medalia and Otto N. Larsen, 'Diffusion and Belief in a Collective Delusion: The Seattle Windshield Pitting Epidemic', *American Sociological Review* 23 (1958), p. 183.
4 Barker, op. cit. p. 112.
5 Hansard (House of Commons), 23 June 1964, Col. 274.
6 Hansard, 27 April 1964, Col. 65.
7 ibid. Col. 71.
8 Frank Elmes, 'Mods and Rockers', *Police Review* XXII (June 1964).
9 Howard S. Becker, *Outsiders: Studies in the Sociology of Deviance* (New York: Free Press, 1963), pp. 152–7.
10 Canon Evans, Chancellor of Southwark Cathedral, at a Christian Action Conference, 7 June 1964.
11 See Tony Palmer, *The Trials of Oz* (London: Blond & Briggs, 1971).
12 See, for example, Gordon W. Allport, *The Nature of Prejudice* (New York: Doubleday Anchor, 1958), pp. 190–3.
13 Lewis Yablonsky, *The Violent Gang* (New York: Macmillan, 1962), p. 210.
14 Edgar Z. Friedenberg, 'The Image of the Adolescent Minority', *Dissent* 10 (Spring 1963), p. 151. Friedenberg suggests a number of other interesting parallels between racial stereotyping and the assignment to the adolescent of minority group status.
15 Hansard, 23 June 1964, Col. 252 and Col. 294–5.

16 Harold Garfinkel, 'Conditions of Successful Degradation Ceremonies', *American Journal of Sociology* LXI (March 1956), pp. 422–3.

17 In the only published research on the Mods and Rockers, Barker and Little write, 'We must shoot down the broken home cliché as well.' This is an example of the tendency to make unjustified assumptions about public attitudes to delinquency. There is no need to shoot down a cliché which is seldom used.

18 In criminology, Sheldon and Eleanor Glueck's popular work is most responsible for perpetuating this analogy. Note David Matza's account of the use of the contagion concept in explaining deviance – *Becoming Deviant* (Englewood Cliffs, NJ: Prentice-Hall, 1969), pp. 101–4.

19 Hansard, 27 April 1964, Col. 52 and Col. 59.

20 Interview, 27 November 1964.

21 P. B. Sheatsley and J. S. Feldman, 'A National Survey of Public Reactions and Behaviour', in Greenberg and Parker, op. cit. p. 174.

22 In one analysis of this subject (Terry Ann Knopf, 'Sniping: A New Pattern of Violence?', *Transaction*, July/August 1969, pp. 22–9), attention is drawn to the receptiveness of American audiences to conspiratorial theories. The classic analysis is Richard Hofstadter, *The Paranoid Style in American Politics* (New York: Knopf, 1966).

23 Robert Shellow and Derek V. Roemer, 'The Riot that Didn't Happen', *Social Problems* 14 (Fall 1966), p. 223.

24 David Downes, 'Clacton and the Dead End', *Observer* (6 April 1964), and 'What to do about Mods and Rockers?', *Family Doctor* (August 1965), pp. 469–71.

25 D. James, MP in *Brighton and Hove Herald* (23 May 1964).

26 L. Seymour, MP, Hansard, 4 April 1964, Col. 42.

27 Jum C. Nunnally, 'The Communication of Mental Health Information: A Comparison of the Opinions of Experts and Public with Mass Media Presentation', *Behavioral Science* 2 (1957), pp. 220–30. While the (very few) studies that exist of public attitudes to deviance do show extreme and misleading stereotyping, such responses have not been compared to those in the mass media, which, perhaps, are even more extreme. See, for example, J. L. Simmons, 'Public Stereotypes of Deviants', *Social Problems* 13 (Fall 1965), pp. 223–32.

28 Edwin M. Lemert, *Social Pathology* (New York: McGraw-Hill, 1952), p. 55.

29 Peter L. Berger and Thomas Luckman, *The Social Construction of Reality* (London: Allen Lane, 1968), p. 131.

30 An identical point about the media response to political demonstrations is made in James D. Halloran *et al.*, *Demonstrations and Communications: A Case Study* (Harmondsworth: Penguin Books, 1970).

Chapter 4

1 Neil J. Smelser, *Theory of Collective Behaviour* (London: Routledge & Kegan Paul, 1962), p. 83.

2 Ralph H. Turner and Samuel J. Surace, 'Zoot Suiters and Mexicans: Symbols in Crowd Behaviour', *American Journal of Sociology* 62 (1956).

3 D. Johnson, 'The Phantom Anaesthetist of Mattoon', *Journal of Abnormal and Social Psychology* 40 (1945), pp. 175–86.

4 Nahum Z. Medalia and Otto N. Larsen, 'Diffusion and Belief in a Collective Delusion: The Seattle Windshield Pitting Epidemic', *American Sociological Review* 23 (1953), pp. 180–6.

5 Norman Jacobs, 'The Phantom Slasher of Taipei: Mass Hysteria in a Non-Western Society', *Social Problems* 12 (Winter 1965), pp. 318–28.

6 See, for example, J. P. Spiegel, 'The English Flood of 1953', *Human Organization* 16 (Summer 1957), pp. 3–5.

7 Turner and Surace, op. cit. p. 20.

8 Johnson, op. cit. p. 186.

9 Jacobs, op. cit. p. 326.

10 Johnson, op. cit. p. 180.

11 Edwin H. Sutherland, 'The Diffusion of the Sexual Psychopath Laws', *American Journal of Sociology* 56 (September 1950), p. 143.

12 See, 'Beachniks – Brighton is Tolerant, But With Reservations', *Municipal Journal* (14 February 1964).

13 Edwin M. Lemert, *Social Pathology* (New York: McGraw-Hill, 1951), p. 447.

14 Turner and Surace, op. cit. p. 20.

15 Isidor Chein et al., *The Road to H: Narcotics, Delinquency and Social Policy* (London: Tavistock, 1964), p. 8.

16 Albert K. Cohen, 'The Study of Social Disorganization and Deviant Behaviour', in R. K. Merton et al. (Eds), *Sociology Today: Problems and Prospects* (New York: Basic Books, 1959), p. 465.

17 These solutions derive respectively from: D. Pulson, *Liverpool Daily Post* (23 May 1964); J. Lucas, *Daily Herald* (19 May 1964); J. B. White, JP in *Daily Telegraph* (22 May 1964). (It is implied rather than explicitly stated that remand in custody *before* conviction is intended); Comment in *Justice of the Peace and Local Government Review* LXXVII (13 June 1964), pp. 401–2.

18 J. E. Lumbard, 'The Citizen's Role in Law Enforcement', *Journal of Criminal Law, Criminology and Police Science* 56 (March 1965), p. 69.

19 The phrase used by Tannenbaum to describe the ritualistic confrontation between the young delinquent and the community: Frank Tannenbaum, *Crime and the Community* (New York: Columbia University Press, 1938), pp. 17–20.

20 James D. Halloran et al., *Demonstrations and Communications: A Case Study* (Harmondsworth: Penguin, 1970).

21 Keith Bottomley, *Prison Before Trial* (London: G. Bell and Sons, 1970).

22 Tony Parker, *The Plough Boy* (London: Hutchinson, 1965), p. 235. For further examples from the Teddy Boy phenomenon, see Paul Rock and Stanley Cohen, 'The Teddy Boy', in V. Bogdanor and R. Skidelsky (Eds), *The Age of Affluence: 1951–1964* (London: Macmillan, 1970).

23 Main source: *Hastings and St Leonard's Observer* (15 August 1964).

24 Kai T. Erikson, *Wayward Puritans: A Study in the Sociology of Deviance* (New York: John Wiley, 1966), p. 103.

25 Thirty-six out of forty-four youths pleaded guilty. It has been noted that many did so on police 'advice'. Others believed that those who pleaded not guilty

were given heavier sentences. Barker and Little note that 'the strained atmosphere of the courthouse seems to have been responsible for this misconception', op. cit. p. 6.

26   See particularly, Richard R. Fuller and Richard R. Myers, 'Some Aspects of a Theory of Social Problems', *American Sociological Review* 6 (February 1941), pp. 24–32 and 'The Natural History of a Social Problem', *American Sociological Review* 6 (June 1941), pp. 320–9. For a critique of the natural history approach, see Edwin M. Lemert, 'Is There a Natural History of Social Problems?', *American Sociological Review* 16 (1951), pp. 217–23.

27   Howard S. Becker, *Outsiders: Studies in the Sociology of Deviance* (New York: Free Press, 1963), Chaps 7 and 8.

28   Sutherland, op. cit.

29   The classic account is to be found in Alfred R. Lindesmith, 'Dope Fiend Mythology', *Journal of Criminal Law, Criminology & Police Science* 31 (1940), pp. 199–208. See also Edwin M. Schur, *Crimes Without Victims: Deviant Behaviour and Public Policy* (Englewood Cliffs, NJ: Prentice-Hall, 1965), pp. 120–68; Jerry Mandel, 'Hashish, Assassins and the Love of God', *Issues in Criminology* 2 (Fall 1966), pp. 149–56 and Roger Smith, 'Status Politics and the Image of the Addict', ibid. pp. 157–75.

30   H. R. Veltfort and G. E. Lee, 'The Coconut Grove Fire: A Study in Scapegoating', *Journal of Abnormal and Social Psychology* 38 (April 1943), p. 141, and R. Bucher, 'Blame and Hostility in Disaster', *American Journal of Sociology* 6 (March 1957), p. 471.

31   Sven Ranulf, *Moral Indignation and Middle Class Psychology* (New York: Schocken Books, 1964).

32   Between 1965 and 1966, the *Morning Advertiser* (the trade paper) showed a marked increase in references to hooliganism in public houses.

33   Forty-fifth Annual General Report of the Magistrates Association, pp. 64–5. See also B. Buchanan, 'Punishment for Disorderly Gangs', *Magistrate*, 20, 12 (1964), pp. 170–1.

34   See, for example, Ralph H. Turner and Lewis M. Killian, *Collective Behaviour* (Englewood Cliffs, NJ: Prentice-Hall, 1957), Part 4; Hans Toch, *The Social Psychology of Social Movements* (Indianapolis: Bobbs Merrill Co., 1965) and Joseph R. Gusfield (Ed.), *Protest, Reform and Revolt: A Reader in Social Movements* (New York: John Wiley, 1970).

35   Smelser, op. cit. pp. 270–312 and 109–20.

36   See Turner and Killian, op. cit. pp. 501–2, and for a particularly clear example, Sutherland, op. cit.

37   Unless stated otherwise, the arguments quoted are from my verbatim recording of the debate in the Seatown Council on 23 May 1966.

38   Alderman K. (Questionnaire).

39   The use of atrocity stories to legitimate forms of control is, of course, a technique well known to moral entrepreneurs. Becker quotes a story of an entire family being murdered by an addict which was used by the Federal Narcotics Bureau in campaigning for the Marijuana Tax Act (op. cit. p. 142). Advocates of LSD control similarly use stories of 'trippers' walking in front of

cars or stepping out of twenty-storey windows. See Mandel, op. cit., for a well-documented account of the mythical nature of one such story.

40 Interview, 20 May 1966.
41 Smelser, op. cit. p. 113.
42 Letter from MP for 'Rockbay' (18 November 1964).
43 Mr H. Gurden, Hansard, 27 April 1964, Col. 31.
44 P. D. Scott and D. R. C. Willcox, 'Delinquency and the Amphetamines', *British Journal of Psychiatry*, 111 (September 1965), pp. 865–76.
45 Mr H. Brooke, ibid., Cols. 89–90.
46 Mr H. Brooke, Hansard, 4 June 1964, Cols. 1249–52.
47 The effect of the Malicious Damage Act 1964 was to extend the jurisdiction of the magistrates' courts and to increase the maximum fine from £20 to £100. It was also made clear that powers to order compensation were not confined to cases where a fine had already been imposed.
48 Mr C. Curran, Hansard, 23 June 1964, Col. 1219.
49 Sir W. Teeling, ibid., Col. 261.
50 Mr H. Brooke, ibid, Col. 242.
51 A. K. Cohen, op. cit. p. 465.
52 Sir W. Teeling, Hansard, 23 June 1964, Cols. 259–60.
53 Mr W. Rees-Davies, ibid., Col. 284.
54 For further elaboration about vandalism, see Stanley Cohen, 'Who are the Vandals?', *New Society*, 12 December 1968, pp. 872–8.
55 Lemert, *Social Pathology*, pp. 65–8. See also Goffman's discussion of the stigmatized person's vulnerability to what he calls 'victimization'; Erving Goffman, *Stigma: Notes on the Management of Spoiled Identity* (Englewood Cliffs, NJ: Prentice-Hall, 1963), p. 9.
56 Lemert, ibid. p. 310.
57 Erikson, op. cit.
58 Peter Laurie, *The Teenage Revolution* (London: Anthony Blond Ltd, 1965), p. 57.
59 Lewis Yablonsky, 'Experience with the Criminal Community', in A. W. Gouldner and S. M. Miller (Eds), *Applied Sociology* (New York: Free Press, 1965), p. 71. For a somewhat different notion of the voyeur role, see Laud Humphreys's sensitive chapter, 'Methods: The Sociologist As Voyeur', in *Tearoom Trade: Impersonal Sex in Public Places* (London: Duckworth, 1970).
60 These quotes are, respectively, from: Resolution passed at Moral Re-armament Easter Conference, 30 March 1964; Speech by Mr F. Willey, Labour Chief Front Bench Spokesman on Education, addressing a meeting of the National Association of Youth Service Officers, 3 April 1964; Telegram sent by Women of Britain Clean Up TV Campaign to Director General of BBC, June 1964; Letter to *Tribune*, 10 April 1964.
61 *The Times*, 23 June 1966. See also M. Wardron, 'Class, Anarchism and the Capitalist Mentality', *Anarchy* 68 (October 1966), pp. 301–4, who includes the Mods and Rockers in a list of strugglers against authority such as the pacifist movement, Oxfam, the campaign against the destruction of wild life, the Welsh Nationalists and the IRA.

Chapter 5

1   See, for example, I. L. Janis, 'Psychological Effects on Warning', in G. W. Baker and D. W. Chapman (Eds), *Man and Society in Disaster* (New York: Basic Books, 1962); S. B. Withey, 'Reactions to Uncertain Threat', ibid. pp. 93–102, and 'Sequential Accommodations to Threat', in G. H. Grosser *et al.* (Eds), *The Threat of Impending Disaster: Contributions to the Psychology of Stress* (Cambridge, Massachusetts: MIT Press, 1964).

2   Withey, in Baker and Chapman, op. cit. p. 114.

3   Withey, in Grosser *et al.*, op. cit. p. 112.

4   Hunter S. Thompson, *Hells Angels: A Strange and Terrible Saga* (New York: Random House, 1966), p. 122.

5   See report in *Daily Mirror* (31 March 1966): 'Spies Warn The Yard of Mods On The Warpath.'

6   For example, L. Yablonsky, 'The Delinquent Gang as a Near-Group', *Social Problems* 7 (Fall 1959), pp. 108–17.

7   The reports of the *Brighton Archways Ventures*, particularly Volume 3, contain much incidental material describing this atmosphere.

8   A highly sensitive portrayal of Brighton some twenty years after *Brighton Rock* – a portrayal which conveys the balance between desperation and release – may be found in the first two volumes of *Generation*, Colin Spencer's projected Quartet: *Anarchists in Love* (London: Eyre & Spottiswoode, 1963) and *The Tyranny of Love* (London: Anthony Blond Ltd, 1967).

9   Erving Goffman, *Where the Action Is* (London: Allen Lane The Penguin Press, 1969), p. 147.

10   Quoted in *Brighton Archways Ventures Report*, Vol. III, p. 64.

11   Paul Barker, 'Brighton Battleground', *New Society*, 21 May 1964, p. 10.

12   Robert Shellow and Derek V. Roemer, 'The Riot That Didn't Happen', *Social Problems* 14 (Fall 1966), pp. 221–33.

13   This type of formulation owes much to the writings of R. D. Laing: see especially R. D. Laing *et al.*, *Interpersonal Perception* (London: Tavistock, 1966), Chap. 3. The possibility of such multiple misinterpretations in regard to gang delinquency is also suggested by Matza. The idea of a commitment to delinquency, he notes, is a misconception both of delinquents and the sociologists who study them. 'Instead, there is a system of shared misunderstandings, based on miscues, which leads delinquents to believe that all others situated in their company are committed to their misdeeds.' David Matza, *Delinquency and Drift* (New York: John Wiley, 1964), p. 59.

14   Extract from youth worker's notes quoted in *B.A.V. Report*, Vol. III, p. 64.

15   The term originally used by Park and Burgess. For an analysis of other forms of milling and social contagion, see R. Turner and L. Killian, *Collective Behaviour* (Englewood Cliffs, NJ: Prentice-Hall, 1957).

16   The discussion on rumour in the rest of the chapter leans on the standard account in G. Allport and L. Postman, *The Psychology of Rumour* (New York: Henry Holt, 1947) and more heavily, the interactionist approach in T. Shibutani, *Improvised News. A Sociological Study of Rumour* (Indianapolis, Bobbs-Merrill Co., 1966).

17 Shibutani, op. cit. Chapter 4.
18 ibid. p. 113.
19 Turner and Killian, op. cit. p. 118.
20 John Harrington, 'A Preliminary Report on Soccer Hooliganism' (Birmingham Research Group, Mimeograph, 1968), p. 37.
21 William Westley, 'The Escalation of Violence through Legitimation', *Annals of the American Academy of Political and Social Science* 364 (March 1966), pp. 120–6.
22 I am indebted to Arthur Chisnell for drawing my attention to this example. One study, however, that shows the need for caution in interpreting such effects is Jerome A. Motto, 'Suicide and Suggestibility – The Role of the Press', *American Journal of Psychiatry* 124 (August 1967), pp. 156–60.
23 See David Caplowitz and Candace Rogers, *Swastika 1960: The Epidemic of Anti-Semitic Vandalism in America* (New York: Anti-Defamation League of B'nai Brith, 1961). A noteworthy feature of this epidemic was that initial reporting indicated other avenues for expressing grievances: at the peak, targets for hostility other than anti-Semitic ones were chosen and, in fact, these general incidents outnumbered the specifically anti-Semitic. This is similar to the widening of the net control of the Mods and Rockers and the ways in which the target changed during the impact. All such processes are heavily dependent on the mass media.
24 See, for example, T. R. Fyvel, *The Insecure Offenders* (London: Chatto & Windus, 1961), and C. Bondy *et al.*, *Jugendliche Stören die Ordnung* (Munich: Juventa Verlag, 1957).
25 See Britt-Marie Blegvad, 'Newspapers and Rock and Roll Riots in Copenhagen', *Acta Sociologica* 7 (1963), pp. 151–78, and Paul Rock and Stanley Cohen, 'The Teddy Boy', in V. Bogdanor and R. Skidelsky (Eds), *The Age of Affluence: 1951–1964* (London: Macmillan, 1970).
26 It is, of course, far fetched to think that such techniques as a total news embargo will 'solve' many problems. Other suggestions which do put the media in a more general political context are more plausible. For a review and references in regard to recent American disturbances, see William L. Rivers and Wilbur Schramm, *Responsibility and Mass Communication* (New York: Harper & Row, 1969), Chap. 6.
27 Peter Laurie, *The Teenage Revolution* (London: Anthony Blond Ltd, 1965), p. 105.
28 Shellow and Roemer, op. cit. p. 223 and Thompson, op. cit. p. 9.
29 See Erving Goffman, *Behaviour in Public Places: Notes on the Social Organization of Gatherings* (New York: Free Press, 1963).
30 Howard S. Becker, *Outsiders* (New York: Free Press, 1963), p. 158.
31 Lewis Yablonsky, *The Violent Gang* (New York: Free Press, 1962), p. 67.
32 Shellow and Roemer, op. cit. p. 226.
33 ibid. pp. 221–31.

Chapter 6

1 See Stuart Hall, Introduction to *The Popular Press and Social Change 1935–1965*. Unpublished MS. Centre for Contemporary Cultural Studies, University of Birmingham, 1971.

2 One of the few serious attempts in this country to deal with both the creative and commercially responsive aspects of pop music is Dave Laing's *The Sound of Our Time* (London: Sheed & Ward, 1969). His Chapters 9 – 'Notes for a Study of the Beatles' – and 10 – 'My Generation' (which deals with the Rolling Stones and The Who) – are important aids to understanding the Mod phenomenon.

3 This account is based on the somewhat fuller analysis I have provided in 'Breaking Out, Smashing Up and the Social Context of Aspiration', in *Working Papers in Cultural Studies*, Spring 1974, pp. 37–64.

   My orientation to the problem is basically the same as those of Paul Goodman in his classic *Growing Up Absurd* (New York: Random House, 1956) and – with particular reference to delinquency in Britain – David Downes in *The Delinquent Solution* (London: Routledge & Kegan Paul, 1966).

4 This is the perspective on adolescence used in Frank Musgrove, *Youth and the Social Order* (London: Routledge & Kegan Paul, 1964). See also the various writings of Edgar Friedenberg.

5 Some further comments on the 'Dream Boys' and 'Ordinary Kids' of the fifties can be found in Nicholas Walter, 'The Young One', *New Society*, 28 February 1963. Just about the only commentary on this period, as it drew to a close, is the work of Ray Gosling. See 'Lady Albermarle's Boys', *Young Fabian Pamphlet*, January 1961, and 'Dream Boys', *New Left Review* 3, May–June 1960, pp. 30–5.

6 This account derives mainly from the work of Downes, and its elaborations by Peter Willmott, *Adolescent Boys of East London* (London: Routledge & Kegan Paul, 1966), and David H. Hargreaves, *Social Relations in a Secondary School* (London: Routledge & Kegan Paul, 1967).

7 The notion of a mood of desperation preceding the drift to delinquency is used by David Matza in *Delinquency and Drift* (New York: John Wiley, 1964).

8 For this whole section I am heavily indebted to the writings of Jeff Nuttall; see particularly *Bomb Culture* (London: Paladin, 1970), and 'Techniques of Separation' in Tony Cash (Ed.), *Anatomy of Pop* (London: BBC Publications, 1970). On the earlier period, Ray Gosling is again invaluable; see his autobiography *Sum Total* (London: Faber & Faber).

9 For details, see Paul Rock and Stanley Cohen, 'The Teddy Boy', in V. Bogdanor and R. Skidelsky (Eds), *The Age of Affluence: 1951–1964* (London: Macmillan, 1970).

10 Colin MacInnes, *Absolute Beginners* (London: MacGibbon & Kee, 1959). See also the essays, particularly 'Sharp Schmutter' (on the clothing style, at the end of the fifties) in MacInnes's *England, Half English* (Harmondsworth: Penguin, 1966). These are among the more noteworthy comments on youth in England during the indefinite transitional stage between Ted and Mod.

11 Nuttall, *Bomb Culture*, op. cit. p. 333.

12 Tom Wolfe, 'The Noonday Underground' in *The Mid Atlantic Man and Other New Breeds in England and America* (London: Weidenfeld & Nicholson, 1968).

13 ibid. p. 101.

14 ibid. pp. 111–12.

15 For details on all these types, see *Brighton Archways Ventures Report*, Vol. 3, Chap. 4.

16 Laing, op. cit. pp. 150–1.
17 ibid. p. 151.
18 See, for example, Roger Williams and David Guest, 'Are The Middle Classes Becoming Work Shy?', *New Society*, Vol. 18, No. 457 (1 July 1971), pp. 9–11. Questions about the supposed allegiance of particular groups to the work ethos need, of course, to be put in a theoretical context which recognizes the inconsistencies and contradictions in value systems about leisure. The classic analysis is David Matza and Gresham Sykes, 'Juvenile Delinquency and Sub-terranean Values', *American Sociological Review* 26 (October 1961), pp. 712–19.
19 Nik Cohn, *Awopbopaloobop Aloopbamboom* (London: Paladin, 1970), p. 141 and p. 145. For a fuller analysis of The Who see Gary Herman, *The Who* (London: Studio Vista, 1971).
20 ibid. p. 164.
21 Nuttall, *Bomb Culture*, op. cit. p. 35.
22 Kai T. Erikson, *Wayward Puritans: A Study in the Sociology of Deviance* (New York: John Wiley, 1966).
23 ibid. p. 69.
24 Laing, op. cit. p. 150.
25 The *Brighton Archways Ventures Reports* give a detailed chronicle of the opposition to the project by the local tradesmen and council. See particularly Volume I, pp. 15–25, and pp. 49–106, and Volume 3, pp. 167–70.
26 Joseph Gusfield, *Symbolic Crusade: Status Politics and the American Temperance Move-ment* (Urbana: University of Illinois, 1963). See especially Chapter 5, 'Moral Indignation and Status Conflict'.
27 Svend Ranulf, *Moral Indignation and Middle Class Psychology* (New York: Schocken Books Inc., 1964).
28 Gusfield, op. cit. p. 112.
29 For a convincing argument about the bases for the societal condemnation of drug-taking, see Jock Young, *The Drugtakers: The Social Meaning of Drug Use* (London: Paladin, 1971).
30 George Melly, *Revolt Into Style* (London: Allen Lane The Penguin Press, 1970).
31 For one account of this transition, see Nuttall, 'Techniques of Separation', op. cit.
32 ibid. pp. 127–8.
33 Howard Becker, *German Youth: Bond or Free?* (London: Kegan Paul, 1946), p. 147.

General Index

interpretation 35–6; inventory
29–34; opinion 52–3, 58;
over-reporting 20–2
Maudling, Reginald 44
Members of Parliament (M.P.s) 37–8,
44; attitude 46–7; control culture
65, 95–6, 98, 101–2, 109–14
milling process 129, 147
mock trials 86
Modernism 2, 155
modes of explanation 56–8
Mods and Rockers 1–2, 6–7, 9–16;
audience 133–5; causation 46–9;
contexts 149, 162–72; control
tactics 73–80, 84–6; crowd scenes
124–33; decline 167–71;
emergence 150–61; exclusive
control 90–115; exploitation
115–19; manufactured news 30–4;
mass media 135–9; opinion 36,
44–5; reaction 49–53, 60; social
control 66; warning phase 121–4
Monkees 169
moral enterprise *see* enterprise
moral panics deviance 1–15; sociology
161–7
morality plays 134
music 151–2, 158–9, 161, 169

National Association of Chief
Educational Welfare Officers 118
National Coal Board 18
National Council for Civil Liberties
(N.C.C.L.) 76–8, 83
National Service 110
Nazis 39
net-widening effect 96
newspapers 18–19, 28–30, 33–4;
attitude 39; causation 46–8;
contexts 160; control tactics 79–80,
112; courts 83, 87, 89; exclusive
control 93, 95, 98–9; impact 135,

136; over-reporting 19–26;
prediction 26–7; public opinion
53–4; reaction 60, 62–5, 110;
spurious attribution 40–1; warning
phase 122–3
No Waiting signs 74
non-event stories 27, 62–3
norm-orientated beliefs 97
Northview sample 49–53, 55, 70, 162,
177

observations 177
obsolescence 170
one percenters 139
one-dimensionality 150
opinion 14, 18, 35–48; control culture
80, 94–6; differential reaction
49–58; mass media 137;
sensitization 63
orientation 37–9, 50, 56, 92
Osborne, John 28
Ostend 32
Oswald, Lee Harvey 47
out-groups 164
outsiders 55–6
over-reporting 19–26
overseas coverage 19
overtime 72
Oz trial 33, 40, 87

pacifism 118
paradox 122
parents 84, 86–7, 108
Parsons, Talcott 11
Pascoe, – 83
Payne, E. 92
penalties 81, 85, 88; control culture
96, 98, 110–11, 113
pendulum argument 46
permissive society 161, 163
persecution 143
petitions 96

Author Index

HOW TO LIVE FOR FREE

80 WAYS TO SLASH YOUR SPENDING

STEPHEN GILES

WHITE LADDER PRESS

new tricks for old dogs

How to Live for Free

This first edition published in Great Britain in 2008 by White Ladder Press,
a division of Crimson Publishing Ltd
Westminster House, Kew Road, Richmond, Surrey, TW9 2ND

16 15 14 13 12 11 10 09   10 9 8 7 6 5 4 3 2 1

A catalogue record for this book is available from the British library.

ISBN 978 1 905410 35 4

Designed and typeset by Julie Martin Ltd
Cover design by Julie Martin Ltd
Printed and bound in Turkey by Mega Basim, Istanbul

FOR
ADA GILES

CONTENTS

ACKNOWLEDGEMENTS

This book would not have been possible without the assistance of the following people, all of whom I acknowledge with grateful thanks: Nikki Locke, Lucy Stone at CAT, Patrick Whetman at Goat Industries, Angi Davies at Liftshare, Stephen Gregory, Esme Barber, Roni Jay and especially Steve Fountain. Thanks also to the many people who came forward with tips, hints and suggestions.

Q: DO YOU WANT TO LIVE FOR FREE?

A: THEN YOU NEED TO BUY THIS BOOK.

No, seriously. It might seem a bit cheeky to suggest that you should start off on a course of extreme frugality by investing in a book, but I can assure you this is money well spent – money that you will quickly recoup in significant and sustained savings.

Let's make it clear from the start, living for free is one heck of a hard slog. But it is just about possible – and if you don't believe me skip straight on to section six for an example of the kind of life you might expect. For most of us, however, this book isn't just about living without cash, it's about making the most of the cash that we have so that we can live free of unnecessary restrictions and of the chains of overwhelming financial commitment.

Because we work so hard for the money that we have, it's more important than ever to be sure that our hard-earned wages are maximised. This means analysing every area of household and personal expenditure and asking some serious questions about what you're paying for and where you should be making savings. But it also means becoming an expert in the long-neglected and misunderstood arts of blagging, ligging, scrounging and scavenging. It means never paying good money for something that can be won, begged for, borrowed or made.

The tangible benefits are all here, on every page there's a saving to be made – slashing hundreds, perhaps even thousands from your expenses each year. If, as a result of this book, you can cut even 20 per cent from your own living expenses, you can put that money towards something important like a holiday or car – you could even work 20 per cent less and spend that extra time with your family or friends instead.

All of the money-saving ideas within *How to Live For Free* are, of course, legal. They have been comprehensively researched – many are tried and tested favourites – and every section is accompanied by detailed notes on how to achieve the aim, the relative advantages and disadvantages, the initial and ongoing outlay (if any) and an indication of how much, on average, this idea may trim from your costs in five key areas: socialising; food and drink; household bills; clothes, toys & other items and sport & leisure.

The ideas range from eco-friendliness to fiscal wisdom and self-sufficiency via downright cheekiness, but each one aims to guide you towards a serious and achievable goal of freedom living. Each idea is given its own 'Freedom living score' that rates how far it will progress you towards the ultimate goal of living for free.

This book doesn't have purely 'green' credentials, nor does it pretend to offer a specific world outlook or a financial quick-fix. It is a compendium of suggestions for further research and investigation from across all of these areas and more. It will give you a starting point for your own journey into freedom living.

"That's all very well," I hear you cry, "but I can't spare the time for all these fancy ideas." And while it's true that some of the suggestions in this book will involve a bit of time, effort and commitment, most of them will fit extremely comfortably into the routine of normal life. The ideas in this book don't require any specialist skills or expertise, just a basic level of practicality, common sense and a desire to see every penny that you spend justifying its outlay.

There may be areas where you don't need to make changes, there may be areas where you are unwilling or unable to do so – perhaps because of a lack of space or resource – but I can guarantee that you'll find something in these pages which will save you money and take you a giant leap closer to living for free.

SOCIALISING

① START A BARTERING COLLECTIVE – TRADE SERVICES AND SKILLS

Do you dream of a world without money – a society in which we are all free from the constraints of earning a crust and free to trade our services in an open and creative environment? Well, someone's already beaten you to it. LETS (Local Employment and Trading Systems, sometimes known as Local Enterprise and Trading Systems, Local Exchange and Trading Systems, or Local Economic Trading Systems) started life in a small community in Canada in the early 1980s as a way for local people to trade goods and services outside of the straitjacket of the national economy.

There are now around 2,000 LETS schemes across the world. In the UK alone more than 30,000 people are involved in about 300 schemes.

Each LETS scheme has its own rules, but in general the system works by creating a bespoke unit of currency and then issuing cheque books to its members with which they can 'buy' services from other members for an agreed 'fee'. No money changes hands between the participants, but everyone pays a nominal membership fee in hard currency to fund the administration of the scheme. Schemes are generally managed on a day-to-day basis by volunteers.

Nikki Locke was a key member of a LETS scheme established in Oswestry. Though the scheme has now closed, it once reached a peak of 100 active members and formed the basis of a crucial alternative local economy. So why did it close? "At its peak, when there was high unemployment, it worked well – it brought together a community of like-minded people," Nikki explains. "Now most people with practical skills are too busy earning money to get involved."

This highlights the greatest disadvantage of LETS, as those people with the time to spend on the scheme aren't necessarily the most skilled workers. Traders that tend to be successful as part of LETS – like builders, plumbers and electricians – find no shortage of paid work when the economy is booming. But even in the good times, there's scope for a LETS scheme to thrive, as long as it can find members who are willing to offer in-demand services like bookkeeping, gardening or painting and decorating.

It's not just a shortage of skills that threaten LETS schemes, there's also an assumption that schemes will take too much time to manage, which, as Nikki Locke explains, isn't really the case: "There is a shortage of people with the spare time and skills to commit to running a scheme, but our LETS scheme took a total of about 140 person hours a year to run. There were usually about five or six people in the main group, plus help from ordinary members, so it was probably less than two hours per person per month."

So if you've got a like-minded group of skilled individuals and you can summon sufficient enthusiasm to devote a couple of hours a month to running the group, what do you do next? The National Association of LETS schemes offers further information on starting your own LETS collective as well as more specific guidance on the legalities of trading schemes. Visit www.letslinkuk.net for more information.

The one essential attribute of a LETS scheme is a strong communitarian ethos – while it's vital that your group is structured correctly, it is more important that you make every member of the group feel like a key part. Creating a co-operative gives all members a role to play, and allows the community to build beyond simple trading into a self-supporting network.

ADVANTAGES: It's great for anyone with a rare (and consequently valuable) skill or trade. It's even better if you can extend your scheme to give members free access to a range of costly 'infrequent use' items like ladders, mowers etc.

DISADVANTAGES: Not a cost-effective option for those of us whose only saleable commodity is the ability to stand up straight. Also not an immediate guarantee of quality service, with much potential for awkwardness in the case of disputes.

INITIAL/ONGOING OUTLAY: cost of membership is approximately £10-£15 per year

POTENTIAL SAVING: A comprehensive scheme gives its members access to a huge range of skills, and the savings can run to thousands of pounds a year. Savings must, of course, be offset by the loss of income on any services you perform for other members of the scheme.

FREEDOM LIVING SCORE: 8 out of 10.

② GO TO THE LIBRARY FOR BOOKS, INTERNET AND COURSES

Pity the poor library; under-funded, under-used and undervalued. They are widely viewed as draughty, forbidding places in which tramps seek refuge, old ladies do battle over the latest large-print Georgette Heyer and school kids pass notes while pretending to do their homework.

In reality, the vast majority of public libraries are modern, well-equipped and extremely useful resources for anyone wishing to live for free. It's not just the number of books available without charge, it's also the wide range of additional services, including internet access, reading groups, free story-time circles and activities for kids and readings from local poets and authors.

For a small fee there's a selection of videos, DVDs and CDs to hire, as well as language courses. Some libraries offer free courses, such as Welsh language courses in Welsh libraries, while others are the local centre for Learn Direct free literacy and numeracy courses (see adult education in section five).

In recent years, the free internet access in libraries, introduced through the People's Network scheme, has been a lifesaver for the crumbling system. Because these facilities are so popular, they are often over-subscribed and it can be hard to get access for more than an hour at a time, which means you have to be pretty focused in your browsing. Remember to take a pen drive with you to download anything you want to take away. And never use a public computer to send sensitive private data such as banking information.

In addition to the cost of hiring CDs and DVDs, there is usually a charge to borrow a book from outside your local council's area. This charge can vary from 80p right the way to a whopping £4 depending on where you live, though if you're astute enough to reside in Wales, inter-library loans are free.

Another way to side-step charges is through a students' scheme called SCONUL Access, which permits the members of nearly 200 participating academic libraries to borrow books from within the network for free. You need to be in education to access the facility, but this scheme opens up a huge network of resources.

ADVANTAGES: Access to a vast catalogue of books – including the latest hardback titles. There are often excellent reference and research facilities. Many larger libraries also stock an impressive selection of newspapers and periodicals. You can also get free literacy stuff and books to keep from the library for kids through the government's Bookstart scheme.

DISADVANTAGES: Some smaller libraries have short opening hours. Internet access is very popular and places are often limited. You may find yourself sitting next to someone giving off a strange smell and talking about the voices in their head. This person may be a librarian.

INITIAL OUTLAY: none

ONGOING OUTLAY: none (CDs/ DVDs and some inter-library loans etc. incur costs)

POTENTIAL SAVING: If you can train yourself to be inquisitive rather than acquisitive, then you'll save a small fortune at the library. The average hardback book costs in the region of £12-£15 and a chart CD will set you back £10. Take a look at the number of books you've bought and never read and the CDs you played just once. I guarantee that'll get you reaching for your library card.

FREEDOM LIVING SCORE: 10 out of 10

3 GET FREE CINEMA, THEATRE AND CONCERT TICKETS BY SETTING UP YOUR OWN LOCAL ARTS WEBSITE OR REVIEWING FOR A LOCAL NEWSPAPER

To get free access to arts events, you need to persuade the promoters that your views are respected. The most convincing way to do this is still to get into print courtesy of your local newspaper, but in the digital age, many local websites have been established for the purpose of providing views and information to locals and visitors, and if you can attract publicity to your website, you can present a pretty compelling case for your inclusion on press lists for all the local arts venues.

If you're interested in the theatre and your local venue deals mainly in touring productions, it might be worth contacting the touring company's press office direct, rather than dealing with the theatre.

In all cases, it's worth your while to show willing. Offer a press officer some advanced publicity (a preview) of their event on your website. This drums up interest in the event and boosts your chances of getting review tickets. Dealing with press offices is a matter of relationship building – if you help them shift a few more tickets for a slow-selling event they'll reward you with plum seats for the best shows/concerts.

As regards the nuts and bolts of establishing a site, you can actually set up a basic website for free using shareware downloaded from the internet. Most web hosting companies offer basic website templates for free to anyone who buys a domain name. If you've got a bit of design flair and basic computer skills, you can buy a do-it-yourself website in a box for around £25 from most computer stores which should suit your needs perfectly.

As for approaching newspapers, well that's a matter of trial and error – it's worth reading the paper's reviews, then writing something on spec that's in a similar format. Don't expect to get paid for the review, only a few papers have any kind of freelance budget any more, but you should at least get two tickets and have the cost of travel reimbursed. It's worth trying regional papers as well, as they may not have anyone covering your immediate area.

The final question is 'what do you write?' It's hard to find something new to say every time an amateur production of *Hobson's Choice* hits the stage, and reviewing theatre can be a hazardous profession unless you're always prepared to back up your comments. To steer clear of libel, remember the old journalists' maxim – 'you should only criticise the performance and never the performer'.

With film, it can be hard to get access for reviewing purposes, especially if you've only managed to make it onto the cinema's 'free list' – the collective of spongers and freeloaders, including staff, that can go to films for nothing on production of a pass. Many new releases at the cinema are specified on the listings as 'free list suspended', which means everyone has to pay to get in. Spoilsports.

ADVANTAGES: Setting up your own site is good for your status and makes you feel important. Getting into print can open doors – if you've got a portfolio of work that can help you get other work, whether reviewing for other papers or possibly features work on the paper you're reviewing for.

DISADVANTAGES: If you're commissioned to do a review you don't get to choose what you'll be watching. Brace yourself for some truly awful (free) nights out.

INITIAL OUTLAY: £25 approx (setting up website), cost of calls/letters to newspapers and cinemas/ theatres

ONGOING OUTLAY: minimal admin costs

POTENTIAL SAVING: Depending on how often you go to arts events, the savings could be anything up to £300 per year at least.

FREEDOM LIVING SCORE: 7 out of 10

④ GIVE AND RECEIVE FOR FREE ON WEBSITES LIKE FREECYCLE.ORG

Established in May 2003, Freecycle is now a global phenomenon, but it has managed to maintain a slightly subversive, underground ethos by focusing its attention on local self-policing groups of individuals who offer goods freely (and for free) amongst themselves. Membership is free and open to all.

So if, for example, you're looking to offload anything from computer equipment to electrical appliances and furniture, get involved in your local community through the freecycle network. You'll find a wealth of like-minded individuals online, all of whom will have something worth passing on to someone. And if there is no local community, consider starting one and invite your friends and colleagues to join.

The main rules of participation are that no money passes hands, no illegal items can be offered and the receiver always collects. Beyond that, it's not a 'trading' service in the same manner as LETS, as it's possible to receive without ever giving, but to fully participate in the communitarian ethos of freecycle, it's worth throwing yourself heart and soul into the process. You never know what you'll find.

ADVANTAGES: In essence, freecycle and its imitators are helping to create a world in which nothing need ever be thrown away. And it certainly bears out the adage that one man's tat is another man's table lamp.

DISADVANTAGES: As an internet-based phenomenon, freecycle is beset by two of the web's greatest ills, spam and sharks. The spam is an inevitable part of being included in a community, and depending on the size of your local group, you may feel overwhelmed by the number of offers and wants you receive on a daily basis. There are also some unscrupulous users who are trying to sniff out valuable items to sell on – there's not much you can do about these blighters, except stick together as a community and try to root them out.

INITIAL/ONGOING OUTLAY: none

POTENTIAL SAVING: limitless, if you strike it lucky, but that's not really the point.

FREEDOM LIVING SCORE: 10 out of 10

5 TRICKS TO AVOID EVER PAYING FOR A ROUND OF DRINKS

It's important to be sociable, even if you're living on a zero budget, but trips to the pub are fraught with potentially crippling drinks bills. These can be avoided but only through the judicious use of monitoring and surveillance tactics. While it's important to avoid meeting the cost of everyone else's drinks, you must also avoid looking like too much of a skinflint, otherwise you'll just stop being invited along.

The following tips should help to ensure you rarely pay for a round, but ought to keep you in the good books of friends and family:

A Pub first, bar last. Make sure you're the first one of your party to reach the pub door as this shows willing. Then hold the door open for everyone else to pass through – this shows a generosity of spirit but it will also ensure you are always the last person to reach the bar. By this time ordering will be underway and your selfless gesture will earn you your first drink.

B Drink with a large, affluent crowd. The people to avoid socially are those who divide bills down to three decimal points. You need to ingratiate yourself with a sizeable party of people who think nothing of throwing in an extra drink for the pretty barmaid. Large crowds are generally good, as the drinks rota is complex and your lack of contribution will, in the short term at least, go unnoticed.

C Drink aware. It stands to reason that you'll spend less if you drink less, but it's equally important to drink at a different pace from the crowd. If you dovetail your drinking to fit with the majority, you will inevitably end up trapped with a large round. If you can tailor your drinking to a smaller subsection within the crowd, you're more likely to be able to manage your place in the round-buying rota, while still enjoying the anonymity of being part of the larger crowd.

D Get out while the going's good. If all else fails and the bell hasn't tolled before your round is due, tactical withdrawal may be your only option. This, again, is a matter of timing. Your excuse must be plausible and sudden – a forgotten promise to be elsewhere, realisation of an early start in the morning, even a hastily arranged phone call. You must offer to buy your round before you leave, but to ensure this offer isn't taken up, you'll need to make it while everyone's glasses are relatively full. Being thus deprived of the chance to be generous towards your friends, you can leave with a clear conscience and the assurance that you will buy the first round next time. Unless you happen to be holding the door that is . . .

ADVANTAGES: You drink cheap

DISADVANTAGES: You look cheap

INITIAL/ONGOING OUTLAY: zero, in an ideal world.

POTENTIAL SAVINGS: Even working on the assumption that you will have to buy the odd drink, these tips should at least halve the cost of a night out.

FREEDOM LIVING SCORE: 5 out of 10

6 SELL ITEMS THROUGH FREE ADS

The eBay generation may have cornered the online marketplace, but it's important to remember that there's a well-established trading network for low priced items in the various free ads publications that you'll find all over the country. While eBay and its clones are great for collectors, or people on the hunt for a new or nearly new bargain, it's not a cost effective place to sell your more tired possessions.

Most free-ad newspapers (easily identified by the garish hue of their paper) offer a free section for people posting low value goods, and local/regional newspapers often have similar free advertising sections. If you insist that the buyer collects the item, you can clear a wide range of items and make a veritable fortune from stuff that would otherwise be cluttering your crawl-space. If you can break up a collection of items without decreasing the value – like an old dinner service for example – then it's worth your while avoiding the advertising costs.

ADVANTAGES: If the altruism of freecycle isn't for you, or if you want to make a few quid from something that's worthless to you, free ads are a lifesaver.

DISADVANTAGES: Low value items are hard to shift at the best of times, and the kind of people who want to pay good money for your broken toaster may not be the kind of people you want in your house.

INITIAL/ONGOING OUTLAY: none

POTENTIAL SAVING: a paid-for ad in a newspaper or shop window can cost anything from £1 per week to £5 per week.

FREEDOM LIVING SCORE: 8 out of 10

7 CREATE A ROTA-SYSTEM BABYSITTING CIRCLE

It can be a nightmare to find a good babysitter, especially as the traditional route of employing a responsible, reliable teenager seems to be fraught with hazard and chronically short of credible candidates.

In the spirit of the LETS scheme, an increasing number of people form their own babysitting circles of anything up to a dozen members. This system allows you to earn credits when babysitting for others, which can then be 'spent' when you fancy a night out without the kids yourself. As with LETS, no actual money changes hands – all new members start with a certain number of credits.

Another similarity with LETS is that the structure and rules of the scheme are vital. It goes without saying that all participants should be known to each other and trustworthy, but it's worth laying down some rules of etiquette at the outset. For example, a six-hour babysitting session with an insomniac toddler is unlikely to have a value equivalent to a two-hour daytime session minding a nine year old. So some kind of points tally must be set and all members must keep full records of the times, durations and nature of the babysitting undertaken.

The scheme should be fairly easy to administer as long as all participants play a fairly active role earning and spending babysitting credits. To make the process even simpler, a pair of far-sighted parents have set up a babysitting circle administration website [www.mynightoff.com] which allows groups to create a bespoke template which all members can then access to book slots.

ADVANTAGES: A babysitting circle established among a group of friends who know each other well should work brilliantly, saving lots of money and stress.

DISADVANTAGES: The reality is that even among friends we have widely differing ideas of what constitutes good parenting. This can lead to possible conflict if you choose to avoid babysitting for a particular member of the group or having them look after your brood.

INITIAL OUTLAY: minimal administration costs

ONGOING OUTLAY: none

POTENTIAL SAVING: One to two nights a month at approximately £5 per hour equals an annual saving of around £400–£500.

FREEDOM LIVING SCORE: 8 out of 10

⑧ CREATE AN AFTER-SCHOOL CLUB

In the same way that a babysitting circle has the capacity to thrive when established by a group of trusted friends, an after-school club, or breakfast club, can function very well when established in a tight-knit community. To work effectively, it depends on the availability of a responsible supervising parent each day and unless everyone lives in mansions the group size needs to be manageable – no more than five or six children.

While it's essential for parents to establish ground rules for the structure, management and operation of the after-school club, the actual nature of the club should be pretty fluid – there's a whole range of alternatives from cooking clubs to reading groups to gardening clubs – anything in fact that reinforces your children's learning and encourages an interest. The larger the group and the more specialised the activity, the greater the likelihood of complications, so if you're aiming to set up a group on a small scale it's best to aim low in terms of the range of facilities offered.

Larger and more ambitious groups do work, but these are best planned in conjunction with a school, and ideally they will take place on school property under correct supervision and within the terms of the school's insurance.

ADVANTAGES: If you're lucky enough to have a self-supporting group of friends then an after-school club is a natural progression from the babysitting circle. If the club is properly managed, no one should feel put upon and your children will thrive in a safe environment.

DISADVANTAGES: In our increasingly litigious world, most people would be concerned about taking responsibility for another child's welfare or handing their welfare to someone without proper training or criminal checks. It goes without saying (hopefully) that you should never arrange to leave your children in the care of someone you don't trust implicitly.

INITIAL/ONGOING OUTLAY: additional cost of drinks/ food for children (estimate a fee of approx £3 each child per session)

POTENTIAL SAVING: £10 per child per week approx.

FREEDOM LIVING SCORE: 7 out of 10

⑨ DO A CAR SHARE FOR LONG JOURNEYS

Car sharing is simply when two or more people share a journey, whether this is travelling on holiday, to university, to a festival or to the airport. According to statistics produced by car sharing website liftshare.org, at present there are 38 million empty seats on UK roads every day. In 2005, more than 60 per cent of the cars on our roads had only one occupant and 85 per cent of commuters travelled alone by car. A two per cent rise in occupancy would result in a reduction of five billion kilometres of road travel.

Car sharing isn't just about long-haul travel – you can car share for any journey you make. It allows people to benefit from the obvious convenience of the car, while reducing the costs and alleviating the associated problems of congestion and pollution. It's also a great way to save money and reduce your carbon footprint.

The website *lift*share.org was originally established in 1998 by student Ali Clabburn. Now, the largest car sharing network in the UK, *lift*share's mission is to "encourage and enable more efficient use of the car". *Lift*share's online network introduces people travelling in the same direction at the same time so they can travel together for their daily commute or for leisure.

According to *lift*share, a typical car-sharer will save themselves around £1,000 and 1 tonne of CO_2 per year by sharing their daily journey - about 10 per cent of an individual's carbon footprint. One *lift*share member saved more than £15,000 in travel costs over five years.

ADVANTAGES: There are many, including saving money and saving the planet, as well as cutting down on all car expenses and turning travelling into a social networking exercise.

DISADVANTAGES: Like all social networking, there's a risk involved. While liftshare wisely detaches itself from any responsibility for who you choose to share your car with, you will need to be careful about selecting a travelling companion. Be sensible about it – never give out too much personal information in advance, meet in a public place and if you have the slightest reservations about your car-sharing buddy, make other arrangements immediately. But don't be put off: as a general rule, the worst that can happen is that you'll be stuck in a conversation about Viking re-enactments for four hours.

INITIAL/ONGOING OUTLAY: none for the free web matching service

POTENTIAL SAVING: the more people you can get to share your car the cheaper/ safer it is. A journey with three passengers will cut your costs by 75 per cent, getting you from one end of the country to the other for £10.

FREEDOM LIVING SCORE: 8 out of 10.

10 CAR SHARE FOR WORK OR SCHOOL RUNS

As mentioned above, car sharing isn't just about one-off journeys, it's also feasible to organise car shares for regular journeys, including the daily commute and the school run.

In addition to its free public access network, *lift*share has developed a consultancy service for business, providing schemes to more than 900 clients, helping them to increase their level of social responsibility and demonstrate a commitment to the environment by cutting congestion and pollution. With additional incentives such as 'guaranteed ride home' schemes and reserved 'green' parking spaces in priority locations, employees of those companies with schemes are reaping the benefits.

In the city, where parking is at a premium, the reduction of a car parking facility by just 50 spaces could save a business up to £2,000 per space. By introducing a car sharing scheme, employers can save money on car park maintenance costs, capital expenditure, administration costs, security, lighting, CCTV and control of unauthorised parking.

It also helps employers to raise their corporate profile by demonstrating their level of social responsibility and their commitment to the environment, cut congestion and pollution. Such schemes can even help to improve the general well being of staff by building a social network and creating stronger ties between colleagues.

*Lift*share Solutions provides public and private schemes to a range of clients from multi-national businesses and local authorities through to small community groups. Even if you don't have the budget to engage *lift*share Solutions, you can formalise your own relaxed car-sharing scheme centred on a school, workplace, football supporters' club or other group.

ADVANTAGES: For employers and schools, the benefits include cutting congestion and potentially reducing the need for parking facilities. It's a good exercise in social responsibility and community cohesion for all involved. Some local authorities, such as South Gloucestershire, have introduced priority lanes on dual carriageways for cars with more than one occupant travelling during peak commuter hours.

DISADVANTAGES: There aren't many, though car sharing does seem to work best when everyone involved works regular hours (for example council staff) as there's less time wasted hanging around while your colleagues finish their day's work.

INITIAL/ONGOING OUTLAY: dependent on circumstances

POTENTIAL SAVING: again, this depends on the number of participants per car and the length of the journey, but savings can range from £20-40 per week.

FREEDOM LIVING SCORE: 6 out of 10

11 DON'T HAVE DINNER PARTIES HAVE POT LUCK DINNERS

Just because you're cutting back on your spending, you don't need to rein in your socialising. If you host a dinner party for all your friends the bill can run into hundreds of pounds, unless you've followed all the instructions in section two (see below) and can provide the vegetables, meat and alcohol from your own reserves. Even so, a dozen hungry guests use up a lot of valuable resources.

That's why a pot luck dinner makes so much more sense than a traditional dinner party. Basically, a pot luck is a dinner in which each guest brings one dish – a starter, a main course or a pudding. The greatest skill involved in planning a pot luck dinner is project management. You must ensure that the meal isn't a conceptual nightmare, with one pizza and eleven desserts (though that's my idea of a perfect menu). So that means subdividing the requirements on a person-by-person basis. The best way to do this is to base it on people's cooking ability. Most people can buy or cook a starter or dessert easily and without fuss, but a decent main course takes time and skill.

With a guest list of 12 friends, you will have four or five good cooks, each of whom should bring a constituent part of the main course, which in the case of a traditional roast meal means a further subdivision between meat, vegetables and potatoes. It's often better to go for cuisine that traditionally involves many dishes, like Indian, Chinese, Greek or North African food. Everyone else can be split between starters and desserts. If there's someone who genuinely can't or won't cook, you can set them the task of bringing cheese and biscuits or even providing extra cutlery, tablecloths, rolls or alcohol.

As a rule, and in the general spirit of community, everyone should bring a bottle too. If you don't have the cutlery or crockery to cope with such a large party, get everyone to weigh in with their own bits and pieces, or buy extra from a charity shop – the great bonus of a pot luck is that as everyone is so relaxed by the spirit of co-operation, no one bothers about such insignificant details.

Assuming your pot luck is a success, you'll have to make your own contributions to other dinners in turn, of course, but the cost will be spread over the year, allowing you to juggle your home-grown resources to maximum effect and minimal impact on your low-cost larder.

ADVANTAGES: Pot luck dinners create a great feeling of community, no one feels put-upon and the host, for once, isn't left with a load of dirty dishes, as these can be taken home at the end.

DISADVANTAGES: Some people feel that the only true spirit of pot luck is to let people get whatever they want without instruction, believing that the organic results are much more interesting. Anyone who has ever eaten a dozen different types of quiche in one evening would disagree.

INITIAL OUTLAY: ideally zero for the host, no more than £5 per guest

ONGOING OUTLAY: £5 per party

POTENTIAL SAVING: In terms of time and effort, £50-£100 per dinner party.

FREEDOM LIVING SCORE: 7 out of 10

12 SET UP A PROGRESSIVE DINNER PARTY CIRCLE

A variation on the 'pot luck' theme, the progressive dinner party, otherwise known in the States as a 'Condo Conga' or notably in Tim Firth's play of the same name as a 'Safari Party', involves the same principle of co-operative cooking, but with the added bonus of co-operative hosting as well.

Progressive parties work well among groups of friends who live close together, but who don't necessarily all have big houses or the space to host a large party. Those people with smaller houses begin the party with appetisers and aperitifs, then the group switches location to a larger residence for starter, then switches again for main course, and so on until another smaller venue can step in for coffee and liqueurs at the end of the evening.

Logistically, few people are likely to stand more than four or five changes of venue, even if the houses are all in the same street, but as with pot luck dinners, it cuts down on the daunting scale of a dinner party and minimises the costs as well.

ADVANTAGES: You can walk off each course. If you aren't comfortable in someone's home — whether because of the doggy smells, the decor or the dust — you haven't got to stay all night.

DISADVANTAGES: It'll be hard to convince any non-participants that a progressive party isn't a euphemism for wife-swapping. Also, five houses have to be frantically tidied for guests rather than just one.

INITIAL OUTLAY: the host pays for their course only, at about £5 per guest

ONGOING OUTLAY: none

POTENTIAL SAVING: about £50 per dinner party.

FREEDOM LIVING SCORE: 6 out of 10 (plus a point for the exercise)

FOOD & DRINK

13 GROW ALL THE VEGETABLES YOU'LL NEED WITHOUT A GARDEN

When we think about providing our own food, it's easy to conjure up the image of 1970s sitcom *The Good Life* – a great big cultivated garden brimming with produce and a huge allotment thrown in. But the reality for most of us is a significantly reduced circumstance. Should it naturally follow that we have reduced ambitions? Not a bit of it.

Even if you've got the tiniest of postage stamp sized yards, you can make the most of your space to produce a plethora of produce. The trick is to think laterally (not to mention vertically and horizontally). Maximising space is the key, and good use of the area should go hand in hand with selection of the best plants, fruit and vegetables for your garden. If you've got no garden at all it's even theoretically possible to grow some fruit and vegetables indoors – a window box of herbs and lettuce should be within everyone's grasp.

If you're planting straight into the ground, you'll need to bear in mind soil type as well as the important factor of the garden's aspect – which areas are in sun and shade, which are protected from the elements and which are exposed. Container gardening, in which the produce is grown in anything from a tub to a Wellington boot, depends less on aspect as most containers can be shifted around according to the conditions.

A small yard of approximately five metres by three metres should give enough opportunity to grow a family's produce, providing it is well planned. Beans, peas, soft fruit trees, apple and pear trees can be trained against a fence to minimise the space used. Potatoes can be grown in a barrel or a raised bed, herbs and tomatoes are attractive components of hanging baskets and cabbages, lettuces and carrots will grow happily in clumps within pots and tubs.

When choosing tubs and pots, go for something that allows for drainage – strong wooden troughs or oak tubs are good, as are porous terracotta pots. You can make a whole range of wooden planters and troughs for very little money and they look pretty handsome when they're filled with trailing produce. But remember that anything can be used as long as it drains well, from milk churns to wheelbarrows, from baby baths to stock pots.

ADVANTAGES: Container gardening allows you to micro-manage your produce. You can bring stuff indoors during extreme cold and heat and you can use vegetables and herbs to decorate your garden.

DISADVANTAGES: If your main concern is yields, container gardening isn't the best option – go for an allotment instead and stick to neat rows.

INITIAL OUTLAY: seeds/compost/containers will cost approximately £15

ONGOING OUTLAY: none

POTENTIAL SAVING: £250-£300 per year approx

FREEDOM LIVING SCORE: 8 out of 10

14 TURN YOUR GARDEN INTO A SPECIALIST VEGETABLE PATCH

If you've got a patch of soil that you're planning to turn over to vegetable or fruit growing, or if you can get hold of an allotment, you've got to think about how to get the best of the space available.

If you plant row upon row of potatoes, you will undoubtedly get a lot of practical produce (providing you like potatoes of course), but spuds are ten a penny, or at least ten a pound, and can be bought or bartered anywhere. If you're on an allotment, there's likely to be a frantic trade in vegetables, as crop yields are invariably higher than one household's needs. So you need to think carefully about how you're going to trade, and whether you can produce a commodity that's so rare, it can be traded for all the common or garden vegetables you need.

While everyone else is sweating over their carrots and runner beans, focus your attentions on asparagus, spinach, globe and Jerusalem artichokes, garlic and rocket. Specialising in 'deli-veg' gives you the edge over your fellow horticulturalists, cuts the cost of buying these pricey but delicious vegetables and means you'll always be in demand when it comes to swapping time.

Think also about how you can raise the profile of the humble vegetable after it's grown – garlic can be smoked (in a smokery, not a pipe) for a really intense flavour, while a Jerusalem artichoke makes a cracking potato substitute, both for chips and, along with beetroot, as thick-cut, hand-fried crisps.

ADVANTAGES: You'll corner the market in fancy foods and mark yourself out as a true specialist.

DISADVANTAGES: Perennials like artichokes and asparagus take a couple of years to bed in, so they are a long term bet. Specialist vegetables sometimes require very specific soil conditions, so plan carefully. And finally, if your fellow allotment holders are all wizened old men in their late 80s, be warned that they might tell you to stick your rocket where the sun doesn't shine.

INITIAL OUTLAY: seeds, off-cuts etc. £10-£15

ONGOING OUTLAY: none

POTENTIAL SAVING: £250 per year

FREEDOM LIVING SCORE: 8 out of 10

15 BREW YOUR OWN ALCOHOL

If you really want to save money on alcohol, your best bet is to avoid drinking it altogether. Winemaking is a rewarding and sometimes challenging hobby that can produce spectacular results but which can also cost a lot of money to set up if you follow expert guidance to the letter and invest in fermentation jars, thermometers and other assorted items from Frankenstein's laboratory. While beer brewing is generally an easier task, it still requires a fair degree of preparation, and unless you can grow the ingredients yourself, it can be hard to source all the constituent parts.

If you are serious about making wine, your best bet is to broadcast this fact widely to friends and family and get them to buy all the necessary equipment over time as Christmas and birthday presents, otherwise you'll struggle to make the kit pay for itself. You can always repay kindly relatives in homemade wine when you've perfected the art.

If you're in a hurry, it is possible to cut corners, although the results may be less than spectacular. In this case it may be better to think more in terms of augmenting low-grade alcohol rather than trying to find it for free. For example, dirt-cheap spirits can be considerably enlivened by the addition of herbs and hedgerow fruits – sloe gin being a particularly good example. In my experience, sloes are also a fine basic ingredient of wine, as are another common foraged fruit, elderberries. In both cases, these freely abundant fruits can produce wonderfully deep, rich, port-like wine.

If, however, you're just looking for bargain basement plonk that tastes OK and achieves the desired effect, there follows a knock-out recipe for knock-out apple wine – recommended by a die-hard freedom living expert who claims to have saved a small fortune thanks to this simple recipe:

APPLE TIPPLE

30 litre food grade plastic bucket with lid
20 litres of apple juice (If you can't juice your own apples then
     supermarket value brands are the best bet)
2kg sugar
10 litres of water
2 teaspoons yeast
Suitable steriliser for the bucket (eg sodium meta bisulphate)

Method: Sterilise your bucket and rinse thoroughly. Add the sugar and a kettle of boiled water then agitate until the sugar has dissolved. Add the apple juice and then top up with water until you have 30 litres. Add the yeast then wait approximately six weeks or until the liquid is clear. You'll then have an apple wine/cider of approximately 11 per cent alcohol content. This is particularly tasty with a splash of sparkling spring water. It's a great everyday drink which can also be used as a present for friends – it's also ideal for trading on the allotment for tips, seeds and vegetables. Source apples for juicing from friends with apple trees – there are always more windfalls than they can cope with.

ADVANTAGES: If you can invest the time and money in equipment, you can produce excellent wines and beer with the minimum of ongoing outlay. Some fruit wines are absolutely delicious.

DISADVANTAGES: Expensive set-up costs and long storage time – most home-brewed wines should be left for at least three months before drinking. And sometimes the results can be absolutely shocking. If you're determined to do the whole thing yourself, be prepared also to spend a long time mashing, pulping, peeling and juicing fruit.

INITIAL OUTLAY: anything from £50-£250 depending on your ambition

ONGOING OUTLAY: minimal for sugar and yeast

POTENTIAL SAVING: depending on typical consumption, from £200-£500 per year.

FREEDOM LIVING SCORE: 6 out of 10

16 GO HEDGEROW HARVESTING FOR FRUIT TO MAKE PIES, CORDIALS AND JAMS

Hedgerow harvesting is a deeply satisfying pursuit for anyone dedicated to living for free. It isn't just the concept of picking nature's bounty without spending a penny of hard-earned cash that's so appealing, but also the image of countless jams, chutneys, cordials, soups and puddings that can be derived from berries, leaves, flowers and fungi.

We might associate hedgerow harvesting with the autumn months, but in truth there's something to be snaffled from springtime onwards if you know where to look. Start with elderflowers for cordial and 'champagne' – though don't take too many or there won't be anything left for elderberry cordial in the autumn. Nettles spring up with alarming regularity as soon as the sun begins to get warmer, and they're a great, nutritious ingredient for soups (see below). Wild strawberries and cherries are excellent summer fruits if you can get to them before the birds.

Mushrooms are, if you'll pardon the pun, in a field of their own and need to be treated with great care by the novice forager. Take a good field guide with you and make sure you're certain which type of mushroom you've picked before eating it. Save a little bit back just in case you get sick, it will help identification (of the mushroom, not of your body) later if needed.

The Food Standards Agency encourages hedgerow harvesting as a natural way to supplement our daily diet, but it also offers the following advice to foragers:

When identifying any berry, fruit or fungi, check several features to be certain (look at leaf, flower, colour, shape and season). If you're unsure, avoid it. Never collect plants and berries growing in industrial or polluted areas or near busy roads. If you do go foraging, only take what you need – always give the plant a fair chance to reproduce. Under the 1981 Wildlife and Countryside Act it is illegal to uproot any wild plant without the permission of the owner. You should never pick any rare or endangered wild plants under any circumstances.

If you stick to the above rules of good practice you'll have many happy hours foraging and harvesting – try canal towpaths, cycleways and byways for the best and cleanest produce. The following is a favourite tried-and-tested foraging recipe:

NETTLE SOUP

20-30 nettle plants
One leek or onion, finely chopped
One potato, diced
One diced carrot, swede or parsnip depending on preference

---

1 litre chicken stock (or vegetable stock if preferred)
Oil or butter

Method: Sweat the onion in the oil/butter, add par-boiled potatoes and root vegetables and simmer together for a few minutes. Carefully wash and pick the nettle leaves and then add these to the pot. Add the stock and allow everything to simmer for about 25 minutes. Finish off with salt and pepper or add some yoghurt/crème fraiche to suit and then blend to required consistency.

ADVANTAGES: Foraging is a satisfying, free and incredibly versatile method of boosting your larder all year round.

DISADVANTAGES: Fungi and berries are potentially hazardous if you don't take due care, but as long as you follow FSA recommendations you should be fine. The greatest disadvantage is that so many people now enjoy hedgerow harvesting you might struggle to find a free spot. If you do identify a plentiful source of berries, freeze some of your pickings immediately to ensure you always have a good, fresh stock available.

INITIAL/ONGOING OUTLAY: for picking and eating, zero. Minimal outlay for making jams and chutneys.

POTENTIAL SAVING: £50 per year

FREEDOM LIVING SCORE: 10 out of 10

17 NO MORE COFFEE CULTURE – DRINK SAMPLES IN STORE

One of the greatest cons of modern society is the growth of the coffee culture. The proliferation of coffee shops has created a civilisation dependent on costly choco-mocha-lattes with hazelnut dusting. While there's never been anything wrong with taking a pause for a quick brew while out shopping, this has now become a miniature meal in itself, with inflated prices to match. There's a difference between pausing for refreshment and burying your head in an over-sized bowl of caffeinated froth and that difference could save you a fortune.

For starters you need to analyse the coffee buying experience – in general this consists of queuing for some considerable hours in a dark coffee shop to then spend five minutes sipping an already-cold coffee while clashing elbows with the fraught shopper next to you. All the good tables are taken by out of work actors pretending to write novels on their I-Books. It's not a value for money situation.

So your best bet is to focus on the 'refreshment' part of the phrase 'refreshment break'. If you need a caffeine hit, head to a deli-catessen, or a retail coffee shop chain where the free samples of coffee are plentiful and the queues are short.

If, on the other hand, you just need a cool glass of water, go to the bank. Most banks have water coolers for customer use, and it's absolutely fine to have a couple of cups while you browse through the latest financial services products. Big department stores and Marks & Spencer are also good bets if you're just after a quick gulp of water.

Some places actively encourage the free consumption of beverages. Members of the free Ikea family card scheme [see www.ikea.com for stores and opening info] are entitled to free tea and coffee in the store's restaurants from Monday to Friday.

ADVANTAGES: You save money, time and the inconvenience of queuing in the 'relaxed' environment of a coffee shop.

DISADVANTAGES: Depending on how much coffee/water you tend to drink, you may have to spread yourself out around the various free sample emporiums in your locality – which won't help much if you live in a village.

INITIAL/ONGOING OUTLAY: none

POTENTIAL SAVING: A minimum of £100 per year

FREEDOM LIVING SCORE: 8 out of 10

18 SNACK FROM DELI COUNTERS AND AT PROMOTIONAL STANDS – ESPECIALLY GOOD AT CASH & CARRY STORES

Getting a hot lunch every day can add a good £15 per week to your outgoings as a minimum, as well as eating into your lunch break while you queue with the world and his wife for service. But if you're lucky enough to live or work in a big town, or within easy distance of a superstore, you can access free, hot food on a daily basis for no cost at all. Welcome to the world of the in-store demonstration.

The best source of demonstration food is the cash and carry store. You will need to organise (free) membership to get access to the in-store delights, but once you're there get set for a feeding frenzy as a whole range of hot snacks, from pizzas to pasta via meatballs and rollmop herrings are generally on offer. Unlike the bafflingly small portions in supermarkets, these are bulk samples. In the course of a trip around the store, it is possible to run through all three courses of a good-sized lunch.

If you're on a lighter diet, or you just fancy grazing as you browse, then supermarket deli counters, town-centre delicatessens and butchers' shops are all regular sources of on-the-counter freebies.

ADVANTAGES: You get to sample a range of food for free while giving the bored shop assistant something to do for five minutes. Everyone's happy.

DISADVANTAGES: As with the free drinks above, it's possible to build up a potentially damaging reputation as a scavenger. Unlike drinks, snack foods are a better bet for a quick 'walk-by swoop' at the deli counter, allowing you to grab a handful of treats and make your getaway unnoticed. Also, living off snack treats may not constitute a balanced diet.

INITIAL/ONGOING OUTLAY: none

POTENTIAL SAVING: @ £15 per week for one year, £780

FREEDOM LIVING SCORE: 8 out of 10

19 GO FISH – HOW TO CATCH A VARIETY OF FISH AND SHELLFISH RELIABLY AND FREELY

Give a man a fish and he'll feed his family for a day, give him a rod and he'll spend the day fishing instead. But the law of averages dictates that he'll actually catch something at some stage. It's important to establish the difference between an angler and a fisherman at this point – rather like somebody who goes paint-balling differs from a soldier. Anglers fish for sport, while fishermen fish for fish. We need only concern ourselves with the latter here.

Rivers in most parts of the UK are controlled by the Environment Agency. You'll need a rod licence to fish these waters legally, as well as a permit from whoever owns the land you are fishing from, and there is a closed season on rivers from March to June each year. While it's not strictly illegal to keep the freshwater fish you catch, it can be frowned upon by sporting anglers. Check out the Environment Agency's web pages for anglers for full details of where to fish inland. Offshore sea fishing doesn't require a licence and you can keep whatever you catch, so if you've got a mate with a boat, that's the safest way to go.

The type of fishing method you use depends on the type of fish you are after – some keep close to the seabed, some swim free. The former are more likely to be caught in a static net or pot and the latter on a hooked line, but net fishing is also pretty profitable for catching fish like herring and mackerel that swim in large shoals.

Back on dry land, it's worth checking out the coastline at low tide for any shellfish and crustaceans that may be going begging. Mussels, clams, whelks, cockles and even crabs can be picked up easily this way and all make delicious and nutritious foodstuffs.

Never collect shellfish from somewhere built-up, or from an area close to a sewage outfall (for obvious reasons), don't eat any seafood that's dead before you cook it. If the pre-cooked shellfish gives some resistance when you try to open it, it's still alive; if it opens easily, it's already dead and should be discarded.

ADVANTAGES: As with any natural resource, fish and shellfish are a great bonus if you're living on a budget. And it's good for your brain.

DISADVANTAGES: Rules, regulations and anglers make fishing for food a bit of a chore in the UK, but sea fishing retains some of the glamour of the good old days.

INITIAL OUTLAY: fishing rod/nets approx. £25-£100

ONGOING OUTLAY: a licence for freshwater fishing costs up to £66.50 (2007/08 prices) per year. Anyone under 12 or over 65 can fish without a licence.

POTENTIAL SAVING: If you eat the government's recommended minimum of two portions of fish a week, you could save anything from £250-£500 per year by catching your own.

FREEDOM LIVING SCORE: 9 out of 10

20 SHOOT WILD ANIMALS

The rules on shooting animals for food are as complex as the rules on gun ownership. It's not possible to give full guidance on the ins and outs of the system here, so before you even think about either owning a gun or killing wildlife, consult an expert. Good places to start are www.defra.gov.uk for the government angle and www.basc.org.uk, the website of the British Association for Shooting and Conservation, which gives a broader industry perspective.

The basic ground rules for shooting wildlife are that most wild birds and mammals are protected in the UK, even on private land. Three categories of animals can be shot: wildfowl (including ducks, geese and woodcock) when they are not in a 'close' or breeding season; pests such as crows, pigeons and magpies may be shot by autho- rised persons under licence from the government; game species, such as pheasant, deer, hares, partridges and grouse may be shot, but again these have specific close seasons depending on species and breeding pattern.

Although this might be a point of argument in the bars of Islington, there is a close link between shooting and conservation, and many of the people who shoot in the UK have a vested interest in the con- servation of the species. Farmers who send cattle to slaughter aren't acting irresponsibly, they're just managing the breed. The same can be said of legal, authorised shooting.

Of course, there are still people who take matters into their own hands, shooting pigeons or shooting and trapping rabbits/hares on common land for the pot. This is a dangerous pastime, not least because of the legal implications for anyone who breaks a walker's ankle with a trap, or takes someone's eye out with an airgun pellet. The best bet is to get decent advice, proper training and effective supervision – then get friendly with a farmer and you've got a ready source of game quarry to aim at.

ADVANTAGES: Sourcing our own food is a natural instinct. Shooting for sport is also a fine skill to master, albeit a difficult and fairly expensive one.

DISADVANTAGES: Shooting is an activity dogged by controversy and misconceptions. If you shoot to eat, you've also got to master the skills of skinning and butchering your kill.

INITIAL/ONGOING OUTLAY: You don't need a game licence in England or Wales, but you do in Scotland. Once you have the necessary gun licence, you can buy a shotgun for anything between £600 and £1,000 new.

POTENTIAL SAVING: If you shoot all your meat, you could save up to £1,000 a year.

FREEDOM LIVING SCORE: 7 out of 10

21 COLLECT AND COOK ROAD KILL

Foraging takes many forms, and while some people might think it is distasteful to eat something that's got tyre marks running along its back, there is a growing movement behind the argument that road kill is a perfectly legitimate and safe source of free meat.

Let's look at the legality first. Even though some of the animals accidentally killed on our roads are protected from hunters while alive, there is no law forbidding the consumption of their carcasses. In the USA, this is a grey area, as some drivers have been found using their vehicles as a hunting weapon, so some states have enforced a ban. But UK law currently allows all road kill to be consumed – from deer to rabbits via pheasants, badgers and hedgehogs.

The practicality of collecting road kill is a major stumbling block. Most of these 'pavement pizzas' come a cropper on busy roads in built-up areas and by the time you've got hold of the remains, there's not much usable meat to be had. Country lanes are a less frequent source of road kill, but the meat is likely to be in a much better state.

The main safety concern regarding road kill is cooking. The meat should be very well cooked, ideally slow cooked in a casserole over some hours to tenderise tough meat. Always check the carcass for structural damage. If bones have shattered on impact, they can render the meat almost useless. It should go without saying that meat which doesn't look or smell fresh must always be avoided.

ADVANTAGES: Meat is very expensive, and cars are everywhere. Road kill is a natural way of taking positives from both situations. Wild animal meat tastes as good as free range.

DISADVANTAGES: Beyond the possible health risks mentioned above there is also a certain stigma attached to the idea of shovelling your dinner off the A412, no matter how cheap it is.

INITIAL/ONGOING OUTLAY: none

POTENTIAL SAVING: anything from £500-£1,000 per year.

FREEDOM LIVING SCORE: 8 out of 10

22 KEEP PRODUCTIVE LIVESTOCK

Keeping animals for your own meat, leather, milk, wool or eggs, or simply for company on those long winter nights, takes you to a whole new level of freedom living. We're now firmly in the realms of the self-sufficient and that means having plenty of space and time to look after the animal(s) in question while ensuring you meet the increasingly lengthy list of obligations imposed by the government regarding the ownership and care of livestock.

If you're still keen then you're a better person than I am, so to reward your commitment, here's a brief guide to the most common small-scale livestock options. For the sake of brevity I'm omitting cows, sheep and pigs as they belong on smallholdings, not in back gardens.

GOATS. OK, so goats belong on smallholdings too, but many people mistakenly believe that you can keep a goat on a small patch of grass and it will act as an effective lawnmower and waste disposal unit while recycling all your lush greenery into delicious milk. In reality goats are inefficient mowers, as they prefer rougher, fibrous food and a varied diet. They may eat some grass, but they are just as likely to completely turn their noses up at the prospect. Goats should never be tethered, they should have freedom to roam in a fairly large paddock with decent stock fencing – they should also have shelter and access to fresh water at all times. The milk is delicious, though, as is the meat.

GEESE AND DUCKS. As lawnmowers, geese are a better bet than goats but they can be awfully temperamental. Ducks are generally more even-tempered and they'll do a bit of weeding if the mood takes them, but both varieties of fowl will produce copious amounts of dung that will need clearing up regularly if you don't want to offend your neighbours. On the upside, both produce eggs fairly regularly under the right circumstances and their meat is delicious. As with all fowl, geese and ducks will need access to a free-flowing water source as well as fencing to protect them from predators and a shelter to sleep in at night.

CHICKENS. The most common domestic 'producing' beast, the chicken is also, in my experience, a vicious little monster, although less susceptible to fits of rage than the goose. Chickens are obviously a good source of eggs and versatile meat. They are happy to eat a combination of greens and grain and they're never happier than when they are scratching about for their own food. Consequently you'll need to allow a sizeable area for exercise that doesn't need to be kept pristine. Predators are a risk again, so protective fencing is a must, particularly around the coop.

ADVANTAGES: Eggs, milk and meat are expensive commodities and buying free range or locally sourced produce is sometimes hard. So there's no better feeling than the knowledge that your meat is home-grown.

DISADVANTAGES: Keeping any animals is hard work, not just in daily feeding and maintenance but also in regular mucking-out, collecting eggs, milking and ultimately taking the animal to be killed at a slaughterhouse (and paying for the privilege). Don't try this at home unless you've got serious time and dedication on your side.

INITIAL OUTLAY: cost of goat approx £50-£300, cost of ducklings/goslings/chicks £5 each, food troughs and fresh water supply £25-£50, shelter and vets bills from £100- £1,000.

ONGOING OUTLAY: Food approx £10 per month.

POTENTIAL SAVING: anything from £500-£1,000 per year.

FREEDOM LIVING SCORE: 6 out of 10

23 THE AVIARY AND THE APIARY

If you've taken a look at the prospect of animal husbandry and can't find anything to suit, don't give up just yet. There are two further options that are suitable for anyone's circumstances – from small-scale residential properties to big country houses. They are relatively low maintenance and low stress. Let me tell you about the birds and the bees.

QUAILS. The birds in this case are quails, small and quite beautiful fowl which have several major advantages over other, larger breeds. First of all, they are happy in a relatively small space – half a dozen quail will live quite happily on the floor of an aviary (if you already keep fancy birds) or in their own high-sided coop. The cage needs high sides because quail can actually fly, especially when disturbed, and will damage themselves in a low-roofed environment.

While quails have the propensity to produce muck in quantities that seem disproportionate to their tiny stature, they are otherwise easy to keep. Like chickens they like to scratch and bathe in the dust, but they are not fussy eaters – which is why they suit an aviary so well, as they will survive on a combination of chick crumb and the seeds dropped by other birds.

The major plus point of quails is that in the right conditions and in good light they will produce eggs prolifically – sometimes as often as one egg every eight hours. Quails' eggs are known as a delicacy, but they are equally useful as a substitute for hens' eggs in everyday cooking.

BEES. The buzzing half of this logical equation isn't so easy to establish, but once they are in situ, you'll have a regular little honey factory throbbing away on your behalf for minimal outlay and effort. If you're serious about beekeeping it makes sense to enrol on a course for beginners before you start, or at least contact your local beekeeping society for advice and recommendations of where you can buy a hive and how you can get hold of your first swarm. It is theoretically possible to make your own hive – after all, bees create their own natural 'hives' in the wild – but for ease of access and maintenance there's nothing to beat the traditional wooden hive.

Once a swarm is established you'll have maintenance responsibilities and, of course, honey collection duties, but otherwise the bees are tremendously self-supporting. For honey collecting you'll need the right protective equipment and a decent smoker to subdue the bees while you nick their precious honey. Don't forget that a bonus by-product of the honey-making process is beeswax, which can be formed into candles and used as a furniture polish.

ADVANTAGES: Both quails and bees are natural scavengers, turning natural resources like nectar and dropped seeds into something practical for you: eggs and honey respectively. They're cheap, low maintenance and interesting too.

DISADVANTAGES: There's little meat on a quail, even a well-fed one, so they're not much of a source of food beyond egg production. They can be flighty and they can stop laying if they're disturbed or their environment is too dark. And bees can sting you, of course.

INITIAL OUTLAY: Quails approx £2-£5 each, water supply £5, bee-keeping kit from £50 second-hand to £150-£200+.

ONGOING OUTLAY: £2 a month for quail food, minimal ongoing costs for beekeeping.

POTENTIAL SAVING: Assuming you substitute quails' eggs for hens' eggs in all your cooking and honey for all sugar, you could save around £150-£200 per year.

FREEDOM LIVING SCORE: 9 out of 10

HOUSEHOLD BILLS

24 CUT YOUR FUEL COSTS BY CONSERVING ENERGY

Heat and power are major costs, and anyone dedicated to freedom living must work hard to minimise the inefficient and costly waste of energy. This isn't simply good news for the wallet, it's essential for the survival of the planet. So before we move on to the wonderful world of generating alternative energy (see below) we need to focus on the greater and more pressing challenge of energy conservation.

Experts at the Centre for Alternative Technology [see www.cat.org.uk], based in Mid Wales, believe that it is possible to slice up to 80 per cent from heating bills with effective conservation. There are many areas of conservation that will make an immediate impact on household bills, including lifestyle changes such as closing curtains, keeping lids on saucepans, only boiling sufficient water for immediate needs, wearing a jumper; insulating your loft, walls and floor; draught-proofing; installing double glazing (or even triple glazing); using more effective heating controls and thermostats; buying energy efficient appliances and turning off appliances rather than leaving them on standby.

Firstly, ensure you choose energy efficient appliances like condensing gas boilers, which run at 90 per cent efficiency compared with traditional boilers, which come in at a pathetic 65 per cent. Secondly, switch every electrical appliance off at the wall, never leave them on standby or in sleep mode. The average home spends £38 per year on electrical items left on standby mode – this wasteful consumption is known as a 'phantom load', and is common in most appliances, such as DVD players, stereos and TVs. Switching off at the wall is the only way to combat this waste.

Finally, insulate your loft to a CAT recommended maximum thickness of 450mm (government guidelines are currently set at 250mm). You can make an average £180-£220 per year saving on household bills by lining an uninsulated loft with 270mm of insulation.

Until you've achieved these aims, there's no point trying to generate your own energy, as the inefficient waste of power will negate any potential cost benefits.

Insulation and other energy-saving tools are often available free to people on low incomes or offered with hefty government subsidies. The Warm Wales scheme is just one of the examples of government- and industry-led initiatives that aim to equip homes with low-energy light bulbs (another great conservation idea) and other cost-saving benefits. Visit the government's energy efficiency website at www.est.org.uk for more information.

ADVANTAGES: Insulating your house and cutting wasteful energy consumption is a no-brainer. Just do it.

DISADVANTAGES: There are none. Get the picture?

INITIAL OUTLAY: cost of insulation material, depending on the size of your loft space. Cost of buying energy-efficient electrical items and boiler (though there are grants available for boilers).

ONGOING OUTLAY: none

POTENTIAL SAVING: Add all the benefits outlined above together and you'll produce an annual heating bill reduction of at least £300 per year.

FREEDOM LIVING SCORE: 8 out of 10

25 CUT YOUR HEATING COSTS BY GOING VICTORIAN

If you're really serious about cutting the cost of heating your house, you could do a lot worse than following the example of our Victorian forbears, who had to cope with the unfortunate consequences of building houses with massive, high-ceilinged rooms. By the time our grandiose ancestors had cottoned on to the idea that hot air rises, they were freezing their whiskers off.

But undeterred by this, they championed a whole series of draught-proofing measures, like excluders under doors, nightcaps (material, not alcoholic), thick lined curtains at windows and on four-poster beds and even the classic wing-backed chair. All of these functional accoutrements are great and sorely under-utilised methods of performing the simple function of keeping the heat where you need it.

ADVANTAGES: You feel as cosy as a Sunday night costume drama.

DISADVANTAGES: Your house looks like something out of a Sunday night costume drama.

INITIAL OUTLAY: minimal. Old blankets work well as window coverings and draught excluders. Wing-backed chairs can be picked up for £30-£40 at a junk shop.

ONGOING OUTLAY: none

POTENTIAL SAVING: as with all insulation, the savings are considerable – anything from £30-£80 per year.

FREEDOM LIVING SCORE: 7 out of 10

26 SWITCH TO WOOD BURNERS

If your idea of burning wood in the home involves a pretty little pile of logs spitting and crackling in the grate, please look away now. What we're dealing with here is the serious business of burning wood for maximum effect – that means acquiring whatever wood you can find, gather and scavenge in whatever form. Barn-dried logs are all very well, but at £5 per small net bag, they're the most expensive way to use wood as fuel.

Step one of converting to wood burners is to select the right stove for your requirements. The size of the stove will depend on the amount of heat you need to generate and whether you intend to use it with a back boiler for heating your domestic water and/or radiators as well. Multi-fuel stoves tend to have small fireboxes and consequently burn fuel inefficiently. Old-fashioned Rayburn or Aga stoves that are used for cooking and as a heating and hot water source, are also fairly inefficient as the demands on one appliance to fulfil all three tasks are excessive. Smaller scale wood burners are sometimes adaptable for water heating as well. Don't be tempted to buy a huge wood burner for a small space. They are very efficient and you'll be wasting money if you have to keep the windows open because you're overheating your room. For an average 15ftx15ft room, the smallest stoves are more than adequate, though again if you're heating water you may need a larger size.

It isn't necessary to buy new – take a look around reclamation yards, where you'll usually find a wide selection of stoves in varying states of decay. Most are salvageable and just need a coat of stove blacking. If you must buy new, source your stove direct from the manufacturer or wholesaler – check prices on trading websites like eBay for the best deals.

For safety and efficiency's sakes, you should always install your wood burner with a properly fitted flue. If you've got a large chimney or inglenook make sure you have a good fireproof register plate fitted – this is the sheet of material that blocks off the chimney cavity. The flue pipe passes through a hole in the register plate, but the heat from the burner isn't wasted heating the chimney cavity.

As regards wood, there are many cheap sources of burning material, as long as you don't mind what it looks like. Furniture manufacturers, timber yards and demolition sites often have off-cuts and surplus timber lying about and are happy for you to remove it for free. Never burn wood that's been painted or treated with a substance that's likely to give off poisonous fumes.

There's not much money to be made from selling logs – even farm gate operations aren't particularly profitable – so you may also find that a farmer or landowner with a lot of surplus wood will be happy to negotiate a hefty discount if you'll remove wood in bulk. It might pay to invest in your own log splitter or chainsaw, as that way you can offer to help cut down problem trees for your neighbours, taking away the remnants in part payment. Never be ashamed of picking up fallen branches when you're out and about in the countryside – they make excellent kindling.

ADVANTAGES: Burning wood is the oldest form of heating and just about the easiest. If your stove is properly installed and sealed, it's also highly efficient.

DISADVANTAGES: Sourcing wood can be a problem in built-up areas. Storage is also a major issue, as the wood needs to be kept dry where possible.

INITIAL OUTLAY: depending on need, a wood burner can cost anything from £150-£1,500. Range cookers are more expensive. The flue and fittings can set you back a further £500, but if you can source your wood cheap you'll earn this outlay back in no time.

ONGOING OUTLAY: cost of wood and chimney sweeping (at £50 a go, twice a year)

POTENTIAL SAVING: an efficient system that provides all the heat and hot water you need could save around £500 a year, while generating 74 per cent of all the energy you need in the home.

FREEDOM LIVING SCORE: 9 out of 10

HEAT YOUR HOUSEHOLD WATER USING SOLAR GAIN

There are two main ways to harness the power of the sun – solar water heating and photo-voltaic panels (more commonly called solar panels) which generate electricity. We'll come back to the latter, more costly method later, but first we'll look at ways to generate hot water only.

The first thing to say is that in the UK you're unlikely to be able to rely on the sun to provide your hot water requirements all year. In the winter months, you will need a back-up, which is why CAT recommends a system that combines wood burners with solar heating.

The most efficient way to generate hot water from the power of the sun is by fitting an evacuated tube system to your roof. These use a low volume of water over a small surface area (approximately $3m^2$ is sufficient to heat the water used by an average sized house). Another popular system is the flat plate collector, which uses a system of insulated black pipes. This is not so efficient, requiring a surface area of 4 sq m to heat sufficient water.

These systems will cost approximately £2,500 installed and fitted. It is possible to buy them as kits and install them yourself, but the cost saving doesn't really offset the hassle of scrabbling around on your roof. There are grants available from the DTI to offset some of the cost of installing these systems.

If you're determined to follow the freedom living principle to the letter and you've got some plumbing experience, you can reproduce some of the benefits of solar heating systems by painting old radiators black, attaching them to your roof and connecting them to the water supply. Obviously, as these aren't designed for the purpose and the volume of water carried is great they are much less efficient than the other methods outlined above. But it does have the advantage that you can pick up the materials for a song from a salvage yard.

ADVANTAGES: As part of an overall system, solar water heating is a low-impact and effective back-up. It'll put an even bigger smile on your face when the sun shines.

DISADVANTAGES: Some people feel the pipes/tubes/radiators look unsightly and the resulting heat generation can be intermittent and disappointing. A bit like the British summer.

INITIAL OUTLAY: £2,500 installed

ONGOING OUTLAY: none

POTENTIAL SAVING: A quarter of our energy use is water heating, so a family house with a £500 heating bill could save around £60 per year and get about 50 per cent of the annual hot water requirements from solar water heating.

FREEDOM LIVING SCORE: 8 out of 10

28 GENERATE YOUR OWN HOUSEHOLD SOLAR POWER

Photovoltaic panels convert the power of the sun into electricity. They are very costly to install – even with a government grant – but are efficient to use and an excellent method of powering small, infrequent use items (which is why they are often seen powering illuminated road signs, for example).

As a principal source of power generation in a domestic environment in the UK they aren't likely to prove terribly cost effective at current prices and don't offer the same year-round reliability as other alternative energy sources. If your house is in the right location, with a roof that faces south without obstructions from buildings or trees, you may even be able to generate sufficient energy to sell some back to the National Grid. If your house isn't connected to the mains, photovoltaic panels are an excellent alternative, though even in this case it is virtually impossible to live on power generated by photovoltaic panels alone because they simply don't get enough sun in winter. Off-grid energy generation usually requires a combination of solar panels and another source, such as wind.

ADVANTAGES: Another reasonably efficient way to convert the sun's power to energy.

DISADVANTAGES: High cost means a very long pay back time.

INITIAL OUTLAY: Systems range in price but an average system can be installed for around £15,000. Government grants were available to cover half the cost of this, but these have recently been capped at £2,500.

ONGOING OUTLAY: none

POTENTIAL SAVING: Savings are difficult to calculate as they are dependent on location and tariff. In the right environment they could save around £240 a year, rising to a potential profit in sales back to the National Grid. Across the UK, the saving is likely to be closer to an average of £120 per year.

FREEDOM LIVING SCORE: 6 out of 10

29 GENERATE YOUR OWN HOUSEHOLD WIND POWER

The old estate agents' mantra 'location, location, location' is never more accurate than when applied to renewable energy sources. As with photovoltaic panels, wind turbines are only truly cost-effective in the right circumstances. If your property is on a hill, with an even and steady wind and with no obstructions like trees or buildings, then a wind turbine may well work for you.

If you're a skilled metalworker you can build your own, providing you also have the technical know-how to connect it to a battery for storage. You're better off buying a ready-assembled turbine for a few thousand pounds.

Wind power is a matter of feast and famine. In a gale, you cannot hope to harness and store the power of the wind, and when it is calm, there's barely enough energy generated to power a small bulb. Consequently, wind power generation on a small scale (as opposed to the giant offshore wind farms around the coast and on bleak moors across the country) is most likely to be feasible as a back-up source of energy only, and could only be considered as the main source of energy for heating a house or a hot water system if you're using a large and expensive turbine along with enough battery power to cope with calm days and/or combining this system with photovoltaic panels.

ADVANTAGES: If you're in the right part of the world, a wind turbine will support your renewable energy system. At least if you're somewhere that doesn't get much sun, the chances are you'll get plenty of wind.

DISADVANTAGES: There are few tangible benefits of small-scale wind power generation in isolation.

INITIAL OUTLAY: wind turbines can cost from £500 to £10,000 depending on size and purpose. At the low end of this scale, the turbine would power a few lights; at the high end, a turbine sited in a good location would power an entire house.

ONGOING OUTLAY: none

POTENTIAL SAVING: £0-£1,020 per year, depending on location and existing tariff. The pay back time is long.

FREEDOM LIVING SCORE: 5 out of 10

30 GENERATE YOUR OWN HOUSEHOLD HYDROELECTRIC POWER

A water source is another potential avenue of energy generation. Again, much depends on the location of your water source. To stand a realistic chance of cost-effective generation you need a combination of factors, namely a fast flowing stream and a good vertical drop. There is a simple calculation to give you a rough idea of the power (in watts) that you can expect to generate from a given water source, which is as follows:

Flow (in litres per second) × Head Height (vertical drop in metres) × 10 (the specific weight of water) ÷ 2 = the power generated.

On a small scale, the most cost-effective turbine is the Pelton Wheel and these require a vertical drop of at least 10 metres.

If you've got this facility available to you, use it. If not, forget it, as you won't be able to make cost-effective use of your water source.

ADVANTAGES: In the right conditions, hydroelectric power is a stable and steady power source.

DISADVANTAGES: The right conditions are hard to find and almost impossible to recreate.

INITIAL OUTLAY: cost of setting up the turbine and power storage = £11,000+, although hydroelectricity costs are very site-specific.

ONGOING OUTLAY: none

POTENTIAL SAVING: £1,000 per year

FREEDOM LIVING SCORE: 7 out of 10

31 SAVE YOUR COMPOST AND WASTE

There is one further power generation method worth mentioning in passing. It's possible to extract gas from human and animal waste to make fuel. While it might seem like a bridge too far for all but the most dedicated eco-warrior, there is an untapped reservoir of power stored up in our dung and kitchen waste which is just waiting to be let out.

So why don't we exploit it more? Well we do, but only on a grand commercial scale at sewage treatment plants. While humans and animals (especially pigs, naturally) have the capacity to produce methane gas and we have the technology to extract and store it, no one has yet made this process viable for the small-scale market as the heat loss is too great on a small scale due to the ratio of volume to surface area. So since we're dealing only with processes that have the capacity to save money, we must discount small-scale gas generation. In other parts of the world, where the climate is more favourable, like India for example, gas from dung is often used as a fuel. But sadly it remains a distant dream in the UK for now.

Never fear, however, as there are other uses for your waste – a compost bin built from a couple of larch lap fence panels is the perfect store for kitchen waste that can be rotted down as a general purpose compost. A composting toilet is a great way to compost human dung which produces the most incredible garden fertiliser – though this should only ever be used around plants and should never come into contact with foodstuffs.

ADVANTAGES: Human and animal waste produces wonderful plant food.

DISADVANTAGES: Getting in touch with nature is fine, but rooting around in your family's dung is a step too far for some of us.

INITIAL/ONGOING OUTLAY: no outlay for composting, £150-£200 to build a basic composting toilet facility.

POTENTIAL SAVING: a composting toilet saves on fertiliser and water usage, to the tune of £50-£100 per year.

FREEDOM LIVING SCORE: 8 out of 10

32 CREATE A 'GREY WATER' REUSE SYSTEM IN YOUR HOUSE

The basic principle behind saving money on water consumption is the same as that for energy consumption – conserve rather than reuse. Commit to fixing dripping taps, take showers rather than baths, put a litre plastic bottle filled with water or a cistern displacement device that is freely available from your water authority in your toilet cistern (never use a brick as these can disintegrate and the particles may cause damage to the toilet), only flush for solid waste, don't let the tap run while cleaning your teeth. All of these tips will cut your water use. If you have a water meter, you'll see the tangible benefits of these measures immediately. And if you haven't got a water meter, ask your water supplier to fit one.

It is possible to reuse water, but with some specific guidelines. Water used in a house takes two essential forms: black water and grey water. Black water is specifically that which has been flushed down the toilet. This water must never be reused. Grey water is the water that is used in the sink, shower or bath and in the washing machine or washing up, in cooking and preparing food. It may contain detergents and will also contain bacteria. Because these bacteria multiply at a frantic rate, grey water must never be stored, but it can be used to irrigate crops and plants. It is theoretically possible to clean grey water using a small-scale filtration and treatment plant, but for domestic use this is neither cost-effective nor energy-efficient.

The simplest way to incorporate a grey water irrigation system into your house is to fit a diverter to the down pipe from the bath or shower. The grey water should then be fed via a system of pipes directly into the plant or vegetable beds. At the Centre for Alternative Technology there is a grey water irrigation system on display which feeds into raised vegetable beds through perforated pipes.

While grey water is generally safe for irrigation purposes, it's worth remembering that the run-off from the washing machine in particular may have quite a high salt content, and so this grey water may have a negative effect if applied to the same area of the garden for too long. It's good practice to spread the watering around as much as possible.

ADVANTAGES: The grey water system is very logical. In the spring and summer we need to shower and bathe more frequently and our plants and vegetables need more moisture. It makes perfect sense to be able to combine these demands on water consumption to our mutual benefit.

DISADVANTAGES: The irrigation system may require a bit of plumbing know-how.

INITIAL OUTLAY: the cost of fitting the diverter (£20-£27) and irrigation system (an old hose pipe, a sink and some plastic piping will suffice).

ONGOING OUTLAY: none

POTENTIAL SAVING: depending on your normal water consumption this could save £40 per year.

FREEDOM LIVING SCORE: 9 out of 10.

33 COLLECT RAINWATER FOR DOMESTIC AND GARDEN USE

Another way to cut consumption of fresh water is to ensure you maximise your use of one of the UK's most abundant natural resources – the rain.

Rainwater is generally cleaner than grey water, though it may also include bacteria from a range of sources – from dead animals in your gutter to pollution from the atmosphere. However, you can save rainwater in butts for some time and reuse this water on the garden. It's also perfectly good for washing the car.

Because rainwater is generally fairly clean, it's also possible to reuse it in the house if you fit a simple sieve-like filter to your down pipes. Once it has been filtered it is perfectly useful as water for the toilet, or even for use in the washing machine.

ADVANTAGES: It's plentiful and free.

DISADVANTAGES: The rain doesn't tend to fall when it's needed most, so you will need to plan an appropriate-sized system of water storage. You'll also need to practise some water-efficient gardening.

INITIAL OUTLAY: the cost of water butts, approximately £25. Some local authorities offer special cut-price water butts to their residents.

ONGOING OUTLAY: none

POTENTIAL SAVING: £12 per year

FREEDOM LIVING SCORE: 9 out of 10

34 'PLAY THE MARKET' WITH ELECTRICITY AND GAS SUPPLIERS

Ever since the energy supply market was opened up, there have been rival companies fighting for our attention, offering great deals, fixed term offers and even free gifts to get us on board.

Along with the proliferation of energy supply companies, there's been a notable increase in price-comparison websites, most notably Uswitch.com, which offer a realistic comparison of the deals offered by the various main players in the market. Although there's no such thing as a completely disinterested comparison site, they are useful to use as a broad benchmark for what's available.

Switching supplier regularly poses more problems logistically than financially, as the administration of such transfers can sometimes become quite complex, involving a lot of time on the phone sorting things out and negating any real benefit of switching, as your chosen supplier will inevitably have to raise their own prices in the end to remain competitive.

The most sensible reason to switch is if you are offered a decent locked-in deal for a fixed period of time. Energy prices are on the up, and they aren't about to decline any time soon, so if you get the chance to cap your price, you're well advised to take it.

ADVANTAGES: If you've never switched electricity or gas supplier, you're almost certainly getting a raw deal, because someone, somewhere will offer you a better deal to secure your custom.

DISADVANTAGES: If you don't choose wisely, or if you swap too frequently, you'll end up paying more in the end.

INITIAL/ONGOING OUTLAY: zero for swapping.

POTENTIAL SAVING: depending on the offer, anything up to £100-150 per year, but if you're offered a good capped deal, think of it as a long-term benefit.

FREEDOM LIVING SCORE: 5 out of 10

35 USE INTERNET PHONE SERVICES FOR FREE NATIONAL AND INTERNATIONAL CALLS

One of the greatest revolutions brought about by high speed internet access is the free VOIP (Voice Over Internet Protocol) call. The most famous global example of this is Skype, an offshoot of eBay, while many people across the globe also communicate using Windows Live Messenger. Providing you and the person you're talking to are both sitting in front of your PCs, are connected to the internet via high speed broadband link and have headphones or a handset connected to your computer, you can make a call from one side of the world to the other without paying a penny for the privilege.

If you've got a lot of family spread out around the globe, the benefits of this are enormous, but Skype in particular is useful for a much wider range of applications – you can effectively use it as a second phone line as it can be used while the landline is busy. But remember that the only free calls are Skype to Skype, all other types of call will cost you, but additional services are available to subscribers.

ADVANTAGES: If you make a lot of international calls, you'll see the immediate benefits on your phone bill. Despite a shaky start, the technology is now pretty sophisticated and clear-sounding.

DISADVANTAGES: Your cousin in Sydney may object to getting up in the middle of the night just to save you a few quid on calls.

INITIAL OUTLAY: a Skype headset (for example) can cost as little as £15. Everything else is free (except for the computer and the broadband)

ONGOING OUTLAY: for Skype to Skype calls, none.

POTENTIAL SAVING: £50-£100+ per year.

FREEDOM LIVING SCORE: 8 out of 10

③⑥ GET FREE TV AND AXE YOUR LICENCE FEE

If you don't own a TV or any device capable of receiving a TV signal, you don't need a TV licence. But doesn't that mean you can't ever watch TV programmes? Not any more. The BBC and Channel 4 have both introduced web-based services for accessing content at a time that suits you.

With the BBC iPlayer [www.bbc.co.uk/iplayer/] you can watch BBC shows after they've happened, although you will need a decent, high-speed broadband connection. Channel 4's on-demand service works in a similar way, although some content is subscription only. In addition to saving you money, these services suit a more flexible lifestyle, rather than being chained to the regular TV schedule. Expect other broadcasters to follow suit – it's the future.

ADVANTAGES: No more missed shows, no repeats, no adverts. It's also great for kids who want to watch shows again and again.

DISADVANTAGES: Not a great viewing experience for anyone who is used to a 40-inch screen and computers often have poor sound quality. Avoiding a TV licence in this way isn't illegal but it's not very communitarian either. Both services are only available to internet users in the UK..

INITIAL/ONGOING OUTLAY: none at present, but expect subscription services to begin soon.

POTENTIAL SAVING: £135.50 per year

FREEDOM LIVING SCORE: 5 out of 10

③⑦ MAKE SURE YOU'RE GETTING THE BENEFITS YOU QUALIFY FOR

There's a fine line between freeloading and getting what you deserve, and for fear of crossing from the latter to the former, many people don't question whether they could be entitled to more government help to supplement their income.

Government support for low-income living is a complex area and depends on individual circumstances, but it is always worth your while asking whether you're entitled to any extra help, both in terms of day-to-day living and with specific events, like giving birth (do you qualify for a Sure Start Maternity Grant?) and entering higher education (do you qualify for a bursary towards your tuition fees?).

One of the best, free places to go for independent advice on your financial well-being is the Citizens Advice Bureau [www.citizensadvice.org.uk] which has branches all over the UK staffed by people who can offer real support and guidance to ensure you're getting everything you deserve.

ADVANTAGES: It's another case of 'if you don't ask, you don't get'. Bursaries and grants are provided for specific purposes, and there's no shame in claiming what's rightly yours.

DISADVANTAGES: Minimal. Some application processes are complex.

INITIAL/ONGOING OUTLAY: none

POTENTIAL SAVING: dependent on circumstances, but possibly £1,000 or more.

FREEDOM LIVING SCORE: 6 out of 10

38 SUPERMARKET LOYALTY CARDS – HOW TO GET THE BEST FROM THEM

Although anyone dedicated to living for free might be forgiven for avoiding supermarkets like the plague, there are some great deals to be had courtesy of certain stores' loyalty schemes. There are three main loyalty cards available: Sainsbury's Nectar card, Tesco

Clubcard and Boots Advantage card. Waterstone's has also introduced a loyalty card for customers, though the benefits are currently limited.

Tesco and Sainsbury's seem to have cornered the market in effective loyalty card administration, mainly by extending their network of associated point-gathering retailers – from car hire firms to restaurants and most trades in between. Nectar and Clubcard points are also used in-store as effective promotion tools. If either retailer wants to promote a new product or service, they often sweeten the pill with a giant points bonus. On a DVD club promotion, for example, Tesco offered 1000 points (£10) to anyone who signed up to their club for a minimum of three months. With a basic monthly fee of £4.47 a month, this meant access to free DVDs for three months for less than a fiver. A good deal.

It's also worth checking for double and treble points deals on specific products. Some of these deals are only available via promotional coupons that you receive with your points statement, so cross-check them carefully to make sure you get the most from your spending.

The final, crucial piece of advice is to check out the dedicated points website for each of the retailers mentioned above. These sites have details of the reward deals on offer to cardholders, which are often better value than simply redeeming your points in store. Again using Tesco as an example, each point is awarded for a pound spent and is worth a penny in store, but it is tripled if redeemed against a voucher obtained via the Clubcard website to be used in selected restaurants, thus turning a £10 Clubcard voucher into a £30 meal ticket. Similar deals are offered on magazine subscriptions and other products and services.

ADVANTAGES: The cards come for free, so if you're spending the money anyway, why not reap the benefits?

DISADVANTAGES: Some people become obsessed with points deals, buying a hundredweight of bananas just because they're on triple points. Try to strike a balance between getting a great deal and keeping a grip on reality.

INITIAL/ONGOING OUTLAY: none

POTENTIAL SAVING: If you maximise your points by getting rewards vouchers, you can save the price of a family meal out each month.

FREEDOM LIVING SCORE: 6 out of 10

39 TAKE ADVANTAGE OF FREE CREDIT ON STORE AND CREDIT CARDS

The credit crunch makes life hard for all of us, but anyone wanting to live for free should seriously dedicate themselves to eradicating their debts. Holding credit cards and store cards that are carrying debt at high monthly interest charges makes no sense whatsoever. Without wishing to sound like an awful daytime TV advert, you need to consolidate and rationalise.

Rationalising your finances is discussed below, but here we need to look at ways to use credit facilities to your advantage. Once you've achieved this, and have successfully cleared your card balance, I'd recommend putting the credit card away for emergencies only.

Interest-free credit and interest-free balance transfers are limited time offers that can help you clear credit card debt. Check the small print of any balance transfer deal, as most include an administration charge. As long as the new card's deal is entirely free, you have a matter of months to clear the balance without incurring interest. If you can't find a good balance transfer deal and still need to clear existing balances, prioritise your payments according to the size of the interest rate. You'll still be paying interest, but at least it won't be top whack.

Finally, before you consider switching to another card, ring your current card company and tell them you're going to jump ship. They'll almost certainly offer you a better deal than the one you're current on if you agree to stay loyal. That might save you the hassle of switching, and a few quid into the bargain.

ADVANTAGES: Credit card companies are extremely competitive, and that's still good news for customers. Check out a price comparison website for a more detailed breakdown of what's on offer.

DISADVANTAGES: If you put anything on credit card, it means you're spending money you haven't got. As a rule, that's a bad habit to get into.

INITIAL/ONGOING OUTLAY: none

POTENTIAL SAVING: this depends on your outstanding balance and the size of your interest payments.

FREEDOM LIVING SCORE: 5 out of 10

40 MAKE SURE YOUR MONEY IS WORKING FOR YOU

Even if you're incredibly sensible with your money and never find yourself in debt that still doesn't mean you're working the system to maximum advantage. Here are some quick tips to make sure your cash is working hard for you:

TAX FREE SAVINGS. If you've got the wherewithal to save some money, make sure you take advantage of cash ISA savings. These are safe, long-term savings accounts that pay a decent rate of tax-free interest.

SELF-ASSESSMENT PAYS. If you're self-employed or are a PAYE employee with other sources of income you'll be required to fill in a self-assessment tax return. This small annual inconvenience can be a massive financial advantage. If you can find yourself a good, cheap accountant, they can advise you on what is and isn't tax deductible. You'll be surprised at just how much you can claim for and what a difference this can make to your annual tax bill.

BE PREPARED. This isn't exactly a money-saving tip, more like a good housekeeping move. Many financial services providers offer good rates of interest on savings accounts providing you open the account with a decent lump sum of money (for example £500). If you can afford to squirrel away this kind of cash you can regard it as a contingency fund, available in an emergency, or to fund big costs like car insurance or tax bills. All the while it's tucked away, it is earning you money, and it saves you from hitting the credit card.

ADVANTAGES: Being smart with your money makes you money and saves you on interest charges and debt.

DISADVANTAGES: High interest accounts sometimes make it hard to access your cash in a hurry.

INITIAL/ONGOING OUTLAY: none

POTENTIAL SAVING: a few thousand pounds saved in an ISA, for example, could be earning you a couple of hundred pounds a year for nothing.

FREEDOM LIVING SCORE: 7 out of 10

41 BE DEMANDING AND WRITE TO COMPLAIN ABOUT POOR SERVICE – GET WHAT YOU WANT OR GET YOUR MONEY BACK

Despite being labelled with a 'mustn't grumble' attitude, we're actually quite effective complainers in the UK. We vote with our feet, and when a service or product hasn't come up to our standards, we'll politely return or refuse it, then walk away and badmouth the offending company to all and sundry.

For this reason, it always pays to contact the company concerned and explain in cool, collected language exactly why they have incurred your displeasure. There's no point in ranting down the phone to the store or tearing a strip off a pimply sales assistant. Even if they are to blame, they don't have the power or the sense to do anything about it.

Instead, get out your best notepaper and compose a letter to the head office customer services department, explaining exactly what happened and how much it has upset you. This letter is the company's lifeline as you are likely to delay your badmouthing until they have responded.

Most companies with any clout or ambition will seize this opportunity to make up for the problem by offering you a satisfactory solution that gives you a better deal than you'd have had in the first place. They avoid a tongue-lashing and you leave with what you wanted, only cheaper/better/twice as much. Whoever said that complaining didn't make people happy?

ADVANTAGES: It puts the customer in their rightful place, at the top of the heap.

DISADVANTAGES: You'll inevitably come across a company that wants to argue the toss, which will cost you stress and time.

INITIAL/ONGOING OUTLAY: minimal

POTENTIAL SAVING: depends on the original product/service

FREEDOM LIVING SCORE: 7 out of 10 (including a point for consumer rights)

42 HOW TO RUN YOUR CAR FROM VEGETABLE OIL

Anyone who's watched the price of fuel creep up to and beyond the £1 per litre mark will have taken an interest in the gathering pace of the biodiesel revolution. Reports in the media give conflicting accounts of the potential damaging effects of biodiesel on an engine, but no one is disputing the fact that a car run on biodiesel is a whole load cheaper than one that takes conventional fuel.

Converting your car to run on biodiesel isn't an easy process and it certainly can't be achieved for free, but the cost of the equipment involved can be quickly and easily offset by savings made on fuel. After a few months of motoring, you'll find yourself sitting on a goldmine.

Patrick Whetman of Goat Industries has been producing biodiesel and vegetable oil conversion kits since the fuel blockade in 2001 threatened the supply of fuel for consumer use. Patrick's firm was the first to be set up in response to the fuel crisis and he has become one of the leading advocates of alternative/sustainable fuel technologies in the UK.

"I set up my first biodiesel plant as a project that interested me. It was something for the future," Patrick explains. "At that time, no one else was doing it – I made a lot of mistakes in the early days, as you never really know how to master the skill until you try it out."

In the relatively short time that Patrick has been producing fuel and supplying equipment for others to do likewise, he's found that demand for fuel – from obvious sources such as chip shops and school kitchens – has increased significantly, while the price of oil has risen accordingly, and has more than doubled in recent years. "There's a high demand for oil now and that will only drive prices upward," predicts Patrick.

In spite of this trend, Patrick is still confident that the production of biodiesel is cost effective for anyone trying to cut fuel costs on an individual basis, especially as it is now possible to produce 2,500 litres of biodiesel for personal use without having to pay any tax on the fuel. Yet there are still some serious pitfalls, as Patrick explains:

"Producing your own fuel involves dealing with dangerous chemicals, which brings with it an element of safety risk. There are other considerations, depending on how you plan to generate fuel – if you use a vegetable oil filtration plant, these are generally cheap but have little functionality and are very messy. You will get covered in oil."

So what does Patrick recommend as a starting point for the wannabe biodiesel generator? "It's important to be well organised," he says. "Make an investment in the best machine you can afford. Get a good machine that is cleanable and that's made from heavy grade materials. A decent quality machine will pay for itself in no time and will be virtually indestructible into the bargain."

ADVANTAGES: Halving the cost of motoring is a pretty appealing prospect. There's also an innate feeling of flicking a devil-may-care finger in the direction of the oil barons.

DISADVANTAGES: Smelly, oily and potentially dangerous working conditions mean that this is an activity geared towards the dedicated. You also need a lot of space for the processing plant.

INITIAL OUTLAY: for a decent quality processor look to spend around £1,000.

ONGOING OUTLAY: you will need to pay for oil and chemicals (though you might get the oil free if you can reach a deal with a friendly chippy).

POTENTIAL SAVING: £1,000+ per year

FREEDOM LIVING SCORE: 7 out of 10

④③ BECOME A SECURITY GUARDIAN OF A PROPERTY AND LIVE FOR NEXT TO NOTHING

Getting a foot on the property ladder is just about the hardest financial step for any young person. Spiralling mortgage costs have driven up rents as well, and the squeeze on wages means that the gap between what someone can afford and what they actually want is growing ever wider.

But there is an alternative for anyone who wants to reduce the costs of living and who doesn't mind a more sociable and potentially varied living arrangement. Property management firm Camelot has a portfolio of extraordinary properties around the UK and Ireland, which it manages on behalf of the owners. The company finds professionals to live in the properties – which can range from penthouse apartments to warehouses by way of farms, manor houses and castles – and these so-called guardians act as a form of security measure for the empty property. Rents are incredibly low (around a quarter of the average) and also include bills.

There is a downside to all this easy living, as the properties are sometimes only available short-term, although the company tries to give residents a three-month stay as a minimum and a month's notice to quit on top of that. Once you are on Camelot's books, they will also strive to find you alternative accommodation if required. Many guardians find themselves in properties for longer-term stays, and even manage to create a cosy living environment in the unlikeliest places. Check out the firm's website at www.camelotproperty.com

ADVANTAGES: Low rents and communal living make this a great option for young professionals who are keen to live independently but also gather some savings for the step up to home ownership.

DISADVANTAGES: It's an insecure life and the company doesn't have a huge portfolio in the UK at present, so there may not be much choice.

INITIAL OUTLAY: £500 approximately deposit, registration fee and fire safety pack.

ONGOING OUTLAY: £25-£60 per week rent.

POTENTIAL SAVING: huge – anything up to £4,000-£5,000 per year.

FREEDOM LIVING SCORE: 8 out of 10

44 MAKE YOUR OWN SOAPS, MOISTURISERS AND TOILETRIES

It had to happen eventually. The more TV adverts we see featuring women washing their hair in waterfalls surrounded by nature's bounty, the more we get wise to the fact that natural, organic products are actually better for us than the long list of pharmaceutical hybrids that drugs companies try to get us to put on our hair, skin and teeth. They've only got themselves to blame.

If you cling to the mumbo-jumbo experts and desire the latest miracle ingredient to send your skin whizzing back through the decades or give your gappy molars the Julia Roberts treatment, then carry on chucking your money away. The rest of us, however, can take a look in the larder for our beauty tips.

Good quality, pure oils – almond, avocado, coconut and sesame are common examples – can form the basis of a range of skin moisturisers. Blend a few tablespoons of your chosen oils with a little cocoa butter and a tablespoon of beeswax (from your own hive, naturally) to make a useful all-over moisturiser.

Rather than wasting money on expensive toothpaste with a baking soda tingle, just use baking soda instead. Wet your brush and drop some powder onto it, or mix up a special concoction using baking soda and herbs like sage or mint with a drop or two of essential oil.

Baking soda mixed with essential oils also makes a reasonable alternative to talcum powder or deodorant. Sweet smelling oils like rose and lavender are especially good.

The drawback of these natural store-cupboard toiletries is that, like all products, they may produce an allergic reaction – especially the essential oils and nut oils. So test a small, discreet patch of skin with any new concoction, and obviously avoid any oils that you wouldn't otherwise ingest.

ADVANTAGES: You look and smell great, feel virtuous and use up all the ingredients from the cupboard that you've never found a purpose for.

DISADVANTAGES: It can feel a little bit like you're basting yourself. Some pure oils can be almost as expensive as the cosmetics they are replacing, so shop with care.

INITIAL OUTLAY: the basic ingredients for the above toiletries should be around £10.

ONGOING OUTLAY: if kept in dry and/or airtight containers, the products should last months.

POTENTIAL SAVING: £50 per year

FREEDOM LIVING SCORE: 7 out of 10

45 EAT HEALTHY, BE HEALTHY

The above statement might sound as if it's from the 'bleeding obvious' school, but it is worthwhile considering exactly how much time (and consequently money) we lose by feeling ill or sluggish because of our diet. The more healthy food we eat, the more energy we have, and the more energy we have, the more we can do with our days.

It can be pretty demeaning to think of the body as a machine in this way, but that's exactly what it is – if we don't provide it with the right fuel it will conk out somewhere between 5pm and bedtime. Aside from the common advice of drinking a plentiful amount of water (up to two litres) each day and consuming five portions of fruit and vegetables daily and two portions of fish weekly, here are a few key tips to keep you thriving:

SUPERFOOD = SUPERPEOPLE. Make an effort to incorporate so-called 'superfoods' like apricots and cranberries into your diet – sprinkle them on cereals if you can't stomach them alone.

BE VITAMIN RICH. Vitamin C is the oldest cold cure even if it's not the most reliable one, and it's present in many more foods than just the humble orange. Eat strawberries, peppers and green vegetables for a varied Vitamin-C rich diet.

GET ENERGY – SLOWLY. There's no point in getting the kind of quick energy hit that soft drinks and sweets give you. Your energy levels will soar briefly and will plummet soon after. Eat slow-release foods like bananas and wholewheat pasta for a more gradual energy hit that will keep you going longer.

CUT SUGAR AND SALT. These ingredients add little to food, and they make you feel very bad. If you're trying to save money, never buy processed food, which is caked in preservatives, sugar, salt and fat. Prepare everything from scratch, it's more fun, doesn't take any-where near as long as you think it will and you can control the ingredients you use. If you must add a sweetener, use natural honey.

ADVANTAGES: If you eat smarter, you'll feel better, look better and save money.

DISADVANTAGES: With no more fast food binges, you'll have to find other ways to amuse yourself after a bad day.

INITIAL/ONGOING OUTLAY: prices from a farmers' market or farm shop are comparable to supermarket prices – and quality is far higher. Anyway, you'll be growing it all yourself, won't you?

POTENTIAL SAVING: by switching from processed to natural foods, you can save around £20 a week from your food bill.

FREEDOM LIVING SCORE: 8 out of 10

46 MEND YOUR OWN CAR AND BUY PARTS FROM SALVAGE

If you must have a car – and the dedicated low-cost life would ideally be free of such a money drain – then it's important to avoid excessive garage bills. There are certain unavoidable running costs like insurance, tax and MOT inspections. But beyond these, the money we spend on services, check-ups and other niggling irritations is a downright waste.

The first thing you need to do is get hold of a decent manual for your make of car – Haynes manuals can be picked up for a few pence from boot fairs, or you can get manuals on most popular makes from the library. Your car's user manual will also have some basic information on general maintenance. Get hold of some basic tools, such as a set of spanners, screwdrivers and pliers and try to learn at the very least the basics of a simple car service.

The more proficient you become at car maintenance, the more money you'll save, and if you do encounter any serious problems which require replacement parts, don't go straight to the main dealer for a costly replacement. Breakers' yards are a great source of spare parts, sometimes in excellent condition and at a fraction of the new selling price. Some breakers' yards, like www.metrosalvage.com offer an online parts sourcing service.

Finally, if you do develop a decent level of maintenance skills, it is easier to maintain an older, more basic car than a newer vehicle with a complex electronic engine management system. As long as your chosen car has strong bodywork and a decent history of maintenance and care, you'll be able to keep it on the road yourself for years to come.

ADVANTAGES: Keeping your car out of the garage makes financial sense, but in general terms it pays to be a bit savvy about car maintenance, both to check the signs of problems in your car before they become serious, and to challenge any unscrupulous mechanic who tries to convince you to part with your cash.

DISADVANTAGES: It's a steep learning curve for many of us, especially as cars are becoming more complex. Like them or loathe them, mechanics are also (generally) good at keeping you safe, so if you are going to take on your own maintenance, you must be dedicated to the craft.

INITIAL OUTLAY: for the manual and basic toolkit, £25 to £50.

ONGOING OUTLAY: parts and oil and so on for annual service around £30-£40.

POTENTIAL SAVING: up to £250 per year in servicing and repair costs.

FREEDOM LIVING SCORE: 7 out of 10

47 USE FREE SALVAGE BUILDING MATERIALS/ LANDSCAPING MATERIALS

Where there's muck, there's brass, as grim northern industrialists are fond of observing. That truism is never truer than when it is applied to demolition sites and building projects, where there's often a huge spill of broken up hardcore or topsoil available for removal by anyone who's got the means to take it.

If you're planning your own landscaping project, or building the world's biggest rockery, this material is a priceless commodity. The only problem is how to find and access this kind of stuff. Fortunately, via the wonderful web, potential large-scale scavengers can visit sites like www.SalvoMIE.com and gain access to a whole network of construction site waste that's ready to be picked up. Some firms will even drop off the offending waste for a small fee if you don't have the transport. The types of material available through this kind of site aren't just limited to landscaping materials. There's also a range of architectural ironmongery and other building products on offer, though the more valuable items are only offered for sale (albeit still at a fraction of the original selling price).

If you're the kind of scavenger that likes to feel their quarry, it's also worth visiting reclamation yards for bargain materials, though these places are a bit more canny than your average construction firm and the prices are often hiked accordingly.

ADVANTAGES: A good, cheap (or even free) source of landscaping materials, and a very fair, satisfying exchange.

DISADVANTAGES: Few people have the capacity to transport the quantities of material involved.

INITIAL/ONGOING OUTLAY: none

POTENTIAL SAVING: depending on the size and scale of project and material involved, a few hundred pounds.

FREEDOM LIVING SCORE: 8 out of 10

CLOTHES, TOYS & OTHER ITEMS

48 GET A PC FOR PENCE

You'd be surprised what you can get just by asking nicely in this world. For example, if you go looking for a cheap PC at local independent computer stores you may just come out with something for nothing.

The reason for this sudden fit of generosity is that because of recycling laws, computer shops have to pay around £20 a time to dump old PCs traded in by customers who buy new machines. So you may be saving the shop money by offering to take one off their hands. It may also be worth asking for a second machine to locate any missing/broken bits for the first one.

Most stores haven't got time to split old PCs into bits and build refurbished machines, so the perfectly reasonable old machines are going begging. Chances are it won't be a ninja PC that plays all the latest games, more like a PC that's three to six years old with a big screen. But this should be absolutely fine for word processing and surfing the net.

ADVANTAGES: It's free for goodness sakes! What more do you want?

DISADVANTAGES: You might need a bit of computer or electrical know-how to make any necessary adjustments to your new machine.

INITIAL/ONGOING OUTLAY: none

POTENTIAL SAVING: around £500 for a new PC.

FREEDOM LIVING SCORE: 8 out of 10

49 BE A SMARTER SURFER

Online shopping is both a blessing and a curse. On the downside it comes with all the inconvenience we associate with catalogue shopping, like not being able to touch the item you're buying and having to wait in for a parcel delivery. But there are great advantages and cost-savings to be had online. Here are a few tips:

COLLECT FROM THE STORE. Some electrical retailers offer a great service for online customers which allows them to reserve a product on the internet and then collect it from the store at a fairly hefty internet-only discount. Other stores may match an online quote, so even if you plan to go into a store to purchase, it's worth your while seeing the prices online first.

CLICKING COUPONS. Before buying anything online, check if there's a money-off coupon that could save you a few pounds. Go to www.google.co.uk and search for the name of the store and the word 'coupon'. You'll have to dig around but it's often possible to locate a code that you enter during the ordering process. This may give you £5 off your first order or free postage. Many major high street stores have online 'clubs' or email newsletters that offer special deals for subscribers – sign-up is free and usually pretty painless. If you're on the lookout for free food samples, cinema tickets and other printable money-off vouchers, try sites like Free Stuff Junction [www.freestuffjunction.co.uk] and www.freeukstuff.com.

GET THE MESSAGE. Message boards are a great help online if you're stuck. Mumsnet [www.mumsnet.com/Talk] is a great online community where you'll find a classified section as well as a free section. You can also ask people if they know where to get something for free or save money. Remember, Mumsnet is for dads too. Also see the money and budgeting section on UK Parents Lounge [www.ukparentslounge.com/forum/index.php] and budgeting sites like www.greasypalm.co.uk and www.moneysavingexpert.com.

ADVANTAGES: The online shopper is a savvy shopper. Websites are always offering great deals to attract first-time users and if you can spare a few minutes to register with the sites, you'll reap the benefits.

DISADVANTAGES: Online shopping is notoriously fraught with peril. Never give your credit card details to an insecure site (you can tell a secure site because it has the code 'https' at the start of the address line and a little padlock in the bottom right-hand corner of your browser). Cheap warehousing sites are also pretty adept at losing your items in the post.

INITIAL OUTLAY: none

ONGOING OUTLAY: whatever you can't resist.

POTENTIAL SAVING: If you can rein in your spending, internet prices can be around 30 per cent cheaper than high street equivalents.

FREEDOM LIVING SCORE: 6 out of 10

MAKE CHILDREN'S OUTDOOR TOYS FROM DISCARDED CAR AND TRACTOR TYRES

Rather like PCs (above), old and worn tyres are more trouble than they're worth for most retailers. They must pay to have them removed, which inevitably results in unsightly stockpiles created by opportunists with a plot of land to spare and no scruples. Now, I'm not suggesting that you tackle these eyesores by going into production as a tyre sculptor, but these humble rubber circles do have a range of uses in the garden and they should be appropriated if possible.

Firstly, you need to get hold of the right type of tyre – for a child's swing you want to ensure there are no sharp edges or rough bits and you will need to clean the tyre thoroughly. Find a strong tree and some good quality rope then attach the swing to the tree, remembering to bore some drainage holes in the bottom of the swing. Tractor tyres also make excellent sand pits if you can persuade a friendly neighbourhood farmer to part with one.

But tyres have uses beyond the play park – a pile of tyres makes a good planter for your potato crop, or a decent compost surround. Again, punch some holes in the tyres for ventilation and drainage.

ADVANTAGES: As a source material for children's toys and garden ornaments, tyres are free, plentiful and can even be painted bright colours.

DISADVANTAGES: Even if you can get the tyres clean, you'll never remove the rubbery smell and that will attach itself to your little ones.

INITIAL/ONGOING OUTLAY: minimal for rope and paints.

POTENTIAL SAVING: £20-£50 on swings and pots.

FREEDOM LIVING SCORE: 7 out of 10

51 TRADE AT THE DUMP

OK, so there is the potential downside that people will start calling you Stig, and that your social life will go out of the window, but in reality trading at the dump is a very good idea. Think of it as a non-virtual freecycle.

While you usually aren't permitted to pick things up that have already been dumped, there are plenty of rich pickings to be had just by approaching people who are in the process of chucking stuff away. Assuming they don't want it any more, it shouldn't make any difference to them whether you get it, and recycling is much better for the planet after all. Some council recycling facilities do actually offer the pick of the dumped items for resale, so it may be worth checking your local tip for knock-down bargains.

It's also worth your while keeping an eye out for things that have been tossed into skips around your neighbourhood – what might be obsolete for a business is fine for an individual. Again, you might be well-advised to check with the owner before hauling anything out, but they're unlikely to stop you.

ADVANTAGES: A completely free source of useful goods.

DISADVANTAGES: Everyone else thinks you're mad.

INITIAL/ONGOING OUTLAY: none

POTENTIAL SAVING: depending on the goods salvaged, anything from a few pounds to a few hundred.

FREEDOM LIVING SCORE: 9 out of 10 (slightly too grim for a perfect score)

52 GET KIDS' TOYS FROM A TOY LIBRARY OR START YOUR OWN

For anyone who's ever spent a fortune on the latest Disney action figure only to see it discarded within minutes by a fickle toddler, toy libraries are an excellent idea. Run on similar principles to book libraries (though sometimes with a nominal fee for lending), the main difference is that these are staffed almost exclusively by volunteers who are keen to promote the value of interactive play for kids and parents alike.

The main advantage is that your child gets access to a range of decent toys without the usual costs – it's a very secure sharing environment, which is also pretty useful for a child's emotional development.

To find out if there's a toy library in your area contact the National Association of Toy and Leisure Libraries (NATLL) on 020 7255 4604. And if there isn't one, ask the NATLL for details of how to start your own.

ADVANTAGES: Kids get bored with toys very quickly, so a wide library of varied toys makes perfect financial and educational sense.

DISADVANTAGES: None.

INITIAL/ONGOING OUTLAY: minimal.

POTENTIAL SAVING: £250 per year in rejected toys.

FREEDOM LIVING SCORE: 9 out of 10

 53 REGISTER FOR ONLINE SURVEYS AND PRODUCT TESTING

Online market research is another boom industry, with a number of sites offering small rewards in exchange for your opinion on a variety of subjects. A couple of the most popular sites are www.toluna.com and www.valuedopinions.co.uk which both give cash rewards to survey respondents. Toluna.com also invites selected members to try out products. The rewards typically range from 75p to £1, although you have to collect a minimum level of rewards (around £10) before you're actually sent the money in the form of a voucher.

So it's not a get-rich-quick scheme, but if you have some spare time on your hands and a fast internet access it's a good way to get paid for telling someone else what you think.

ADVANTAGES: The more involved you get, the more surveys and products you are given. It's quite an interesting way to find out what companies are planning.

DISADVANTAGES: The surveys are often very repetitive and slow.

INITIAL/ONGOING OUTLAY: none.

POTENTIAL SAVING: anything from £10 to £50 per year, depending on how often you take part.

FREEDOM LIVING SCORE: 5 out of 10

54 TAN YOUR OWN ANIMAL SKINS TO MAKE LEATHER GOODS

Now we're really getting back to nature. If you've got the stomach to kill and butcher an animal and flay the hide from its carcass, then you're well on the way to being able to produce your own high quality leather goods. Even if you can't bear the idea of all that butchery, you may be able to find a slaughterman who will prepare the hide of your slaughtered goat or sheep. You can even use rabbit skin for clothes and shoes.

The three basic types of home tanning are known as brain tanning (so-called because it uses a combination of wood smoke and emulsified oils in the tanning process and one of the most common natural sources of this oil is the brain of the departed animal), bark tanning and chemical tanning.

Brain tanning is the most popular of the above methods as it produces effective results in a matter of days, though not many people are brave enough to use brains in brain tanning any more and prefer to buy their emulsified oils elsewhere. Animal hide that has been brain tanned is called buckskin, a versatile, breathable material that is also washable, and so makes great outdoor clothing.

Bark tanning takes longer and produces a stiffer resulting product, and chemical tanning produces similar results to brain tanning, though in a less 'natural' way. For more information, take a look at www.braintan.com

ADVANTAGES: Leather and hide clothes, shoes and bags are tough and durable. It's the ultimate reuse of animal waste products.

DISADVANTAGES: Buckskin is tough, but not waterproof. You need a strong stomach to prepare the hides.

INITIAL/ONGOING OUTLAY: cost of oils or chemicals, £10-£15.

POTENTIAL SAVING: £50-£100 on a good winter coat.

FREEDOM LIVING SCORE: 7 out of 10

55 MAKE FURNITURE FROM JUNK

Almost all discarded materials can be reused as furniture, home decoration or as garden ornaments. Anything that you can source from building sites, timber yards, beaches and skips that you can't or won't use as fuel can be put to good use as building material.

Driftwood, for example, is a very versatile source material. Not necessarily strong enough in itself to form the structural basis of a chair or table, it can be used creatively and cosmetically to give a finish to a piece of furniture – a driftwood-topped table for example, or driftwood cladding for a bookcase or wardrobe.

Found items like shells and broken pottery can be set together to create a mosaic effect that covers a pot table constructed from a more rudimentary material, like a broken down pallet for example. The simplest, most functional wooden or plastic chair can be rescued with a padded patchwork throw of brightly coloured fabric offcuts from a textile store.

In fact anything that can be safely cut, shaped or moulded can be put to a more practical use, from pebble doorstops to plastic sheeting table mats via coathanger topiary trainers and papier mâché picture frames.

ADVANTAGES: Reusing found materials in the home is a fun creative activity, and it's virtually free.

DISADVANTAGES: Obviously, you'll need some creative skills, and some decent tools which might offset the cost benefit of reusing junk.

INITIAL/ONGOING OUTLAY: none.

POTENTIAL SAVING: £200-£500 per year on furniture.

FREEDOM LIVING SCORE: 8 out of 10

56 MODIFY AND MAKE YOUR OWN CLOTHES FROM CAST-OFFS

If you've really got the creative bit between your teeth, you could try your hand at making your own clothes. Again, a degree of skill is required, and if you don't want to be spending long hours over the same shirt, you'll probably need to invest in a sewing machine too.

Making dresses, shirts, skirts and trousers is a bit of a dying art, but that fact weighs in your favour. Material (especially when bought from a market or textile factory shop) can be extremely cheap and you can pick up basic patterns for pence from charity shops. Try looking online for free patterns and templates as well.

If you're not quite so adept at sewing or knitting, but you still want to save money on clothes, consider modifying plain clothes from a charity shop or from a textile store. A simple embroidered pattern turns a bland T-shirt into a unique piece of clothing, even sewing accessories to a plain top, skirt or trousers can give them a serious lift.

ADVANTAGES: Another creative, frugal art form – developing the ability to sew also enables you to repair clothes and extend their usefulness.

DISADVANTAGES: Hand-sewn fabrics aren't always as hard-wearing as commercially produced items, so if you're aiming to make clothes for everyday use, you might have to get used to running repairs.

INITIAL/ONGOING OUTLAY: cost of fabrics, cotton, sewing accessories, £100.

POTENTIAL SAVING: £200-£500 per year on clothes.

FREEDOM LIVING SCORE: 7 out of 10

57 GROW YOUR OWN DYES FOR CLOTHES

If you're serious about making your own clothes from scratch it also makes sense to grow the natural products that can be used to dye the finished items. As a general rule, it's easy to guess which plants and berries make good dyes by their natural colour, but some produce more effective dyes than others. Here's a brief outline of some common natural dyes:

PLANTS AND FLOWERS: Onion skin (orange), roses and lavender (pink), red cabbage (purple), spinach, nettle (green)

BERRIES: Strawberries, cherries (light red/pink), juniper (brown), elderberries, mulberries, blackberries (all purple)

Chop the flowers, leaves or berries and boil in a pot with two parts water to one part ingredient. Strain after an hour or so of gentle simmering. Before adding the material, soak it for an hour in a fixative of salt and water or vinegar and water, rinse and then place the material and the dye together in a dye bath. Leave to soak until the required colour is achieved.

ADVANTAGES: For a truly organic experience, you can't beat home-dyed, homemade clothes.

DISADVANTAGES: Home-dyed materials must be washed separately in cool water, which makes laundry a pain.

INITIAL/ONGOING OUTLAY: minimal.

POTENTIAL SAVING: £100+ per year.

FREEDOM LIVING SCORE: 7 out of 10

58 DON'T PAY TO HAVE STAINED CLOTHES OR FURNITURE PROFESSIONALLY CLEANED

Natural, simple stain removal is a lost art, like pinhole photography and making crystal radio sets. But unlike these other pursuits, there's actually some point in learning how to get stains out of a huge range of items easily, quickly and, above all, cheaply. Esme Barber, an expert in stain removal, recommends the following tips:

To get **candle wax** off a carpet, wait until it has hardened, scrape off as much as you can and then, using a cool iron and a piece of brown paper or blotting paper, iron the paper onto the wax, which draws out the greasy residue. Freeze **chewing gum** stuck on carpet or rugs with an ice cube and then chip it off.

To get rid of **grass stains** on non-washable fabrics, use a paste of warm water and cream of tartar. To remove **blood stains** from clothing, soak the fabric in warm, salted water, and to remove a **red wine stain** from a carpet, douse with white wine. To cover a **scratch** on a table, use a paste of coffee and water. To remove a minor **carpet stain**, cut a potato in half and rub the fresh half directly onto the stain.

If you've got a **table** that's stained, greasy or oily, rub tea over it and the tannins will draw out the grease. Similarly, you can use weak tea to clean stained **mirrors**. To clean tarnished **copper** use a mixture of vinegar and salt.

ADVANTAGES: These cheap stain removal tips save a fortune on dry cleaning for clothes and professional cleaning for carpets and rugs. Most expensive chemical products are no more effective than the remedies above.

DISADVANTAGES: none.

INITIAL/ONGOING OUTLAY: minimal.

POTENTIAL SAVING: £50+ per year on cleaning products.

FREEDOM LIVING SCORE: 8 out of 10

59 MAKE YOUR OWN CLEANING PRODUCTS

About ten years ago, when daytime TV turned us all into obsessive cleaning monsters, someone remembered (probably after a freak accident in a chip shop) that vinegar was a magic ingredient.

You can use it to clean windows, floors, furniture; anything that's afflicted by a layer of grime (but don't use it on teenagers). The cleaning product manufacturers quickly got wise and tried to pretend they'd invented the craze by introducing new 'with vinegar' products left, right and centre. These were swiftly replaced by 'orange essence' or 'lemon zest', which have the distinct advantage of not smelling like vinegar.

But the essential message remains the same – the acids in vinegar (acetic) and citrus fruits (citric) are good cleaning agents, as is that other 'wonder product' baking soda. Mix these cheap and easily available items with a little water and give expensive cleaning products the heave-ho. Esme Barber offers more top cleaning tips using vinegar and baking soda:

Baking soda, mixed in equal parts with vinegar and water, produces the most effective **sink and drain cleaner** – shifting fat, food and even hair.

Rather than buying fabric deodorants, **freshen cushions and settees** that smell smoky by sprinkling with baking soda and then leave for a couple of hours. Brush them off and the smell should be gone.

If you drop something pungent like **sour milk**, douse it with vinegar which will (ultimately) neutralise the smell.

And finally, if you want a cheap and effective alternative to **toilet cleaners**, look no further than a bottle of cheap, flat cola. It really does work wonders.

ADVANTAGES: Commercial cleaning products are a chronic waste of money. These perfect substitutes cost pence and they're just as effective.

DISADVANTAGES: Vinegar has a pungent smell, especially when used as a floor and surface cleaner.

INITIAL/ONGOING OUTLAY: 30p-50p a time for vinegar or value brand citrus fruits.

POTENTIAL SAVING: up to £100+ per year on cleaning products.

FREEDOM LIVING SCORE: 8 out of 10

60 ONLY SUBSCRIBE TO FREE TRIALS FOR SUCH THINGS AS DVD CLUBS

Free or cheap DVD subscription clubs have sprung up all over the place in recent years, rather like the book and video club boom of the 1970s and 80s.

Like their forebears, these clubs work on the theory that momentum and the pace of life will stop you cancelling the contract before the end of the free trial. But some of them actually offer incentives – money or free DVDs – to take part in the trial, effectively paying you. There is no contract or obligation to stay involved.

If you're really careful with your timings, and make a note on your calendar of the exact date for cancellation, you can exploit this and try the service for nothing while pocketing the freebie. Of course, there is an outside possibility that you'll decide to keep the service anyway.

ADVANTAGES: It's a rare example of marketing actually working in your favour in an (almost) foolproof way.

DISADVANTAGES: As the club has your contact details it will bombard you with offers to retain your custom after you've cancelled. Of course, that disadvantage may work in your favour if you decide to take them up on a good deal.

INITIAL/ONGOING OUTLAY: none (though you may have to give them your debit or credit card details as part of the enrolment procedure).

POTENTIAL SAVING: they pay you – or at least give you a DVD. What a result.

FREEDOM LIVING SCORE: 8 out of 10

61 SELL YOUR HOME WITHOUT AN ESTATE AGENT

This one is a real challenge. There are two ways of looking at estate agents – they are either incredibly useful middle-men who ensure the complex transaction of a house sale goes smoothly and without confrontation, or they are a thorough pain in the neck designed to complicate a simple process for their own financial ends. Having moved house myself several times, I'd say they are actually somewhere between the two, but whatever your definition of an estate agent, you'd be hard pressed to find anyone willing to buy or sell a house without one.

The question you need to ask is why? Here are the main reasons:

ESTATE AGENTS PROVIDE A DEGREE OF SECURITY. They aren't permitted to make false descriptions of properties, but in reality this liability extends as far as a tape measure, as they have to give accurate room sizes and that's about it. Most agents specifically distance themselves from any responsibility for checking appliances and services, and they have no interest whatsoever regarding legal ownership of a property. So any potential buyer can overcome this first objection by checking the measurements for themselves.

ESTATE AGENTS HAVE A CODE OF ETHICS. Well, hopefully we can all lay claim to having ethics, even though we don't all write them down. Unfortunately, it's natural to mistrust the person you're dealing with, which is why both sides need a good solicitor (no financial shortcuts here, I'm afraid, unless you're married to one). But again, estate agencies don't really earn their crust as beacons of virtue.

ESTATE AGENTS HAVE THE BEST MARKETING REACH. This one's hard to argue with. Estate agents spend a lot of money on advertising both in print and on the web and they are a powerful force to contend with. They may seem fiercely competitive, but they are actually pack animals, preferring to band together in big online enclaves like rightmove.co.uk and primelocation.com. In the newspapers, the story is the same, with dedicated property sections that are filled with seductive ads.

So in brief, it you want to go it alone, you have two options. You can use a low-key web-based service that will charge you around £50 for a basic package of a photo and listing on a website. You pay more for a 'For Sale' board and other extras. Or you can go it alone, make your own sign, website and newspaper ad, as well as copies of details to hand out to prospective buyers. Even though you aren't subject to any regulation as a private seller, do be as honest as possible on the details – it will save hassle later.

ADVANTAGES: Estate agents' fees are huge, from 1.5 per cent right up to 3 or 4 per cent of the sales value of your house. By doing it yourself, you keep hold of the process and the communication channels.

DISADVANTAGES: It's a lot of work, especially if you aren't comfortable negotiating and getting tough on price. There's still a lot of sheep-like resistance among buyers who assume you must be working some kind of con, so it may take much longer to sell.

INITIAL OUTLAY: from £50 for a serviced package. If you do it all yourself then expect to pay around £100+ for one week's newspaper advertising plus £50 for literature and £50 for your web costs.

ONGOING OUTLAY: none, if the advertising works, otherwise it's fair to assume you'll need to spend an extra £100-£150 every six weeks or so to keep interest going.

POTENTIAL SAVING: on a £200,000 house, with 2 per cent fees, you should make a saving of around £3,500.

FREEDOM LIVING SCORE: 7 out of 10

62 GO TO TRAINING HAIR SALONS AND EAT AT TRAINING RESTAURANTS

If you've got a technical or vocational training college near you, the chances are it will have a trainee hairdressing salon and a trainee catering school. Both of these are a rich seam of young talent, eager to try out their new-found skills on willing guinea pigs, sorry, members of the public.

The salons and training restaurants are often open and available to the public during regular hours in term-time. The restaurants sometimes have special theme nights – like Valentine's and Christmas meals – or gourmet nights where the young chefs flex their culinary muscles.

The great upside of all this vocational endeavour is that much of it is carried out at a fraction of the price of normal service. The hairdressing trainees and the chefs work under the strict guidance of their instructors, so you also know you're getting an excellent level of service. Check your local college's website for details of opening hours and special events.

ADVANTAGES: You could be the inspiration for the next Nicky Clarke or Gordon Ramsay.

DISADVANTAGES: These are popular activities, so there's a lot of demand. Remember it's a training activity so you may have to be patient. In the unlikely event that you get duff service you might end up with hair that looks like linguini and linguini that looks like hair.

INITIAL/ONGOING OUTLAY: half the cost, or better, of the same services in the high street.

POTENTIAL SAVING: £10-£20 per hair appointment/£15-£30 per meal.

FREEDOM LIVING SCORE: 6 out of 10

63 GET SHAREWARE OFF THE INTERNET

There seems to be a plethora of free software available on the internet, but as a general point you should be careful before downloading it to your PC. So-called 'free' software that you can download from the web often – but not always – comes with spyware that uses up valuable resources on your PC and secretly reports back to a website about your surfing habits (so the website owners can bombard you with spam/junk emails). Free software has been known to contain viruses too.

Microsoft charge a small fortune for their Office suites. Open Office [www.openoffice.org/] from Sun Microsystems is a free alternative with many similar and compatible applications for word-processing, slide presentations and more. It's 100 per cent free – and it's a top-quality product used by major businesses.

Security companies will often provide free versions of their software for home users (not for business), saving you from shelling out £30-50 a pop to protect your PC. Try Avast! [www.avast.com] for anti-virus protection, Zone Alarm [www.zonealarm.com] for a firewall and Spybot [www.safer-networking.org/en/] for squishing spyware. You may have to look around the menus to find the product that's free to home users.

ADVANTAGES: Avoid the trap of expensive and bug-ridden 'popular' software products and still get the same user benefits. That's smart surfing.

DISADVANTAGES: Sorting the wheat from the chaff. On the internet there's so much chaff and much of it will do your computer harm, so if you're at all suspicious about a download, avoid it.

INITIAL/ONGOING OUTLAY: none, although some products may be available as time-limited trials only. You are not obliged to buy the full version after the trial has finished.

POTENTIAL SAVING: Depending on your software needs, anything from £250-£1,000.

FREEDOM LIVING SCORE: 7 out of 10

64 STAY COOL IN THE SUMMER WITHOUT AIR CONDITIONING

In the light (or should that be gloom) of recent British summers, it might seem farcical to suggest that air conditioning is a necessary component of any home, but it wasn't so long ago that we were racking up temperatures of 100F on a regular basis. The increasing popularity of sun rooms and conservatories means that the average UK house has the capacity to become incredibly hot in the summer months, and that can mean danger for anyone, old or young, who can't regulate their own heat so well.

So how do you stay cool without investing a fortune in a cumbersome and noisy air conditioner? The first thing to remember is that, as your house traps the heat, so it also traps the cold when the sun goes down. So open windows and doors between sundown and bedtime to draw in cool air, then seal it in by closing everything up tight overnight. The cool night air will keep the heat at bay for a while at least in the morning.

The second thing to remember is that if you can't cool your room down, you can at least cool yourself. Drink iced water regularly in hot weather – it keeps you hydrated and moderates your temperature. Keep a plant sprayer in the fridge filled with water and give yourself a quick misting if you get too warm; again this will keep you cooler without having to jump in a cold shower.

ADVANTAGES: Air conditioned houses, like air conditioned cars, are invariably sealed boxes which circulate bad air. They aren't healthy places – much better to keep a natural flow of air whenever possible.

DISADVANTAGES: If you open your house up at night, you'll attract all sorts of little bugs and beasties. Go the American way and fit a fly-screen to any open doors and windows – they let air in but keep pests out.

INITIAL/ONGOING OUTLAY: minimal.

POTENTIAL SAVING: air conditioning unit + power = £200-£500 minimum per year.

FREEDOM LIVING SCORE: 7 out of 10

65 HOW TO ENSURE YOU ENTER COMPETITIONS YOU ARE LIKELY TO WIN

How often have you said: "I never win anything"? And how many competitions do you enter? One, maybe two a year, I'd guess. Success in competitions, like most things in life, depends on a combination of luck, judgment and probability. Here are some valuable tips on how to maximise your chances of success:

DON'T THINK TOO LITERALLY. If a competition offers something popular, like a holiday or a trip to a spa, everyone will want a piece of it and your chance of winning is severely diminished. If the competition is for a set of coins commemorating the opening of the Telford bypass, not so many people are going to want this, and so your chances are improved. So far, so simple. But someone will want the product ultimately, so if you enter and win, you'll have something to trade. A coin collector may pay handsomely, or may swap the prize for something you do want. So never turn your nose up at the chance to win a prize, however ridiculous it may seem.

INCREASE YOUR ODDS. On a similar logic to the above, if the *Daily Mail* is giving away a speedboat, two million people will see this offer and a small percentage will try to win it. If the Bognor Times is giving away two pantomime tickets, about a thousand people will see it and only a couple will enter. In my newspaper days, competition winners were rarely chosen at random, as this increased the likelihood of the same old names getting every giveaway, such was the paucity of entrants. So enter smaller, less well-publicised competitions in local newspapers and promotional brochures. Radio competitions are often under-subscribed as well.

AIM HIGH. Though it might seem a complete contradiction to the above points, there are never as many entrants in seriously fancy competitions as you might expect. This is because people are natural pessimists and assume that the bigger the prize – like a car, or a trip to the moon – the less their likelihood of winning, so they don't bother. That can significantly increase your odds.

USE YOUR LOAF. If you have a particular gift for words and can craft a well-made rhyme or slogan, use this skill in those 'say why you like our outboard motors in no more than 250 words . . .' competitions. Always make sure the slogan you devise is a good match with the product – and don't be tempted to employ a scattergun approach here. Take your time and do each entry from scratch. A successful slogan is a carefully wrought combination of rhyme and rhythm, which must work as a spoken statement as well as a written one.

Humour is another vital ingredient of a winning slogan. Remember that your competition entry will be read by a human being, or at least by an editorial assistant. They have feelings too, and if you make them laugh then you're already half-way to that fortnight in the Bahamas.

ADVANTAGES: There are many free competitions around. Enter as many as possible, as you'll lose nothing and by the nature of probability, you'll end up with something worth something to someone. For free.

DISADVANTAGES: Once you start entering competitions it can become addictive. Many come complete with time-consuming customer surveys, so it's worth checking whether you need to do the survey to qualify for the prize. In fact you should always check the small print just to be sure you aren't committing yourself to a lifetime of spam emails or junk post.

INITIAL/ONGOING OUTLAY: none.

POTENTIAL SAVING: thousands, if you're lucky.

FREEDOM LIVING SCORE: 8 out of 10

66 HAVE A 'PRESENT AMNESTY' WITH FAMILY

A present amnesty means that you and your nearest and dearest (or at least your siblings) agree that no one will buy presents for each other, consequently saving everyone money.

This is very much a matter of personal taste; some people put a great deal of effort into the presents they buy for family on birthdays and at Christmas. Most of us just get something from the Body Shop or the off-licence at the last moment and hope it will do, which rather defeats the object of buying presents in the first place.

You have to be brave to initiate negotiations about a present amnesty, just in case your sister-in-law has come to depend on the honey and coconut bath bombs you've given her every year for a decade, but frankly most people will be relieved that there's one fewer present to buy when the festive crush comes around once more.

You could suggest a more communitarian alternative, such as a huge family party (see pot luck dinners above) instead of present-giving. That allows everyone to feel that they've made a special effort without being out of pocket.

ADVANTAGES: Avoids the unpleasantness of having to graciously receive awful presents. Also cuts down on Christmas shopping.

DISADVANTAGES: Introducing the concept could make you appear a touch Scrooge-like. Best approach is to say "Hey, everyone, I was talking to a friend and they've come up a fantastic way to be caring and save money ..."

INITIAL/ONGOING OUTLAY: none.

POTENTIAL SAVING: this depends on how generous you've been in previous years, but even at a conservative estimate it'll save you £100-£200 per year.

FREEDOM LIVING SCORE: 9 out of 10

67 **LEARN HOW TO SPOT COLLECTABLES AND BARGAINS AT BOOT FAIRS**

If ever there was a grim microcosm of life, it's the boot fair. They're more accurately described as table-top sales as there aren't many people who sell direct from their car boots, or sell their car boots, or sell boots. However, the phrase boot fair does sound a little like boot camp, and it would serve you well to regard it as a military exercise.

Some of the best buying at boot fairs is conducted before the tables are loaded. Swarms of bargain hunters collect around the unloading vehicles and try to pick off the best bits before they're even unboxed. If you fancy joining this pack of desperadoes, you may get an early deal from an inexperienced trader looking to cover the cost of their pitch. But an early deal isn't necessarily the best deal. No self-respecting car-bootee would sell to these vultures, but it will pay you to hang around in earshot, as you'll get an idea of what's worth fighting over later.

It's far better to take your time and be patient. Assess the various traders – some will be experienced pros but others will be occasional traders, or even boot fair virgins. This is where to focus your efforts, as they'll have little knowledge of the value of their items and/or may be willing to sell everything just to get shot of it.

In terms of the items to choose, focus on specialist items like sailing and camping equipment and sporting accessories. These big-ticket items might be evidence of a hobby gone sour and you could get a massive saving. It's always worth taking a punt on art, sculpture and ceramics, especially if the former is an original artwork, or if the latter has a maker's mark. Books and older hand tools and garden tools can also be good buys.

Finally, in the words of Eric Idle, you've got to haggle. It would be criminal not to.

ADVANTAGES: Boot fairs offer the cut and thrust of the open market, the community spirit of a recycling network and the smell of fried onions. Where else can you get all three?

DISADVANTAGES: If you're tempted to buy electrical goods or suspiciously cheap DVDs, you're about to get ripped off. Some electrical stuff may be OK, but you'll never get the chance to bring anything back.

INITIAL/ONGOING OUTLAY: it can be fun to set a small budget (say £10) and see how much you can make with it.

POTENTIAL SAVING: you can easily make ten times your outlay on the right item.

FREEDOM LIVING SCORE: 7 out of 10

HOLIDAYS, LEARNING, WORK & LEISURE

68 GET FREE ADULT EDUCATION TRAINING

One of the greatest regrets that most people have later in life is that they didn't capitalise on learning possibilities when they were young. But it's easy to see why people might want to shy away from further education given horror stories of student debt and costly tuition fees. So it might be sensible to assume that living for free and studying on a structured course are incompatible pursuits, right? Wrong, go to the back of the class.

The basic rule of thumb regarding free adult education is that the more you need it, the cheaper it is. If you want to study the mating habits of elephants in the Thai jungle, you'll have to fork out for it yourself. But if you want to improve your literacy, maths or even foreign languages, there's plenty of free help available. Learn Direct is one of the UK's largest providers of training for adults, both privately and through the workplace. While many of the vocational courses do have a charge, free literacy and numeracy programmes are available.

Depending on where you are in the UK, other sources of free help may also be available, such as Cornwall's excellent Link into Learning scheme and similar services operating in Wales and Scotland in conjunction with the regional assemblies. In some towns and cities of the UK, regional BBC offices have Open Centres, which combine open internet access with free courses on a range of multimedia skills – visit www.bbc.co.uk/bus for more information. The BBC also offers basic online training in literacy, numeracy and languages, and there are various internet-based providers of training [such as www.creatingcareers.net] which offer free courses in a variety of vocational subjects.

If your aim is less vocational and more educational then the Open University has launched an excellent, entirely free service to all, called Open Learn. While participants don't study for a specific qualification, they are able to access a huge catalogue of the university's materials, and participate in structured units of study, forum-based discussion groups as well as keeping a learning journal that allows the individual to track their own progress through a subject. While the scheme can be seen as a recruitment drive for the university's fee-based courses, it's also a very worthwhile exercise in open access learning in its own right.

ADVANTAGES: If you're looking to change jobs and/or if you have specific literacy or numeracy needs, these free courses are a great way to change your life without spending a penny. Most of the courses can be taken online, which means they are convenient and can be built around a busy life.

DISADVANTAGES: Most free training is limited in scope and is useful only to those with fundamental learning needs. General online resources are useful and expanding, but of course they are dependent on computer literacy and internet access (to access free training in both, see libraries in section one).

INITIAL/ONGOING OUTLAY: zero for basic literacy and numeracy training, other training courses may charge fees dependent on status.

POTENTIAL SAVING: difficult to put a value on training, but you could save around £500 - £1,000 on private training costs.

FREEDOM LIVING SCORE: 8 out of 10

69 GET A GRANT OR BURSARY TO STUDY LATER IN LIFE

If you're looking for more structured or academic study, but you still want to avoid the fees, there's plenty of help and support available. In this case, the amount of support you receive will be directly related to factors such as age, previous educational experience, geographical location and income, but the sheer volume of support available to anyone who shows a commitment to return to education means that there is almost certainly some form of help for everyone in the form of a grant, loan or childcare subsidy.

A good first port of call is the Educational Grants Advisory Service [www.egas-online.org], which provides free advice and information on funding for education and training from 16+ including loans, grants, benefits, access funds, hardship funds, bursaries and charitable trusts. Also worth checking out is www.offa.org.uk – an independent public body that aims to provide fair access to higher education for all.

Individual training bodies like City & Guilds and Lifelong Learning offer money or bursaries to adults wishing to return to learning. Conditions and application criteria differ between organisations – though again the EGAS should be able to help provide full details of charities and other bodies offering help.

If you're a member of a trades union or a professional organisation, you may find another way into education through one of their bursaries or scholarships. A number of the students at Oxford's Ruskin College, a leading centre for adult education in the UK, have their studies part-funded in this way. Ruskin, which has been providing training and academic courses for a century, offers lots of information and advice for potential students who need help with fees.

In certain cases, adult learners can even qualify for a maintenance grant as well as the cost of their tuition fees – check with your local education authority for more information on discretionary grants. All in all, it pays to take a 'gap-decade' before continuing with your studies post-school.

ADVANTAGES: As an adult learner, you are more likely to be focused on your studies than the other students, who are generally just focused on each other, the dirty devils. As a way to change direction in your career or simply expand your mind, taking a serious course of study later in life can be hugely liberating.

DISADVANTAGES: If your idea of hardship is going without an olive in your Vodka Martini, then you might baulk at the thought of surviving on a grant, that's if you're one of the lucky few who qualifies for one. Otherwise you'll just have to get by on savings and your wits, which makes this an option only for the determined.

INITIAL/ONGOING OUTLAY: potentially zero, depending on status.

POTENTIAL SAVING: At least £10,000 for a degree course.

FREEDOM LIVING SCORE: 9 out of 10 (if you stick to it)

70 **EXERCISE IN THE PARK AND ON THE BEACH**

Going to the gym is a thorough waste of money. There, I've said it. The pointless pounds that you spend in a futile attempt to shed weight or build muscle could be vastly better spent on hiring a bike for a day, rowing on a boating lake, swimming in the sea or just running around the park with a weighted backpack. This way, you also get to avoid smelling other people's sweat and being blasted with MTV at full volume.

Seriously, parks and beaches are excellent open spaces for running, stretching and yoga – parks sometimes cater for tennis, boating and basketball at nominal cost. And now, in one Manchester park at least, they are providing serious open-air gym equipment.

Designed with older people in mind, and based on similar sites in Germany, the gym park features a range of equipment that works to tone hips, legs and upper body. A couple of hours' exercise a week should keep your average mature person lithe and fit. And the best thing? It doesn't cost a penny.

The beach is another haven of healthy reflection, especially out of season, when huge expanses of beach open up to anyone brave enough to face the elements. Kite flying, running and beach cricket are all year-round activities on the sands that will keep you ticking over better than any circuit trainer ever will.

ADVANTAGES: Parks and beaches are wonderful resources, even just for a brisk walk. Exercising in the open air makes you feel better, you get Vitamin D from the sun and fresh air in your lungs.

DISADVANTAGES: You can feel pretty self-conscious doing your press-ups in the open air. But get there early and you'll avoid the dog walkers, drunks and yobs.

INITIAL/ONGOING OUTLAY: none

POTENTIAL SAVING: if you quit the gym, you'll save at least £500 per year.

FREEDOM LIVING SCORE: 9 out of 10

71 WORK TO TRAVEL – FRUIT PICKING AND TEACHING

OK, let's define some terms pretty early on. Neither of these activities constitutes a holiday. They are good ways to get yourself to another country, and to fund your travels around that country, but in themselves, they are no picnic. The hours are long and the work is demanding.

But don't let that put you off. Take fruit, for example. Many beautiful countries of the world need seasonal labour for fruit picking – all of the great wine-producing countries for starters, but especially Australia and New Zealand. There are plenty of opportunities in Italy, Spain and Greece to help with the olive harvest, and even countries like Denmark, which you wouldn't ordinarily think of as a fruit-producing nation, are always looking out for good seasonal staff.

Teaching is more of a grey area. Most recognised schools (that is, the ones that will pay you in currency rather than magic beans) require a TEFL (Teaching English as a Foreign Language) qualification, which costs about £1,000 and a lot of hard work to acquire. Other, less scrupulous schools may take on a graduate without qualifications as long as you speak good English and look half-way presentable. You'll teach large classes, most likely of children and young adults and you'll be paid a pittance. But it's a fun way to meet people.

ADVANTAGES: Having a skill that gets you from destination to destination is a must for the dedicated traveller. The more experience you gain, the more you'll find your skills in demand – heck they might even start paying you something.

DISADVANTAGES: All the above – long hours, backbreaking work, poor conditions. You may get accommodation thrown in, you may find yourself drinking away your earnings just to get through the contract.

INITIAL/ONGOING OUTLAY: none

POTENTIAL SAVING: If you do save some earnings, these could fund a holiday at the end of your working contract, maybe up to £500 in total.

FREEDOM LIVING SCORE: 7 out of 10 (for effort)

72 GO ON A WORKING HOLIDAY

Now this is a holiday, a proper one with evenings off and nice accommodation to boot. The only downside is that you're not paid. Actually, you'll have to pay for it yourself.

The thing is, working holidays are part of the eco-industry, offering people the chance to savour a once-in-a-lifetime experience while making a contribution to the health of the planet. Far-flung holidays are available through organisations like Earth Watch, which involve participants in the ecology movement, while the fees help to keep the organisation's work going forward.

For the sake of this book's focus, we need to concentrate a little closer to home, on the budget volunteering holidays offered by organisations such as the National Trust, the BTCV (British Trust for Conservation Volunteers) and RSPB.

These holidays are for two to seven nights, and start from as little as £60 per week including food and accommodation.

But probably the biggest benefit of a working holiday is that each working party is led by a trained expert, who will pass on valuable skills and experience. Take a look at www.nationaltrust.org.uk, www.ecoholidaying.co.uk and www.wwoof.org for more information.

ADVANTAGES: Get valuable experience, meet like-minded people, get fit and pay just a few quid for the privilege.

DISADVANTAGES: Single-sex dormitories and no alcohol makes for a very different ambience to a Club 18-30 break. And it's hard work, too.

INITIAL/ONGOING OUTLAY: from as little as £60 per week all in.

POTENTIAL SAVING: over a package holiday, £250-£350 at least.

FREEDOM LIVING SCORE: 8 out of 10

73 WORK YOUR PASSAGE ON A LUXURY YACHT AS A CREW MEMBER

If you're looking to get around the world in style for free and you fancy yourself as a bit of a seadog, you can work your passage on a yacht in a couple of different ways.

First of all, there's the delivery crew. This is a pretty relaxed environment, just getting the yacht from A to B, or Antigua to Bermuda. If you're an experienced sailor you'll be well in demand for this kind of work. You may not get paid, but the trip will be an uneventful and free ride.

Then there's crewing for races, or for cruising. This can be a bit more formal, it doesn't necessarily take you in a straight line, or indeed anywhere very fast at all. It's more of a job than a travel option, and accordingly you'd expect to get paid for the privilege. You won't necessarily need sailing experience, as you may be needed for catering, waiting or cleaning duties.

Whatever takes your fancy, try a crew/yacht matching website like www.jobsonluxuryyachts.com to see what's on offer.

ADVANTAGES: Good experience and cheap travel for anyone who loves to sail.

DISADVANTAGES: There aren't that many luxury yachts flitting across the Atlantic on a regular basis. Places may be limited.

INITIAL/ONGOING OUTLAY: none

POTENTIAL SAVING: hundreds of pounds.

FREEDOM LIVING SCORE: 7 out of 10

GO ON HOLIDAY TO 'LIVING MUSEUMS' – AS A VOLUNTEER/EXHIBIT

There are few better things in life than getting paid for doing something you enjoy, so if you're one part thespian to two parts historian you'd thrive as an 'exhibit' in a living museum.

There's a multitude of these interactive learning experiences around the country, each of which uses seasonal staff to act as guides or to provide local colour. So if you fancy yourself as a Viking marauder or a Victorian schoolmaster, check out your options at a heritage portal like www.britainsfinest.co.uk or try the venues direct. Remember that most venues will recruit for their busy summer season in January and February.

If you just fancy getting involved on a smaller scale, museums and exhibits around the country welcome volunteers who want to give up a day or two each week to act as guides. You still get to meet people and learn new skills.

ADVANTAGES: It's a great chance to dress up, teach and have fun yourself.

DISADVANTAGES: Like all contract work, if the job starts to get monotonous, motivation can be hard. Unlike fruit picking, however, you've got to be fresh every day.

INITIAL/ONGOING OUTLAY: none

POTENTIAL SAVING: you may be given a family season ticket to the attraction you're working in, which could save a couple of hundred pounds in admission fees.

FREEDOM LIVING SCORE: 6 out of 10

75 DON'T PAY FOR A HOLIDAY – DO A HOUSE SWAP INSTEAD

House swapping is not a new phenomenon, but its popularity has only recently started to grow following a succession of daytime TV shows on the subject.

In essence, a house swap is a step up from a pen pal, in which you establish a long-distance relationship with someone until you become sufficiently secure to offer them the use of your home in exchange for theirs for an agreed period. This is a process that's made considerably easier by the advent of the internet, and well-established home-swapping companies like www.homelink.org are now big businesses, with contacts all over the world.

The length of time it takes to become confident that you'll trust someone else in your home differs from person to person. The average American may exchange homes after the first email, the average Briton may wait a few years, but generally any reservations we have about letting someone else take over our property are usually banished after the first positive exchange. In more than 50 years of operation Homelink hasn't yet had an incident of theft or vandalism.

As a rule, home exchanges only work if everyone's very upfront about what their home and neighbourhood offers when they enter their property and location details on the website. So don't be tempted to maximise the glory of life in Goole just so you'll be able to swap for a Miami condo. It's a short-term policy that will inevitably end in tears. If you can make a match with another home, always ensure that you leave your property immaculate for the new guests and that you provide copious notes with emergency contacts as well as advice on what to do and what to avoid. Take all this on board, and house swapping can become a passport to incredible foreign travel experiences.

ADVANTAGES: Home swaps are a great way to see another culture away from the usual tourist routes. If you have detailed notes of what to do and see it's as good as having the services of a local guide. And you'll never have to worry about your house being empty while you're away.

DISADVANTAGES: If you book a hotel and don't like the room, you can swap, but a house swap is fixed for the duration of your holiday, so it's important to ask any questions before you commit.

INITIAL/ONGOING OUTLAY: If you arrange the swap through a site like Homelink (which is recommended) you'll have to pay around £115 to list your property and a few pounds for a printed copy of the directory.

POTENTIAL SAVING: If you can get good flight deals, you may save at least £1,000 on a family holiday.

FREEDOM LIVING SCORE: 8 out of 10

76 BECOME A COUCH SURFER AND SEE THE WORLD (OR ITS LIVING ROOM)

A slightly odd amalgam of lift sharing and house swapping, couch-surfing is an internet craze that might involve loaning out your sofa for the night. But in return, you could get to kip in another country for free.

As the couch surfing website [www.couchsurfing.com] explains, the idea represents a new way to make friends around the world. But it's also for people who want to travel on a shoestring.

First, you look up a country on the site and find people willing to let you sleep at their property for free for one night or more. You contact them to see if this is OK and make some arrangements. They may offer you a room – or maybe just a garden where you can pitch your tent.

Having arrived, the website suggests that, in return, you help out your hosts by offering to do the washing up or other jobs around the house. Of course, the hope is that you'll also become such good friends that maybe one day you'll return the favour to your hosts. Site founder Casey Fenton says the idea has taken off at great speed, but more members are welcome – especially from the UK.

But what's to stop shady characters or anti-social free-loaders from becoming unwelcome guests in your home? Well, Fenton is aware of this risk and the site states that safety is a top priority. As a result, users can choose to become a 'verified member' so others can see they've gone the extra mile and had their name and address confirmed through credit card records and a letter sent to their home. It's also possible for couch-surfers to 'vouch' for each other, rather like providing good feedback for other members to read.

Even so, the website says it's still OK to refuse someone a couch for the night if you feel uneasy – or it's just not convenient.

ADVANTAGES: No more hotel fees or booking hassles and you may just make some good friends too.

DISADVANTAGES: You may feel honour-bound to return a favour to someone that you'd never normally dream of having in your home. And there's always an outside chance that you'll find yourself sold into slavery.

INITIAL/ONGOING OUTLAY: it's totally free to become a couch-surfer, although PayPal donations are invited.

POTENTIAL SAVING: £50–£100 per night.

FREEDOM LIVING SCORE: 8 out of 10

 ## DON'T PAY FOR A HOLIDAY – BECOME A HOUSE/PET SITTER

This version of a free holiday is a bit like couch surfing with added freedom and responsibility. Your role is to make sure the house is safe, tidy and that the pets are happy for the duration of the owners' absence. This can be for a weekend, for a fortnight's holiday, or even for a much longer period of time while the owner is away. The advantages to the homeowner are clear – providing you are a trustworthy person, they have complete peace of mind. For you, it's a question of whether you're comfortable hopping from house to house and living out of a suitcase.

As with house swaps, there's a booming market in online 'brokers' for these types of service, as well as franchises that operate nationwide. Check out www.petpals.com and www.housecarers.com as a couple of popular examples. As a house-sitter advertising your services on a website, you'll have to pay a membership fee, but otherwise most of the costs involved in your stay should be covered by the person vacating the house – though don't treat this as carte blanche to start making long-distance calls.

Many people who are looking for house/pet sitters search these sites because they feel more reassured that the house sitter will be trustworthy, but there's nothing to stop you setting up alone, especially if you can do a few trial 'sits' for friends and add their testimonies to your CV. One writer that I know has been living this way successfully for the best part of a decade.

Pet sitting requires a bit more of a grown-up attitude and a genuine affinity with the animals in your care. It isn't an easy way to get a free holiday as there's a degree of chore and stress involved, though if you'd like a pet but don't want the year-round commitment, it's another bonus.

ADVANTAGES: If you can establish a good reputation you can hop from home to home and save a small fortune, especially if you move in the right circles – anyone you know who owns multiple houses should become your new best friend.

DISADVANTAGES: Unless you're very lucky, it's not necessarily a year-round occupation. House sitting can also leave you feeling rootless and insecure. Try counting the money you've saved, it'll make you feel better.

INITIAL/ONGOING OUTLAY: to register as a house sitter on a website costs around £20-£30 per year.

POTENTIAL SAVING: around £6,000-£7,000 a year in rent/mortgage and other costs.

FREEDOM LIVING SCORE: 9 out of 10

78 COLLECT AIR MILES – HOW TO GET THE MOST, QUICKEST

Owned by British Airways, Air Miles, like supermarket loyalty card points, are collected every time you spend a certain amount of money. You can earn the points on a Lloyds TSB credit card, or on a loyalty card available from the Air Miles website [www.airmiles.co.uk]. Points can be gained from other retailers and by shopping through the Air Miles online shopping section for a variety of goods and services.

Accruing Air Miles is a daunting task – the website gives an example of how to get a free flight to New York that involves spending approximately £30,000 in 12 months. If you don't rely on the Air

Miles to get you all the way to the Big Apple, you could alternatively use your Miles to get alternative rewards, such as trips out to theme parks and activity experiences.

ADVANTAGES: If you're a big spender, or a business customer, you might find yourself quickly picking up enough points for a European return flight.

DISADVANTAGES: Air Miles have suffered as a result of the general disquiet over excessive air travel. If you do manage to build up enough Miles for a flight, you'll find the range available is quite limited.

INITIAL/ONGOING OUTLAY: none for the card.

POTENTIAL SAVING: anything from £150 to £1,500 depending on your points total.

FREEDOM LIVING SCORE: 5 out of 10

79 CHECK OUT RESIDENTS' DEALS AND SEASON TICKETS AT TOURIST VENUES

Have you ever found yourself going to a particular attraction time and again? It may be because your children love the facilities, or because you love the peace and quiet. Whatever the reason, most tourist attractions around the country offer special deals for the returning visitor. Season tickets or family passes are usually double the price of a standard admission, but with frequent use they soon pay for themselves. I've used them for zoos, heritage sites and National Trust properties and they are a great way of expanding your horizons without spending too much money every time.

Another possible way to save at local attractions, whether or not you're a frequent visitor, is to check out any local residents' deals offered by the venue. Many attractions, and particularly those that rely on council or government sponsorship, have a special tariff for people who live locally. These should be clearly advertised, but as people rarely visit attractions close to home, you may have missed some incredible bargains. It's worth checking the availability of these kinds of deals with your local tourist information centre.

ADVANTAGES: If you find a place you trust and that holds everyone's attention on repeated visits, you're onto a goldmine.

DISADVANTAGES: Children are changeable souls, so choose wisely before investing in a costly season ticket. Not all activities and benefits may be open to season ticket holders — check the small print when you sign up.

INITIAL OUTLAY: twice the price of standard admission (approximately).

ONGOING OUTLAY: none

POTENTIAL SAVING: between £60 and £120 per year, depending on frequency of use.

FREEDOM LIVING SCORE: 7 out of 10

80 GET GREAT HOLIDAY DEALS BY BOOKING ONLINE

There's money to be saved on travel in a number of ways, most of which revolve around the internet (sorry to sound like a stuck record). Here's the pick of them:

BOOK LATE. Websites such as www.lastminute.com often do great deals on reduced entry to attractions as well as hotel rooms. Check the coupons idea mentioned in 'be a smarter surfer' (above) for two-for-one deals and discount coupons at tourist attractions in the UK and overseas (they are particularly popular in the US). Also visit the websites of any motorway or roadside services you may be passing. These may have a voucher page that gives you up to 20 per cent off the price of a meal.

BOOK EARLY. If you're taking an early flight or simply travelling a long distance, you can save lots of money on functional overnight accommodation by booking well in advance with Travelodge. The hotel and motel firm offers a saver rate of just £19 on rooms that are booked at least 18 days ahead of travel. You can also make incredible savings by booking train travel well in advance. Again, places and travel times may be limited. And finally, book your airport parking well in advance to save stress and money too.

ADVANTAGES: Many people focus their energies on the cost of the main holiday and forget how much the extras, like food and pre-flight accommodation, can add up. Checking these out in advance is one less thing to worry about and will save money.

DISADVANTAGES: If you book too soon, you may pay a penalty if your plans change. If you wait, there may be no availability. It's a gamble.

INITIAL/ONGOING OUTLAY: none

POTENTIAL SAVING: £50–£100+

FREEDOM LIVING SCORE: 6 out of 10

 GET FREE TICKETS TO TV SHOWS

There are many ways to experience a live TV show: you could marry your crack-smoking mother-in-law and get on a daytime show, you could become a contestant on one of the few quiz shows that survived the 'fixing' cull. But it's far easier and more enjoyable to get tickets to the recordings of shows and it's also an extremely interesting way to get an insight into how they're put together.

For a while now, tickets to all the main shows have been available through (guess what?) a website, namely www.applausestore.com, which handles audience tickets for all of the main broadcasters – including free group bookings. The BBC still manages tickets for some of its audience radio shows [see www.bbc.co.uk/tickets].

Tickets for the most popular shows are in serious demand at both outlets. You can register on applausestore.com to get your name down for tickets, but don't be surprised if the main shows have been snapped up. The site makes its money by offering a premium 'members-only' priority booking service which costs £15 to join. This will dramatically increase your chances of getting the tickets you want. The BBC allows people wanting tickets to sign up for email updates of recording schedules.

ADVANTAGES: Watching the recording of a show can be as entertaining as a night at the theatre. There's often a warm-up act and a real sense of camaraderie as the audience works to try and build up the performances.

DISADVANTAGES: There's a lot of rubbish on TV, and you'll probably end up watching some of it live, which means it's the same rubbish, just much slower. Just as a lively audience can raise a TV show, a dull audience can kill the atmosphere.

INITIAL/ONGOING OUTLAY: none for basic membership.

POTENTIAL SAVING: on a night at the cinema and theatre, up to £30 a go.

FREEDOM LIVING SCORE: 9 out of 10

CONCLUSION

THE ULTIMATE FREEDOM LIFE – WHAT IT TAKES TO LIVE FOR FREE

Meet Ken and Barbie (not their real names). They live in London, and combine house sitting with pet sitting, and occasional couch-surfing. They haven't had a home to call their own in eight years, but then they haven't paid a penny in rent or bills either.

Ken is a carpenter and Barbie gives Indian head massages. They trade their services for goods and food. Barbie sometimes gives massages to customers in charity shops, for which the customers make a donation to the shop, and in return Barbie has the pick of donated clothing for her and Ken.

Ken was given a free laptop computer in exchange for a rather nice set of shelves he built from wood reclaimed from a demolition site and erected for his friend who runs a computer shop. Ken uses this laptop and the free internet access he gets in his house sitting residence to manage his pet-sitting and couch-surfing, to co-ordinate his LETS scheme (his management hours offset any membership fee), to trade on freecycle and to organise travel using liftshare. He and Barbie are extremely popular travelling companions via the latter, despite the fact that they can offer no financial input – Ken is an expert motor mechanic, and happily helps many of his friends maintain their vehicles in exchange for transport. And Barbie is always on hand with a head massage at refreshment breaks on long journeys. They enjoy volunteering holidays around the UK.

Ken and Barbie spend their free time exercising in the park, or reading books, newspapers and magazines in the local library. If they want to see live entertainment, they go to a recording of a TV show. They earn no money and spend no money. And yet somehow they are blissfully happy. Go figure.

OK, so Ken and Barbie are figments of my fevered imagination, but their exploits are just about plausible. When we talk about living for free, and particularly when we disparage the idea, it is always with a focus on independent living – having your own house, your own heating source, your own food source and so on.

But true freedom living isn't some survivalist hokum about living apart from society, it's about being an integral, inter-connected unit of society, but without the restraints and restrictions of financial need and want. Granted, if everyone did it there would be no houses to sit for, no yachts to crew, no cars to share. But then not everyone will do it. Doesn't stop you, though, does it?

CONTACT US

You're welcome to contact White Ladder Press if you have any questions or comments for either us or the authors. Please use whichever of the following routes suits you.

PHONE: 01803 813343

EMAIL: enquiries@whiteladderpress.com

FAX: 0208 334 1601

ADDRESS: 2nd Floor, Westminster House, Kew Road, Richmond, Surrey TW9 2ND

WEBSITE: www.whiteladderpress.com

WHAT CAN OUR WEBSITE DO FOR YOU?

If you want more information about any of our books, you'll find it at **www.whiteladderpress.com**. In particular you'll find extracts from each of our books, and reviews of those that are already published.
We also run special offers on future titles if you order online before publication. And you can request a copy of our free catalogue.

Many of our books also have links pages, useful addresses and so on relevant to the subject of the book. You'll also find out a bit more about us and, if you're a writer yourself, you'll find our submission guidelines for authors. So please check us out and let us know if you have any comments, questions or suggestions.

How small groups can raise BIG FUNDS

Jessica Ruston

So you need to raise money for a good cause – a favourite charity, the church roof, a new community centre, or a campaign to save the local wildlife sanctuary. How much do you need: a few hundred? Maybe a few thousand or so?

It's not easy, is it? There's only so much money to go round, and the big charities employ professional fundraisers. That doesn't give smaller groups or individuals like you much of a look in. Unless, that is, you have a few tricks up your sleeve...

Jessica Ruston has talked to plenty of people just like you who have successfully raised money for all kinds of causes. Whether you want to run a marathon or put on a fete, hold a charity auction or organise a quiz night, or even ride a bike across the Indian subcontinent, she's got hundreds of fundraising ideas including:

- community events
- sponsored events
- major missions
- balls and banquets
- auctions and sales

You'll also find plenty of advice on getting support from celebrities and businesses, and on how to organise and publicise your events. Let the big charities keep their professional fundraisers. You won't need them once you've read this book.

£7.99